IN DEFENSE OF JUSTICE

THE ASIAN AMERICAN EXPERIENCE

A list of books in the series appears at the end of this book.

In Defense of Justice

Joseph Kurihara and the Japanese American Struggle for Equality

EILEEN H. TAMURA

UNIVERSITY OF ILLINOIS PRESS
Urbana, Chicago, and Springfield

Manufactured in the United States of America
C 5 4 3 2 1
∞ This book is printed on acid-free paper.

Library of Congress Cataloging-in-Publication Data
Tamura, Eileen H.
In defense of justice: Joseph Kurihara and the Japanese American struggle for equality / Eileen H. Tamura.
pages cm. — (The Asian American experience)
Includes bibliographical references and index.
ISBN 978-0-252-03778-8 (cloth : alk. paper)
ISBN 978-0-252-09506-1 (e-book)
1. Kurihara, Joseph Yoshisuke, 1895–1971.
2. Japanese Americans—Evacuation and relocation, 1942–1945.
3. Manzanar War Relocation Center—History.
4. Tule Lake Relocation Center.
5. Japanese Americans—Social conditions—20th century.
6. Japanese Americans—Cultural assimilation.
7. Japanese Americans—Ethnic identity.
8. Japanese Americans—Biography.
I. Title.
D769.8.A6T37 2013
940.53'1779487092—dc23 [B] 2013001410

*Dedicated to World War II incarcerated Nikkei,
especially those whose experiences in WRA camps
led to torments known and unknown to others.*

CONTENTS

Foreword by Roger Daniels ix

Preface xi

Acknowledgments xiii

Introduction 1

Chapter 1. Growing Up American 9

Chapter 2. A Yank in France, a Jap in America 24

Chapter 3. To Manzanar 39

Chapter 4. Resistance in Manzanar 51

Chapter 5. Stepping Back 68

Chapter 6. Isolating Citizen Dissidents 81

Chapter 7. Turmoil at Tule 96

Chapter 8. Renunciation 115

Chapter 9. Japan 132

Afterword 146

Notes 153

Glossary 199

Bibliography 201

Index 223

Illustrations follow p. 80

FOREWORD

Eileen Tamura, whose earlier book in the Asian American Experience series remains the outstanding study of the Nisei of Hawai'i, here examines the life and significance of the Hawai'i Nisei Joseph Yoshisuke Kurihara (1895–1965), who became, for a time, the most notorious Japanese American for his role in fomenting the Manzanar Riot of December 6, 1942, during which American soldiers shot and killed two unarmed incarcerated young men. Although Kurihara's actions on the fatal day have figured in dozens of accounts of the ordeal of Japanese Americans during World War II, he has remained, until now, a shadowy figure. Tamura has, through extensive research, discovered and described the pattern of his life in Hawai'i, the United States, Europe, and Japan.

In a fast-moving narrative, Tamura traces Kurihara's life on the outskirts of Honolulu and his decision in his teens to switch from a free public school to a Catholic school whose modest fees would have seemed large to him. While many ambitious Nisei, in both Hawai'i and on the mainland, opted for Christianity as a way of conforming to American mores, the choice of Catholic Christianity was highly unusual. Tamura explores the dimensions of Kurihara's encounter with Catholicism, which continued after his migration to California, where he attended a Catholic high school and eventually converted. She also explores her subject's encounter with blatant American racism in Progressive Era California—quite different from what Kurihara had experienced in Hawai'i. Enlisting in the army when the United States went to war, Kurihara served in France and Germany before coming home and resettling in Los Angeles. He graduated from a commercial business college, achieved lower-middle-class economic status during the prosperous 1920s, and maintained it in the Depression. On December 7, 1941, he was at sea as the navigator of a tuna clipper and returned to an America at war with Japan, a place he had never even visited and had little or no interest in. Tamura's sensitive exploration of Kurihara's life after his renunciation of American citizenship and resettlement in war-torn Japan provides for the first time an extended account of those parts of her subject's life.

The most important contribution of this work lies in Tamura's detailed analysis of Kurihara's three-plus years of captivity in various parts of an American archipelago of penal sites built to imprison Japanese Americans of all ages, genders, and beliefs, none of whom were charged with any crime. They were prisoners without trial. Kurihara was originally in the Manzanar concentration camp run by the War Relocation Authority—not for anything he said or did but because his parents had been born in Japan. Enraged that his government ignored his voluntary military service, he rejected the government. What he said and did at Manzanar resulted in his being sent to even more remote, small, semi-secret penal camps. His final cage was the Tule Lake concentration camp, which had been transformed from a normal American concentration camp into a camp for dissidents and troublemakers who were shipped from the normal camps and penal sites and where the WRA found it expedient to construct a stockade—a prison within a prison run by U.S. Army military police—where conditions were so deplorable that it can be called a precursor of Abu Ghraib. Tamura's exposition and analysis of these facilities and what Kurihara did in them are an important contribution to the history of the wartime ordeals of Japanese Americans.

But also important is her contribution to Japanese American historiography. By the mid-1970s historians were beginning to recognize that what one of its earliest critics had called "our worst wartime mistake" was instead a logical result of centuries of American racism. Most of the scholarship focused on the "loyal" victims, most often stressing the heroism of the veterans of the 442nd Regimental Combat Team. During and after the Vietnam War the focus began to shift to loyal dissenters who refused to go to camp quietly and challenged the government in court, and then to those young men who had resisted the draft in and out of camp without the option of fleeing to a welcoming Canada, which, during World War II, established camps for its Nikkei population. Tamura's lucid account of Joseph Kurihara's wartime rebellion takes the process one step further, pointing to the need for studies of some of the other hundreds who took the path of renunciation and for a deeper examination of the process by which the American government, for the first time, actively facilitated the cancellation of native-born citizenship.

Roger Daniels

PREFACE

I first became aware of Joseph Yoshisuke Kurihara in the late 1980s when I read a passage from his unpublished autobiography. It caught my attention because of its direct, forthright, and passionate style, so different from the image I had of Nisei men. My own observations and what I had read about them indicated characteristics of self-restraint, control of emotions, deference, reticence, nonverbal communication, and composure in the face of hardship. This was not to say that Nisei men lacked feelings, but that they tended to eschew public displays of their emotions. While Kurihara was not the only exception to this generalization, as Arthur Hansen has demonstrated, its validity was strong enough to cause scholars—among them Frank Miyamoto, Stanford Lyman, Minako Maykovich, William Caudill, Harry Kitano, and Akemi Kikumura—to remark on it. Because behavior attributed to the Nisei did not accord with Kurihara's style of verbal assertiveness, confrontation, bluntness, and spontaneity, I wondered, "Who was this man?"[1]

Following the publication of my book on the Nisei in Hawai'i,[2] I began to explore Kurihara's place in the incarceration of Japanese Americans during World War II. I also began to explore his earlier life experiences. After several years of digging, I interrupted my research in order to pursue other projects. When I resumed my focus on Kurihara, I was pleasantly surprised to find that I had no trouble—despite the long hiatus—in re-immersing myself in the twists and turns of his multilayered experiences. I hope that you will find his story as compelling as I do.

This book is organized chronologically. After an introduction, which orients the reader to the book's purpose and scope, chapter one focuses on Kurihara's youth, growing up and attending schools in Hawai'i, followed by his arrival in San Francisco to continue his schooling. Chapter two has Kurihara volunteering as a soldier in World War I and then settling in Los Angeles to continue his schooling and find employment. Chapter three takes the reader to the eve and aftermath of the Pearl Harbor attack as it affected Kurihara and other Japanese Americans. Chapter four lays out the main events that led to the revolt at Manzanar, one of the ten concentration camps to which ethnic Japanese were exiled. Chapter five steps back from the revolt to assess the highly charged emotional setting in which the inmates found themselves. Chapter six examines the interpersonal dynamics that occurred at two largely invisible citizen isolation camps, created for dissidents who were removed from their families without having been charged with any crime. Chapter seven recounts the turmoil at Tule Lake, designated a segregation camp for those labeled "disloyal." Chapter eight examines the renunciation fiasco that brought fear and hysteria to thousands of inmates. Chapter nine discusses the aftermath of Japan's defeat for Kurihara and others who left the United States for life in that war-torn country. And finally, the afterword explores Kurihara's three major life themes that explain his words and actions, and his sense of himself as an American.

ACKNOWLEDGMENTS

During my many years on this project, individuals have wondrously given me their time and expertise. Three historians gave me untold assistance. Roger Daniels expressed interest in my project when I considered it some twenty years ago. He pointed to valuable sources, and with his wealth of knowledge on Japanese Americans and their World War II incarceration, he provided constructive comments on my early drafts. Arthur Hansen suggested that I delve into this project, after I had read his amazing, in-depth interview with Harry Ueno and asked if anything had been published on Ueno's friend Kurihara. Throughout my research and writing he was absolutely generous in offering ideas, resources, and critical comments. Idus Newby gave the manuscript a careful read, offering excellent insights that strengthened my analysis, and editorial suggestions that improved my narrative.

I am extremely thankful to Kurihara's family for their encouragement and generous help. My letter to the editor in a Japanese American newspaper led to my friendship with Kurihara's niece, Grace Fukumoto, who helped me decode the Kurihara family register filed at the Japanese Consulate in Hawai'i, provided me with priceless family photos, and introduced me to Kurihara's other family members. Hanako Marubayashi, another niece of Kurihara, spoke with me about her reminiscences of Kurihara, his parents, and his siblings. Raymond Kurihara, Joe Kurihara's nephew and son of younger brother Roy Kurihara, corresponded with me by e-mail, recalling the 1930s when Joe lived with Roy's family in Los Angeles. Kurihara's grandnephew Henry Fujita showed me a news clip of Kurihara, letters Kurihara wrote to Fujita's mother, and World War I artifacts he sent her. Joe Wilfred Fujita, another grandnephew, spoke to me of his conversations with Kurihara during the 1950s in Japan. For all the help that Kurihara's family offered me, I am forever grateful.

I truly appreciate the people who so willingly allowed me and others to interview them, and those who permitted their interviews by Densho volunteers and staff to be stored in the Densho Digital Archive, a repository of valuable material on the Japanese American experience. Former renunciants who agreed to be interviewed were forthcoming about their thoughts and feelings. I thank them for their courage and generosity in sharing a part of their painful past.

Father Michael Kotlanger, S.J., was most supportive during my visit to the University of San Francisco Archives, and after my visit he suggested secondary sources that gave greater depth to my understanding of issues affecting Kurihara's life. Patricia Alvarez oriented me to Catholicism and helped me think through the possible influences of Catholic schooling on Kurihara; both she and Ann Marie Ryan provided helpful comments on my section on Catholic education. Lloyd M. Pierson took me on a personal tour of the isolation camp at Moab and provided me with photos of it; Mary Monkoski-Takemure, Reiko Monkoski, Ruriko Kumano, and Aya Inoue translated materials from Japanese to English; Aiko Hirota and Jan Holmes helped me in my research on Kurihara's life in Japan; and Dwight Hoover critiqued portions of the manuscript. Aiko Herzig-Yoshinaga, Teruko Kumei, Yoshi Komori, Brian Hayashi, Pedro Loureiro, Shigeru Sugiyama, Greg Robinson, Eiichiro Azuma, Brian Niiya, and Kenji Tagumi pointed me to valuable resources.

I would like to thank archivists at the National Archives and Records Administration, the Hawai'i State Archives, the Bancroft Library at University of California Berkeley, Department of Special Collections of the Charles E. Young Research Library at University of California Los Angeles, St. Louis School Archives in Honolulu, and Eastern California Museum in Independence, California; Jean McDowell, curator-director of the Dan O'Laurie Museum of Moab; Mako Rova of the Xavier Catholic Mission in San Francisco; Linda Whisman of Southwestern Law School Library; Dore Minatodani of Special Collections and Ross Togashi of the Map Collection, Hamilton Library, University of Hawai'i Manoa; Glen Creason of the Los Angeles Public Library; and Tami Suzuki of the San Francisco Public Library.

The person who has been with me throughout this endeavor is my husband Dave Raney, who not only discussed ideas with me and helped me explore several archives, but also remained a keen supporter during the entire project.

I gratefully acknowledge the Civil Liberties Public Education Fund of the Civil Liberties Act of 1988, Public Law 100–383, for a grant in support of research for this project.

Parts of chapters 1 and 4 are from previously published works.

"Searching for America: A Japanese American's Quest, 1900–1930," in *The History of Discrimination in U.S. Education: Marginality, Agency, and Power* edited by Eileen Tamura, 91–116 (New York: Palgrave Macmillan, 2008), used with permission from Palgrave Macmillan.

"Value Messages Collide with Reality: Joseph Kurihara and the Power of Informal Education, *History of Education Quarterly* 50, no. 1 (2010): 1–33, used with permission from Wiley-Blackwell.

INTRODUCTION

> What is there for us to be ashamed of being a Jap? . . . To live as Jap is the greatest pride we can enjoy in life, and to die as Jap under the protection of the Japanese Flag which has weathered through many national storms without a defeat for 2,600 years is the greatest honor a man can ever hope to cherish. I, in the name of the Niseis proclaim ourselves Japs, 100 per cent Japs, now, tomorrow, and forever.
>
> Tenno Hei Ka Banzai! Banzai! Banzai!
> Dai Nippon Teikoku Banzai! Banzai! Banzai!
> Zai Ryu Dobo Banzai! Banzai! Banzai!

Joseph Yoshisuke Kurihara proclaimed these incendiary words in 1942 while an inmate in Manzanar, one of ten U.S. concentration camps to which Japanese Americans were relegated during World War II.[1] Kurihara, an American citizen who had served in the U.S. Army during World War I and was a member of the Veterans of Foreign Wars and the American Legion, had become one of Manzanar's leading dissidents.

His words reflected his stance in the middle of war and contrasted markedly with his attitudes and behavior prior to the war. Though Kurihara had felt the brunt of anti-Japanese hostility, especially in California in the decades before World War II, he had remained adamantly positive about the prospects of his own life in America. The forced removal and incarceration of ethnic Japanese destroyed that perspective.

This study recreates the story of Kurihara's life to provide a window into the history of Japanese Americans during the first half of the twentieth century. From his youth and until World War II, Kurihara pursued a path that he believed (naively, I can say in retrospect) would enable him to live the American life, as envisioned in the Progressive Era phrase, "the promise of American life." He enrolled in schools that offered a quality, Western-oriented education. He embraced Christianity, the essential source of Western cultural identity at the time, endured anti-Japanese hostility directed at him, and fought as a soldier in the U.S. Army during the Great War. This dogged pursuit of a place for himself as an American in the face of jarring discouragements enabled Kurihara to absorb Western modes of thinking and behavior. As a result, he was able to navigate his way in two cultural worlds, European America and Japanese America.

With the entry of the United States into World War II and the consequent incarceration of the Nikkei (ethnic Japanese), whether resident aliens or American citizens, Kurihara's attitude and behavior changed radically. His resulting disillusionment turned to bitterness when he realized that his status, both as a U.S. citizen and a combat veteran of World War I, was of no import to the government. For Kurihara this was betrayal by a country that professed the ideal of equality and justice. In 1944, after two years of incarceration because of his ancestry, Kurihara renounced his U.S. citizenship, and the following year, at the age of fifty, an age at which major cultural adjustments are problematic at best, he boarded a ship to Japan, a country he had never even visited. And he never returned to the United States, though he lived through another twenty years of profound changes in Japanese-American relations. So radical a change in circumstances and perspective provides a clear demonstration of the ways in which arbitrary acts of injustice can completely overturn the mindset of an avowedly patriotic person.

As a youth and young adult, Kurihara not only pursued an American education, but in converting to Christianity, he chose not Protestantism but the more disciplined and authoritarian Catholicism. In doing so he also rejected the dominant religion among the Nikkei, Buddhism, which Caucasians in Hawaiʻi considered an alien, even pagan, religion, while equating Christianity with Americanism and civilization.[2]

From his family, his schooling, and his religion, he internalized values and acquired knowledge and skills that he hoped would make him a productive, integrated, and accepted member of American society. From his parents he learned the value of work and perseverance. At school he learned the particulars of Catholicism and Christianity, and also the values and viewpoints of American and Western thinking, including American mannerisms and ideals. Years later, during his interrogation at one of the isolation camps for dissident Japanese Americans, he told his inquisitor, "[W]e were taught in school to think like Americans, live like Americans and standup and fight for our rights like Americans[.] So I have fought, and will fight for right and justice."[3]

Long before he made this statement (and many others like it), Kurihara had been one of the dissident leaders in Manzanar, one of the concentration camps the U.S. government set up in World War II to incarcerate Nikkei then residing on the West Coast. In this role he had been and continued to be a distinctive if not unique man. At Manzanar he had made emotional, often inflammatory speeches attacking the U.S. government for its treatment of the Nikkei. He openly, vociferously, and provocatively professed loyalty to Japan to any and all who would listen. Yet in his feelings of rejection, despair, anger, frustration, and bitterness, Kurihara very much reflected the group of which he was a part. Because he dared to say to camp administrators what other detainees, even the most docile and cooperative, thought and felt at different levels but dared not voice openly, he became a spokesperson for camp inmates.

Kurihara's story personifies the processes of identity formation in their ethnic, cultural, social, and national dimensions and contradictions. What he learned abstractly and how he interpreted and reconciled it with his experiences were bound together with his ongoing re-creation of his self-image. Through it all and despite his decision to become an expatriate, he continued to maintain an American identity. Even after he renounced his citizenship, he maintained, "I will voice my conviction like a man and will fight like an American."[4]

Kurihara's story also personifies as it illuminates the tragic injustice of the forced removal and incarceration of the West Coast Nikkei by the U.S. government, even as it dramatizes the heroic resistance to that injustice. If Americans seek to be true to their professed democratic values, as they must, it is crucial that they—and we—understand resistance among those they have or their government has unjustly treated. This study seeks to illuminate dissent, chiefly at Manzanar, but within the context of resistance at other concentration camps. In so doing, it addresses issues of citizenship renunciation and expatriation, the complexities of such subjects as loyalty and patriotism, and the constitutional issues raised by incarceration itself as well as by the existence of the "Isolation Centers" of Moab and Leupp, places where citizens were denied hearings while never charged with any crime.

Kurihara's story further personalizes the contradictions between rhetoric and reality in American society. Despite the anti-Japanese hostility that he encountered in California, he continued to believe in his country, volunteering for the army when the United States entered World War I. After returning home as a veteran, he continued to maintain a positive outlook, despite the mounting anti-Japanese hostility he and fellow Japanese Americans had to endure. But the shock of incarceration during World War II, solely because of his ancestry, was a disillusionment he could not shake. It convinced him that he must reject the country that he had so passionately sought to be a part of. He then realized how naïve his belief in the rhetoric of American democracy had been, and his reaction to that realization was profound. Kurihara's renunciation of his U.S. citizenship was an extreme act of defiance, but hardly more extreme than the cause that provoked it. It is a stark manifestation of the often invisible emotional scars that immigrants and children of immigrants carry when they are confronted with a polity that insists on making them forever an alien, an Other. This study maps the ways in which Kurihara perceived, experienced, and interpreted the world around him. In doing so, it sheds light on the ongoing processes of constructing and reconstructing the self.

• • •

The literature on the incarceration of Japanese Americans during World War II is massive and varied. In it, discussion of Joseph Kurihara appears regularly though briefly as one of the leading dissidents protesting the injustice of imprisoning men, women, and children for nothing more than their ethnicity. Yet little is known about him. For example, what in his early life best helps to explain his actions as an adult? What motivated him to say and do what he did? This study answers these questions and corrects published misconceptions about him.[5]

Studies of Nikkei resistance in the U.S. concentration camps demonstrate conclusively that inmates did not acquiesce passively to their imprisonment but engaged in subtle as well as overt forms of opposition. My study adds to this literature by examining the theme of resistance through the personal experiences of an individual man. Building on previous works that examine the performance of government officials and administrators, my study reveals intra-group differences, including conflicts and even violence among the Nikkei themselves. In this context Kurihara emerges as a human being with both admirable and questionable attributes.[6]

Kurihara was a controversial figure in the camps, often characterized as an "agitator" and "troublemaker" by fellow inmates as well as camp officials. Succeeding generations, on the other hand, have depicted him as an admirable, even heroic figure. This study re-creates the story of Kurihara in the concentration camps while illuminating his own understanding of his life and actions. While Kurihara deserves praise for his protests against the victimization of innocent Nikkei by the U.S. government at Manzanar and then by Nikkei radicals at the Tule Lake concentration camp, his call for justice does not vindicate his advocacy to violence at Manzanar.[7] To be sure, he believed that those he opposed were informers for the FBI or Manzanar administrators, and he sought to protect Nikkei from unjust accusations.

Reflecting in a Japanese American newspaper in 1946 on Kurihara's actions, Togo Tanaka, who had been one of those targeted for violence by Kurihara and others in Manzanar, recalled that Kurihara believed passionately that the Nisei—American citizens who were children of Japanese immigrants—needed "aggressively [to] guard their rights as American citizens." Tanaka further noted that Kurihara's ultimate decision to renounce his U.S. citizenship was "not so much evidence of 'Japanism' . . . as it [was] a symbol of U.S. wartime racist injustice to little people caught in the frustrating mesh of a raw deal that got an easy okay during war under the mask of 'military necessity.'"[8]

Despite Tanaka's open commentary on wartime racism, most of those who had been incarcerated said little, in the early years after the war, about that or any other aspect of their experiences. From the end of the war in 1945 until the mid-1960s, most Japanese American families and the larger ethnic community spoke little if at all of their incarceration. Those who had been imprisoned saw it as a shameful experience, one that was better unrecounted to those who came after.[9] Yet what had happened remained with them—if only in the recesses of their minds. As Sethe, the lead protagonist in Toni Morrison's *Beloved*, states, "Some things go. Pass on. Some things just stay. . . . Places, places are still there. If a house burns down, it's gone, but the place—the picture of it—stays, and not just in my rememory, but out there, in the world." The filmmaker Chris Marker put it another way: "Remembering is not the opposite of forgetting, but rather its lining."[10]

In the late 1960s, the situation within the Nikkei community began to change. Third-generation Japanese Americans, known as Sansei, almost all of whom were born after the end of the war, joined other Asian Americans on college campuses in calling for courses in their own history. Inspired by the civil rights and Black Power movements, and fueled by anti-Vietnam war protests, many in this younger generation became activists for a yellow-power, Asian American movement.[11]

In this context the Nisei, most of whom had suppressed their memories of exile, began during the 1970s to allow themselves to bring these memories to the surface. But how they remembered their experiences conflicted with some of the cultural imperatives of the generation born after the war. While the Nisei largely stressed endurance and making "the best of it," the Sansei, who were supported by some Nisei, stressed oppression and resistance. Disputes resulted "about different frameworks for collective memory." Much of this controversy dated back to animosities within the concentration camps themselves, between members of the Japanese American Citizens League, for example, and those who accused them of serving as spies for the FBI or collaborators with camp officials.[12]

During this time, both Nikkei and non-Nikkei scholars began to unearth documents that implicated U.S. government officials, and a movement for redress gained momentum, culminating in a reparations law that was eventually followed by redress payments. With the success of the movement and the growing studies on the incarceration, the Nisei have been more willing to bring the skeletons out of the closet.

One of the skeletons was the issue of renunciation. Amid the strikes, martial law, tanks, arrests, imprisonment in the stockade, pressure groups, threats, and violence, over fifty-seven hundred Japanese Americans renounced their U.S. citizenship.[13]

After the war and in the decades that followed, renunciants said little to others about their past. During their sixty years of silence, they bore the label "disloyal" and were invisible in an ethnic community that sought acceptance in mainstream society.[14] The heroes were the war veterans, who were glorified and honored for their patriotism and valor. As a result, renunciants were for many decades erased from the community's memory. Glorifications on the one hand, silences and erasures on the other. This was the prevailing mindset.

As late as the 1980s and 1990s, most renunciants refused to be interviewed. A few were willing to share their memories only if they remained anonymous. One man who recounted his experiences to me refused to discuss a fractious occurrence at one of the camps. Another man whom I phoned to inquire if he would be willing to speak with me refused with palpable hostility. Ironically, he was neither a dissident nor a renunciant. However, he did have a rather prominent role in one of the camps, and his memories may have been difficult for him to reconcile. Since the early years after 2000, former inmates, including former renunciants, have been more comfortable in telling their stories and revealing their identities to the public. The redress law signed by President Reagan, the letter of apology signed by President Bush, and the redress payments all helped to heal the bitterness, confusion, and shame that they had held for so many years.[15] Moreover, pilgrimages to Manzanar and to Tule Lake, the most turmoil-ridden of the camps, provided a space for people to allow their memories to emerge and healing to take place.[16]

In writing Kurihara's story, I have been conscious of the importance of words in creating images in our memories. For almost a generation after the war, most of those who wrote about the incarceration used the language of euphemism to soften the jarring realities a harsher terminology would convey. In this study I avoid the language of euphemism: evacuation, Assembly Centers, relocation, Relocation Centers, and internment camps. Instead, I use a language Kurihara would have agreed with: forced removal, exclusion, exile, incarceration, imprisonment, and concentration camps. This last term is especially helpful in understanding the significance of my choice of words. The camps for Japanese Americans during World War II have often been referred to as internment camps or relocation centers. In the early 1970s, some scholars began to call them "concentration camps." Those who rejected that term made the obvious point that the camps for Japanese Americans were not like the Nazi death camps for Jews and other "undesirables."[17]

That point was well made. But U.S. government officials themselves used "concentration camps" to refer to the Japanese American camps. They did so because the term broadly defined is amorphous enough to cover a wide variety of places: a guarded compound to which persons are confined without being charged with crimes and held without due process.[18] As the notoriety of Hitler's concentration camps spread during the course of the war, U.S. officials replaced "concentration camps" with the more benign term, "Relocation Centers." But this is inaccurate, misleading, and inappropriate for what the camps were—sites where authorities wielded power over defenseless people thrown together because of their ancestry. To distinguish the Japanese American camps from the Nazi death and slave labor camps, the historian Roger Daniels has used the term "American concentration camps."[19]

As for "internment," that is a legal state defined and regulated by the 1929 Geneva Prisoners of War Convention. During World War II, about eight thousand Japanese nationals, as well as two thousand German and a few hundred Italian nationals, were interned in camps run by the U.S. Immigration and Naturalization Service (INS), a component of the Department of Justice. The U.S. State Department "insisted that Geneva Convention conditions be maintained [in the INS internment camps] . . . in the hope that the Axis powers . . . would reciprocate" in their treatment of Americans in their custody.[20]

Unlike the internment camps, the War Relocation Authority camps, which held citizens and noncitizens, did not follow Geneva Convention rules. There were no agreed-upon standards for these camps, and as a result, living conditions were far inferior to those in the internment camps. Moreover, ignoring the Geneva Convention allowed the U.S. government to place citizens in the stockade for more than thirty days, and remove others to isolation camps away from their families—all without due process.[21]

As Daniels said, "Words do matter."[22] They matter because they invoke images in our minds and memories. The words we use to reconstruct the past and transmit this reconstruction largely determine what we remember about the past.

CHAPTER 1

Growing Up American

Joseph Yoshisuke Kurihara was born January 1, 1895, on the island of Kaua'i in what was called the Republic of Hawai'i. This was two years after the overthrow of the Hawaiian monarchy and three years before the U.S. Congress passed a joint resolution that resulted in the occupation of the islands as an American territory.[1]

Kurihara's father, Kichizo Kurihara, was among the many farmers in southwestern Japan who had been hit hard by the economic transformations brought about by the Meiji government in the last decades of the nineteenth century. Like many others in the Ōshima district of the Yamaguchi prefecture, he and his wife Haru responded positively to the call for plantation workers in the distant and unknown Hawaiian Islands. With high hopes, they left their home and their homeland and arrived in 1888 in what was then the Kingdom of Hawaii. The Kuriharas were one of the relatively few married couples who joined the migration of Japanese nationals to Hawai'i. Like the Chinese who came to the islands before them, the overwhelming majority of Japanese migrants, who became known as Issei, first generation, were men.[2]

They were not the earliest migrant workers in the islands from Japan. An earlier group of 148 Japanese had arrived in the islands in 1868, but the Japanese government halted the emigration of laborers due to internal needs as well as political and diplomatic developments. Then in 1885, Japan and the Kingdom of Hawaii reached a new agreement governing the migration of Japanese nationals to the islands. As a result of this agreement, in the next twenty years, tens of thousands from Japan would arrive in Hawai'i, each obligated to a term, usually three years, of labor on sugar plantations.[3]

The Kuriharas settled in Hanama'ulu, two miles northeast of the main town of Lihu'e, on the island of Kaua'i. Hanama'ulu was a component of the fifty-thousand-acre Lihue Plantation.[4]

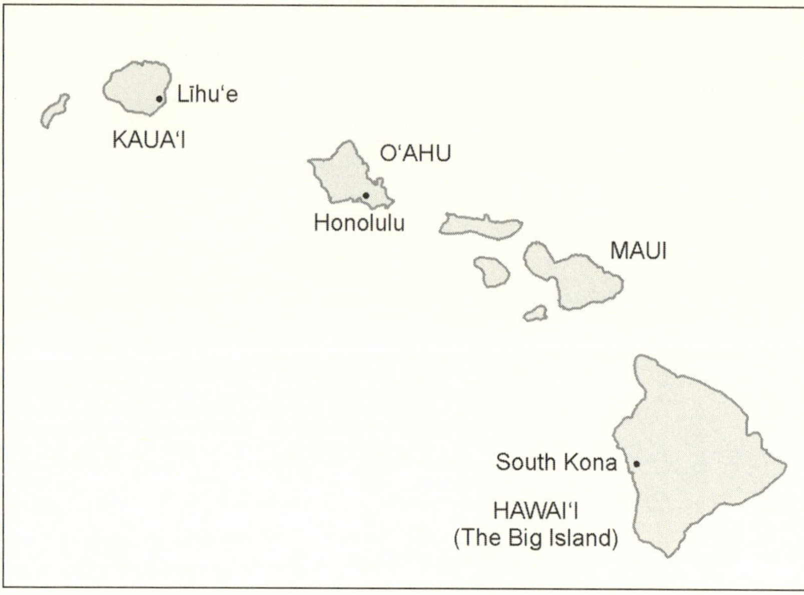

Map 1. Islands of Hawai'i. Map by Dave Raney

At the plantation Kichizo Kurihara found himself in the harvesting season facing the task of performing strenuous physical labor for ten to twelve hours a day under the scorching sun in dusty air amid razor-sharp cane leaves and buzzing wasps and yellow jackets. It was an oppressive, debilitating, onerous, relentless routine. In it he worked alongside Japanese and Chinese nationals, Hawaiians and other Pacific Islanders, as well as Portuguese and a few Spaniards. (Portuguese, like the less numerous Spaniards, had been recruited as laborers and were therefore considered distinct from other Caucasians.) Germans, too, worked for the plantation, but as more highly paid skilled workers and field foremen. During this time the Kuriharas lived in a single room in a long hut in a camp in which Japanese were segregated from those of other ethnic groups.[5]

The Japanese camp, like camps of other plantation workers, was situated in the midst of a vast sugar cane field. The Hanama'ulu site included a sugar mill[6] and a plantation store at which families purchased food and household essentials, charging them to accounts identified not by the name of the family head but by his plantation identification number, called *bango*—a Japanese word meaning "number"—which had been issued to each plantation worker. To supplement the provisions at the plantation store, peddlers from nearby villages came with their wares and foodstuffs. Japanese families were especially fond of their own ethnic foods such as soy sauce, tofu, and Japanese sweets.

Kichizo Kurihara worked at Lihue Plantation from 1888 to 1890.[7] Leaving the plantation was a momentous decision for someone who had little command of English and few skills beyond farm work and the pidgin language that foreign workers used to communicate across ethnic lines in Hawai'i. In making the decision Kurihara was rejecting the poor pay, grueling field labor, and harsh treatment of plantation foremen—*luna*—in favor of confronting the daunting challenges of unknown work ahead. In this he was like many other plantation laborers who left the plantation at the end of their three-year contract.[8] By this time his wife was expecting their first child.

It is not clear what type of work Kichizo found after leaving Lihue Plantation, but all five of the couple's children were born on Kaua'i: Kikuno, a daughter, in 1890, followed in the next year by Taiji, a son; Kawayo, a second daughter, in 1893, then Yoshisuke (Joseph) in 1895, and finally Saiichi, the third son, two years later.

When Yoshisuke—he would give himself the name Joseph at age twenty—was two years old, the family moved to Honolulu, the seat of government of the Republic of Hawaii and the urban center of the island of O'ahu, in search of better economic opportunities.[9] The next year the United States occupied the Hawaiian Islands and in 1900 incorporated them into the American union as a territory. The acquisition of the island chain, strategically located in the Pacific Ocean, was one result of a late-nineteenth-century U.S. imperialistic enterprise that included war with Spain and later the Philippines, with the resulting possession of the Philippines, Guam, Puerto Rico, and the temporary control of Cuba.

Honolulu in 1897 was a bustling little city of twenty-nine thousand inhabitants, almost a third of the population of the archipelago. The Kuriharas settled there, in the Palama district, on Asylum Road, so-called because it led to the Oahu Insane Asylum. Nearby was O'ahu's Reform School.[10] The family rented a simply constructed wooden cottage, one of many clustered in the area. The Kurihara residence was surrounded by homes of other struggling, working-class families. People cooked on wood-burning stoves and lit lamps fueled with kerosene. Ox carts and horse-drawn wagons traveled unpaved dirt roads, which sloshed with mud during and after heavy rains.[11]

Located immediately west of downtown Honolulu, Palama was home to both middle-class and working-class families, many of them Native Hawaiians. About three years after the Kuriharas arrived in Honolulu, a catastrophic fire a few blocks away in the Chinatown section of downtown Honolulu changed the face of Palama and much of the rest of the surrounding community. In the fall of 1899 the world pandemic of bubonic plague reached Honolulu. The outbreak occurred in Chinatown, an overcrowded, squalid section of the city, and threatened to spread everywhere. In their attempt to eradicate it, health officials ordered the controlled burning of rat-infested tenements in Chinatown. One of the resulting fires set in January 1900 became a spreading conflagration when unexpectedly powerful and relentless winds whipped the flames out of control. In the aftermath, thirty-eight acres—about a fifth of downtown Honolulu—lay flattened and charred, and five thousand people—largely Chinese but also Japanese and Native Hawaiians—were left without homes, businesses, and personal belongings.[12]

Government officials ordered the rapid building of two- and three-storied tenements in Palama, to which the displaced Chinatown residents were directed to move. The resulting over-crowded conditions in Palama disrupted the water system and caused the sewer systems to malfunction, and as a consequence, middle-class families moved out of the area. Thereafter Palama became known as the poor, "rough" part of town, where youth gangs picked on newcomers and got into fistfights.[13]

Despite these problems, Palama maintained a vibrancy of its own. During the first decade of the twentieth century, the district—only a mile from busy Honolulu Harbor, which accommodated increased shipping of raw sugar to U.S. markets—offered a rich amalgam of rural and urban life. Within Palama and its adjoining Kalihi district stood a soda bottling company, a soy brewing company, a poi factory, churches, clusters of wooden cottages, tenement houses, and small family shops offering meals, produce, and supplies. Intermingled with these businesses and dwellings were fields of taro patches, rice paddies, banana groves, and farms of vegetables, chickens, pigs, and dairy cows. Only a mile or so away from the harbor, acres of sugar cane grew under the blazing sun.[14]

After a decade on Asylum Road, the Kuriharas moved less than a mile away, to Houghtailing Road, named after a prominent family who lived on fifteen acres of land abutting the road. There the family rented half of a small duplex near King Street, an unpaved dirt thoroughfare busy with horse-drawn vehicles and fronted by family-operated shops and large-scale businesses. Kurihara's father drove a hack, one of many horse-drawn cabs that transported passengers.[15] After a few years he became a drayman, an independent businessman who transported heavy loads in his own wagon. A few years later he opened a new business, listing himself in boldface in the city directory as a "Contractor for Stone Wall, Step and Cement Work, Dealer in Black and White Sand, Coral Rock, Foundation Stone and All Kinds of Soil."[16]

The Kuriharas sent their children to public grammar school, but each of the three older ones attended for only a few years. Kurihara's eldest sister, Kikuno, wanted to continue her schooling, but she had to quit at the end of her third year to take care of her younger brothers, Yoshisuke (Joseph) and Saiichi. In time, Kikuno formed a close bond with her charges, and throughout her life she continued to maintain a protective and supportive relationship with them.[17] By the time Kurihara decided that he wanted to continue in school, his parents had no objections. By then they were financially secure enough that they had no need for him to work to augment the family income.

Kurihara first attended Kaiulani School, less than a mile away from his home. The school had been named after the heir apparent to the Hawaiian kingdom, Princess Kaiulani, who died in 1899, the year the school opened. With 407 students enrolled in its first year, the school helped ease the overcrowding in other Honolulu schools. The island's Reform School, which had been on a lot adjacent to Kaiulani School, had been removed to a new location just before the grammar school opened.[18]

Kaiulani School was an attractive, two-story brick-and-stucco structure with large windows. This solid, contemporary-styled building, like others constructed in the islands at the turn of the twentieth century, helped to demonstrate that Hawai'i was no backward way-station but on the contrary, a prosperous, progressive economy and polity in step with the United States.[19] Such evidence ostensibly endorsed the efforts of the republic's white political and business leaders, who had orchestrated the overthrow of the Hawaiian monarchy and then engineered an occupation of the archipelago by the U.S. government.[20] As part of their effort to show that Hawai'i was Americanized, these men enacted a law that provided for free public schooling and made schooling compulsory for children aged six to fifteen. As the schooling record of Kurihara's family demonstrated, however, the law was poorly enforced.[21]

On his first day of school in September 1903, eight-year-old Kurihara walked barefoot to Kaiulani School, one of nineteen public grammar schools in a city of thirty-nine thousand inhabitants. Like his classmates, many of whom were also children of immigrants, Kurihara was a U.S. citizen because he was born in Hawai'i. According to the Organic Act, which created the Territory of Hawaii, all who had been citizens of the Republic of Hawaii—which meant those born or naturalized in the Hawaiian islands—were "declared to be citizens of the United States."[22] In race-conscious America in the early twentieth century, however, the meaning of citizenship for racial and ethnic minorities was amorphous. Thus Kurihara and other Asian Americans were often treated as noncitizens or as "new" Americans. During the first half of the twentieth century, the unmodified word "American" referred to white Americans. The territory's public school reports, for example, included teachers' names and "nationality." The reports reserved the term "American" for Caucasians, while calling Asian Americans Japanese or Chinese.[23]

As a first-grader, Kurihara shared his teacher with forty other students. By today's standards, such a student-teacher ratio is abysmal. But Kurihara was more fortunate in this respect than most of his peers, some of whom sat in classrooms with as many as sixty students. By the time Kurihara reached the eighth grade in 1910, overcrowding had become an even greater problem, with some classrooms in urban Honolulu having as many as fifty to eighty students. Kaiulani School's student body, which grew from 569 to 952 during the first decade of the twentieth century, reflected this increase in class size.[24]

Kurihara's teachers were white and female, which was the norm in the territory's public schools. His classmates were predominantly Native Hawaiians and Chinese, with some Japanese (these terms refer to their ethnic background and not their nationality). While the proportions of ethnic groups varied from school to school, the predominant groups enrolled in the territory's public schools during the first two decades of the twentieth century were, in order of numerical size, Japanese, Native Hawaiians, Portuguese, and Chinese.[25]

Those attending the territory's private schools that year, including Catholic schools, constituted 21 percent of the student population. Of the 5,525 private school students, 35 percent were Hawaiians or Part-Hawaiians, 21 percent Portuguese, 13 percent Japanese, and 12 percent Chinese. While Caucasians constituted 7.7 percent of the territory's population, their children were only 3 percent of public school students and 14 percent of private school students.[26]

The ethnic diversity that surrounded Kurihara in his youth meant that, aside from his white teachers, most of his interactions were with people of color. This ethnic mix would change abruptly when he moved to northern California.

While Hawai'i included a unique combination of ethnic groups, ethnic diversity in schools in the major cities of the United States in this period was not unusual. In 1908, for example, 72 percent of all students in New York City schools were immigrants or children of immigrants, and the percentages in other cities were also high: 67 percent in Chicago, 64 percent in Boston, 60 percent in Cleveland, and 58 percent in San Francisco. In matters of curriculum, too, Hawai'i's public schools reflected U.S. trends. During each of his grammar school years, Kurihara's course of study included language, arithmetic, nature study, geography, physiology and hygiene, reading, writing, manual work, calisthenics, and music. In his fifth through eighth grades, history was also part of the curriculum.[27]

When Kurihara was sixteen years old, he completed the eighth grade at Kaiulani School. He spent the next two years working to accumulate savings to pay for future schooling. Then in September 1913 he enrolled in the Catholic, all-male St. Francis School as a ninth grade student, with tuition a dollar a month.[28] Why did he opt for a private school that charged tuition?

The only public high school on O'ahu at the time, McKinley, was noted for its high academic standards, and was not only free but accessible to Kurihara by trolley car. The answer to that question is unknown, but the question itself invites speculations that go to the root of Kurihara's distinctiveness. The option he took was one of a series of radical, almost unique choices for a young Japanese American in 1913: to begin high school at the age of eighteen; to opt for a liberal arts rather than a vocational course of study; and to enroll in a Catholic school with a Western-oriented curriculum. In combination, these actions suggest a deliberate decision to reorient the course of his life in a most fundamental sense. He would become culturally an American rather than a Japanese or Japanese American, a Christian rather than a Buddhist or unbeliever. All of these choices are vital to self-identity, to self-creation, to making an individual into the person he or she wants to be, and to be identified as such.

None of this might have occurred to Kurihara on any conscious level. On the surface at least Kurihara might simply have been inspired by some of the things he had come to know and believe about Catholicism. Yet here, at the point at which he became seriously attracted to Catholicism, may be the pivot of Kurihara's life, the turn that set him apart from his Nisei peers, whose typical life course he had heretofore generally followed.

Situated near his home at the corner of College Walk and Kukui Street, St. Francis was a charity school attached to St. Louis College, a high school run by the Brothers of Mary and known to give its students a sound education. In his class of forty-six students, Kurihara was the only one of Japanese descent, but Chinese Americans constituted 44 percent of his classmates, while 37 percent were whites and 17 percent were Hawaiians and Part-Hawaiians. Chinese immigrants had arrived in Hawai'i a generation earlier than the Japanese, and they and their offspring were more open to Christianity than the Japanese.[29]

The ethnic makeup of Kurihara's class mirrored the student body of St. Francis and St. Louis College. In 1913–14, only nine of 726 males enrolled at one or the other of the two schools were Japanese. In his history of the Catholic mission in the Islands, Father Reginald Yzendoorn noted the scarcity of Japanese students at Catholic schools in the first two decades of the twentieth century, in contrast to the more numerous Chinese students. As more Japanese American children reached school age in the 1920s and 1930s, however, their numbers in Catholic schools grew, and some of them converted to Catholicism. Nevertheless, the Japanese Americans attending Catholic schools remained a small minority.[30]

Kurihara's attraction to Catholicism was an anomaly in his family and among the Nikkei. He was the only one in his family of Buddhists to attend a Catholic school or to "embrace" Catholicism. Historically, most Nikkei who became Christians chose Protestantism, suggesting the distinctiveness of the life course Kurihara had chosen.[31]

His curriculum at St. Francis included English, algebra, U.S. history, shorthand, and bookkeeping, as well as elocution, which would continue in his later schooling. Important also is that he learned lessons in manners and morals, as the Brothers who taught at the school did not refrain from proselytizing their non-Catholic students. Catholic students took religion courses, while non-Catholics like Kurihara enrolled in ethics classes in which they received a strong dose of Catholic teachings. His teachers were preoccupied with "character formation," viewing their task as not so much to "instill knowledge but to make good men." With this emphasis, St. Francis School, like St. Louis College, succeeded in converting many of its non-Catholic students. In 1913–14, when Kurihara was at St. Francis, about thirty boys at the two schools were baptized. Although Kurihara was not one of them, his classmates' conversion made an impression on him, for immediately after moving to San Francisco, he was baptized as a Catholic.[32]

Kurihara left St. Francis School in March 1914. By then he had decided that he wanted to become a doctor and continue his schooling on the U.S. West Coast. Knowing that his family could not support his educational aspirations, Kurihara worked for a year in road construction in South Kona, on the island of Hawai'i, in "probably the most uninhabited section of the island." When he had earned enough money, he quit his job and moved to San Francisco.[33]

Life in San Francisco

In July 1915 Kurihara made the eight-day journey to San Francisco aboard the steamship *Sierra*, one of several vessels of the Oceanic Steamship Company of San Francisco and one among many that serviced the busy seaport of Honolulu. With Kurihara were twelve other passengers as well as mail and cargo.[34]

Once in San Francisco, Kurihara needed a job so that he could "accumulate as much as possible" in order to attend school. Learning that farms in the Sacramento valley needed laborers, he went there, and soon found himself toiling "under the over-bearing heat" alongside other seasonal workers, most of them Nikkei. In the 1910s, farm labor was the work most available to Nikkei in California. Many of the employers were Japanese immigrants, Issei. At the time Kurihara worked in the Sacramento delta, Japanese farmers leased 27 percent of the cultivated land there, growing onions, beans, asparagus, celery, berries, potatoes, and cantaloupes. Although the Issei dominated the cultivation of such crops in the area, California's alien land laws prevented them from purchasing the land. Instead, they operated farms on land owned by white landlords who profited from the labor of the Nikkei.[35]

Once employed in the delta, Kurihara found food plentiful. Although the work was strenuous, he enjoyed his life there because fruit, fish, and game were abundant. Life in the city of Sacramento, however, he found "appalling." "While walking on K St.," he later wrote, "a fairly well-dressed person came and kicked me in the stomach for no reason whatever. . . . I watched his next move, maneuvering into position to fight it out the best I could, since my nature [would] not permit me to let it go unchallenged." The fight would have proceeded, had another man not stepped in to stop it. "I then went my way," Kurihara recalled, "feeling terribly hurt." In another instance, youths threw rocks at him and a Nisei friend as they walked down a residential street. "As we went toward them, they ran and hid. It was really aggravating." "Feeling perplexed" about the unprovoked hostility, Kurihara turned to his friend for an explanation. "'It's discrimination,'" his friend responded, an understatement of the naked racism that confronted Nikkei in California and the West Coast.[36]

With these experiences Kurihara realized that he had entered a place where whites—immigrants and American citizens alike—had little or no tolerance for people of color, a place where stoning, assaults, and vandalism toward them was not unusual. What happened to him in Sacramento reflected the racial hatred in California and other Western states toward the relatively small number of ethnic Chinese and Japanese, whether U.S. citizens like Kurihara or alien residents. Like the Chinese who had arrived earlier, the Japanese were needed as laborers for farms, railroads, lumber mills, salmon canneries, and coal and copper mines, at the same time that they were despised as outcasts. Eight years before Kurihara arrived in the Bay Area, race riots had erupted in San Francisco and Bellingham, Washington, as well as farther north, in Vancouver, British Columbia, where angry white mobs wreaked violence on Japanese, Chinese, and South Asians who seemed to threaten the economic, racial, and social status quo. Whether or not he knew about these riots, Kurihara understood that he and other Asian Americans were despised because of their ancestry, and he must have pondered what this meant for him as a Japanese American in the United States.[37]

While discrimination existed in Hawai'i, the violence he met in California surprised him. "No such thing ever happened where I came from," he recalled. "It was disgusting. At the time, I felt homesick for my good old native land." Yet his revulsion to the racial hostility confronting him neither deterred his aspirations nor caused him to return to the islands. On the contrary, continuing to believe that his country had a place for an American like him, he was determined to move forward with his dreams. He had gone to California with high expectations, and he continued to believe that possibilities for a bright future lay ahead. "Hard and discouraging as it was," he recalled, "I resolved ever more to carry my ambition through to success."[38]

After a couple of months in Sacramento, Kurihara returned to San Francisco to attend school. As the "financial and social center of the West," the city was growing rapidly, teeming with merchants, financiers, professionals, small-business people, trades people, laborers, sailors, fishermen, and a host of other workers. Having recently recovered from the devastating 1906 earthquake, San Francisco demonstrated its resilience in 1915 with the Panama-Pacific International Exposition, which opened just a few months before Kurihara first arrived in the city. Despite war in Europe, the exhibitions welcomed 20 million visitors.[39]

Soon after returning from Sacramento, Kurihara joined the St. Francis Xavier Japanese Catholic Mission, established for Nikkei Catholics in San Francisco. Having recently borne the brunt of anti-Asian hostility, Kurihara found the mission a sanctuary, as it was for other Nikkei Catholics, unwelcomed in most Catholic churches. Like other whites, white Catholics held an "intense racial prejudice and hatred of Asians." As a result, the St. Francis Xavier Mission in San Francisco, located on Buchanan Street in the "Japan town" section of the city, served as a place of both refuge and spiritual sustenance.[40]

Named after the Jesuit priest who, in 1549, had led the first Christian missionaries to Japan, the San Francisco mission had been established in 1913 as part of an effort by the Maryknoll Catholic Foreign Mission Society to open schools for and minister to the spiritual needs of Japanese Catholics along the West Coast. Father Albert Breton, who had previously lived and proselytized in Japan, had begun this effort by opening a mission in Los Angeles in 1912 and, the following year, another in San Francisco, naming both after St. Francis Xavier.[41]

In 1914 the Society of Jesus took over responsibility for the San Francisco mission. Father Julius von Egloffstein, who headed the mission for the Jesuits, had previously served in Japan as a missionary and was thus familiar with the customs of the Japanese community. On November 15, 1915, he baptized twenty-year-old Kurihara, who took the name Joseph.[42] During the early to mid-twentieth century, changing one's name was common among immigrants and their children. This facilitated their interactions with those unaccustomed to non-English names. In addition, Joseph—which has a similar-sounding first syllable as Yoshisuke—was an appropriate name for a Catholic.

By embracing Catholicism, Kurihara affirmed his commitment to Westernization. Why choose Catholicism over Protestantism? His later perfect scores in behavior at St. Ignatius, the Jesuit high school he attended in San Francisco, suggest that he found the exacting precepts of the Catholic Church appealing. Apparently he believed that Catholicism was part of mainstream America, in contrast to Buddhism, his family's religion. At the time he converted, he was probably unaware that he had chosen a denomination that was, ironically, itself marginalized by mainstream American society, dominated as it was by Protestantism.

The small community of Japanese Catholics in San Francisco helped Kurihara adjust to life in his new surroundings and pointed him to two Catholic institutions of higher learning—Santa Clara University just south of San Francisco, and St. Ignatius in the city itself. Kurihara first visited Santa Clara, the flagship Jesuit educational institution in the West. Although there was a high school attached to the university, Kurihara asked to enter the university. Attempting to do so without having completed high school indicates a sense of confidence, or, one might say, an inflated sense of oneself, a characteristic that reappears throughout his life. At Santa Clara he learned that he would need to pass an entrance examination as well as have a high school diploma. Disappointed but undaunted, he returned to San Francisco, enrolling in the high school attached to St. Ignatius University.[43]

There Kurihara attended classes in the school's box-like building on Hayes and Shrader Streets. This "temporary" structure—used from 1906 to 1927 and nicknamed "the shirt factory"—had been constructed quickly after the 1906 earthquake had demolished the original building. Kurihara's teachers were priests or brothers, all of them whites, as were most of the school's students. In 1915–16, when Kurihara was a ninth grader at the school, he was the only nonwhite in his section. There was a black student in the other section of his class, but the rest of the 188 students in the high school were white. In the following school year, Kurihara was the only nonwhite among the school's 186 students.[44]

This was a far cry from the ethnic diversity that had characterized Kurihara's schools in Hawai'i. Yet the fact that St. Ignatius admitted Asian Americans was more than noteworthy; it was an oddity in a city that maintained a segregated public school for Chinese, to which the school board attempted unsuccessfully to direct Japanese youths. To be sure, some of California's public high schools admitted Asian Americans, and California universities enrolled a few Asian and Asian American students.[45]

Nevertheless, anti-Asian animus was the prevailing sentiment everywhere in California, despite tiny numbers of Asians and Asian Americans there. In San Francisco during the first two decades of the twentieth century, the Chinese proportion of the population decreased from 2.5 to 1.5 percent, while the Japanese constituted 1.1 percent. Unlike the Chinese, who were concentrated in the city's Chinatown, the Japanese maintained their shops and homes in small clusters scattered within the city.[46]

As in Sacramento, the "atmosphere" in San Francisco was often unpleasant for Kurihara. During the two years he lived there, he had to endure "the distasteful word, 'Jap.'" "Never had I heard this word Jap in the islands," he declared, "but . . . in California it was almost a universal title used to address the Japanese. Many times, trying to be broad-minded, I soothed my feelings by interpreting it as an abbreviation of the word Japanese." But whenever the speaker used the word with "an ugly expression," Kurihara knew that it was meant to be an ethnic slur.[47]

The two years of his sojourn in the city coincided with a period of rabid anti-Japanese agitation. Led by San Francisco Mayor James D. Phelan, labor unions, and the Asiatic Exclusion League, white Californians campaigned to bar Japanese from entering the state and the rest of the country. Although the campaign was unsuccessful, they were able to convince the California legislature in 1913 to pass an alien land law that was aimed at the Japanese, who were gaining a foothold in farming. The law prohibited "aliens ineligible for citizenship"—a phrase referring to Asian immigrants, who were barred from naturalization by federal law—from owning agricultural land and limited their leasing of such land to three years. (In 1920 and 1923 the legislature added more stringent amendments to the law.)[48]

"Disregarding the conditions," Kurihara later wrote, "I decided to weather it through." He found a place to live on Fulton Street in a residential neighborhood several blocks from St. Ignatius School. To pay his tuition and room and board, he did a variety of janitorial chores for the apartment building in which he lived. Among other things, he operated the boiler that heated the building, cut firewood for the boiler, and on weekends swept the building's hallways, polished the brass work, and scrubbed the back stairs. About this experience he later wrote, "[The pay] was so small . . . [but] I was satisfied because . . . I wanted an education which I was unquestionably getting."[49]

St. Ignatius differed markedly from the Catholic schools that enrolled most of the few Japanese Americans who became Catholics. The Xavier Mission School in Los Angeles, for example, opened in 1921. Operated by Maryknoll Sisters, this school taught students in both Japanese and English, with the aim of having them become bilingual and bicultural. The St. Paul Miki School in Portland did the same thing. Both of these schools were similar in purpose to the ethnic parochial schools that served millions of European immigrant children in the nineteenth and early twentieth centuries.[50]

St. Ignatius, in contrast, taught in English only, and offered a curriculum that was thoroughly Western-centered. There, the "Ancient [Western] Classics

[held] the first place." At the same time, in response to a nationwide push to Americanize immigrants and their children through the school system, and to demonstrate the American-ness of the education offered in Catholic schools, St. Ignatius offered courses aimed to instill so-called American values in its students.[51]

As a college-preparatory school, St. Ignatius offered four years of coursework. In each of his two years there, Kurihara took classes in religion, Latin, history, elocution, English rhetoric, algebra, and elementary science. In his second year, he had the option of taking either drawing or a modern language.[52]

A young man of twenty when he entered St. Ignatius, Kurihara was a highly motivated student. And as a convert, he was serious about his Catholic faith, receiving scores of 96 and 97 percent in religion classes during his years at the school. Dedicated to the idea that religious learning should "permeate the whole atmosphere" of the institution, teachers at St. Ignatius emphasized the "development of Christian manhood." This meant that the school emphasized the development of character according to the precepts of Roman Catholicism. School expectations included "punctual attendance, strict obedience, assiduous application and blameless conduct," with students receiving "conduct" grades monthly. For his conduct, Kurihara received a perfect score of 100 every month, the only one to do so among his classmates during his two years at the school. Long after he departed St. Ignatius School, he continued to carry with him the idea of righteousness.[53]

The St. Ignatius curriculum had a strong impact on Kurihara. Designed for college-bound students and future civic leaders, the course of study included a grounding in Latin and Greek and the works of classical authors as Cicero, Ovid, Virgil, and Homer. "Embodying the ideals of the Renaissance world in which they arose," the historian Gerald McKevitt notes, "Jesuit schools [like St. Ignatius] . . . embraced the [Western] classics, because they seemed the ideal instrument for an education centered on ethical training and the development of effective rhetorical style and leadership skill." These themes—of ethics, rhetoric, and leadership—would play themselves out in Kurihara's activities during his incarceration years later at Manzanar and elsewhere.[54]

Kurihara did well in his courses in Roman and Greek history. In view of his later opposition to the incarceration of Nikkei, his first-year textbook, Evelyn Shuckburg's *A History of Rome for Beginners*, is of particular interest. One of the book's five parts focuses on the constitutional history of Rome and the continual "struggles of the plebeians for equality" and "civil rights."[55] These ideas, whatever the intentions of their English author, served the school's effort to promote concepts in keeping with "Americanism," as did other parts of the book, narrating themes of civil strife and revolt by the less powerful. One wonders if, years later, Kurihara saw parallels in the situation of the Nikkei and that of the plebeians and slaves in the civil wars in ancient Rome.

Kurihara also studied elocution, to which he had been introduced earlier at St. Francis School, and to which he was especially attracted. St. Ignatius awarded a gold medal for the winner of its annual elocution contest. Participation was voluntary, and Kurihara took up the challenge: during his sophomore year at the school, he was one of only two students in his class who participated. By this time his grade in elocution had improved from a fair-to-middling 75 percent in his freshman year to an impressive 93 percent in his sophomore year. This was a major achievement, especially considering his language background. He had grown up in a household in which Japanese was the primary language. At home he spoke rudimentary Japanese, and with his siblings and friends he spoke a creole language derived from the languages of Hawaiian, Chinese, Portuguese, and Japanese. His high elocution grade in his sophomore year at St. Ignatius, coupled with his participation in the elocution contest, demonstrate his proficiency not only in English, but also in standard English pronunciation. His participation in the elocution contest further demonstrates his obvious gain in confidence as a public speaker and his understanding of the pleasure and power of effective oratory. Years later at Manzanar he would use what he learned to his advantage in his many speeches that sought to convince his fellow inmates of the injustice of their incarceration.[56]

For the contest, Kurihara selected "Rienzi's Address to the Romans," part of a larger production written by the English playwright Mary Russell Mitford. Kurihara memorized this poem and learned to recite it with passion, appropriate emphasis, and what elocutionists call "expression."[57]

The Roman Rienzi had led a successful revolt against the nobles, after which he became a tribune, whose role was to protect the people against oppression, in the course of which he introduced many popular reforms. In the address that Kurihara recited, Rienzi calls on the people to rebel against an oppressive government in the name of freedom. The parallels between the circumstances that Rienzi's oration recalls, and the situation Kurihara and his fellow Nikkei inmates found themselves in, are striking, as are the points Kurihara made over and over in speeches and talks with his fellow inmates, urging them to protest their incarceration. While one should not read too much significance into one episode two decades earlier, it should be noted that Kurihara had memorized the speech for the elocution contest, and the meaning, if not the exact words, would have remained in his memory long after he left the school.

Selections of other students participating in the elocution contest embodied themes of resistance to oppression, noble struggles, principled action, forgiveness, redemption, and heroism. Such was the paradoxical nature and inherent tension in Kurihara's Catholic schooling: within a hierarchical system, his religion classes and the school's expectations emphasized respect for authority and obedience to Catholic doctrine at the same time that his history and elocution lessons exposed him to notions of freedom, heroic action, and resistance. To be sure, this paradox of schooling—the tension between ideas of democracy and the realities of school life—was not unique to Kurihara's experience, nor to that of his schoolmates and other students enrolled in Catholic schools, nor can it be said that Kurihara was bothered by it or even aware of it. More important was what St. Ignatius gave Kurihara: a nurturing of notions of justice for ordinary people, and an appreciation of the power of oration in persuading them to defend their rights. These ideas helped shape the way in which he responded, years later, to the incarceration of the Nikkei during World War II.[58]

CHAPTER 2

A Yank in France, a Jap in America

While Kurihara was pleased with the education he received at St. Ignatius, the racial atmosphere in San Francisco troubled him. So when a friend suggested a move to Michigan, he responded favorably. "Unexpectedly my friend from Sacramento called and persuaded me to go East," he later remembered. "He vouched to me that the American people east of Chicago are very friendly and kind. They do not discriminate just because we are Japanese. They will treat us as one of their equal. I could not believe it, but the news was very tempting after experiencing much unpleasantness for two years." In June 1917 the two young men took a train to Chicago. Upon arrival they saw a "Japanese boy . . . walking down the street with an American girl, arm in arm." Kurihara's friend exclaimed, "See what I told you? They don't discriminate . . . out here."[1]

Among the jobs open to them in the American Midwest were dishwashing in Milwaukee and houseboy service in Minnesota. They chose instead to work as bellhops at a hotel at Mt. Clemens Mineral Springs because of its proximity to the University of Michigan, where they intended to enroll in the fall. While Kurihara had completed only two years of high school, he believed that he would be able to enter the university. But America's entry into World War I changed his plans.[2]

Three years earlier, in August 1914, war had erupted in Europe. Gripping that continent during Kurihara's years at St. Ignatius, the war eventually pulled the United States into it. On April 2, 1917, President Woodrow Wilson asked Congress to declare war on Germany, and four days later Congress did so.

On May 18 Wilson signed the Selective Service Act. As preparations were being made under that act to register men for the draft, a First Expeditionary Division was formed from men already in the U.S. Army and those who had volunteered soon after Congress had declared war. The division left for France on June 14 under the command of General John J. Pershing.[3]

Meanwhile, on June 5, 1917, the federal government held a national registration day. Kurihara, who at the time had not yet departed San Francisco for Michigan, and his younger brother Roy (Saiichi), who was still living with their parents in Honolulu, were among the 10 million men who reported to registration boards in what John Chambers describes as an amazing response of "mass compliance" that resulted from "propaganda, hoopla, and peer pressure." James Montgomery Flagg's famous Uncle Sam "I Want You" recruiting poster was symbolic of the government's intensive publicity campaign and appeal to national patriotism. From the overwhelming number of men registered, local draft boards selected draftees, while regional boards monitored the process, heard appeals, and responded to the labor requirements of their respective areas. In eighteen months the process brought 2.8 million men into the army.[4]

Kurihara was not one of those drafted; instead, he was among the 28 percent of draft-eligible men who volunteered. He was not employed in agriculture or an industry that was deemed essential to the war effort, was twenty-two years old and single, and in good health. He knew that it was likely that he would be drafted. At the same time, the "sound of the band, the beating of the drums" stirred in him powerful feelings of patriotism, moving him to purchase five one-hundred-dollar Liberty Bonds (together worth more than $8,000 in 2012 dollars), one for each of his five nieces and nephews in Hawai‘i. He later recalled that as a youth attending Japanese language school, he had taken to heart the notion of *koku on*, which his teachers explained, meant "to be true to the country [the United States] to which [they owed their] living."[5]

Kurihara went to the draft board in Mt. Clemens and explained that he had already registered in San Francisco and wanted to enlist immediately. At five feet two inches tall and over 118 pounds, he met the height and proportional weight requirements, and the board accepted him. His brother Roy, who had relocated to California and found work there as an agricultural laborer, did not volunteer and was not drafted.[6]

Kurihara was sent to Camp Custer for basic training. Situated three-and-a-half miles west of the little town of Battle Creek, Michigan, the camp was one of thirty-six cantonments built hurriedly to meet the demands of war. In fact, construction had begun only a few weeks before the first contingent of soldiers arrived. On that rainy day in late July, the men were greeted by "acres of mud chewed up by construction trucks, acres of raw pine buildings springing up in the rain like mushrooms, lumber and litter everywhere." Like the thousands of recruits who followed them, the men had to walk the mile from the railroad station to the cantonment. Once at the camp, they were told to fill sacks with straw for their beds. They also had to wait weeks for their uniforms, and for a long time they had no rifles.[7]

The camp for the newly created 85th Division would eventually include two thousand buildings on four miles of hills overlooking the Kalamazoo River, and house as many as thirty-six thousand men at a time, all of them enlistees from Michigan or Wisconsin. Among the buildings were facilities for the YMCA, the Knights of Columbus, and the American Library Association, offering books, motion picture viewing, game rooms, and reading rooms. A "Liberty Theater" seated an audience of five thousand, and a large gymnasium was built from funds donated by residents of Michigan and Wisconsin.[8]

New arrivals soon received their assignments. Kurihara, who arrived on November 2, 1917, was assigned to be a cook. When he objected, telling his superiors that he aspired to be a doctor, they assigned him to the medical department of the 328th Field Artillery. During the day, Kurihara and his fellow soldiers were variously occupied with bivouac and artillery practice, trench digging and mock trench warfare, bayonet drills, hiking, and marching. In their spare time they participated in team sports, took classes, and enjoyed movies and other forms of recreation. Through the War Camp Community Service, in which families in nearby communities entertained off-duty soldiers, Kurihara enjoyed the hospitality of the families of Homer Knight, a physician in the nearby town of Charlotte, and William Green, president of an advertising company in Detroit. In his several visits to their homes, he was "treated like a prince." He was deeply touched by their kindness, which helped to sustain his positive identity as an American and made him even more determined to "fight and die for the U.S."[9]

Kurihara was evidently a willing, even eager participant in the War Department's effort to Americanize recruits who were immigrants and sons of immigrants, who constituted more than 18 percent of all soldiers. This figure reflects the millions who had arrived in the United States during the previous three or four decades. In the cantonments, ethnic community leaders participated in the Americanization push by teaching English, giving patriotic speeches, and translating patriotic literature and other forms of war propaganda. At the same time, they advocated successfully for the cultural and religious needs of immigrant soldiers. As a result of their efforts, for example, the military granted leaves for religious holidays and welcomed the services of immigrant clergymen.[10]

This enlightened treatment was aimed at immigrants from Europe. American Indians, Mexicans and Mexican Americans, Asians and Asian Americans, and African Americans were not of primary concern in this accommodation effort. In addition, while the larger society categorized each nonwhite group separately, the U.S. Army recognized only two groups of soldiers: white and colored. In this simplistic binary system, everyone not of African descent was classified as white.[11]

With this dual classification, the U.S. government kept no figures based on ethnicity or language. It is thus uncertain just how many Japanese Americans like Kurihara, or Asian Americans and Asian immigrants, served in the military during the war, or how many were drafted or volunteered. While there was a segregated unit of 838 noncitizen Japanese from Hawai'i, all other Asian immigrant and Asian American soldiers were dispersed throughout the army. Thus Kurihara, who enlisted in Michigan, was assigned to the 85th Division, and within the division to Battery F, Medical Department, in the 1,100-man 328th Field Artillery. He was the only nonwhite and the only soldier of Asian ancestry in the 328th.[12]

In contrast to what he had experienced in California, and despite the increasing tensions between Japan and the United States during the war, in his training at Camp Custer and on the battlefields in France, Kurihara encountered little or no anti-Japanese sentiment or behaviors. This gave him a feeling of belonging in the army and in his unit, and fed into his identity as an American. In the army, he had become a "Yank," as the American soldier was familiarly known.[13]

Kurihara embraced "the hyperpatriotic atmosphere of the war, in which all were called to demonstrate their 'unqualified loyalty.'" He also embraced the idea that wartime military service was "the ultimate test of a man's Americanness." He was enthusiastic about demonstrating his American identification with and loyalty to the United States. Like other servicemen from marginalized ethnic groups, he hoped his service would give him and his group respect from the larger community, thereby improving their social standing.[14]

This hope was indifferently realized at best. Since the war began, military boosters had argued that military service was a sure-fire way to Americanize alien soldiers and build a common national identity. To this end, Congress passed in 1918 a law designed to expedite the process by which aliens who served in the military could become citizens. The focus of the legislation was on European immigrants, but Asian immigrants also seized onto this idea with enthusiasm. However, the law was applied unevenly because it was interpreted differently by different federal judges and naturalization examiners. As a result, some Asians were granted citizenship while others were not. It was not until 1935, well after the war ended, that Congress passed the Nye-Lea Act that finally granted Asian veterans the right of naturalization.[15]

The Nightmare of War

In all, 4,800,000 Americans served in the U.S. Army, Navy, and Marines during the war, two million of whom crossed the Atlantic to serve in France. With the influx of so many American soldiers into France within a short span of time in the midst of heavy warfare, confusion, mix ups, errors, and changes in plans were bound to occur, and they did. Nevertheless, the American contribution to the Allied effort would be decisive in bringing about the needed breakthrough that led to the end of the war.[16]

At Camp Custer, Kurihara's 85th Division received its overseas orders.[17] With eight months of training under their belts, the men cleaned out their barracks, packed their belongings, and otherwise prepared for departure. On July 16, 1918, Kurihara and his regiment boarded the train amid great noise and excitement. "[M]en, women, and children shouted and waved small flags; whistles blew and bells rang; girls ran up to the soldiers leaning out of the coach windows"; "women passed out coffee, apples, cigarettes." The train took Kurihara and his fellow soldiers to New York, the port of embarkation for most of the soldiers who were transported across the Atlantic. While waiting to board their ship, the men "underwent final inspections, waited until all the paperwork was in order, drew new clothing, if needed, steel helmets, and gas masks."[18]

On July 30, the men boarded the S. S. Mauretania. Except for a detachment that was dispatched to Russia, the troops eventually arrived at Liverpool, England, and then traveled to Southampton by train. There the men boarded ships for France. In France, the demands of the war forced the division, like other divisions, to detach units to support and replace others already on the front lines. What was left of Kurihara's division was sent to Camp Coetquidan (see map 2), the French artillery school, where they spent six weeks of training in day and night maneuvers. From there the men were transported eastward to the front in railroad boxcars with floors "saturated with urine" from horses and mules that had been transported previously in them. In this way the men endured the journey to Toul, attempting to sleep despite hard, filthy floors and strong, foul odors.[19]

Once in Toul, Kurihara's unit marched sixty-two kilometers northeastward (see map 3). In contrast to the grand parades in Michigan, which had inspired him to volunteer for military service, the march of two days and two nights from Toul was "hellish." The men "waded through" "sticky mud that became part of [their] breeches," and slept in dug-outs "bothered by rats." Bathing was a luxury they could not afford. "Many boys were dropping off to the roadside," Kurihara recalled, and even the animals suffered. "[T]wo horses simply

Map 2. Movement of 328th Field Artillery (Kurihara). August 8–November 11, 1918. Map by Dave Raney. Sources: Barraclough, The Times Concise *Atlas of World History*, 118–19; Bonjour La France, "France Map."

squatted and refused to pull the artillery any further. . . . I brought up the rear and wondering [*sic*] if I could make it." "Going through woods, over hills and ravines, we saw numbers of dead soldiers, left to the mercy of the weather, rotting and stinking. . . . [M]aggots were oozing out of their eyes, ears, noses and mouths. . . . The air was so foul." Elmer Sherwood, another soldier in the war, described similar experiences in his diary. Because of the intolerable stench, the decaying flesh, the multitude of maggots and flies, and the serious menace to health and morale, special units—when they could be spared—were given the task of burying the dead.[20]

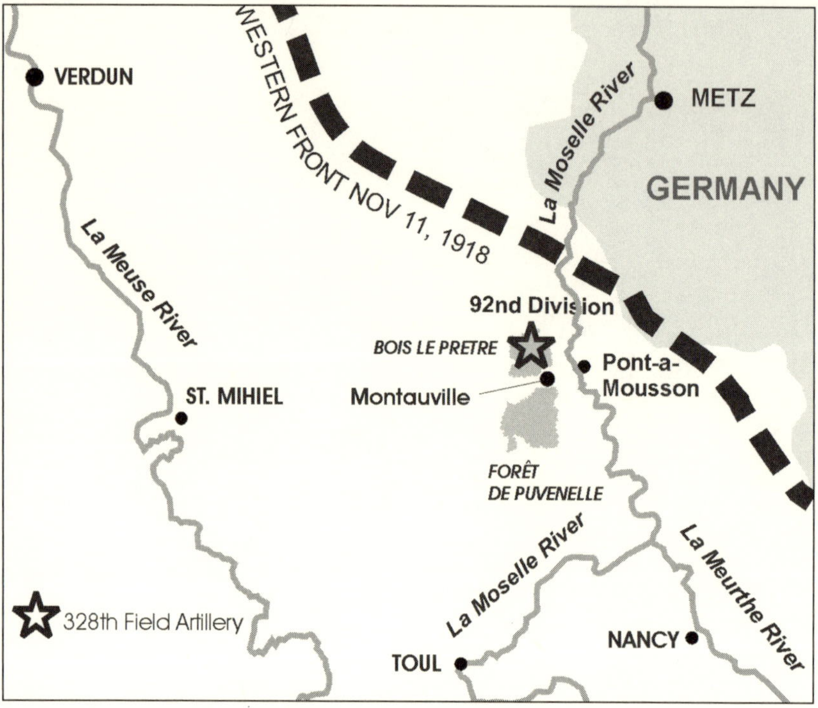

Map 3. Position of 328th Field artillery, November 11, 1918 (Armistice). Map by Dave Raney. Sources: U.S. Surgeon-General's Office, *The Medical Department of the United States Army in the World War*, Plate L; Stamps and Esposito, eds., *A Short Military History of World War I*, Map 69; Hanson, *World War I, I Was There*, 56–57; Murray, *The "Fortnightly" History of the War*, 126.

On October 29, 1918, Kurihara's 328th Field Artillery arrived at the front, just southeast of the major Allied offensive between the Meuse River and the Argonne Forest, just above the town of Pont-a-Mousson. The unit entered an extensive wooded area called Bois le Prêtre. There they relieved the soldiers of the all-black 92nd Division. "The roaring of the cannon was plainly audible," Kurihara later wrote, "and the flares at night became distinct. . . . Shells were bursting everywhere. The queer sensation of despair was creeping up our backs. Unintentionally we said our prayers figuring that our time on this earth was only a matter of minutes and seconds." As William Hanson, a physician who served in the medical corps during the war, notes, "It is hard for anyone who was not there to understand the tremendous pressures on those who were at the Front. . . . The tension was constant and there was no getting used to it."[21]

Once at the front, Kurihara's unit prepared for an offensive aimed at the strategically important town of Metz, which served as a German hub, a heavily fortified railroad center "entirely surrounded by a chain of permanent forts mounting heavy long-range guns."[22] On November 11, 1918, as the men were preparing the assault, the Armistice was declared, recalled Kurihara, bringing "joy and relief" to the soldiers. American forces had suffered casualties in proportion to their time in combat: 49,000 killed and 230,000 wounded, numbers that were dwarfed by those of the Europeans, who had fought much longer.[23]

Twenty-two years later, on the eve of America's entry into another war, World War II, Kurihara told readers of the Los Angeles *Kashū Mainichi*, "Let those who agitate for war fight it out." As one who had experienced the nightmare of battle, he declared, "Let them carry that heavy pack and hike to the front for days and nights without a decent meal. Let them drink the muddy water, and let them go without a bath, so the cooties can flourish on their filth! If such is not enough, let them sleep in a rat-ridden, cold and damp dugout. Let them stand guard and freeze in bitter cold. Let them live under bombardment with death staring them constantly in the face, and see if they ever will ask for another war!"[24]

Within two years after he had penned this exhortation, Kurihara found himself incarcerated by the government of the country for which he had risked his life. Ignoring the patriotism he and other Nisei veterans had demonstrated in World War I, the government now treated them and other Nisei who lived on the West Coast as—in the words of Mae Ngai—"alien citizens." While they were U.S. citizens, their loyalty was questioned, and they "remained alien in the eyes of the nation." As the chapters to follow demonstrate, Kurihara did not take this affront quietly, and while incarcerated he became a vociferous and impassioned dissident.[25]

But at the end of World War I, Kurihara was unaware of what would happen decades later. With the armistice that ended that war, he volunteered to join a Captain Schiewetz as a dental assistant in the German town of Coblenz, which served as headquarters of the American occupation army. While there, he was pleasantly surprised to find the German people "just as human as any other race. . . . I learned to like these people because they were kind and sincere." His experience contrasted with American propaganda, which had referred to German soldiers as "Huns" and pictured them in posters as dark, brooding, and bloodstained. During a two-week furlough, he enjoyed himself by visiting Cologne, Brussels, Ypres, Paris, and other places of interest. Kurihara remained in Germany almost a year, until September 1919, when he returned to the United States. He was discharged from the service on September 30, 1919, at the Presidio in San Francisco.[26]

If Kurihara in civilian life expected appreciation and respect for his military service, he was quickly disabused of the notion. While still in his army uniform on a streetcar in San Francisco, he was spat at and called "Jap." "I looked at him sternly," Kurihara recalled of the spitter. "He kept quiet, which avoided an incident." This confrontation showed him that the racial climate in the city had not improved for Asian Americans, even for those who had fought for their country. In fact, anti-Japanese hostility on the West Coast was rising, eventually peaking in 1924, when Congress passed an immigration law that stopped the migration of Japanese to the United States. (Other Asians had been barred previously.)[27]

Life in Los Angeles

Upon his discharge, Kurihara received transportation fare to Hawai'i, where he visited his very ill father and his mother. He also spent time with his elder sister Kikuno, his elder brother Taiji, his younger sister Kawayo, and their families. At this time, after thirty-one years in the islands, his parents had decided to return to Japan. Kurihara reached Hawai'i in December 1919, three days before their departure; his father died on the day his ship arrived in Japan.[28]

After a few months in Hawai'i, Kurihara left for Los Angeles, where among other things he joined the American Legion (AL), an organization of the veterans of World War I. He did so as a public profession of his patriotism and as an expression of his commitment to the Legion's aggressive promotion of the notion of "100% Americanism." He had passed the Legion's "test of Americanism" by being willing "to lay down [his] life for [his] country." He also joined the more selective Veterans of Foreign Wars (VFW), open only to those whose service had taken them to Europe. He remained a member of both organizations until he was forced into World War II camps for Japanese Americans, at which time he disavowed his membership in the AL.[29]

Both the AL and the VFW were strong advocates for veteran benefits. Believing that all veterans had proved their patriotism, both joined the struggle to allow Asian veterans to become naturalized U.S. citizens. The effort came to fruition in 1935 when Congress passed the Nye-Lea Act.[30] This support for Asian veterans contrasted with other positions the AL took before and during the war (and in subsequent decades) on matters relating to Asian Americans. In the early 1920s, for example, the AL had lobbied Congress to close the doors to Asian immigration and supported anti-Japanese land laws on the West Coast. Then, with the U.S. entry into World War II, the organization pressed for the removal of all Nikkei from the Pacific Coast, including veterans of World War I, and supported President Franklin Roosevelt's decision to issue

Executive Order 9066, which forced the Nikkei into American concentration camps. Finally, forty years later, in Congressional hearings on reparations for the Nikkei who had been incarcerated, both the AL and the VFW testified against redress.[31]

As sensitive as Kurihara was on ethnic issues that affected him, he must have known of the AL's positions. By the time of his incarceration, he had disassociated himself from the group, saying that its "button [didn't] have any weight." He would once again have been disappointed, if not bitter, had he been alive when the AL and the VFW opposed reparations for the Nikkei, an idea he had advocated years earlier when he was incarcerated in the camps.[32]

But I am moving ahead of my story. In 1920, when he returned to Los Angeles after visiting his family in Hawai'i, his main concerns were to find a job and continue his schooling. "Though my ambition to make a man of myself still remained," he later wrote, "my desire to be a Doctor of Medicine and Surgery was changed to . . . [becoming] a Business Executive." He decided that Los Angeles offered the best opportunities for him to realize his ambition. He began taking bookkeeping courses at California Commercial College, hoping to work as a bookkeeper while continuing his education at a university.[33]

By 1920 Los Angeles had become a major port city of well over half a million residents, primarily Caucasians, including many European immigrants. The Nikkei constituted only 2 percent of the population. There were some Chinese Americans and larger numbers of Mexican Americans and African Americans, but together they and the Nikkei were only 9 percent of the city's inhabitants. Ten years later, while Kurihara was still there, the city's population had escalated to 1.2 million. Among the residents were 97,116 Mexicans and Mexican Americans, who were classified as white. The nonwhite population included the following ethnoracial groups: 21,081 Japanese, 3,009 Chinese, 616 Indians, 38,894 Blacks, and 3,748 all other nonwhites, primarily Filipinos. Together, the Mexican and nonwhite population had grown to 14 percent.[34]

In the 1920s and 1930s, the city was by today's standards thoroughly segregated along ethnoracial and socioeconomic lines. Affluent and middle-class whites lived in the city's west side, which included Beverly Hills and Hollywood. Because of "restrictive covenants" that controlled 95 percent of residential areas, nonwhites and foreign-born whites lived on the east side, which included working-class neighborhoods, the industrial zone, and the red-light district. "Little Tokyo," in the east side, included Japanese shops and small businesses, Buddhist temples, and residences. It was the hub for Nikkei engaged in agriculture and fishing, their two most important sources of employment. Little Tokyo provided the Nikkei with goods and services as well as cultural and religious activities, and also served the wider community with its boarding houses, employment agencies, restaurants, pool halls, brothels, and bars.[35]

Constituting about 20 percent of the residents of Little Tokyo, the Nikkei lived in rental homes and rooming houses interspersed among blacks and foreign-born whites, as well as Mexicans, Filipinos, and Chinese, and their American-born children. Kurihara lived just outside Little Tokyo, on South Flower Street. Surrounding the apartment building in which he lived were numerous other apartment buildings, small hotels, and stores. While the Nikkei clustered in and around Little Tokyo, and blacks did the same around Central Avenue just to the south, the two areas overlapped considerably. Thus, while minority groups tended to congregate among themselves, their proximity to each other and to working-class whites meant that they would inevitably and regularly interact with one another.[36]

Living and working in Los Angeles reminded Kurihara again of the racial and ethnic discrimination not only of Asian Americans but also of African Americans and other minority groups. Years later, while incarcerated for the ostensible offense of being a Japanese American who lived on the West Coast, he denounced this second-class status in his speeches, decrying that the "rights [of blacks] heroically earned" in World War I were nonetheless "submerged completely beneath the rights and pride of the whites."[37]

The Nikkei in the Los Angeles area were able to survive, and some of them could even prosper, by specializing in economic enterprises that others ignored or rejected—catching fish and abalone, and practicing labor-intensive farming that required less land. They cultivated fruits, vegetables, and flowers, and created a distribution system to market these crops. More specifically, they dominated the growing of celery, peas, beans, cauliflower, and berries, selling the produce to Nikkei wholesalers who distributed it to Nikkei retailers, who in turn sold it at numerous fruit and vegetable stands.[38]

Their success in these endeavors bred resentment that built on longstanding anti-Japanese sentiment in Los Angeles and elsewhere in California. Kurihara had arrived in Los Angeles during a push to amend the 1913 California alien land law that forbade Issei and other aliens ineligible for citizenship from owning agricultural land. This effort succeeded in convincing the legislature to pass a 1920 amendment forbidding Japanese immigrants from leasing and corporations from owning agricultural land, and a 1923 amendment prohibiting Japanese from sharecropping. Issei farmers circumvented these amendments and the original law itself by leasing land in the names of U.S. citizens like Kurihara and other Nisei.[39]

In this hostile racial climate, Kurihara had disagreeable encounters. "[M]any times I was turned out of restaurants catering to customers of the working class," he later recalled. "Practically in all of these restaurants . . . there [was] a sign reading, 'We reserve the right to refuse service to anyone.'" "Such things," he declared, "must not be allowed if America is to be the Democratic standard bearer of the world." In another instance, in an "electric train" heading southward to San Pedro, he sat down by a woman who told him, "I don't want a Jap to [sit] next to me." She moved when he retorted, "Sorry, madam, I paid my fare. If you don't like my looks, why don't you move?" In yet another instance, as he was walking to his bookkeeping class, one of three boys who passed him in the opposite direction spat at him. While he was short, Kurihara had a sturdy build and was fearless in his response. "Throwing my books down," he later recollected, "I jumped at his throat. He didn't expect such a sudden charge. The force threw him off balance and he fell backward, striking his head on the walk with a thump. He was wiggling and groaning with pain." Kurihara then "picked up [his] books and continued on [his] way." As these instances demonstrate, Kurihara had a fighting spirit, a sense of justice, and a forthrightness that administrators at the World War II camps holding Nikkei would later remark on and admire.[40]

Such disagreeable experiences were not unique to Kurihara. Nikkei, like other ethnoracial groups, were forced to cope with constant discrimination and intimidation. According to Daniel Widener, the "desirability of maintaining white racial control" led to job discrimination and "racially circumscribed" transportation and housing. In fact, he notes, "Violence and law intertwined . . . forcing black, Filipinos, Japanese, and Mexicans to cope with repeated assaults that recalled a legacy of nineteenth-century violence." In the 1920s in Los Angeles, Ku Klux Klan marches and threats became both visible and common.[41]

In this environment, Kurihara completed his bookkeeping course and, on the advice of one of his professors, decided to study accounting, which was, Kurihara decided, a "wide and lucrative" field. Kurihara also noted that accounting would be a "valuable base" for him as a future businessman and "executive." With this in mind, he enrolled at Southwestern University while working part time as a bookkeeper. Here he demonstrated his characteristic earnestness and determination. "Many, many times I went with only two meals a day," he wrote twenty years later. "To work through school is not an easy task. It requires super-human determination. . . . My body trembled and I experienced fainting spells frequently. . . . I saw boys and girls heading for picture shows while I had to stay in and study. I saw people going to a picnic party while I had to work. It really was discouraging at times but I felt and know, to succeed I must deny all pleasures however painful it may be."[42]

Southwestern University, then located on Spring Street, a short distance from Kurihara's residence, offered degrees in law and commerce. From its earliest days in 1911, the school had encouraged women and minorities to enroll. In 1921–22, Kurihara's first year there, the school had 510 students, of whom thirty were women and ten Asian Americans, all males.[43]

In addition to courses in accounting, Kurihara took classes in economics, finance, marketing, commercial law, and banking, as well as English, mathematics, and other general subjects. Research for his thesis, "The Farmer and Politics," undoubtedly helped him understand the activities and rhetoric swirling about him in the campaign for restrictive land laws and immigration exclusion against Japanese in the early 1920s.[44]

The "greatest and the most glorious day of my life," he later recalled, arrived in June 1924 when he received his bachelor's degree in commercial science as well as a certificate of accountancy. Kurihara graduated from Southwestern when it was rare for Japanese Americans to attend a university. Most of them were born after 1910 and not yet of college age in the 1920s. Furthermore, older Nisei children, like Kurihara's oldest sister and brother, had had to work to help support their families. Later, such older siblings sometimes helped younger siblings financially as the latter attended high school and college. Kurihara was the fourth of five children and did not have to work to help support younger siblings, but he was on his own financially when he attended high school and college.[45]

After graduation from Southwestern, Kurihara worked in a number of office and administrative jobs—as an accountant, as part owner and operator of two wholesale produce companies, as an auditor and then manager of a seafood packing company, and as a salesman of scales and other equipment for supermarkets. These jobs were bounded within the narrow economic sphere opened to ethnic Japanese—food production and distribution. "No job was open to my kind," Kurihara explained years later, "and I had to make my living among the Japanese people the best I could." Like their parents, Nisei living in Los Angeles and the rest of the U.S. West Coast during the first four decades of the twentieth century found job opportunities largely limited to farming, fishing, gardening, domestic service, and work related to food distribution. Other areas of employment were closed, even to the university graduates among them.[46]

If Los Angeles was so hostile to the Nikkei, why did Kurihara move there after being discharged from military service instead of returning to Honolulu or even to Michigan, where he had had such positive experiences? In recalling his life in the 1920s and 1930s, Kurihara never addressed this question directly. However, one can speculate that with a large population in Los Angeles and a high concentration of Nikkei there, Kurihara saw greater opportunities for himself, albeit within the confines of the Nikkei community. And in fact, during the decade-and-a-half after his graduation from Southwestern, he was able to achieve a degree of economic prosperity.[47]

That he did so was a result, in part, of his success in negotiating his way outside the Nikkei community. While his work placed him in the heart of Little Tokyo, Kurihara lived elsewhere—on Flower Street during his schooling at Southwestern and then on East Pico Boulevard after graduation and through the 1930s. In this way he kept one foot outside the Japanese community. As in San Francisco, where he attended a predominantly white Catholic school, and in Michigan and Europe, where he trained and fought as a soldier integrated into the U.S. Army, in Los Angeles both his education at Southwestern and his subsequent employment involved interactions with whites—school officials, classmates, business people, government officials, and others. While not of the white world, he was relatively conversant in its modes of thinking and behavior. This enabled him to bridge the Nikkei world with that of the larger society.[48]

After nine years in the world of small business accounting and management, Kurihara turned to his love of the sea for a job. Toward that end he learned how to operate a radio, and then how to navigate at sea. He did the latter under the tutelage of a Captain Thoresen at San Pedro, the port of Los Angeles, and in doing so, he benefited from his previous study of mathematics and accounting.[49]

By this time Kurihara was living with his brother Roy, two years his junior, Roy's wife Kinu, and their three children, May, Raymond, and Jeanne. This arrangement enabled Kurihara to have a place to stay during the intervals when he was not at sea. The family's wooden, two-bedroom rental house on East Pico Boulevard was eight blocks south of Little Tokyo. While there, Kurihara slept on a foldout sofa in the living room. Many of their neighbors were Japanese, but Mexicans, blacks, and whites also lived there. It was a mixed-use area; interspersed among their homes were grocery stores, a zipper plant, a coffee-roasting plant, a lighting fixture store, and a house of prostitution.[50]

For eight years until the turmoil of World War II began, Kurihara worked as a navigator for fishing boats, eventually landing a premium job on a Portuguese tuna clipper. His long hours at sea afforded him time to reflect and put his thoughts in writing. He found an outlet for them in the English sections of two Japanese ethnic newspapers, the *Kashū Mainichi* and the *Rafu Shimpō*. By this time he was in his forties, and as an older Nisei, he saw his role as one of advisor to younger Nisei, most of whom were either approaching or in their twenties. Recognizing the difficulties they faced, he offered them advice, chiefly on economic and social matters. Despite discrimination and hostility toward the Nikkei and other minorities, he remained positive about life in America. In "Go East, Young Man, Go East," he advised young Nisei to take up farming in southern Illinois or South Carolina, where rents were low and the soil "exceedingly rich." "Why toil under tremendous handicaps [in California]?" he asked. Referring to the limited opportunities for Nisei there, he continued, "Why not go into a locality where you will be respected . . . your industry will be appreciated, and where your unselfish toil will bring you much wealth and happiness?" In "Jobs and Leisure" and "How to Make Best of a College Education," he admonished jobless college graduates for "wasting their valuable time in and around pool halls" because they were "too proud to do manual labor." "Don't let your false pride govern your destiny," he wrote. "Any work is honorable." And in "Let's Not Pass the Buck" he urged the Nisei to lay a solid economic foundation for their children.[51]

But not all of his advice concerned economic issues. In "Sun Suits and Temptation," for example, he urged young women to refrain from wearing "sun suits" in the streets. Bluntly, he warned them that by showing "their shapely legs and forms," they tempted men who were "starving sexually!" Kurihara himself never wrote, in his newspaper column or elsewhere, of his own romantic inclinations or his sexuality, and I have not been able to find verifiable evidence on the subject.[52]

He did, however, share his personal observations, in "Strange Facts" and "Strange but True," on Mexico and Central America, where his tuna clipper docked when it ventured south of California. It was during one of those trips south, when he was aboard the *Belle of Portugal*, that the Japanese bombed Pearl Harbor and war was declared between the United States and Japan.[53]

CHAPTER 3

To Manzanar

At the time of Pearl Harbor, Joseph Kurihara was on the high seas navigating the *Belle of Portugal,* a handsome, state-of-the-art, 130-foot craft, the second largest tuna vessel based in California. The *Belle* was one of many Portuguese-owned boats, which dominated tuna-fishing out of San Diego. Kurihara spent many months at sea on this craft in search of tuna, venturing as far as the Galapagos Islands, nearly three thousand miles south of San Diego.[1]

Tuna fishing was strenuous work, both physically and mentally. A typical fishing trip lasted seven or eight weeks, covering round-trip distances of six thousand to eight thousand miles from southern California down the coasts of Mexico, Central, and South America, and westward about 850 miles. Tuna boats held from 150 to 350 tons of fish, with crews of twelve to twenty men, depending on the size of the vessel.[2]

The boats traveled the seas in search of widely scattered schools of yellowfin and skipjack tuna. Of the two species, yellowfin was much larger, with individual fish weighing up to several hundred pounds, while skipjack rarely attained thirty pounds. Yellowfin tuna was the predominant species, brought higher prices than skipjack, and were the prized catch, but both species were caught and sold.[3]

The catching of tuna alternated between long periods of mundane activities relating to searching for tuna and live bait, and icing down the catch, and then relatively brief periods of intense and strenuous activity, excitement, and risk.[4] When a school of tuna was located, a frenzy of activity ensued. Live bait was tossed in the water as chum to attract the tuna to the boat. When the tuna were biting, a crew of fishermen might haul in as many as twenty to fifty tons on a good day.[5]

To facilitate the fishing, the aft section of tuna boats rode low in the water. The men stood at or below water level, outside the boat itself, on special walkways lowered from the sides of the boats. They used poles and hooks, and the "weight and the muscles of [their] arm[s] and back[s]" to haul in the tuna. To land an especially large fish required as many as five fishermen and five poles for a single hook. While fishing a school of small tuna, a man could be pulled into the water by the unexpected arrival of an especially large fish. In rough seas, the men fished in waist-deep water with waves crashing on them. In this backbreaking and exhausting endeavor, the men might work from dawn to dusk, using their "every ounce of strength and energy."[6]

Kurihara was spared the risky and strenuous tasks of fishing. As navigator he had a key role. Not only did the captain and crew expect him to navigate with precision, they relied on him to find schools of tuna. This job placed him in the pilot house on the upper deck, where he commanded a wide view of the surrounding ocean, helpful for spotting the flocks of seabirds, schools of porpoises, and patches of roiled waters indicating the presence of tuna schools.[7]

The search for tuna took Kurihara far from shore for weeks at a time, with the success of each voyage depending on how well he and the crew dealt with the conditions they encountered at sea. Tuna schools chose when and where they would appear. Storms and high waves could emerge without warning and sweep over the fishing vessel. These were challenges tuna fishermen honed their skills to meet. For Kurihara, however, there were additional forces at work that would soon prove a far greater challenge than any he encountered at sea.

Kurihara was employed in an industry that provided one of the relatively few opportunities for good, well-paying jobs open in California to persons of Japanese ancestry. Hundreds of Japanese worked as tuna fishermen on Japanese fishing vessels or in the canneries and other businesses related to the tuna fishing industry, both in southern California and in the Mexican territory of Baja California. This concentration of Japanese along the west coasts of the United States and Mexico did not go unnoticed as tensions rose between Japan and the United States through the 1930s.

Following Japan's invasion of Manchuria in 1931, the U.S. Office of Naval Intelligence (ONI) became concerned about Japan's long-range military ambitions and the evident need to counter those ambitions, even to the point of preparing for a possible war with Japan. Those preparations included significant increases in intelligence activities designed to detect and counter potential or suspected espionage by Japanese agents and sympathizers.[8] ONI officials focused particularly on the U.S. West Coast fishing fleet owned and operated by persons of Japanese descent, due to the proximity of the fleet and its workers to harbors and naval bases.[9]

Naval intelligence officials also believed that Japanese fishing and commercial enterprises in Mexico, specifically in Baja California, served as fronts for Japanese espionage networks and potential bases for attacks on the United States should war erupt between the two countries. The most compelling case for concern over Japanese activities in Mexico was provided by the Japanese government itself. By August 1940, U.S. intelligence had succeeded in breaking the code the Japanese used to communicate with its overseas embassies. A process known as MAGIC had been developed to intercept, decode, and translate secret Japanese worldwide diplomatic messages. A message intercepted in July 1941 stated that, because of its geographic location, Mexico was and would be the main site for gathering intelligence on the United States as long as Mexico did not officially join the war on the American side. During the preceding three years, ONI had been picking up persistent rumors from other sources alleging subversive activity by Japanese agents stationed in Mexico. Before the MAGIC intercept, however, ONI had not been able to verify any of those rumors. Yet none of the information from MAGIC ever implicated any Japanese American in espionage or other subversive activity.[10]

More than six decades later, Michelle Malkin, in a book defending "racial ethnic, religious, and nationality profiling policies," used the MAGIC intercepts to justify the forced removal and incarceration of the Nikkei. She furthermore argued that the Nikkei were not the only ones who suffered in the war: Italians, Germans, and others were excluded from sensitive areas, and hundreds of thousands of servicemen were killed or wounded. Were Kurihara alive to learn of the MAGIC intercepts and read Malkin's statements, he would remind her emphatically that no Japanese American was ever implicated in the messages. He would further state that, yes, others also suffered in the war, but using that fact to justify the incarceration of the Nikkei misses the core of his argument, that people—whether Nikkei or non-Nikkei—are unjustly treated if they are incarcerated solely because of their race (or for that matter, their ethnicity, religion, or nationality) without evidence of any crime committed.[11]

While ONI fretted over Mexico, it became more concerned about possible espionage activities in southern California. In 1937, about seventy vessels, of which fifty were "larger tuna boats 90 feet or more in length," constituted the tuna fleet operating off the California coast. These boats were owned and operated by men of various nationalities, predominately Japanese, Italians, and Portuguese. At that time, some twenty-five hundred persons of Japanese ancestry lived in "tiny wooden shacks" "cramped together" on Terminal Island in San Pedro Bay, the Los Angeles harbor. Some were fishermen but more worked in the canneries and processing plants located on the island and associated with the fishing industry. Because Japanese on Terminal Island lived adjacent to Reeves Field, a naval air base, a confidential Navy report identified them as potential security risks.[12]

Some of the Japanese owners and operators of fishing fleets based in Los Angeles or San Diego were long-time residents but not citizens of the United States. Because U.S. immigration law barred alien Asian residents from obtaining citizenship, the fishing fleets were technically owned by Japanese nationals, even though those persons did not reside in Japan. To further complicate matters, some of the fishing vessels were registered in Japan and flew the Japanese flag on the high seas, and some of their crewmembers were contract workers from Japan.[13]

Following a change of command in May 1938, ONI's 11th District Office, based in San Diego, increased its surveillance of the Japanese fishing fleets. The newly arrived commander, Ellis Zacharias, a veteran intelligence officer, was convinced that the fishermen posed a major security threat, that San Diego was "the very hub of Japanese espionage," and that this hub centered on "the fishing fleets in which scores of Japanese espionage agents sailed [U.S. waters]." Accordingly, ONI initiated intensive scrutiny of the Japanese fleets, which included detailed information on each boat and its owner and skipper.[14]

It was in this atmosphere that Kurihara came to the attention of U.S. officials. He and his crewmates had been at sea near the Galapagos Islands when Japanese bombers attacked Pearl Harbor. Soon after the attack, the Navy ordered all U.S. vessels to return to their home port. After some hesitation, Captain Souza of the *Belle* decided to ignore the order, reasoning that his boat was of Portuguese registry, and Japanese submarines were unlikely to venture so far south. Moreover, Souza wanted an additional one hundred tons of tuna before heading home. After a number of days, Souza reached this goal and directed Kurihara to head the *Belle* north to San Diego.[15]

As they neared Cedros Islands, off the coast of Baja California and three hundred miles south of San Diego, Souza and his men spotted U.S. airplanes hovering above them. Kurihara "felt proud" as he watched the planes fly back and forth, trying "to determine the name of the boat."[16]

At daybreak on December 29, the *Belle* entered San Diego Bay. Before it reached the dock, however, a navy patrol boat stopped it and several officers came aboard. After examining the boat's papers, the officers took Kurihara and two of his Portuguese sea mates to the navy wharf, where they waited for several hours. After receiving no orders concerning the detainees, the navy officers returned the three men to the *Belle*. Immediately upon boarding the boat, however, Kurihara was singled out by an intelligence officer. "Hey! You Jap, I want some information. You better tell me everything or I'll kick you in the ____." Kurihara recalled that his "blood boiled," and he "felt like clubbing the man's head off." "What did you call me?" Kurihara asked him. "If you want any information from me, you better learn to address a man properly." Their altercation ended there, for another officer quickly intervened and asked Kurihara to go with him to the immigration office. After sitting in the office for six hours, ignored and without food or water, he learned that he had been brought because of instructions to question all Japanese in the fishing fleet. After a feeble attempt at interrogating him, an officer told him that he could leave.[17]

Kurihara's experience was played out many times over and often for the worse, not only for Issei—Japanese nationals—but also for Nisei—U.S. citizens. A Nisei named Togo Tanaka, for example, the English-language editor of the *Rafu Shimpō,* a Japanese vernacular newspaper, who was to become Kurihara's adversary at Manzanar, was also arrested by the FBI and jailed for twelve days. A Nisei friend of Kurihara who was a radio operator on a fishing vessel had a more embittering experience. Returning to San Diego soon after the attack on Pearl Harbor, he and his Japanese crewmates were thrown into jail where they were held for a month with no charges made against them, and where they were forced to sleep on the concrete floor without mattresses and forbidden to bathe. Kurihara soon learned that this was only the beginning of worse things to come.[18]

After his last voyage at sea, Kurihara had intended to return to Los Angeles, but he remained in San Diego at the request of Captain Souza, who had asked him to delay his departure for a few weeks. Not yet realizing fully the intensity of suspicions directed at all Nikkei on the West Coast, and looking for ways to be useful to the American cause, Kurihara went to see the San Diego port master. Since Kurihara had a captain's license, which permitted him to navigate, he asked for a permit "to sail the sea," so that he would be ready in the event that his services were needed for the war effort. "No permit for any Jap," the port master said bluntly. "Get out or I'll throw you out." Unwilling to accept such treatment meekly, Kurihara retorted angrily, "I . . . served in the U.S. Army and fought for Democracy. . . . [Y]our pronunciation tells me you came to this country not long ago. . . . I may be a Jap in feature but I am an American."[19]

Undaunted by the port master's hostility, Kurihara looked for other ways to help the American cause. He went to the Consolidated Aircraft Corporation in San Diego to see if the company could use him as a navigator of bombers that needed to be flown to war zones or other places. Rejected again, he went to San Pedro, to the merchant marine office, then across the harbor to the California Shipbuilding Company and the Bethlehem Steel Company, both on Terminal Island. Everywhere, his offers to be of service were rebuffed. Returning to San Diego, he reacted with disgust when his landlady told him that the FBI had searched his room while he was away. It was then that he recalled noticing a man trailing him before he had left for San Pedro and Terminal Island.[20]

After Kurihara had been in San Diego for three weeks, Captain Souza, accompanied by an ONI intelligence officer, visited him and told him with regret that Souza's request to have Kurihara retained as navigator of the *Belle* had been denied by the War Department. While Kurihara was disappointed at the news, he was pleased to know that the captain, an exacting man who was difficult to satisfy, had made every effort to have Kurihara continue as his navigator.[21]

As Kurihara's experiences show, the attack on Pearl Harbor accomplished what some members of the California legislature had sought years earlier, the demise of the Japanese fishing industry on the West Coast. Opposition to the Japanese fishing operations had begun as early as 1899, as soon as Japanese fishermen and their entrepreneurs began to make inroads into the industry. Anti-Japanese fishing bills were introduced repeatedly in the state legislature between 1919 and 1933. White cannery owners as well as Nikkei community organizations opposed such legislation, and all but one of the bills failed to pass, and that one was later declared unconstitutional by the courts.[22]

Yet the effort to prevent the Nikkei from fishing continued up until the outbreak of World War II. Although the Japanese tuna fishing fleet was criticized for taking away jobs from U.S. citizens, no evidence was presented to support those accusations. Quite the contrary: Wiley Ambrose, president of the Westgate Sea Products Company, testified at the California legislature that Japanese fishermen were not displacing American fishermen, since very few Americans were willing to work on tuna fishing boats.[23]

Others who opposed the Japanese fishing industry considered them a threat to American security. Despite their suspicions, however, ONI officers were unable to identify and document espionage activities among the fishermen. And among the rest of the Nikkei population on the West Coast, there was only one case in which three Japanese nationals living in southern California were found to have cooperated with a Japanese naval officer, Tachibana Itaru, in his attempt to gather intelligence on the U.S. Pacific Fleet. In this instance, Tachibana operated through a Japanese national, Kono Toraichi, to try to obtain intelligence from a retired U.S. Navy officer. The Navy officer reported Kono's actions to ONI and cooperated in setting up a sting operation. On June 9, 1941, Kono and Tachibana were arraigned on charges of espionage; a search of Tachibana's apartment by ONI officers produced a treasure trove of information on the U.S. Navy and national defense. Ultimately Tachibana's case became a matter of negotiation between the U.S. and Japanese governments; as a result, Tachibana was allowed to leave the United States. He departed for Japan on

June 21, 1941. With Tachibana gone, the Justice Department was forced to drop its cases against Kono and two others, Furusawa Takashi and his wife Sachiko, a Japanese couple who helped Tachibana collect information.[24]

As she did with MAGIC, Malkin in 2004 pointed to Kono and the Furusawas as reason to incarcerate all West Coast Nikkei, and again, were Kurihara alive to read Malkin's argument, he would think it absurd to take sweeping punitive action based on the deeds of a few. He would have told her in no uncertain terms that even if one or a few Nikkei had acted treasonously, this would not have justified the government's punishment of more than one hundred thousand innocent Nikkei.[25]

With the exception of the sensational and well-publicized Tachibana case, ONI never uncovered any espionage activities among the Nikkei, despite efforts by Japan's intelligence services to recruit agents within the Nikkei community, and despite ONI's efforts to ferret out such activities. A special investigation undertaken by the State Department in September 1941 at the request of President Franklin Roosevelt also failed to identify any espionage or sabotage activity among the Nikkei. Curtis B. Munson, who conducted this investigation, concluded that the Nisei were patriotic U.S. citizens and that the Issei were basically loyal to the United States.[26]

While ONI was unable to find further evidence of espionage by Nikkei, it did uncover cases of espionage directed from the Japanese embassy or conducted by Japanese agents in the United States posing as language students or naval attaches. Furthermore, ONI was able to prosecute successfully a few cases of espionage involving white Americans.[27]

One of these was Harry Thompson, a veteran of the United States Navy. Thompson used personal connections to gain access to Navy vessels and obtain information to sell to a Japanese contact, Lieutenant Commander Miyazaki Toshio. Miyazaki, a graduate of the Japanese Naval College and an expert on torpedoes, was in the United States as a language student at Stanford University. In July 1936 Thompson was tried, convicted, and sentenced to fifteen years imprisonment. Miyazaki left the country before the Thompson case came to trial.[28]

Another espionage case involved the Drummond brothers, one of whom was an employee of the Northrop Division of Douglas Aircraft in Los Angeles. He was able to smuggle out photographs and blueprints of a new Navy bomber under development at Northrop. The brothers tried unsuccessfully to sell their information to Japanese contacts, and were eventually arrested and successfully prosecuted.[29]

The impact of the Tachibana case was immense. It convinced the U.S. intelligence community of the need for increased vigilance. Furthermore, it shocked and worried the Nikkei, who feared that the publicity it generated would intensify suspicions against them.[30]

Forced Removal

Even before the Tachibana case surfaced, the FBI and military intelligence agencies had been wary of Nikkei loyalty. In 1939, the agencies began keeping lists, primarily of Issei, whom they labeled as "dangerous enemy aliens," and after Pearl Harbor, the FBI arrested those on the list. In their endeavor to ferret out these "enemy aliens," intelligence agents had gained the cooperation of Nisei leaders of the Japanese American Citizens League (JACL). As a result, these JACL leaders were deeply resented by many Nikkei, who took this resentment with them to the concentration camps.[31]

But even the Nisei were suspects. Before the attack on Pearl Harbor, three separate investigations into Nisei loyalty had been made—one, mentioned earlier, by special investigator Curtis B. Munson, another by the ONI officer Lieutenant Commander Kenneth D. Ringle, and a third by the FBI. All three concluded that despite widespread suspicions against them, most Nisei were loyal citizens, and neither they nor their parents were likely to engage in disloyal or subversive acts. The bombing of Pearl Harbor did not change this conclusion. In fact, in internal administrative discussions, Ringle and Munson urged the federal government to "engage the Nisei in the war effort." Moreover, the FBI Director J. Edgar Hoover advised against removing all Nikkei from the West Coast, an idea then being promoted by army Provost Marshal General Allen W. Gullion and Major (later Colonel) Karl R. Bendetsen, head of the Aliens Division in Gullion's office. In time Gullion and Bendetsen succeeded in convincing Assistant Secretary of War John J. McCloy and Secretary of War Henry L. Stimson, and through them, President Franklin D. Roosevelt, that on the West Coast the Nikkei were a security threat.[32]

On February 19, 1942, the president signed Executive Order 9066. With a stroke of his pen, and without regard for the U.S. Constitution, the president set in motion the process of forced removal and incarceration of an entire people charged with no crime. As Eiichiro Azuma notes, this episode was not so much "our worse wartime mistake," as Yale law professor Eugene Rostow had labeled it. Instead, it was "a historical moment when the cultural, racial, and national Otherness of the Asian was most lucidly articulated, most undisputed, and most resolutely dealt with by the American citizenry and state."[33]

The executive order gave the Western Defense Commander, Lieutenant General John L. DeWitt, the power to exclude from designated "military areas" "any or all persons." Neither "Japanese" nor "Japanese Americans" were mentioned in the order, but it was clear that they were the targets. DeWitt in turn designated as military zones the western half of California (later the entire state), western Oregon and Washington, and southern Arizona.[34]

Nikkei living within DeWitt's exclusion zone were then herded into temporary detention centers, officially called "Assembly Centers," managed by the Wartime Civilian Control Administration (WCCA), an agency of the army's Western Defense Command (WDC). (Several thousand had left legally before DeWitt's March 27 deadline.) "Without charges, without proof, without hearings, with only a few days' to a few weeks' notice, and forced to leave behind their furniture, appliances, farm equipment, automobiles, and other possessions, they were placed in makeshift barracks at racetracks and fairgrounds in and near the major West Coast cities."[35]

With the Nikkei in temporary detention centers by the summer of 1942, a newly created civilian agency, the War Relocation Authority (WRA), assumed responsibility for the imprisoned people. Milton Eisenhower, the first director of the WRA, attempted to convince governors in the mountain west states to allow the Nikkei to resettle in their states, but none would do so. Unable to overcome the governors' resistance, the WRA decided to designate ten sites for the incarceration of the Nikkei. Officially called "Relocation Centers," the sites were in desolate and forbidding environments.

Nativist groups, with long histories of racial animosity toward the Nikkei, cheered their forced removal. The removal was also endorsed by the country's political majority, who believed that ethnic Japanese were "genetically untrustworthy and racially unassimilable." The attack on Pearl Harbor only "confirmed" that view. General DeWitt, the man who oversaw the removal to the temporary camps, shared the sentiment. To him the Nikkei was an "enemy race," a perspective endorsed by such officials as Secretary of War Henry Stimson and Navy Secretary Frank Knox. Roosevelt himself was ambivalent at best concerning the Nikkei. Widespread nativism in the country and Japan's rising military strength and increased aggressiveness in the 1930s influenced his image of Japanese Americans as essentially foreign and "potentially dangerous."[36]

Ironically, in Hawai'i, where martial law was declared after the bombing of Pearl Harbor and where the Nikkei population was larger than in California, the Nikkei's fate in World War II was far different. Although anti-Japanese hostility existed there too, the small geographic area meant that Nikkei interacted more frequently and familiarly with non-Nikkei, which made them seem less a threat to many whites. Moreover, concerted efforts by multi-ethnic leaders in the community succeeded in squelching the attempt to remove the Nikkei wholesale. Then, too, there was the prohibitive cost of removing the

158,000 Nikkei to a small island in the territory and maintaining them there, or removing them to the continental United States. And finally, because the Nikkei constituted as much as 37 percent of the population, their labor was vital to the islands' economy. Thus the military governor of the islands, General Delos Emmons, opposed removing the Nikkei, and with the help of McCloy, Emmons persuaded Stimson to drop proposed plans to do so. As a result, some fifteen hundred Nikkei, most of them Issei, whom someone in the nation's security apparatus deemed dangerous, were incarcerated in the islands, and some seventeen hundred, similarly singled out, were sent to mainland camps. The others, well over 150,000 of them, continued to live their lives as normally as possible under martial law.[37]

An interesting footnote to this story of the Hawai'i Nikkei is that Emmons, the military governor who opposed Nikkei removal, replaced General DeWitt in September 1943 as head of the Western Defense Command. In that capacity, he lent his support to the War Department's rationale of military necessity and internal security as justification for removing all Nikkei from the West Coast. A year later, however, after being informed of the "tenuous legal basis" for continued mass exclusion, he worked with John McCloy of the War Department to find a way to end it in favor of individual exclusion.[38]

One of DeWitt's justifications for removing the Nikkei from the West Coast had been the claim that there had occurred shore-to-ship communication that aided Japanese submarine attacks on mainland targets. Yet DeWitt had no evidence for his claim, and no Nikkei was ever charged with such actions. Moreover, there were only a few sporadic submarine attacks on the West Coast, and all of them were inconsequential. In contrast, attacks along the U.S. Atlantic coast and on transatlantic American shipping were numerous and often deadly. German submarines destroyed hundreds of Allied and neutral merchant ships in the Atlantic and for a long time posed a serious threat to the Allied war effort. Furthermore, military officials had concluded even before President Roosevelt issued Executive Order 9066 in early 1942 that there was no threat of a Japanese invasion of the West Coast.[39]

DeWitt had also justified the removal by arguing that especially Issei but also Nisei ties to Japan made them a danger to national security. West Coast congressmen and Departments of Justice and War officials agreed by pointing to the matter of dual citizenship, whereby Japanese Americans were citizens of the United States and simultaneously subjects of the emperor of Japan.[40]

Like most nations, including the United States, Japan adopted the concept of paternal *jus sanguinis* (right of blood), by which a child born to a male national also became a national of the country, no matter where the child was born. In addition, the United States held to the concept of *jus soli* (right of soil), by which a child born in the United States automatically became a citizen. Because of these laws, ethnic Japanese born in the United States before 1916, like Kurihara, were nationals of both the United States and Japan. In response to requests from Japanese Americans, Japan revised its nationality laws in 1916 to allow Nisei under the age of eighteen to expatriate. (Eligibility for military service began at age eighteen.) In 1924 Japan further revised the law, allowing Japanese Americans to expatriate at any age, and no longer holding to the concept of *jus sanguinis* for children born after 1924 unless their parents registered their births at a Japanese consulate. Most Nisei responded to these changes in Japanese law so that in 1941, Kurihara was among the minority 10 to 15 percent of Nisei who remained dual citizens.[41]

It should be noted that Germany and Italy also followed the practice of jus sanguinis. As a result, there were more than a million German and Italian Americans in 1941 who were also dual citizens. Yet the U.S. government focused on Japanese Americans while ignoring the dual citizenship of German and Italian Americans.[42]

The order to move from the West Coast, which forced families to leave behind most of their possessions, infuriated and dismayed Kurihara. In early February 1941, even before Roosevelt signed E.O. 9066, Kurihara had seen Terminal Islanders "thrown into turmoil" by the order to leave the island at once. Mothers were "completely bewildered with children crying from want and care." With most of the men gone, having earlier been arrested as security risks, the women were taken by surprise when the Department of Justice ordered them off the island. Kurihara saw "peddlers taking advantage and offering prices next to robbery." "Here my first doubt of American Democracy . . . crept into the far corners of my heart," he recalled, "with the sting that I could not forget."[43]

Knowing now that he was excluded from the war effort, that he could no longer work as navigator of the *Belle*, and that Nikkei were being evicted from their homes and jobs, Kurihara decided to return to Los Angeles to join other Nisei to fight the order to move. Two days after Roosevelt signed E.O. 9066, Kurihara wrote a letter to Togo Tanaka, editor of the English-language section of the *Rafu Shimpō*. Kurihara did not know Tanaka personally, but only as the editor of the opinion pieces Kurihara had contributed to Tanaka's newspaper. In his letter, Kurihara asked Tanaka if anyone was taking the leadership in speaking up for the Nisei against the forced removal. If not, he stated with some desperation, "[M]ay I ask if you can obtain the sanction of the Niseis to delegate the position to me?"[44]

Soon after writing his letter, Kurihara departed for Los Angeles. On the evening of his arrival, he attended a meeting of the Citizens Federation of

Southern California, a Nisei organization affiliated with the Japanese American Citizens League (JACL), founded in 1929 to promote Americanism among its members. There he heard Mike Masaoka, JACL field secretary, tell the audience that he had recently met with General DeWitt. Masaoka urged his audience to comply voluntarily with the order to move. Kurihara "felt sick" when he heard this. While the prospect of forced removal had angered him, Masaoka's effort to assist the government in the unjustifiable expulsion of innocent and defenseless people was too much for Kurihara to stomach. These so-called leaders, he concluded of the JACL leadership, were "a bunch of spineless Americans" whom he would "fight" and "crush" "in whatever camp [he] happened to find them." He would take this determination with him to Manzanar.[45]

CHAPTER 4

Resistance in Manzanar

Kurihara was among the Nikkei assigned to Manzanar, one of ten concentration camps for Nikkei, citizens and alien residents alike. Located at the base of the Sierra Nevada in eastern California, Manzanar was in a desert land of extreme temperatures, high winds, and harsh climate. It was isolated from everything: the nearest town, ironically called Independence, was five miles to the north. Manzanar's only concession to aesthetics was the majestic Mount Williamson, towering 14,375 feet in the distance.[1]

Situated in the Owens River watershed, the area had been used for centuries by the Paiute and Shoshone Indians. In the late nineteenth century, white settlers moved into the fertile, then-well-watered areas, establishing ranches, apple, pear, and peach orchards, and a town they called Manzanar ("apple orchard" in Spanish). In the early decades of the twentieth century, leaders in the rapidly growing city of Los Angeles, 225 miles to the south, seized on the bonanza of the watershed and declared it as the answer to the city's water needs. They had an aqueduct built that eventually diverted the underground water to the city. Manzanar farmers and ranchers responded by setting off explosions on the aqueduct and wells, but they were unable to stop the loss of water. By the 1930s Los Angeles owned most of the land and water rights in the area, which by then had become a wasteland. In 1942, with the removal order creating a need for land on which to house the Nikkei, the Los Angeles Department of Water and Power willingly agreed to lease six thousand acres of otherwise useless land to the federal government.[2]

Because time was short and much had to be done to prepare the site and build the camp for the thousands of Nikkei who would arrive in a matter of weeks, the federal government turned for assistance to Father Hugh Lavery of the Los Angeles Maryknoll Mission, which was a central place for Nikkei seeking information and assistance during this time of anxiety and confusion.

The government wanted volunteers to help build the camp and prepare it for people to live there. The Maryknoll Mission organized and coordinated this volunteer effort, recruiting a thousand men for this decidedly ambiguous enterprise.[3] Among them was Kurihara.

Kurihara's decision to volunteer was reluctant and came only after much urging from Father Lavery. While Kurihara was a "devout parishioner" who normally would have been more than willing to help those in need, in this case he was unenthusiastic. He could not see "why he should help the Government build prison camps for aliens and citizens against whom there were no charges, no trials, no convictions, for either sabotage or espionage." Father Lavery told Kurihara that being able bodied, single, and without dependents put him in an ideal position to help the thousands of Nikkei who would be sent to Manzanar. Furthermore, the army promised that the Nikkei men who joined the construction crew would earn "prevailing wages and special privileges."[4]

Years later, Kurihara recalled bitterly, "The Army made fools out of us volunteers, and a liar out of a Catholic priest." He was referring to the low wages paid to the Nikkei construction crew, and to a promise from the government, repeated by Father Lavery, that relatives of the volunteers would join them in Manzanar. However, Kurihara's two cousins and their families were sent to Poston, Arizona, and his brother and family were sent to Rohwer, Arkansas. Kurihara asked the priest to intervene, to have him and his relatives united in the same camp, but to no avail.[5]

In early March 1942, however, Kurihara was unaware that the promises made to him and other men would not be kept, and in good faith he decided to volunteer. On March 23 he arrived in Manzanar with the other volunteers. "The wind blew with such ferocity," Kurihara recalled, "at times I thought the building was going to be carried away. Dust [was] everywhere [and] sandstorms were so bad [they] obscured the sun." Of daily life, he noted, "We . . . slept in the dust, breathed the dust, and ate the dust." "For two weeks," he added, "we had to go without a bath."[6]

Construction at the site had begun a few days before Kurihara arrived. The Nikkei volunteers joined hundreds of workmen; together they cleared brush, dug ditches, laid foundations, and nailed together prefabricated sections of the barracks. Trucks roared into the site, carrying lumber, sewer pipes, water pipes, cement, tarpaper, and other building supplies. Construction was still continuing in April, when hundreds and then thousands of Nikkei began arriving at the camp.[7]

By the end of May most of the men, women, and children assigned to live in Manzanar had arrived. They were housed into some 575 wooden barracks within a square mile that was surrounded by barbed wire, guard towers, and armed guards. Each of the barracks was divided into rooms measuring 20 by 25 feet or less, with one family per room. The barracks were built with plywood walls covered with black tarpaper. Cracks between the planks and the absence of insulation allowed the desert heat, the dust of swirling storms, and the freezing winter weather to penetrate into the rooms.[8]

Sixteen barracks formed a block, which included a mess hall, laundry facilities, and latrines. A total of thirty-six blocks held as many as ten thousand people, the peak number in Manzanar at any time during its three-year existence. Also enclosed were a rudimentary hospital, a store, a church, an orphanage, administrative housing, support facilities, and other buildings. Just beyond the barbed wire there would eventually be a reservoir, a sewage treatment plant, agricultural fields, and a cemetery.[9]

In contrast to the stark living conditions of the inmates, WRA employees, all of them white, lived within Manzanar in apartments with showers and toilets, stoves and refrigerators, and, occasionally, air coolers. Moreover, they were paid "prevailing wages," while the Nikkei who worked earned $16 a month, or $19 if they worked as doctors or lawyers.[10]

On June 1, 1942, the army's Wartime Civil Control Administration (WCCA), which had been running Manzanar, turned over its administration of the camp to a civilian agency, the War Relocation Authority (WRA).[11]

The Revolt

Six months after the WRA took control of Manzanar, the camp experienced a revolt that ended in the death of two innocent young men, shaking the confidence of administrators and the sense of security of the inmates. At 8 PM on December 5, 1942, six masked men entered the barracks apartment of Fred Tayama, a thirty-seven-year-old Nisei with a wife and an eleven-year-old daughter, and assaulted him with clubs. A female passerby heard the noise and screamed, causing the men to flee and a neighbor to call for an ambulance. Tayama's injuries were significant but not life threatening. He identified one of his assailants: the thirty-five-year-old Kibei-Nisei Harry Y. Ueno. (A Kibei-Nisei is a Nisei who went as a youth from the United States to Japan to be educated for a number of years before returning to the United States.) As a result, Ueno was arrested and removed from Manzanar to the jail in nearby Independence.[12]

On a number of occasions prior to the assault, Ueno had clashed verbally with Tayama, who was one of the leaders of the Japanese American Citizens League (JACL), an organization of Nisei who declared their undivided loyalty to the United States despite their own involuntary incarceration. Ueno, like many other inmates, despised Tayama for what they regarded as his unethical actions toward fellow Nikkei going back for some years before the incarceration. Ueno and other Nikkei regarded Tayama contemptuously as an informer for the FBI and camp administrators, a betrayer of his fellow Nikkei at Manzanar. They called him an *inu* (dog), a hated "stool pigeon."

Earlier, Ueno, who was a cook in Mess Hall 22 and head of the Kitchen Workers' Union—in other words, a "troublemaker"—had accused Assistant Project Director Ned Campbell and Chief Steward Joseph Winchester of stealing meat and sugar intended for the inmates and selling them for personal profit outside the camp. Inmates believed that this accusation was the reason that Campbell, who was unpopular among the Nikkei, had Ueno removed from Manzanar.[13]

The morning after the assault on Tayama and the removal of Ueno from Manzanar, about two hundred inmates, most of them from Ueno's Block 22, met in the block's mess hall to discuss what to do about the situation. After some discussion, they decided to adjourn and meet again at 1 PM, this time with the entire camp's block managers and mess hall workers. News of the meeting spread throughout the camp, and the incensed feelings over Ueno's removal brought more than two thousand people, so many that the meeting had to be moved outside to the nearby firebreak area. There, from atop an oil tank, speakers addressed the crowd using a microphone and loudspeakers so that everyone could hear what they said. Members of the Kitchen Workers Union first told the crowd "of the unselfish efforts and sacrifices made by Mr. Ueno for the benefit of the people."[14]

Then Kurihara mounted the oil tank and looked out over the crowd. By then a forty-seven-year-old balding and portly man of short stature, and older than almost all of the Nisei at Manzanar, Kurihara began by reminding the crowd of Ueno's work on their behalf. "Please do not forget to thank Mr. Ueno, your benefactor, in your nightly prayers," he told the crowd. "He has done more for us than any man." "[S]hall we permit the Police Department to arrest and jail Mr. Ueno [based on] the questionable words of that sneak, Mr. Tayama," Kurihara asked, "or shall we unite and fight to have Mr. Ueno, your benefactor, be brought back to Manzanar?" Kurihara continued by reviewing recent upsetting developments at Manzanar, and spoke of Tayama's role in those developments.

> His past records in Los Angeles prove beyond all question of doubt that he has been informing on you, and betraying you, and since his arrival here in this camp, he has been very active . . . in his nefarious work as an agent of the F.B.I. I have definite proof to substantiate my charges. Are you going to tolerate it any longer? Why permit that sneak to pollute the air we breathe? Let's kill him! Let's

> kill him and feed him to the roving coyotes! . . . He is now in the hospital. Let him not escape.
>
> If the Administration refuses to listen to our demand, let us proceed with him and exterminate all other informers in this camp. There are tens upon tens of them amongst us. I will name some of them to you now. There is that Tokutaro Nishimura otherwise Slocum, informer No. 2, and Togo Tanaka, Tom Imai, George Hayakawa, James Oda, Joe Masaoka, Ted Uyeno, John Sonoda, Satoru Kamikawa.
>
> We are now going to demand the return of Mr. Ueno to this camp. Let us fight and fight to the finish![15]

In the aftermath of Kurihara's agitated exhortation, the crowed formed a Committee of Five to negotiate the release of Ueno. The committee consisted of three Issei, one Kibei-Nisei, and one Nisei, Kurihara, who was the oldest member of the committee. Other members were a Kitchen Workers' Union leader, a chef, and two block leaders; they selected Kurihara as spokesperson for the committee because of the respect they had for his outspokenness and fearlessness in criticizing camp administrators.[16]

When he heard that a mass meeting was occurring, the chief administrator of the camp, Project Director Ralph Merritt, became alarmed and asked Captain Martyn Hall of the 322d Military Police to have his men stand guard outside the center's entrance. Then Merritt and Acting Chief of Internal Security John Gilkey drove to the meeting. Upon arrival, they learned that the meeting was over, but that the Committee of Five was walking toward his office to talk with him. They also learned that Tayama and other alleged stool pigeons were put on a blacklist at the meeting. Merritt and Gilkey returned to the administration building, and soon the Committee of Five arrived, accompanied by a large crowd of inmates.[17]

The committee, urged on by the unruly crowd, demanded the release of Ueno. At first Merritt refused, but after an hour of back-and-forth talk, interspersed with taunts and jeering from the crowd, and after the crowd refused to disperse, Merritt—in consultation with Hall and Gilkey—decided to respond positively to what had become a volatile situation. Since Ueno's arrest, investigations into Tayama's beating had found no evidence that Ueno was among the assailants. Moreover, the Committee of Five had warned Merritt that it could not control the crowd, and they urged him to concede before something unfortunate occurred.

Merritt and the committee then conferred apart from the crowd, and after some discussion they agreed that Ueno would return to Manzanar, provided that the crowd disbanded immediately, that no mass demonstrations occurred until Ueno's case was settled, and that no attempt be made for Ueno to escape from his confinement. According to an official investigation conducted after the revolt, Kurihara "then burst into a fanatical tirade, disclaimed loyalty to the United States, expressed the hope that Japan would win the war, and threatened death to all informers." When he was reminded of the terms of the agreement, "he subsided." He then explained the agreement to the crowd, asked the people to return to their barracks, and promised that at 6 PM that evening in the mess hall of Block 22 he would report to them on Ueno's return. Satisfied, the throng returned to their barracks. Kurihara later noted that he had spoken to the crowd in a Hawaiianized-form of Japanese, which made it difficult for most of them to understand fully what he said.[18]

At mid-afternoon Ueno arrived at the Manzanar jail. Merritt then met with Ueno and the Committee of Five, repeated the terms of the agreement, and shook hands with them. At 6 PM, when the committee arrived at the mess hall to make its report, a crowd of two thousand to four thousand Nikkei awaited them. The committee reported that Ueno was now in the Manzanar jail and, believing that it had accomplished its mission, attempted to resign. The crowd would have none of it, instead calling on the committee to demand the "return of Mr. Ueno to his home [that night], 'unconditionally.'"[19]

In a dark mood, the crowd agreed to divide into two groups. One group marched to the hospital to find Tayama and finish the job begun earlier; the other group headed to the jail to release Ueno. Unaware of the crowd's decision to split in two and fearing that the angry mob might do something rash, Kurihara and the other members of the Committee rushed to the jail.[20]

The first group reached the hospital but was unable to find Tayama because sympathetic Nikkei hospital workers had hidden him. The crowd then decided to split into smaller groups and locate Togo Tanaka, Tokie Slocum, and other suspected informers. Forewarned, Tanaka and the others also went into hiding.

Tanaka later recalled that at 7 PM a "mob" "ripped" open the door to his family's barracks room, where they found his wife, baby, parents-in-law, and father. Just a few minutes earlier, Tanaka had fled to a friend's place to borrow clothes to disguise himself. He then joined the mob as it approached his barracks. "There was much conversation," he recalled, "as the crowd [picked] up newcomers along the way." Walking near the rear of the mob, Tanaka wondered "whether [he would] live to see the dawn." Several of the men, carrying knives and a club, marched into his family's room and demanded his whereabouts; after fifteen minutes of threatening, searching the room, and not finding him, they left.[21]

Meanwhile, a throng of about five hundred men and boys were marching toward the police station with the Committee of Five. Robert Matsushita, who was in his room at the time, recalled hearing a loud, "enormous buzz," like the sound of a "thousand bumblebees swarming." Curious, he peeked outside his door and saw the "mob" as it passed his barrack.[22] At 6:50 PM this crowd arrived at the police station. They surrounded the jail, which was a section of a barrack with a window that would enable Ueno to escape. Although urged to climb out of the window, Ueno refused. "[T]he window was wide open," he later noted. "I could have gotten out anytime I wanted to. But I didn't want to break my promise to the negotiating committee, so I stayed in there."[23]

At this point Assistant Chief of Internal Security Arthur Williams phoned Merritt, described the situation to him, and advised him to stay away from the police station because the crowd threatened to become unruly. Believing that the effort to free Ueno breached the agreement with the Committee of Five and that violence might occur at any moment, Merritt asked Captain Hall to send in the military police to maintain order. Merritt then attempted to join Hall, but the volatile situation prevented him from doing so. He therefore went to a nearby building and watched the scene from a window with other administrators while communicating with Williams by phone.

Kurihara, now fearful that violence would occur, admitted that the committee could no longer control what he thought had become an angry mob, and he pleaded with Hall to allow Ueno to return to his barracks temporarily as a form of appeasement. But Hall refused.[24] As the night wore on, the crowd became increasingly menacing—variously taunting and jeering at the soldiers, singing Japanese patriotic songs, and throwing stones, sand, bottles, and lighted cigarettes. After several attempts to convince the crowd to break up, Hall decided that in order to disperse them he had to order the soldiers to use tear gas grenades. In the ensuing smoke, panic, and confusion, two soldiers, with no order to fire, shot into the crowd. At the same time, someone in the crowd turned on the engine of a nearby automobile, which rolled, driverless, toward the police station. Unaware that the vehicle was without a driver, a soldier shot at the car. The crowd dispersed in panic. When the dust and smoke cleared, seventeen-year-old James Ito was dead, twenty-one-year-old Jim Kanagawa died soon after, and ten others were injured. It was 9:30 PM.[25]

In recalling these events, Kurihara stated that he and others had overheard "a Sergeant going from soldier to soldier, [telling] them, 'Remember Pearl Harbor'"—a direct provocation to the soldiers. Bitter over the senseless shooting at the crowd, Kurihara called it "murder in the first degree, unpardonable and unforgivable."[26]

Throughout the night kitchen bells tolled and military police patrolled the camp. Those who had been threatened or assaulted as stool pigeons were taken to the Administration Building for their own safety. A few days later, these sixty-five individuals were transported to an abandoned Civilian Conservation Corps camp in Death Valley, where they remained for a few weeks until they were released and relocated to Chicago and other cities.[27]

A different fate awaited Ueno and the Committee of Five. They were arrested, taken to the jail at Bishop, fifty miles north of Manzanar, and a few days later transferred to the jail at Lone Pine, ten miles south of Manzanar. In the days following December 6, others whom the authorities suspected of being troublemakers were also imprisoned at Independence and Lone Pine. As a result of the revolt, a total of twenty-six Nikkei found themselves behind bars in the two towns. Within a few weeks, ten of them were returned to Manzanar. The remaining sixteen were kept at the Lone Pine jail as federal officials pondered what to do with them.[28]

Events Leading Up to the Revolt

The assault on Tayama and the subsequent arrest of Ueno were the catalysts that triggered defiance and revolt on December 5 and 6. But long before that explosion of hostility, there had been strong undercurrents of resentment at Manzanar that went back ultimately to the frustrations of Nikkei rooted in the long history of discrimination they had endured, especially in California. These frustrations fed the bitterness and sense of helplessness that welled up among the vast majority of Nikkei as they realized that they had been singled out by the U.S. government for exile for no other reason than their ancestry, and in the process compelled to abandon their homes, property, and means of livelihood. What began as bewilderment and anxiety evolved into anger and resentment as they realized that they would be imprisoned behind barbed wire indefinitely. When a Nisei nurse learned that the Office of War Information was producing a film entitled "How We're Treating the Japanese," she responded bitterly that, since 70 percent of those incarcerated were American citizens, the film "should be titled 'How We're Treating Americans.'"[29] Some, like the nurse, verbalized their anger; others suppressed it. Kurihara, more loudly and forcibly than most of the Nikkei at Manzanar, articulated the growing resentment toward imprisonment.

During the first months of incarceration, when Manzanar was under the jurisdiction of the army's WCCA, poor planning, lack of facilities and equipment, and overcrowded and unsanitary conditions fed resentments the inmates brought with them. This was hardly surprising, since ten thousand people were moving into a mile-square area while constructing and organizing of camp operations were still underway.[30] When the WRA assumed control of Manzanar on June 1, 1942, morale at the camp was already deteriorating. Events during the next six months only accelerated the deterioration. Among the reasons for complaints were seemingly arbitrary and discriminatory WRA directives, as well as widely believed rumors that sugar meant for the Nikkei was being siphoned off by camp administrators.

While these problems took their toll on Nikkei morale, the particular chain of events that set off the revolt related to differing cultural perspectives within the Nikkei population, differences camp administrators were evidently unaware of and thus unprepared to recognize or deal with. In "The Manzanar Riot: An Ethnic Perspective," Arthur Hansen and David Hacker examine two "cultural themes" in the Nikkei community in the decades before the war. The first was a commitment to and respect for traditional forms of social hierarchy based on age, generation, and sex. In this hierarchy, leadership and power in family and community life went to older men and immigrant (Issei) parents. It is no surprise, therefore, that the Committee of Five, formed to secure Ueno's release, were older males, three of whom were Issei.[31]

Hansen and Hacker's second cultural theme emphasized group solidarity over individual interests. As one Nisei explained, Issei did not talk about themselves: "Japanese don't even use the pronoun 'I.' They imply it in a sentence without using it. So you don't know whether they're talking about one person or two people or ten."[32]

These two themes—so distinct from those of the dominant American culture and of the cultural understandings of WRA camp administrators—were central to the world view of the Issei and of the Kibei-Nisei, who were more proficient in Japanese than in English, and in Japanese than in American social and cultural mores, and thus culturally more similar to Issei than to Nisei. The Nisei, who had had greater contact with the larger American society, shared the cultural perspectives of the Issei and Kibei-Nisei, but to a lesser extent. As scholars like Lon Kurashige, Brian Masaru Hayashi, John Stephan, and Jere Takahashi have argued, during the decade before the war, Nisei attitudes toward the culture and politics of Japan on the one hand, and the United States on the other, were ambivalent, diverse, and complex. Moreover, especially during the first year of their incarceration, some Nisei and probably most Kibei-Nisei and Issei favored a Japanese victory in the war, believing that it would benefit them more than an American victory.[33] Under the shocking circumstances of their forced exile, that belief certainly had some credence.

In contrast, there was a small group of members of the Los Angeles JACL at Manzanar. This group was much more conditioned by American cultural perspectives and norms. They therefore enthusiastically supported a U.S. victory in the war and believed that a kind of pro-American acquiescence was the best way to achieve acceptance for Japanese Americans into the larger American society once the war was over. So while the Issei and Kibei-Nisei gravitated together in the face of harassments and discrimination, the JACLers "advertised their Americanism."[34]

Although Kurihara had shared the JACL enthusiasm for Americanization before his incarceration, his reaction to the forced removal and exile of himself and other Nikkei contrasted sharply with the JACLers' perspective. While the JACLers accepted their incarceration as unavoidable, Kurihara was offended by their public avowals of compliance. Kurihara believed that his Americanism demanded that he stand up and fight for his rights as a citizen of an ostensibly free country.

The JACLers' pride in their American citizenship led them to distance themselves from the notion of Issei leadership. After the bombing of Pearl Harbor, Fred Tayama, Tokie Slocum, Togo Tanaka, Joe Grant Masaoka, and Tad Uyeno had formed themselves into an Anti-Axis Committee that reported to the FBI what they thought were suspicious activities among the Issei. This of course provoked widespread hostility toward them: Issei, Kibei-Nisei, and Nisei alike generally believed that these men and others in the JACL were "sacrificing the community's welfare" for their own "aggrandizement."[35]

The animosities these disagreements produced continued in Manzanar. Unaware that the JACLers were detested by other Nikkei as informers and even traitors, camp administrators relied on them for information and advice. In turn, the JACLers willingly took the role as spokespersons for camp inmates.[36]

To complicate these matters, some Nikkei at Manzanar were Communists, the most visible of whom were Karl Yoneda and Koji Ariyoshi, who supported the United States in its war effort against what they called the "fascist" government of Japan. On the surface, Yoneda and Ariyoshi seemed to camp administrators to be united with the JACL leaders because both groups supported and cooperated with WRA administrators. In reality, hostilities that went back to the 1930s sharply divided the two groups. At Manzanar, they tolerated each other's presence, but they were never more than allies of convenience.[37]

Because Yoneda and Ariyoshi, like the JACLers, supported camp administrators and were suspected of being informers, they, too, were generally despised by the Nikkei. Still other Nisei—non-ideological, like those on the Manzanar police force and those working with camp administrators on the camp newspaper, the *Manzanar Free Press*—were also suspect. In their anger toward informers, activist Nikkei placed JACLers on a deathlist and Communists and other suspected *inu* (dogs) on a blacklist.[38]

The Nikkei directed their anger toward the JACL and others believed to be collaborators largely because their primary targets of resentment—the U.S. government, General John DeWitt, government officials, and xenophobic white Americans—were beyond their reach, distant figures "against whom no direct action could be taken." This redirected anger, coupled with differences in worldviews concerning social hierarchy and group solidarity, which separated the JACLers and Communists from most other Nikkei, underlay the emotional upheavals that erupted in Manzanar.[39]

On July 12, 1942, Fred Tayama and other JACLers and the Communists organized the Manzanar Citizens' Federation. The purported purpose of the federation was that Issei could not represent the Nisei point of view in matters relating to camp governance or in dealings with camp administrators because Issei were not citizens, and only American citizens could fight discrimination and educate Nisei for leadership and good citizenship. The Federation Chair Koji Ariyoshi opened the first meeting on July 28. As speaker after speaker supported the federation's views, the Nisei audience cheered heartily. When the floor was opened for discussion, however, Kurihara rose to challenge the views of the speakers. He declared that he would speak "honestly and fearlessly, regardless of the consequences." Before he was forced to leave his home, livelihood, and family, Kurihara explained, he had been "100 percent American." But on the day the army forced the banishment of the Nikkei, he continued, "I [swore] severance of my allegiance to the United States, and became 100 percent pro-Japanese." Pointing to the denial of the "civil rights" of Kibei-Nisei and Nisei alike, he asked those of them in the audience, "Why seek to remain as citizens of a country which denies us . . . rights which are guaranteed [to us] . . . by the Constitution of the United States?"[40]

Kurihara went on to say that he was an American citizen who had served "under fire" in France as a soldier in the U.S. Army in World War I. Despite that service, he noted, he was now in "this prison." "You're all American citizens," he told his audience. "You're all here, too, with me. I've proved my loyalty by fighting other there. Why doesn't the government trust me?" When Tokie Slocum responded, "We're here because of military necessity," Kurihara shot back. "Tokie, why are you in here? . . . Isn't it because you're a Jap? Isn't it because the government doesn't trust you?"[41] "Why didn't the government give us the chance to prove our loyalty instead of herding us into camps?" he continued. "It is not because we are unloyal. It is because we are what we are, Japs! Then, if such is the case, let us be Japs! Japs, through and through to the very marrow of our bones!"[42] This theme, of becoming the pariah that government officials labeled them to be, became central in Kurihara's pleas to the Nikkei, and it found growing resonance, particularly among the Kibei-Nisei and Issei.

Kurihara's insistent remarks "drew forth spontaneous expressions of heretofore dormant feelings." "The entire floor was electrified," Kurihara later recalled, and "after more [of my] verbal blasting . . . the hall resounded with cheers, whistling and stamping. . . . I had turned the table with unquestionable success."[43]

A second public meeting organized by the Citizens Federation occurred ten days later. "The hall was filled beyond its capacity," recalled Kurihara, "and there were many hundreds crowding at every opening, doorways and even in the immediate rear of the speakers' platform." This meeting ended with results similar to the first one. Yoneda began the meeting by urging the Nisei to work in the camouflage net factory for $16 a month as a gesture of their American patriotism. When Kurihara rose to speak, he later noted, the "audience broke into the most grateful cheers I ever heard. Much as I was convinced that I had unquestionably turned the table at the previous meeting," he continued, "my conviction was totally confirmed on this night. I felt elated." Kurihara then responded to Yoneda's plea by declaring that people working in defense plants outside the camp earned $40 or $50 a week. Kurihara asked Yoneda why he had not fought "for fair wages for the Nisei instead of asking them to work for a mere pittance."[44]

Historians Arthur Hansen and David Hacker have argued that these meetings, together with the Federation's petition to the U.S. government to draft Japanese Americans, convinced many Nisei to reject the JACL perspective: "Increasingly, the Issei and Kibei-Nisei point of view was expanding into an Issei, Kibei-Nisei, and Nisei point of view." Reflecting back on the months leading up to the Manzanar revolt of the preceding December 6, Togo Tanaka concluded that Kurihara and other spokesmen for his views articulated what became the dominant sentiments of the Nikkei, and as a result Kurihara and other like-minded activists eventually assumed the "leadership of Manzanar's population."[45]

After the second meeting sponsored by the Citizens Federation, Kurihara set out to organize a countergroup called the Manzanar Relocation Center Federation. This group was to act as an intermediary between camp administrators and the vast majority of the Nikkei population not represented by the JACL or the Communists. This alternative federation would function according to "democratic principles" and adopt a constitution that was in accordance with the U.S. Constitution. The Assistant Project Director Ned Campbell denied Kurihara's petition to organize the group, as well as a Kibei-Nisei request to organize another group. Kurihara's effort here was significant. It showed that despite his rhetoric and declaration of being "100 percent Jap," his instinctive model of civic functioning was American democracy.[46]

As they increasingly felt the brunt of discrimination and as their bitterness over WRA policies swelled, more and more Kibei-Nisei began to follow Kurihara's lead in speaking openly in favor of a Japanese victory in the war. When they learned on July 20, 1942 that the Kibei-Nisei would be prohibited from leaving the camp on work furloughs, they were incensed. As American citizens, they believed that they should be treated as other Nisei. The contradiction in U.S. policy was not lost on them. As Kurihara noted, when U.S. officials needed the Kibei-Nisei for their bilingual skills, the U.S. Army recruited them as translators and interrogators of Japanese prisoners. Otherwise, because they had lived in Japan, they were suspects and denied furloughs that would allow them to work outside the camps.[47]

The prohibition led the Kibei-Nisei leader Ben Kishi to call a meeting for August 8. Four hundred Kibei-Nisei, two-thirds of their population at Manzanar, plus sympathetic Issei and Nisei, attended. Fred Tayama, who would be beaten four months later on that fateful evening of December 5, described the meeting's proceedings in a confidential report to camp administrators, the army, and the FBI. The first speaker, Raymond Hirai, spoke of Nikkei grievances regarding medical care, school facilities, food, housing, wages, and self-government. On self-government, Hirai complained that current block leaders were not speaking for the Nikkei community but merely taking orders from Manzanar administrators. He called for new elections for block leaders. "I demanded many . . . things of [Roy] Nash," Hirai reported of a meeting he had had with the camp director, "and Nash told me, 'I am the project director here and I can do anything the way I want it to be done,' so I told Nash, 'You are like Hitler and Mussolini combined,' and Nash replied, 'I am,' so I demanded [that he put] what he had said in writing and immediately Nash turned around and said that he had never said such a thing. That is the type of director we have here."[48]

Kiyoshi Hashimoto then stood up to speak, but when he hesitated and seemed overwhelmed, Kurihara stood up to encourage him. "Why be afraid to say what we [want] to say?" he asked. "We, the citizens of the United States, were orphanized by this government and were forced to be Japanese. If such is the case, let us be Jap, 100% Japs." This declaration was greeted with "roaring applause and stamping of feet." When another speaker, Masaji Tanaka, declared that Kibei-Nisei were Japanese and not Americans, and thus owed no loyalty to the United States, his statements were also greeted with loud applause.[49]

In contrast, when Karl Yoneda tried to speak, he was greeted with boos and told to "shut up." When he said that despite "their segregation and hardships, the Japanese must still participate in the country's war effort, the heckling was so loud that it was impossible to hear all that he said."[50] Such conduct bore witness to a growing sentiment of in-group solidarity that reinforced negative feelings about camp administrators and the U.S. government they represented.

The Kibei-Nisei meeting prompted Project Director Roy Nash to issue a bulletin that banned the use of Japanese in public meetings, which further infuriated and antagonized the Issei and Kibei-Nisei, whose first language was Japanese. Nash also reported to the FBI that about six hundred people had attended a meeting at Manzanar in which speeches "of a subversive nature" were given. In response to Nash's report and to a letter from a Nikkei informer, the FBI sent Special Agent Robert Van Wagoner to Manzanar, where he interviewed administrators and Nikkei. His detailed report noted that Henry Brown, engineer and construction director, for whom Kurihara worked at Manzanar, said that Kurihara served as a supervisor of a carpenter crew and was "a very good worker and a leader." However, the Manzanar Police Department characterized Kurihara as "an agitator, trouble-maker, and pro-Japanese."[51]

As a result of Wagoner's report, FBI Director J. Edgar Hoover wrote a memo in October to Assistant Attorney General Wendell Berge, asking "whether or not . . . the individuals confined to such camps [could] be technically charged with a violation of the Sedition Statues as a result of remarks made to other members of the camps." Berge's response several weeks later was that "the facts disclosed in the [report] do not warrant prosecution . . . under the Sedition Statutes." When a second FBI investigation was initiated in November, followed by another report, this one by Special Agent William McCormick, Hoover sent another inquiry to Berge. In his response, dated January 30, 1943, Berge enclosed a Justice Department memo by Laurence Bailey, which stated that there was no violation of the sedition law, and that the "riotous conduct at [the Kibei-Nisei meeting] was simply a spontaneous expression of discontent." "It is noted," wrote Bailey, "that Kurihara, the one making the most damaging statements, is a World War overseas veteran. It is doubtful that such tenuous [accusations of] treason would be sufficient to get a conviction, in the face of this past evidence of loyalty."[52]

Another major source of unrest was a directive in early September 1942 from the WRA office in Washington D.C. that took political power from the Issei and gave it to the Nisei. Specifically, the directive stipulated that each camp would have a council of elected block leaders, and only U.S. citizens could be elected, overturning the previous organizational structure in which Issei were eligible to serve as block leaders. This WRA policy triggered bitter protests, since at the time about two-thirds of block leaders were Issei.[53]

To implement the new policy, the project director appointed a seventeen-man commission of Nisei to draft a charter for the new government, thus excluding not only Issei but also Kibei-Nisei from the process.

As a result of the issues just discussed—organization of the Manzanar Citizens Federation, exclusion of Kibei-Nisei from participating in the furlough program, and wresting of political power from the Issei—conflict and "feuds" erupted among the Nikkei, creating turmoil in Manzanar. Furious over the stance taken by Nisei supporters of the administration, Kurihara sought out

Tayama, Slocum, Yoneda, Ariyoshi, and Tanaka, challenging each to a "public debate." The question: Should the Nisei affirm their "allegiance to the United States" under existing circumstances, or should they highlight the hypocrisy of America, reject the United States, and affirm their Japanese identity? All of the men declined the challenge. Tanaka explained that he did not wish to exacerbate the existing rancor among the Nikkei.[54]

Kurihara, on the other hand, was eager to engage his adversaries in public debate. His high school elocution experiences at St. Ignatius, coupled with the effectiveness of his efforts to sway Nikkei opinion at the Manzanar Citizens Federation meetings and the Kibei-Nisei meeting, had given him confidence in his public-speaking abilities.

Ueno, who accompanied Kurihara when he issued his challenge to Tanaka, also declared that the Nisei should affirm their allegiance to Japan. Many Nisei realized that this was unrealistic, because they were not subjects of Japan, either because they were born after 1924, when Japan renounced its claim on them, or because they had renounced their Japanese citizenship after Japan had changed its citizenship laws. Tanaka also told Ueno that his view was based on the belief that the Nisei would be accepted in Japan. Tanaka believed, to the contrary, that the Nisei would be mistrusted and treated as enemies, and that the Nisei themselves would learn that they were too Americanized to be comfortable living in Japan.[55]

Meanwhile, a Manzanar Work Corps was being formed ostensibly to represent the rights and interests of Nikkei workers. Because the corps was sponsored by JACLers, however, most Nikkei showed little interest in it. Ueno believed that the corps was another administrative tool to control workers. Instead, he organized the Kitchen Workers Union. Because mess hall workers were primarily Kibei-Nisei, and the Kibei-Nisei constituted about fifteen hundred of the four thousand Nikkei workers in Manzanar, Ueno's union became a group to be reckoned with because of its potential for mobilizing community action.

Ueno's success in forming the Kitchen Workers Union and growing opposition to the Charter Commission, the body that would institutionalize changes in the election of block leaders, were indicators of rising and widespread opposition to JACLers and like-minded supporters. At a meeting on November 25 to discuss the proposed charter, newly appointed Project Director Ralph Merritt, who had arrived at Manzanar only the day before, was confronted with the mood of the camp. "Look out the window and what do you see?" a Nikkei asked those at the meeting. "There is barbed wire, there is a watch tower, and there is a soldier who guards us by day and night and shoots us if we break the law. Because . . . we have no self-government, I move that the damned charter be thrown out the window." The motion was passed without dissent. Because of the events of the next two weeks, the charter was never put to a vote and thus never ratified.[56]

By this time Ueno had emerged as a vocal critic of the administration and the JACLers. Fluent in Japanese, he was a persuasive speaker. He became a special problem for the administration when he accused Assistant Project Director Ned Campbell and Chief Steward Joe Winchester of taking sugar meant for the Nikkei and selling it for personal profit. An investigation concluded that the Nikkei were indeed being shortchanged in their sugar allotment, but no evidence emerged that Campbell and Winchester were the culprits. Nevertheless, Ueno's charge made him popular among his peers, who believed that he had their interests at heart.[57]

In contrast to Ueno, Tayama by this time was largely despised. Before Pearl Harbor, Tayama had been president of the Los Angeles chapter of the JACL, as well as owner of a chain of restaurants. A successful businessman, he had a large home and drove a "fancy" car, but his restaurants were known among the Nikkei for their poor working conditions, low wages, and opposition to unionization. Nikkei saw him as an aggressive opportunist uninterested in their welfare. It was said that, as co-owner of the Pacific Service Bureau, he charged Issei exorbitant prices for such vital services as filing alien travel permits and obtaining or transferring business licenses. In spring 1941, prior to the bombing of Pearl Harbor, he had formed a committee of Nisei to gather information on suspected subversive activities by Issei, and turned the information over to the U.S. Office of Naval Intelligence. After Pearl Harbor, his committee's activities expanded and accelerated.[58]

At Manzanar Tayama's leadership in the Citizens Federation and the Work Corps only intensified the disdain of his fellow Nikkei. Then in mid-November, as camp administrators attempted to convince the inmates to accept the revised form of self-government that would replace the Issei with the Nisei in positions of power, Tayama and Kiyoshi Higashi, another JACL leader, went to Salt Lake City to represent Manzanar at the JACL National Convention. There, WRA leaders met with Nisei representatives from all ten WRA camps to determine policy affecting the Nikkei. Manzanar inmates were outraged that Tayama would present himself as their voice. Their outrage neared the breaking point when the *Manzanar Free Press* reported that at the convention, Tayama had proposed that Nisei be recruited as soldiers in the U.S. Army. His proposition elicited "profound disgust."[59]

In light of widespread animosity toward Tayama, it is not surprising that upon his return to Manzanar, he was beaten on December 6, and that "the overwhelming majority of internees fully endorsed this beating." According to a WRA report, "Not one person interviewed in camp following the riot had a good word to say for Tayama." It is thus understandable that when Harry Ueno was arrested for the beating, thousands protested to compel his release. The Nikkei at Manzanar believed, overwhelmingly so, that no one should be punished for beating Tayama. To them, Tayama—as the very antithesis of communitarianism and the embodiment of self-aggrandizement—thoroughly deserved the treatment he had brought down upon himself.[60]

What happened at Manzanar, as well as events before Pearl Harbor, challenge statements made by Roger Lotchin, who in 2011 attempted to justify the imprisonment of innocent Nikkei during the war. While Lotchin agreed that the decision to order Nikkei into concentration camps was a civil rights violation, he argued that racism was negligible prior to Pearl Harbor and played a minor role in the pressure to exile the Nikkei. (He defined racism as belief in the biological inferiority of a group.) Moreover, Lotchin wrote, life in the camps was humane, democratic, and no worse than life outside. Were Kurihara alive to read Lotchin's essay, he would likely respond that his own experiences in California (in contrast to Michigan) in the decades before World War II bore witness to a racial hatred among many whites there toward Nikkei. And while Lotchin might not call that racism, Kurihara would declare that such racial animosity was clear and palpable. Kurihara would also point out that the WRA directive denying Issei the right to vote for community block leadership excluded a key constituency and thus made a sham of the rhetoric of democracy in the concentration camps. Based on my knowledge of Kurihara, I am certain that he would declare Lotchin's piece a whitewash (a word in keeping with Kurihara's language) and the author an apologist for unforgiveable actions that caused the ruin of innocent lives. In Kurihara's words, what happened at Manzanar was a "damnably disgraceful and irreparable action against the very principal[s] of democracy."[61]

CHAPTER 5

Stepping Back

Among the men with whom Kurihara clashed at Manzanar were Tokie (Tokutaro) Nishimura Slocum, Togo Tanaka, and Karl Yoneda. The background of these men and their disagreements with him are part of Kurihara's story. Like Kurihara, Slocum was a veteran of World War I and a member of the American Legion and the Veterans of Foreign Wars. And like Kurihara, he was forty-seven years old when he entered Manzanar with his wife and two children.[1]

Despite the suggestiveness of his surname, Slocum was born in Japan and had arrived in the United States with his parents when he was ten years old. The family settled in North Dakota, which adds to the singularity of his experience. In North Dakota, he was adopted by the Slocum family in circumstances and for reasons unknown to me, but that led to his adoption of the Slocum family name. He eventually attended the University of Minnesota and then Columbia University Law School. When the United States entered World War I, he left Columbia to enlist in the army. For his valor in the war, he was promoted to the rank of sergeant-major, an unusual achievement for an Asian who was not even an American citizen.

In May 1918, when Congress passed a law allowing the naturalization of alien soldiers, Slocum became a U.S. citizen. His citizenship was threatened, however, when in 1925 the U.S. Supreme Court ruled in *Toyota v. United States* that Issei veterans were not covered under the 1918 statute.[2] Although the Bureau of Naturalization decided not to enforce this decision, Slocum feared that if he and other Issei exercised their rights as citizens, they might well be challenged. As a result, he devoted his next ten years working with individuals and organizations to convince Congress to pass a bill that would give citizenship to Issei veterans of World War I. The eventual result was the 1935 Nye-Lea Act, which gave all World War I veterans of Asian descent the right to naturalize. Slocum's significant achievement in this effort, however, was later eclipsed (in the opinion of most Nikkei in Manzanar) by his subsequent actions during World War II.

As war between Japan and the United States grew imminent, Slocum gained the reputation of being an informer for the FBI and Naval Intelligence. After the bombing of Pearl Harbor, he publically accused some Issei leaders of engaging in subversive activities and accompanied FBI agents when they went to arrest the men. Because of such conduct, most Nikkei at Manzanar considered Slocum "dogmatic" in matters related to the way in which they should respond to government actions, as well as "obnoxious" in his public behavior. Like Tayama, he was thoroughly despised. His response was to let it be known that he was in constant communication with the FBI and was unconcerned by the acrimony the Nikkei displayed toward him.[3]

Another object of acrimony was Togo Tanaka, a Nisei who was two decades younger than Kurihara. Born on January 7, 1916 in Portland, Oregon, Tanaka had grown up in the middle-class, white community of Hollywood in Los Angeles, where his parents operated a fruit and vegetable market. He attended Hollywood High School and then the University of California, Los Angeles (UCLA), where he majored in political science and graduated Phi Beta Kappa in 1936. During his junior year at UCLA he worked as associate editor of the English-language section of the *Kashū Mainichi*, a Japanese vernacular newspaper. A year-and-a-half later he left the *Kashū* to join Louise Suski as co-editor of the English-language section of the *Rafu Shimpō*, a leading Los Angeles Japanese American daily, where he also served as personnel manager of sixty employees. By late 1941, at age twenty-five, Tanaka had become relatively prosperous. He owned some real estate and was vice president of, and a stockholder in, a wholesale produce company. At the *Rafu Shimpō*, Tanaka had had some correspondence with Kurihara, who regularly sent unsolicited opinion pieces to the newspaper. Of their exchanges, Tanaka later recalled that Kurihara had been "friendly and outgoing," wrote "very directly," and gave his readers "no difficulty knowing where he stood."[4]

In October 1941 the *Rafu* publisher sent Tanaka to Washington, D.C., to request that the newspaper be permitted to continue publishing in the event of war between the United States and Japan. It may have been this trip that led to his arrest in the wake of Pearl Harbor. In any case, he was held for twelve days, during which he was denied permission to contact his wife. No charges were ever made against him, and he was released without explanation.[5]

In Manzanar, Tanaka disliked what he believed was destructive finger pointing by his fellow JACLers. And unlike Tayama and Slocum, he wrote no secret reports to the FBI or camp administrators. In Manzanar, he was a WRA "documentary historian," a job he held with Joe Masaoka. He was open about the numerous reports that he wrote on happenings in the camp. Moreover, while he cooperated with camp officials, he was an independent thinker who was unafraid of disagreeing with officials, and when he did so, he did it with civility. Because of his role as documentary historian, however, Nikkei dissidents targeted him as an informer and included him on their death list. Decades later, in recalling his time at Manzanar, Tanaka noted that Kurihara had urged him and Masaoka to stop writing their reports, which Kurihara thought could be used against the Nikkei. But Tanaka and Masuoka disagreed, believing that their reports served to promote a positive image of the Nikkei and would be useful to future historians.[6]

After Tanaka and others were convoyed to Death Valley in the wake of the Manzanar revolt, Professor Dorothy Swaine Thomas of the University of California at Berkeley, and director of the Japanese Evacuation and Resettlement Study, asked him to write reports for her on the Nikkei and their Manzanar experiences. The results were insightful, in-depth essays on the Japanese vernacular newspapers, the JACL, and the Manzanar revolt.[7]

In reflecting on the months of turmoil at Manzanar, Kurihara remembered Tanaka as a "most worthy opponent . . . a very brilliant young man." "Though we disagree politically," Kurihara wrote, "I have great esteem for [him]." The respect was mutual. According to Tanaka, Kurihara was "the most eloquently persuasive fellow in Manzanar. We [JACLers] were no match for him." Their respect for each other reflected their shared belief in stating their positions openly and honestly.[8]

Tanaka and Kurihara had both lived and worked before the war in the larger American society, but their responses to incarceration contrasted markedly. While Kurihara was embittered and disillusioned, Tanaka maintained to the end an optimism that "things would get better." While Kurihara felt betrayed that the government failed to acknowledge his service in World War I, Tanaka, a generation younger, had no such prior experience. He also had white American friends who rejected and denounced the incarceration of the Nikkei, which he believed was a hopeful sign about the future of the Nikkei in postwar America.[9]

Karl Yoneda was another man whose views and activities at Manzanar brought him into conflict with Kurihara. Born in 1906 in California, Yoneda was sent to Japan at age seven, and he remained there through his next formative thirteen years. As a young man in Japan, he evidently encountered the ideas of Karl Marx and Marx's analysis of capitalism, class struggle, and the material basis of society. In any case, he became attracted to labor organizing, and upon returning to California he became an active union organizer and member of the American Communist Party. It was in Los Angeles that he met his future wife, Elaine Black, who was also a labor activist and Communist Party member.[10]

Like Kurihara, Yoneda volunteered as a construction worker in the first group of Nikkei to go to Manzanar, and like Kurihara, Yoneda was a passionate idealist. His ideals, however, took him in a direction quite different from that of Kurihara. Unlike Kurihara, he refused to speak out against DeWitt's removal orders. Because by this time the United States and the Soviet Union were allies in the war against Nazi Germany, the Communist Party of America had decided to support actively the struggle against fascism. Yoneda and other Nikkei Communists felt that they had no choice but to "accept the racist U.S. dictum" of incarceration "over Hitler's ovens and Japan's military rapists of Nanking." Fearing "the menace of worldwide fascism," they vowed "to do everything to insure Allied victory." Yet, because Yoneda was a Communist, the Manzanar Chief of Police Kenneth Horton kept him "under close observation."[11]

Because of his strong pro-American stance in the war, his campaign to send Japanese American soldiers to the front lines, his distinctiveness as a "dangerous red," his marriage to a white woman, and his non-Japanese way of life, Yoneda was unpopular with many of Manzanar's Nikkei. In addition, he was seen as an informer, a "stooge." Indeed, like Tayama and Slocum, Yoneda reported on Nikkei meetings in confidential letters to camp administrators.[12]

Word of what Yoneda had written in his report about the Kibei-Nisei meeting of August 8 spread among the Kibei-Nisei. One evening two weeks after the meeting, fourteen Kibei-Nisei entered his barracks room, demanding that Yoneda retract what he had written in the report. For thirty minutes, their shouts and threats terrified Yoneda and his wife, and especially their three-and-a-half-year-old son, Tommy, who later repeatedly referred to the episode in fear. His mother believed that the trauma of that evening caused Tommy's ensuing nightmares and years of poor health.[13]

Yoneda's encounters with his opponents, including Kurihara, did not deter his eagerness to support the American war effort. When the first Military Intelligence Service recruiting team arrived at Manzanar soon after the above encounter, Yoneda and his fellow Communist Koji Ariyoshi were among the fifty men who volunteered to serve. Only fourteen of the fifty volunteers—Yoneda and Ariyoshi among them—passed the physical, oral, and written examinations and were accepted. On December 2, four days before the revolt, the men left for Minnesota.[14]

On December 6, when a large crowd protesting Ueno's arrest had formed near the administration building, Kurihara spoke atop a truck to the crowd in Japanese. As he did so, Elaine Yoneda arrived at the building with her son Tommy to see if his permit to return to the exclusion zone—that is, California—had been approved and had arrived. There she overhead Kurihara and then another speaker, Ben Kishi, saying "Yoneda" a number of times. Two men translated Kurihara's remarks, telling her that he said that Yoneda had left Manzanar, but that his son was there so they could still "get him." Stunned, Elaine Yoneda ran with Tommy to the police station for protection. Receiving no help there, they returned to their barrack room, where she barricaded the door with a table. At 4:30 AM the next morning, with increased anxiety, she dressed Tommy up as a girl and ran with him to the administration building, where she found sixty men, women, and children who had gone or been brought there for protection. Three days later, she, Tommy, and the rest of the group were convoyed to Death Valley, where they stayed at an abandoned Civilian Conservation Corps (CCC) camp. When Tommy's travel permit arrived on December 19, he and his mother departed for Los Angeles. As noted earlier, the other Nikkei at the CCC camp eventually resettled in Chicago and other cities.[15]

In view of these experiences, it is not surprising that in the campaign for redress in the 1970s and 1980s, when a younger generation of Nikkei wrote glowingly in newspaper articles of Kurihara's heroism, the Yonedas dissented strongly. In a letter to the editor, Karl wrote that Kurihara's "destructive activities . . . [had] resulted in the bloody 'Manzanar riot.'" Elaine was even more outspoken. "Some call Kurihara a 'patriot' and/or 'hero,'" she wrote in 1983. "To me, he . . . was an embittered manipulator who helped turn some camp residents' frustrations into a pro-Japan cause, with a small number foolishly . . . shouting for "Victory for Japan," which to me meant and still means plaudits for the rapists of Nanking and Hitler's butchers."[16]

Whatever one's ultimate view of Kurihara, the activities in which he played so prominent a part at Manzanar showed clearly that many did not accept incarceration fatalistically, as those protesting crowds numbering in the thousands showed. Some commentators, however, have too loosely used the Japanese phrase *shikata ga nai* to characterize the Nikkei response during the war, especially among Issei and Kibei-Nisei but also many Nisei. They cite statements such as those of the Nisei Alice Imamoto Takemoto, who, when asked how she felt to be incarcerated when she had done nothing wrong, responded, "An interesting thing about Japanese people is that they're fatalists. There's an expression—*shikata ga nai.* It means . . . [i]t can't be helped. . . . When you have that kind of philosophy you just take it," you don't blame anyone. In the same way, Kurihara himself once noted that the Nikkei allowed themselves to be "corralled like a bunch of sheep . . . [and] made wards of the government overnight."[17]

Yet this mentalité of *shikata ga nai* can clearly be superseded by feelings of betrayal. Such became the prevailing attitude at Manzanar, where events coalesced to create just such feelings. Aside from Kurihara and a few other Nisei, the leaders of the revolt at Manzanar were Issei and Kibei-Nisei, which indicates that *shikata ga nai* did not apply in this case, even among those closest to the Japanese cultural perspective. As Kurihara himself noted, contradicting his earlier statement, "[A]s a matter of fact, we Japanese are not what [Assistant Project Director Ned Campbell] figured we were. . . . He tried to enforce his domineering will over the Japanese and failed."[18]

As *shikata ga nai* did not represent the mindset of the Manzanar dissidents, neither did the label of disloyalty. Yuji Ichioka, in his study of the controversial Nisei Buddy Uno, who worked for the Japanese government during the war, reminded his readers of the importance of understanding the conditions and circumstances in which people find themselves. "What is the meaning of loyalty in a racist society?" Ichioka asked. "[H]ow can the category of a disloyal Nisei have any meaning in a society that overwhelmingly rejected the Nisei on racial grounds?" His point was well taken, as was that of Naoko Shibusawa, who warned against the "false binary" of categorizing the Nikkei as either loyal to Japan or to the United States.[19]

In *American Inquisition*, Eric Muller reveals that none of the three federal agencies that "made [official] loyalty findings"—the Western Defense Command, the War Relocation Authority, and the Provost Marshal General's Office—had a "coherent definition of loyalty *even for itself*." Moreover, their notions of Nikkei disloyalty were not based on the behaviors of the Nikkei. "Each agency's conclusions . . . ultimately reflected much more about the agency and the context in which it operated than about the American citizens whose cases it was judging." As Muller also noted, there are fundamental problems with labeling people as loyal or disloyal: "People can be utterly disgusted with their nation and yet have not the faintest inclination to betray it. . . . People can feel strong affection for another nation . . . without risking subversive conduct. And people can be quite attached to their own country and nonetheless betray it for other reasons, such as love or money. The two attributes—feeling and action—simply do not belong on a single continuum."[20]

In the case of the Manzanar Nikkei dissidents, it would be likewise a mistake to label them as disloyal and pro-Japan, as press reports did at the time. A block manager who was interviewed by Morris Opler, the Community Analyst who arrived in Manzanar in the wake of the revolt, assessed its causes, saying that it stemmed from a multitude of decisions, actions, events, and interpersonal clashes that arose soon after the Nikkei arrived at Manzanar and continued for months: false promises; poor pay; high turnover of administrative personnel, in particular the ever-changing project directors, five in nine months;

Campbell's domineering ways; and the discriminatory policies toward Issei and Kibei-Nisei. After examining a plethora of documents and interviewing many other participants, Opler himself concluded that the low morale among inmates was intensified by general animosity toward the JACLers whom many Nikkei saw as traitors and spies; rivalry between the Issei and JACLers for leadership positions in inmate governance; administrative actions that undercut the leadership of the Issei; and the absence of more accommodating Nisei and Kibei-Nisei who had voluntarily left Manzanar temporarily to harvest crops for farms some distance away, or permanently to attend college or U.S. military language schools.[21]

WRA administrators, too, recognized the fallacy of oversimplification. Reflecting on the anomalous position of the Issei, Ralph Merritt and his assistant Robert Brown wrote, "The fact that they were denied citizenship hangs as a heavy load over their understanding of America. . . . [They say], 'We have never been wanted—the evacuation proves it, so let's *be* Japanese.'" Similarly, Manzanar attorney Robert Throckmorton concluded, "[T]he primary reasons for the demonstration did not involve the question of loyalty or disloyalty. . . . The primary causes appear to be (1) those which led the people to believe that Uyeno [*sic*] had been unjustly arrested; and, (2) those which led them to hate Fred Tayama, other JACL leaders and certain members of the Administrative staff." Likewise, Togo Tanaka noted that prewar animosities toward JACLers that were intensified in Manzanar, as well as "clashes of personality," led to the revolt. By early December 1942, he wrote, "Manzanar was like a powder barrel. . . . One single incident—the attack on Fred Tayama and the subsequent arrest of Harry Ueno—ignited the whole barrel." These explanations, while valid, fail to identify the incarceration itself as the root cause of Nikkei anger and bitterness. Yet they do recognize the fallacy of accusing the dissidents of disloyal conduct. Having been rejected by the U.S. government and American society because of their ancestry, Kurihara asked, "Could America blame us for the change of our mind . . . [after being] ostracized and corralled like a bunch of prisoners . . . ?" While their resistance did not free protesters from their physical confinement, it did allow them to assert themselves in a way that expressed their individual sense of dignity and their collective sense of pride in their ethnoracial identity.[22]

As noted above, the key players in the revolt were whisked away from Manzanar. But in the ensuing months the resistance continued. In February 1943, the WRA and the Army developed what became a controversial registration program. Questionnaires were administered in all the camps in order to recruit volunteers for a Japanese American combat unit as well as to determine who could leave the camps. Confusion arose over the wording of two "loyalty" questions: Question 27 asked if the inmates would be willing to serve in the U.S. armed forces, and Question 28 asked for "unqualified allegiance to the United States." At Manzanar, only ninety-four male citizens—4 percent of those eligible—eventually entered military service, and—more than any other camp—52 percent of male Nisei and 45 percent of female Nisei either answered "no" to the question on "unqualified allegiance" or refused to answer it.[23]

By mid-1943, vocal Issei dissidents from all the WRA camps had been removed to internment camps for aliens, administered by the Immigration and Naturalization Service. At the same time, vocal Nisei and Kibei-Nisei dissidents had been taken to the citizen isolation camp at Moab. Later in the year, those who had responded negatively or not at all to the loyalty questions on the questionnaire were taken to Tule Lake, the designated "Segregation Center" for dissidents. As a result of these removals, visible forms of dissension among those who remained became much less apparent.[24]

Kurihara: Hero or Villain?

Older than most Nisei, Kurihara was a self-proclaimed leader at Manzanar. In his remembrances of the camp, he recalled settling several heated disputes that would have led to violence—one involving about 50 carpenters, another involving 170 members of the Construction Department, and a third involving 200 gang members. There is no independent confirmation of these episodes, but there is no reason to doubt Kurihara's account. His supervisor, Construction Director Henry Brown, attested to Kurihara's stature as a leader. Tanaka, too, noted that Kurihara "commanded a respectable numerical following" among Nisei truck drivers, food handlers, warehouse workers, and other young men.[25]

Kurihara also aroused passions. He called on his fellow Nikkei to "get" "traitors" such as Fred Tayama, Tokie Slocum, Togo Tanaka, Joe Grant Masaoka, Karl Yoneda, and Koji Ariyoshi. According to Tanaka, Kurihara's threats were not idle chatter, nor were they mere rhetoric. Tanaka believed that Kurihara was "deadly serious" when he made them. In his speeches, Kurihara repeatedly referred to a deathlist and often named people whose names were on it.[26]

Such threats against people's lives could only have the effect of encouraging others to violence. The beating of Tayama, which sparked the Manzanar revolt, was not the only act of violence at Manzanar. There were other beatings that were not publicized. Tayama's became the most well known because of the widespread animosity he engendered.[27]

A group whose actions demonstrated the sharp conflict between supporters and detractors of the administration was the Black Dragons, who took their name from the Black Dragon Society in Japan, an ultranationalist organization that encouraged Japan's expansionist foreign and militarist policies after 1910 until the 1930s.[28]

At times the Manzanar Black Dragons, also called the Blood Brothers, could be violent. In June, months before the December 6 revolt, Yoneda and Slocum were sitting on the steps of a barrack when a truck displaying two flags—one of a white skull and crossbones and another with the words "Manzanar Black Dragon Association"—headed straight toward the men. The men jumped aside just before the truck ran over and crushed the steps. Subsequently, when a camouflage net project began, the Black Dragons posted flyers in latrines threatening those who worked there. In November, as plans were being made for residents to vote on a proposed charter, inmates serving on the Charter Commission received letters warning them to end their cooperation with the farce of self-government. Besides writing intimidating letters, Black Dragons also posted warning notes on walls and doors. All of this was done anonymously. Because the Black Dragons advocated victory for Japan in the war, Yoneda and others believed that Kurihara and Ben Kishi were leaders of this group. Both men denied the accusations, pointing out that they expressed themselves openly and thus had no need to "run around in the dark putting up bulletins or sending anonymous threat letters."[29]

Yoneda and other Nikkei refused to believe these denials and asked camp administrators to remove from Manzanar those they believed were Black Dragons. Assistant Project Director Ned Campbell responded to their request by saying, "You are all Japanese and will have to live together."[30]

While camp administrators refused to intervene in such intra-Nikkei conflicts, they took seriously Kurihara's declaration of being 100 percent Japanese. Both Project Director Roy Nash and his successor Ralph Merritt made unsuccessful attempts to have Kurihara prosecuted for sedition. As discussed earlier, after the Kibei-Nisei meeting, Nash initiated an inquiry into Kurihara's role there, to which the Justice Department concluded that Kurihara had not violated the sedition law. After the Manzanar revolt, Merritt had a file prepared on Kurihara, recommending that Kurihara's case be "referred to the Department of Justice for federal prosecution for the crime of sedition." To his disappointment, however, a board of review concluded that the evidence did not justify referral for prosecution.[31]

Despite Kurihara's incendiary speeches, some WRA administrators came to respect him. Raymond Best, a project director at Moab and then Tule Lake, wrote of Kurihara, "In my experience, [he] always was responsive to honest and fair treatment. He never requested or expected any special favor or consideration from me in spite of our intimate acquaintance." Francis

Frederick, who was in charge of internal security at Moab and then Leupp, wrote similarly, "One outstanding characteristic of Kurihara is his honesty. He can be depended upon to hold up his end of any agreement if the other side holds up their end."[32]

Other administrators admired his fearlessness in speaking his mind, and "were, in general, sympathetic with him." In August 1942, after Kurihara had made speeches that some thought subversive, an administrator reflected, "I find Joe Kurihara very bitter about the entire situation, but he is bitter and sore in quite an American way." Ned Campbell, with whom Kurihara had argued repeatedly and heatedly at Manzanar, noted that Kurihara was "one of the few Japanese in the Center who would openly tell Administration leaders what he really felt." On another occasion, Campbell remarked, "If I were Joe Kurihara, I'd be mad, too. He was a veteran of the World War, was discharged . . . honorably, had done his part as a citizen. It's just as if I had saved one of you guys from getting stabbed or killed in a street brawl, and you rewarded me by kicking me into the gutter. Hell, sure I'd be bitter."[33]

Had Kurihara heard Campbell's comments, he would have agreed that he had what he believed to be an American behavioral style. Explaining his reaction to incarceration and his boldness in speaking against it, he said, "When I was a kid in school in Hawaii, I was told I was an American and I must stand up and fight like an American." He also believed that Nisei who grew up in Hawai'i had a "superiority complex" over those who grew up on the West Coast. This was because in Hawai'i "the Japanese predominate." In contrast, on the mainland, they are "the smallest of the minority parties" and thus "go about with the feeling that [they] are nobody." He rejected such sentiments. Instead, because of his self-confidence, he was "not going to let [whites] slap [him] a second time." "I'll defend my self," he declared, "and fight like a man."[34] Kurihara was correct in sensing that the Hawai'i Nikkei experienced less overt racism than Nikkei on the mainland and particularly on the West Coast, and were therefore less tolerant of discrimination based on their ethnicity. Nevertheless, Kurihara's stance was the result of his own temperament and personality, which led him to be direct and sometimes blunt and confrontational.

With these matters in mind, a question arises: What was Kurihara's role, if any, in the December 5 beating of Tayama? In an interview with Karl Yoneda in 1972, Satoru Kamikawa said that he had attended the Kibei-Nisei meeting on December 5, the night of Tayama's beating. Kamikawa recalled that about forty to fifty people were at the meeting, and that "Ben Kishi, Joe Kurihara, and others were talking about going to Fred Tayama's place to give him 'a lesson' because of his participation at the Salt Lake City meeting that led the JACL to request the U.S. government to draft all Kibei-Nisei and Nisei." Yoneda kept the interview transcript in his files, which were later deposited at the University of California Los Angeles library. One can surmise from the transcript how Kurihara was present at the discussion yet not be the instigator of the beating. Moreover, Yoneda is not the best source for this allegation since he had been at odds with Kurihara at Manzanar, and his feelings of antagonism toward Kurihara continued long after their encounters there.[35]

Yet a letter from project director Merritt to M. M. Tozier, chief of WRA Reports Division, has a similar thrust. Merritt had visited Kurihara in Tule Lake in November 1945, after the war ended, at which time Kurihara agreed to respond to questions about the Manzanar revolt. According to Merritt, in their hour-and-a-half conversation Kurihara confessed that he had organized the group that beat up Tayama. Kurihara showed Merritt copies of reports that Tayama had sent to the FBI concerning Kurihara and other dissidents at Manzanar. According to Kurihara, Tokie Slocum—who worked as a police officer on the night shift in order to copy records from administrative offices—gave Kurihara copies of Tayama's reports. What led Kurihara to want "to kill Tayama," he told Merritt, was Tayama's report on Kurihara's speech at the Kibei-Nisei meeting.[36]

It was not that Tayama had lied; in fact, Tayama's report was remarkably similar to what Kurihara himself later recalled about his speech. What infuriated Kurihara was Tayama's enthusiastic support for the interests of the FBI and camp administrators rather than those of the Nikkei.

In his letter Merritt concluded with an uncomplimentary appraisal of Kurihara, characterizing him as lacking intelligence and generally inarticulate. According to Merritt, Kurihara had not been taken seriously by other Nisei. What made him a leader among the dissidents, Merritt opined, was his fearlessness and verbosity at meetings. Merritt, in other words, was completely disparaging of Kurihara.

But would Merritt lie in a letter to a WRA official on so important a point? Much of the substance of Merritt's letter is consistent with information in other documents, including statements Kurihara himself made. For example, Merritt wrote that Tayama had been seen numerous times with FBI Agent McCormick; this was similar to what Kurihara had told Chief of Internal Security Francis Frederick at the Leupp Isolation Center. Also consistent with Merritt's letter to Tozier, Kurihara further stated to Frederick that Slocum had made copies of Tayama's reports to the FBI and had given the evidence to Kurihara. According to Frederick, Kurihara then continued:

> With what intention he . . . gave me this evidence I do not know, but I am sure he must have known that it would produce the result he desired. Tayama and Slocum

> had a heated argument and called each other terrible names. Both were acting in the capacity of stool pigeons. Slocum in order to distract the people and place all blame on Tayama must have tried to use me as a stool to broadcast the news. . . . [Tayama's] reports against those who spoke at the Kibei-Nisei meeting were purposely distorted to create bad impressions.[37]

As a result of Tayama's reports, Project Director Nash had ordered Kurihara's arrest, but Chief of Police Kenneth Horton refused to make the arrest, saying that Kurihara had the right to say what he had said.[38]

Merritt's statement that Kurihara had organized Tayama's beating may have been Merritt's conclusion instead of Kurihara's admission. Or, having decided to leave the United States, Kurihara may have deliberately chosen to spare others by taking the blame. To be sure, Kurihara had placed Tayama on his deathlist. Furthermore, Kurihara may have blamed himself for indirectly causing the fatal shooting of the two bystanders. But would he have organized a group to beat up Tayama? As Kurihara noted to Frederick, "It is my nature to be alone, work alone and fight alone." He said this of his personality: "I go from one extreme to the other. I sympathize, cry and give my last penny to save a person in a worthy cause but I can be mean and devilish when I am aroused." Yet, he emphasized, "I do not indulge in gang fights or personal fights. I think it is very debasing and cowardly. But I will fight and champion a cause if it affects the Japanese people as a whole."[39]

Nevertheless, Kurihara's alleged confession to Merritt is supported in part by a memo from FBI Director J. Edgar Hoover to Assistant Attorney General Herbert Wechsler. In his memo, Hoover quotes from a report by FBI Special Agents Edward Kirby and John Quill, who interviewed Kurihara at Moab in April 1943. Kirby and Quill reported that Kurihara "assisted them in the preparation of [a] statement but refused to sign it," stating that an attorney "once told him he should never sign anything in haste and regret it at leisure." Nevertheless, Kurihara apparently spoke without hesitation. Kurihara said that many Nisei wanted to beat up Tayama: "I held the boys off and advised them not to take any action until they obtained concrete evidence which would justify giving him a thrashing." After Tokie Slocum had given him "absolute evidence" that Tayama was a "stool pigeon," Kurihara showed the evidence to a certain man and to gang leaders who wanted to beat up Tayama. "I told them, I can no longer hold you back if you want to thrash him." When asked, Kurihara refused to identify these men. "I am certain . . . who beat him up but I would not reveal their identity because I consider that Tayama as a Stool Pigeon is a coward and too low to deserve to live, and I think that he got exactly what was coming to him." Because Tayama and Harry Ueno were "bitter enemies," continued Kurihara, Tayama accused Ueno as his assailant, and as a result Ueno was arrested. At the end of his interview, after discussing the jailing of Ueno and the subsequent mass meetings of December 6, Kurihara stated, "I was the 'brains' and instigator of the Manzanar incident." Here, however, he was probably speaking of events after the beating and not the beating itself.[40]

The details in Kirby and Quill's report are consistent with what Kurihara said and wrote elsewhere. The only new information in their report are Kurihara's alleged conversations with men who wanted to beat up Tayama. In his own writing about the revolt, Kurihara said nothing to implicate himself or anyone else in the beating. After examining three reports on the beating and none by Kurihara himself, I am left with the conclusion that Kurihara did not actually organize the beating but probably did discuss it with men who were intent on doing so. In this instance, Kurihara was neither hero nor villain, but a person fighting to maintain his dignity and the dignity of other Nikkei caught in the tangled mesh of the incarceration.

Kurihara's parents, Kichizo and Haru Kurihara, circa 1890. Courtesy Grace Fukumoto.

Fifth graders during arithmetic lesson, Kaiulani School. This photo was one among many taken in spring 1900, during the school's first year of operation. Officials were proud of the school's state-of-the-art structure and furniture. Some classrooms had moveable chairs and tables, while others like this one had desk-chairs that were bolted to the floor. Courtesy Hawai'i State Archives.

Kurihara's parents, Kichizo and Haru Kurihara, with two children near their home on Houghtailing Road, c. 1910. Kichizo Kurihara transported passengers in the horse-drawn carriage shown next to them. Courtesy Grace Fukumoto.

Kurihara and first-year high school classmates, St. Ignatius School, San Francisco, May 1915. Courtesy University of San Francisco Archives.

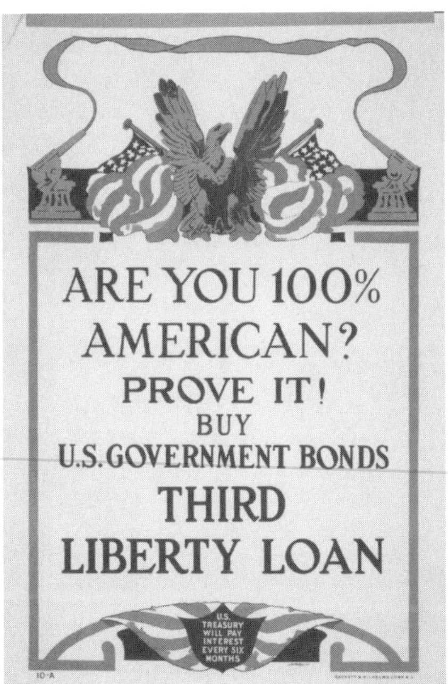

World War I Poster, "Are You 100% American?" This is one of many posters aimed at instilling patriotism during the war. Courtesy Library of Congress, Prints & Photographs Division, WWI Posters, LC-USZC4-8075.

Kurihara in World War I army uniform, with unidentified man, circa 1918.
Courtesy Grace Fukumoto.

Joseph Kurihara, circa 1937. Courtesy William Hohri.

Manzanar from guard tower, showing barracks, roads, and the Sierra Nevada in summer heat, 1943. Ansel Adams, photographer. Courtesy Library of Congress, Prints & Photographs Division, LC-DIG-ppprs-00201.

Dalton Wells Civilian Conservation Corps Camp, Moab, Utah, circa 1935. In 1943, this site became a citizen isolation camp for Kurihara and other dissidents. Note the highway with power poles fronting the camp. Courtesy National Archives, Rocky Mountain Region, Denver.

Men in front of mess hall at the former Leupp Indian Boarding School, December 1943. During World War II, Leupp replaced Moab as a citizen isolation camp for dissidents. Courtesy Harry Ueno.

Men boarding first post-war transport for Nikkei destined for Japan, Seattle, November 1945. Courtesy National Archives.

Kurihara with sister Kikuno Nakahara, who was visiting him in Japan, 1954. Courtesy Grace Fukumoto.

CHAPTER 6

Isolating Citizen Dissidents

Moab Isolation Camp

After their arrest in the wake of the Manzanar revolt, Kurihara and the other members of the Committee of Five were taken with Ueno to the jail in Bishop, and after a few days, to Lone Pine. Eventually the group at Lone Pine grew from six to sixteen after other dissidents from Manzanar were brought there.[1]

As the men awaited their fate, federal officials explored the possibility of prosecuting them. "Unless the evidence [justified] a fairly long prison term," wrote Deputy Director E. R. Fryer and Assistant Solicitor Lewis A. Sigler in a memo to the WRA Director Dillon Myer in late December, "it is recommended that prosecution" of the "leaders in the Manzanar incident" and those who made "threats of death to informers" "would be undesirable. But this recommendation was "conditioned," continued the memo, "upon the immediate availability of an isolation center to which the group can be sent. If for any reason that center should not be available immediately, prosecution in the local courts would be the only feasible method of holding the men until the isolation center can be made ready." The goal was to keep the men away from Manzanar.[2]

On the basis of this recommendation, prosecution was held at bay, since WRA officials were able to secure a temporary isolation camp near the town of Moab, Utah. Meanwhile, in a show of support, the Nikkei at Manzanar sent the men gifts and food. They also formed a negotiating committee of 105 representatives, which in turn appointed a Committee of Four. The latter then attempted to negotiate the return of the men to Manzanar. But their efforts were unsuccessful. On January 9, the men at Lone Pine received a letter from Merritt, stating that they would be taken immediately to the camp near Moab, that Myer had established a three-person hearing committee to review their cases, and that they would be given "a fair and speedy hearing."[3]

Thus on that cold, wintry day, the sixteen men left Lone Pine on a Greyhound bus that took them south to Barstow, California. From there they boarded a train traveling northeast. Guarding them were sixteen soldiers, including a lieutenant and an assistant chief of police. During the trip the soldiers cooked the meals and stood guard in the coaches and in the rest room. On January 10 they reached their destination, a barren, isolated former Civilian Conservation Corps camp that was, according to Kurihara, "the size of a single block of Manzanar." Ueno later recalled, "All around [the barracks], nothing but sagebrush, not even trees." This was to be their home for the next two-and-a-half months.[4]

The isolation camp was fourteen miles from Moab. Located near the Colorado River in the southeastern Utah desert and surrounded by breathtaking red rock formations of Arches and Canyonlands National Parks, Moab is today a frequently visited tourist center. In the 1940s, however, it was a sleepy town of a thousand residents, one elementary and high school, three churches, and a Main Street that boasted a bank, the office of the *Times Independent* newspaper, and various retail stores.[5]

The isolation camp was on Highway 191 at Dalton Wells, a remote site reachable only by gravel road. Because it was to be a temporary WRA camp, no fence or other improvements were made, but the men were kept under constant military guard. Except for brief mentions in the local paper, "the whole operation was kept pretty quiet in Moab," and the rest of the country knew even less about it. Most Americans, in fact, were unaware of its existence.[6]

The Moab camp was designed specifically for Nisei, who, as U.S. citizens, could not be transferred to the enemy alien internment camps operated by the Immigration and Naturalization Service (INS). On the other hand, because of an informal agreement between Myer and Edward J. Ennis and Thomas Cooley of the Alien Enemy Control Unit, noncitizens at Moab could be transferred to the INS internment camps. Thus, after a month at Moab, the Issei from Manzanar were removed to the INS camps, "although"—as Ennis noted to J. Edgar Hoover—"their conduct did not establish subversive activity under the standards heretofore applied." The informal agreement also enabled the WRA to send Issei dissidents directly from other WRA camps to the INS camps.[7]

Within several months after the Manzanar sixteen had entered the Moab camp, other dissidents arrived from the Gila, Manzanar, and Tule Lake camps. No formal charges were made against any of these men either. Rather, they were sent at the discretion of the WRA camp project directors. The lack of due process resulted in innocent men being sent to Moab—one for calling a Caucasian nurse an old maid, for example, and others because of mistaken identities. Still others were men who made life difficult for WRA administrators: those "accused of having instigated work stoppages; of having made bravado statements of disloyalty; of throwing jars of filth in apartments of informers;

of making pin-ups of Japanese soldiers"; and of causing "agitation and unrest." At its peak, the Moab camp housed forty-nine men.[8]

At Moab, Kurihara took an immediate liking to Project Director Raymond R. Best. According to Kurihara, unlike Merritt and Campbell, Best treated the men with respect, understanding, and fairness. He was, in Kurihara's words, "very nice and gentle to us," and "responsible for my conduct. Returning good for good."[9]

A week after arriving at Moab, Kurihara wrote: "To the People of Manzanar, Mr. Best . . . is the *best* of all the Project Directors I have met. . . . So, like a gentleman, I will co-operate with a gentleman." Indeed, Best reported to Myer that Kurihara was "a real leader" who "prevented many serious outbreaks caused by this detention." Best continued, "I feel that he will respond to proper treatment and still can be a useful citizen." According to Best, "four men [were] excellent residents" at Moab: Yoshiro Kaku, Bill Kuga, Joseph Kurihara, and Maesaki Tanaka. Kurihara reciprocated, often declaring his willingness to cooperate with WRA administrators at Moab—a behavior he continued when he was later transferred to the Leupp isolation camp and then to the Tule Lake concentration camp. He declared that his changed behavior was due to the kindness and fair treatment he and others received from Best and other camp officials. "I am very, very happy," he wrote Best, "that you were the one I have met when bitterness was boiling at its height."[10]

This posture by Kurihara followed the Manzanar upheaval, an experience that shook him profoundly. Speaking of the deaths of James Ito and Jim Kanagawa, the two young men killed on that fateful night, Kurihara later wrote, "I [had] never felt so bad in my life before." It was soon after those senseless deaths that Kurihara made a firm decision to expatriate to Japan.[11]

At Moab he kept largely to himself, reading the Bible for solace and studying Japanese in anticipation of his life in Japan. According to Mamoru Sasaki, a friend and fellow inmate at Tule Lake, where Kurihara and other Nisei were taken in December 1943, Kurihara told him that since leaving Manzanar, he had refused to become involved with any protest because he wanted no responsibility for anyone being shot or otherwise hurt as a result of a demonstration. Despite this stance, Kurihara continued to believe passionately that the incarceration and treatment of the Nikkei were grave injustices. To vent his feelings he wrote essays denouncing the U.S. government for its actions against innocent people. At Moab, for example, he penned "Murder in Camp Manzanar," in which he stated, "The deliberate firing on the backs of the fleeing crowd had blacked [*sic*] the pages of American History. Could America continue to preach Democracy . . . to the world? No!"[12]

As the foregoing demonstrates, Kurihara's decision to cooperate with camp administrators did not end his anger at his status as prisoner. On the contrary, at Moab he and his fellow inmates bristled at being treated as dangerous criminals. Soldiers with loaded and bayoneted guns followed them everywhere, hovering over them day and night, and even into the early morning hours when the temperature dropped to well below freezing. Throughout the humiliation of this ordeal, Kurihara's religion helped him maintain his composure. In another letter from Moab to "the people of Manzanar," who continued regularly to send the men gifts to let them know that they were not forgotten, Kurihara wrote, "God of Justice is giving us the strength to bear this predicament . . . and his divine light [will] guide us in the hour of our need."[13]

On February 12, 1943, a month after being transferred to Moab, each of the inmates received a letter from WRA director Myer. "I have appointed a board of review in my office," wrote Myer, who "has recommended that you not be permitted to return [to Manzanar], and I have approved that recommendation." This was another disappointment and disillusionment, the decision having been made, as Kurihara noted, without the promised hearing. "There was no bona-fide charge against me," protested Kurihara, only the "flimsy charge" "that I [spoke] at the Kibei meeting. . . . If such was the charge, *WHY* then the others who spoke that night of the meeting, numbering around twelve, were not taken into custody and later segregated and isolated to this lonely canyon?"[14]

The men had hoped to return to Manzanar. They had pinned their hopes on the success of the Committee of Four, who had tried to negotiate the return of the men. Project Director Merritt, however, in effect stonewalled the committee, whose members concluded not only that their efforts were futile, but that it would be in the best interests of the Nikkei in Manzanar to cooperate with Merritt. Frustrated with what they believed was a betrayal by the committee, the men at Moab wrote its members a bitter letter, accusing them of deception and urging them to act on their behalf. Nothing came of this plea.[15]

A month-and-a-half later, ten of the Moab inmates wrote Best, asking him to inform them of the charges for which they were "segregated and isolated." Best reported these letters to Myer, and after some discussion among themselves, WRA officials made no response. The die was cast. The men would not return to Manzanar.[16]

Meanwhile, trouble had been brewing at the isolation camp. Earlier, while they were at the Lone Pine jail, Ueno had accused Ben Kishi and Tamotsu Kono, two fellow jail mates, of being traitors because they had previously done furlough work topping beets in Idaho. "It was hard for us to understand why Uyeno [*sic*] had to say that to us," wrote Kono to a block leader in Manzanar, "because after all we were in jail for his sake." At Lone Pine Ueno also called the Committee of Four—who were then trying to negotiate the release of the jailed men—"dogs."[17]

The trouble at Moab began the day after the sixteen arrived, when they received "work order slips" directing them to clean the mess hall, carry coal, and perform other chores. Ueno, Koichi Tsuji, Frank Ego, and Bob Matsuda refused to work and told the others to do likewise. But Kurihara and the others decided to cooperate with camp administrators. The four men responded by threatening violence, overturning some beds, drenching other beds with water, throwing others' personal belongings into the stove, and threatening to burn the barracks. These actions continued for a month. "There were many sleepless nights," wrote Kono, "but we did not want to report . . . the distressing situation, fearing that someone might get hurt." Kono continued, "On the day we received the letter from Washington [saying that we could not return to Manzanar], Tsuji and Uyeno [*sic*] said to us that they would 'kill anybody who goes to work' and told Matsuda to 'shut both doors and don't let them go out.' Matsuda shut the door and attacked Yamaguchi without reason. We stopped it. Then Tsuji and Uyeno said: 'You return your work slips; we'll kill you if you don't.'" The four men then crushed a bucket and "threw an ink bottle" against a window, smashing the glass. "They also shouted that they would burn up the place that night." When the project director learned of this situation, he isolated the four men in another building, Barracks 2, where they were watched by soldiers with bayonets "at meal time, in the shower room and at the lavatory."[18]

Associate Chief of Internal Security Francis Frederick said of this situation that some of the men were "bitter and uncooperative in the early days of this center, taking the attitude that if [they were] prisoners, [they would] act like prisoners," and refusing to work "until they had been given a fair trial. . . . Kurihara helped break the ice by signing up for work and setting the example for others." Frank Ego, who later recalled his refusal to cooperate with the WRA administrators at Moab, said of Kurihara, "He never made any trouble at Moab and Leupp. He was very quiet. He did not agitate people."[19]

At Manzanar, the 105-member negotiating committee, having seen Kono's letter as well as the letter from Moab accusing the Committee of Four of deception, called a special meeting to discuss the situation. Because the letter from Moab was unsigned, the negotiating committee was unsure whether it expressed the sentiments of all of the sixteen men. Tom Ozamoto of the Committee of Four stated that he and the other three on the committee were not only wrongly accused by the men at Moab, but they were also caught between those at Manzanar who demanded concessions from administrators, and the project director's refusal to meet those demands. Ozamoto and his fellow committee members thus felt themselves "under constant threat and intimidation." Moreover, their parents were seriously concerned for their safety, and Ozamoto's wife was "confined to the hospital due to mental worries." To ask them to serve further as negotiators, Ozamoto declared, "was to sentence them to slow death." After further discussion, the attendees voted unanimously to accept the resignation of the Committee of Four, and furthermore, to disband the 105-member committee.[20]

Meanwhile, at Moab, the inmates were still, so to speak, at each other's throats. The continued infighting led some of them to inform Best that Ueno had been "the leader of the gang that beat up on Tayama," and that Koichi Tsuji had been one of the assailants. They told Best that, had they known "what sort of a person Uyeno [*sic*] really was, [they] never would have had a riot at Manzanar." The men offered no proof for these accusations, which they may have made falsely in order to get Ueno and Tsuji in trouble with Best. In an interview forty-four years later, Ueno denied any involvement in the beating of Tayama.[21]

For three months at Moab, Ueno, Tsuji, and Ego continued to threaten and intimidate the other men. Meanwhile Matsuda had discontinued his association with the group, and Frederick and his staff were receiving complaints from inmates that they lived "in constant fear of physical violence and possibly death" as a result of "threats [being] made to them." Although the complainants refused to name those who threatened them, saying they feared retaliation, Frederick learned that Ueno, Tsuji, Ego, and three other men living in Barracks 2 were behind the threats. When a new group of inmates arrived from Tule Lake, the men of Barracks 2 convinced a number of them to join the campaign of harassing and threatening the "stool pigeons" for cooperating with the administration.[22]

On the night of April 13, seven men from Barracks 2 went to Barracks 7, where Kurihara and others who had been cooperating with the administration lived. The men from Barracks 2 tried to initiate a fight, but those in Barracks 7 prevented it by locking their doors. The next morning, Frederick, acting project director in Best's absence, assembled the barracks representatives and distributed to them a written general order that forbade a "resident of one barrack to visit any other barrack unless permission was first obtained and that the resident desiring to visit [had to] be accompanied by a Caucasian escort and all intercourse during this visit [had to] be in the English language." Anyone violating the order "could expect the maximum penalty of three months imprisonment and loss of all pay privileges." Because Barracks 2 did not send a representative to the meeting—the only one who refused to do so—a copy of the order was delivered to its residents.

At 1:15 PM that day, twenty-one men carrying bags packed with their belongings "stormed into the administration building" and stated that they would not comply with Frederick's order and were ready to go to jail for three months. Frederick responded that since they had broken Moab rules by barging into the Administration Office without first requesting a meeting via the Internal

Security Office, he would satisfy their request by conducting trials for all of them. At the trials that began two hours later, he found the men guilty of violating Administrative Instruction #85, which forbade unlawful assembly. The first six men to be tried—Ueno, Tsuji, Ego, Tsutomu Higashi, Hisato Kitadani, and Yoshio Saika—had all announced their intention to renounce their U.S. citizenship. A seventh man, Kentaro Takatsui, a recent arrival from Tule Lake, had been "constantly agitating" during his ten days at Moab. All seven men were convicted and sentenced to three months' imprisonment. They were sent the next day to the Grand County Jail in the town of Moab. Because of lack of additional space at the county jail, an eighth man, Teruyoshi Harada, also from Tule Lake, was jailed in a separate barracks within the Moab camp.

The remaining thirteen men said that as recent arrivals, they had not understood the situation at Moab, and that the six men from Manzanar who had just been convicted had misled them about Moab's rules and procedures. As a result of their statements, ten were put on probation and three were acquitted.

Once Ueno and his cohort were removed from the Moab isolation camp, tension dissipated and the remaining men began to speak more freely with the administrative staff. Frederick learned that the original seven convicted men, led by Ueno, Tsuji, Ego, and Higashi, had talked of beating or killing men they considered traitors. The plan was to do this soon after their transfer to the Leupp isolation camp, a larger facility that was being prepared to house the Moab inmates and other dissidents yet to be sent from various concentration camps. The idea was that the confusion of moving to a new location would make it more difficult for officials to prove who had committed the crimes. Among the men they intended to attack were Kurihara, Kishi, and Kono, who had taken leading roles in supporting Ueno during the crisis at Manzanar, but who, upon their removal to Moab, had decided to end their hostility toward WRA administrators. In fact, according to Frederick, Ueno and Kurihara had once come "virtually to blows" at Moab. (The two men later reconciled their differences and re-established their friendship at Leupp.)[23] Also on Ueno's list was Matsuda, who had earlier aligned himself with Ueno and Tsuji when the Manzanar sixteen had first arrived at Moab, but who later distanced himself from them. Other targeted inmates included Shigetoshi Tateichi, Yoshiro Kaku, Kameichi Fukumoto, and George Yamashiro. Even Moab's Project Director Best was on the list to be attacked physically, although the preferred action was to force him out of Moab by collecting signatures for a petition requesting his removal and causing so much trouble for him at the camp that administrators in Washington, D.C., would conclude that he lacked the ability to control the inmates. For one reason or another, the plan was never set in motion.

Leupp Isolation Camp

On April 27 the inmates at Moab were transferred to a larger isolation camp for "troublemakers." Located in north central Arizona, eighteen miles from the town of Winslow, the camp occupied the physical remains of what had been a boarding school for American Indian children. The school had been named for Theodore Roosevelt's commissioner of Indian affairs, Francis E. Leupp, a name inherited by the isolation camp.[24]

Most of the men traveled to Leupp by bus. But Frederick put Ueno and four others who had been imprisoned in the Moab jail in "a four-by-six-foot box on a pickup truck with a hole in the back end of the box, which was only about two by two feet." Traveling in the box from Moab, Utah, to Leupp, Arizona, the five men endured thirteen hours of suffocating dust, heat, and humidity over rough, unpaved roads. Ueno wrote in his diary, "The dust was so thick that I needed to press a handkerchief against my face. . . . [T]he rough movement made you feel like your insides were being forced up." "In 36 years of my life," he later recalled, "this was the first time I had ever experienced such a painful, agonizing, and helpless feeling."[25]

The ordeal increased Ueno's ire over his incarceration and his resentment at the treatment he was receiving from the WRA. Upon arriving at Leupp, Ueno wrote a letter to his wife, Yasako. Telling her that he believed that Japan would win the war, he declared that he intended to renounce his U.S. citizenship. "Our victory is approaching day by day. . . . If you have a chance to [renounce your citizenship] you do it," he told her. "I would like to renounce the children's citizenship too." At this time, in spring 1943, other Kibei-Nisei also believed that Japan would win the war. As Frank Ego noted, "[At Moab and Leupp] we listened to the short-wave radio and heard Japan propaganda. They did not say they were losing the war. And we Kibei were educated [to be proud of Japan]. So we believed that Japan would never lose a war."[26]

Neither Ueno nor other men with wives and children would be able to see their families in the months ahead. In preparing the isolation camp at Leupp, the WRA chief Myer noted that it would be unable to accommodate families, which was further punishment for "troublesome" inmates. This unfortunate decision was made poignant by individual examples, like that of twenty-two-year-old Ben Kishi, who had never seen his newly born baby, who remained with its mother at Manzanar.[27]

Nevertheless, the camp at Leupp was a physical improvement over the one at Moab. Unlike Moab's long, drab wooden barracks that included no partitions separating forty beds, Leupp "was like a high-class, two-story concrete apartment building." Corridors separated rooms, each sleeping about ten men on bunk beds.[28] But Leupp was surrounded by a "man-proof fence" with a guard tower in each corner of the compound manned by a soldier with a machine gun. In a further attempt at intimidation, the soldiers drilled regularly just outside the compound. The Nikkei, whose population at Leupp ranged from about forty-five to sixty, occupied two buildings: a mess hall and living quarters. There was no fraternization between them and the 150 soldiers stationed there. The soldiers lived in another building and ate in a separate mess hall. Leupp Project Director Paul Robertson and his wife and two children lived in the former school superintendent's three-bedroom home and ate regularly with the military officers.[29]

Robertson had replaced Best in late July, when the WRA transferred Best to the Tule Lake camp to became its project director. Within the limits of the circumstances at Leupp, Robertson was fair and humane, an official who worked for the best interests of the inmates. While "Best thought everyone had to obey him automatically," the Kibei-Nisei Frank Ego recollected, "Robertson listened to you. He had an entirely different personality." At Leupp, Ego and Ueno had the task of "throwing office papers at the dump. At first the MPs would follow and watch us," Ueno remembered, "but later they didn't. So we would go through the papers." Reading the discarded sheets made the men realize that Robertson was trying to help them. "He wanted the families united," said Ego. "He wrote a letter to [WRA head] Dillon Meyer asking for a hearing for us." Because Robertson was not afraid to remind Myer and other WRA officials in D.C. of the need to proceed with due process and justice in mind in dealing with the inmates, he could be a thorn in their side.[30]

The attitudes these comments reflect were widespread among the other inmates. At the farewell party that marked the closing of the Leupp Isolation Center in late 1943, Kurihara spoke on behalf of the Nikkei: "I wish to thank you Mr. Robertson for the kindness which you have lavished on us. Ever since that day when we first met at Leupp, we learned to like you and that liking . . . grew into a genuine friendship." Frederick, who had transferred with the others from Moab to Leupp and who kept his position as Associate Chief of Internal Security, said similarly of Robertson, "Finest guy I have met yet in WRA. Honest, sincere, law trained, capable, and *likes* Japanese."[31]

Frederick had begun his stint with the WRA in 1942, when he became assistant chief of internal security at the Gila River camp. Disagreements in administrative approaches as well as internal politics at Gila led to conflicts between Frederick and his immediate supervisor, W. E. Williamson, as well as Project Director Leroy Bennett. When Moab needed someone to handle internal security, Frederick was transferred there.[32]

While at Gila River, Frederick had developed a friendship with Robert Spencer, then a research assistant in Dorothy Thomas's Japanese American

Evacuation and Resettlement Study (JERS), and after Frederick left Gila River, the two men corresponded. In his letters, Frederick indicated that he wanted to be known by the Nisei as a "tough guy," yet his letters reveal perceptive understandings and insights of the Nikkei. Based on interviews with the men and observations of them, Frederick wrote some seventy case histories with recommendations for the WRA. He sent the case histories to Spencer, who showed them to Thomas, who in turn had them copied by typists and returned to Frederick. In a letter to Spencer, Frederick reported that Robertson told him that the case histories were "hot" and took them to the WRA office in D.C. Frederick believed that there would be repercussions for his nemesis Bennett of Gila River and other project directors who failed to follow WRA procedures in sending men to Leupp without justification. Frederick, who was known to promote himself, later credited his case studies with prompting the WRA office in D.C. to "release nearly all of [the] inmates" from Leupp to other camps. While Frederick likely exaggerated his influence, Robertson did support the thrust of his meliorating profiles of the Nikkei. In his letters to Myer, Robertson recommended strongly that many of the Nikkei should be returned to the "relocation centers" instead of being isolated at Leupp.[33]

Aware that men were being sent to Leupp without justification, Myer issued a memo on June 5, 1943, announcing a change in procedures. Previously project directors were told that in order to maintain order in the WRA camps, they could send men to Moab and then Leupp without holding hearings. "As we . . . see more clearly the implications of isolation, however, it is becoming increasingly evident that transfer to the isolation center is a punishment." Therefore, Myer mandated, every inmate accused of being an "incorrigible trouble-maker" would need a hearing before he is transferred to the Leupp camp. The hearing need not be held in a public location, but it should be fair, with the accused present, informed of the charges against him and presented with such evidence as can be disclosed "without revealing the identity of informants or other confidential sources of information." A report of the hearing must then be sent to Washington, where the board of review and the director would make the final decision concerning a transfer.[34]

Despite this new directive, project directors continued to send men to Leupp without due process. Two months after the June memo, Robertson wrote to Myer that only two cases warranted removal to Leupp. "In reviewing the dockets of [the men]," Robertson wrote, "I was very much amazed at the lack of evidence which I had believed necessary to warrant a transfer to this center." For example, two men from the Jerome camp had nothing in their dockets explaining why they were sent to Leupp. The only thing that Robertson could say about them was that they were "thoroughly Japanese." A second example was twenty-year-old George Hamanishi, "timid and well behaved," who had been involved in a carpenters' strike at the Granada camp. Because he spoke English better than the other sixty carpenters, most of whom were Issei, they made him spokesperson for the group. As negotiations over the strike progressed, he asked to be reassigned to work elsewhere. Instead, he was removed to Leupp without a hearing or even an interview. Still another example was a group of young men removed to Leupp because of their roles as leaders of the Gila Young Peoples Association, an organization "believed to be strongly pro-Japanese." However, the organization had been chartered by the Gila River project director and was allowed to continue its activities even after its officers had been taken to Leupp. Robertson noted that the young men held "positions of trust [at Leupp] and cooperated 100% with the Administration."[35]

In view of such circumstances Robertson recommended that hearings be held for men already unjustly transferred to Leupp, preferably at the camp of origin, where there would be witnesses and other forms of evidence, or that the men be told that there would be no hearings on the issue of their transfer. He further recommended that the men be told that they had been "suspected of causing trouble," and that when they were "ready to live in peace and harmony with their fellow men," they would be transferred from Leupp to another camp. He then recommended that forty-one of the sixty-seven men at Leupp be transferred to other camps, among them Kurihara and Kishi. Three weeks later Robertson received a response from Myer, who approved the transfer of thirty-six men, including Kishi but not Kurihara.[36]

At the same time that he reported unjustified transfers to Leupp, Robertson gained approval from the WRA office in D.C. to transform Leupp from a disciplinary camp to a rehabilitation center. As a result, the inmates were told that case histories were being written for each of them, a written record was being made of their behavior, and recommendations for releases to other camps would be based on these records. They were further told that while the administrative staff "couldn't force them to work, refusal to work would be regarded as an uncooperative attitude which fact would hardly be conducive to a speedy release." From that day forward, no inmate refused to work.[37]

As with Moab, the existence of Leupp was kept out of public discourse. When an investigative committee of the U.S. Congress, the so-called Dies Committee, made a tour of the WRA camps in 1943, it failed to visit Leupp, as Frederick and the inmates there had expected it would. The Nisei were "ever prepared to tell [the committee] the works!" declared Frederick. "But they never did come." Frederick speculated that the committee was ignorant of Leupp's existence, "especially since" it "recommended a program of Americanization for the centers [it did visit]." "How in hell can you Americanize the Japs," Frederick wrote Spencer, "when Gestapo methods are used in sending them to Leupp—no warrants, no trials, no sentence, separated from their families?"[38]

Despite Frederick's apparent concern for their well-being, the Nisei did not warm to him. "We called him 'See Me,'" recalled Ueno. "Everytime he said, 'See me.' In other words, 'report to me.' Nobody liked him. He was a dictator." Kurihara, in turn, thought that Frederick was conceited, acted arbitrarily, and lacked tact in dealing with inmates. Frederick, on the other hand, drew a sympathetic portrait of Kurihara: "Kurihara is very proud and for this reason does not want to ask for any favors." Frederick recognized the "necessity of treating Kurihara as an equal rather than as an inferior. . . . Kurihara does not expect any special consideration but does insist upon justice and fair dealing."[39]

Robertson, too, made a positive assessment of Kurihara, saying that he "seemed to have gained the confidence of all." "As the days passed," Robertson added, "more and more of the boys would listen to [his] counsel. . . . Most any evening you could find a large group of boys sitting in a circle with Kurihara in their midst and the group listening to him intently."[40]

Despite this evident amiability, Kurihara distanced himself from the politics of camp life and spent much of his time alone. Having decided at Moab to live in Japan after the war, he developed a "disciplined routine—rising early, walking for a certain length of time, [and] devoting so many hours a day to studying Japanese and reading his Bible."[41]

Despite this decision to keep to himself, Kurihara retained his antagonism toward those Nisei with whom he had clashed at Manzanar. While at Leupp he wrote two angry poems and sent them to Kiyoshi Higashi at Manzanar.

From
J. Y. Kurihara
Leupp Rel. Ctr. Leupp, Ariz.

To
K. H. (Slacker)
Manzanar Police Dept
Manzanar, Calif.

Rats, Sneaks and Scums

You! who swore an allegiance
You! who swore vaunted vengeance
You! who renounced your race to fight
For America, the meddler

Who trampled and jeered at our rights
Do not pride yourself as Japanese!

You are just as much a traitor!
You are just as much a hater!
You're just as much an enemy!
Of Japan, and her destiny
As those shameless rats, sneaks, and scums
Tayama, Yoneda, and Slocum.

Let not those who died in their teens
Let not those who died for the King
Let not those who died for us all
Bear untold agony of woe
Through your treacherous mask, you foe
Claim and pride yourself as Japanese!
by J. K.

Why are you not in the Army?
You circulated a Petition for second
front to President Roosevelt, have
you not?
Don't be a Slacker if you want
to be a Leader. Prove
your metal [mettle]. J. K.[42]

Furthermore, despite his cooperation with camp authorities at Moab and Leupp and despite distancing himself from camp politics, Kurihara remained steadfastly certain of the injustice of the incarceration. Hoping to communicate his thoughts to the outside world, he sent a twenty-page essay, "Niseis and the Government of the United States," to the *Saturday Evening Post.* The essay accused the government of "one of the greatest errors since the founding of this great Nation, and without question the greatest injustice against . . . its citizens." Calling for reparations, he asked, "Will [the government] admit the wrong and compensate the Nisei for the injustice, or will it white-wash [its actions]?" Kurihara also drew parallels between the treatment of the Nisei and the treatment of African Americans. "Why are [*sic*] they not been given the right to vote in many of the Southern States?" he asked. "Why are they not enjoying equal rights as citizens of the United States? . . . Those same promises made to the colored boys [who served in the U.S. army] in the first world war are being repeated to the Niseis today." To believe in those promises, Kurihara contended, was to "be made Jack-asses in this war." Instead of publishing the essay, the *Post* sent it to the FBI.[43]

This was not Kurihara's first attempt to communicate to the world outside the Nikkei community or to point to the commonalities of the Nisei and African American experiences. A confidential memorandum in the administrative file in Manzanar stated that Kurihara had written a letter to "a pro-Japanese negro suspect on August 28, 1942, from Manzanar, in which he stated that he expected to make a speech within the following fortnight in which he would set forth his ideas regarding internal conditions at Manzanar, a speech for which he said he probably would be picked up by the Federal Bureau of Investigation." Kurihara, the memo continued, was said to have "contemplated having this speech published in a negro newspaper."[44]

Unlike Kurihara, WRA Director Dillon Myer did not dwell on the injustice of the incarceration of the Nikkei. However, he was concerned about the questionable legality of placing U.S. citizens in isolation camps without regard to constitutional guarantees of due process. In an interview on September 29, 1943, with Morton Grodzins, a research assistant in the JERS project, Myer spoke frankly about the lack of due process in sending men to Moab and Leupp. After the Kibei-Nisei meeting at Manzanar and subsequent signs of tension and unrest there and at other camps, Myer explained, he had been urged to "remove the troublemakers." The results, Moab and Leupp, he admitted, were "pure accidents." "Nobody knew what Moab was or what it was going to be. We didn't know whether it was a jail, a rehabilitation camp, or what. We still don't know about Leupp." In the final analysis, Myer conceded, these isolation camps became places where the WRA would "keep people whom we consider trouble makers but whom, speaking very frankly, we don't have enough evidence to take into Civil Courts." "I have said from the first that it's illegal," Myer continued, "and I still think so." To prevent legal challenges, Myer told the American Civil Liberties Union (ACLU) Director Roger Baldwin and the ACLU National Committee member and legal scholar Alexander Meiklejohn of his plans for Moab and asked for their sympathy and understanding in this "emergency matter"; the two nationally known civil libertarians complied with the request, thus making the supposed watchdog organization, in the words of Richard Drinnon, "toothless and barkless."[45]

By the time Myer spoke to Grodzins, he had begun the process of closing Leupp. A few weeks after the interview, he told project directors that "all troublesome cases" had to be handled at their camps through "judicial action" or by transfer to Tule Lake, the designated segregation center. In an October memo to Myer, Community Management Division Chief John Provinse and Solicitor Philip Glick, both of the Leupp Review Committee, noted that Leupp was "not to be explained as a mistake, despite the fact that it was unfortunate that such a center had to be established."[46]

Leupp effectively closed on December 3, 1943, when the last of the inmates, including Joseph Kurihara, departed for Tule Lake. They left by train from the nearby town of Winslow, traveled to Stockton, where there was a long delay, and finally arrived in Klamath Falls, Oregon, on the morning of December 6.[47]

During his nine months of incarceration at the two citizen isolation camps, Kurihara behaved like a model prisoner. Because he had decided that he could no longer live in the United States, he used his time at Moab and Leupp to prepare himself for life in Japan by concentrating on learning how to read and write Japanese. One might say that he was a changed person, but that would be a superficial assessment. Although he removed himself from most of the politics in the isolation camps, he remained convinced that the U.S. government had committed an inexcusable act of betrayal toward its people.

CHAPTER 7

Turmoil at Tule

Situated at the northern end of California, thirty-five miles southeast of Klamath Falls, Oregon, and ten miles from the town of Tulelake (named after nearby Tule Lake), the Tule Lake concentration camp was flat, treeless, dusty, and desolate. At four thousand feet above sea level, its long winters were cold, its summers hot and dry. The address for the camp was Newell, the name of the nearby post office, general store, and gas station.[1]

Construction of the camp began in April 1942; in late May, five hundred Japanese American volunteers from the temporary detention camps at Portland and Puyallup arrived to help set up the camp. They were soon joined by Nikkei assigned to Tule Lake in the original peopling of the concentration camps. Within months, discontent over poor food and substandard living and farm-working conditions led to protests and strikes.[2]

This early discord escalated into a crisis during the loyalty-questionnaire fiasco of February 1943 (see chapter five), which caused "fear, confusion, and utter chaos" among the Nikkei and resulted in the label of "disloyal" for those who gave "no" answers to one or both of the two contentious questions about their national loyalties or who refused to answer the questions. As Michi Weglyn noted, their negative responses "had little to do with [their] disloyalty to America. . . . Though generally interpreted as a dereliction of allegiance, it was a registering of grief, disappointment, anger, and sometimes rage, against what the Nisei and Kibei considered disloyalty on a mammoth scale—America's disloyalty to them."[3]

Four months after the questionnaire debacle, which was replicated across all of the concentration camps, WRA officials decided to designate Tule Lake as a "Segregation Center" for incarcerated Nikkei deemed disloyal. To free up space at Tule Lake for the "disloyals" from other camps, Tule Lake administrators in the summer of 1943 asked those who had answered "yes" to the controversial questions to move to other concentration camps. About six thousand did so, while some four thousand refused to leave, and thus they remained with the forty-five hundred dissident Tuleans. When the ensuing transfers of "loyals" and "disloyals" were completed, the Tule Lake population had grown to eighteen thousand people, including about twenty-seven hundred from Manzanar.[4]

Those arriving from other camps were taken aback by living conditions at Tule Lake. As one of them noted, "Everything was dirty: the barracks were dirty, the showers were dirty, the mess halls were dirty." Noburo Shirai, an Issei and an old Tulean—one of the original Nikkei at Tule Lake—wrote of this situation, "Those who had left Tule Lake had taken everything they could carry with them and hadn't bothered to clean up behind themselves. They had given away their bulky furniture—their tables, chairs, and sofas—to their friends. Not a stick remained for the newcomers." These conditions fueled anger and resentment among the new Tuleans.[5]

As more segregants arrived, more barracks were built to house them, more soldiers came to guard them, and more watchtowers were added within a perimeter surrounded by a six-foot-high chain-link fence topped with barbed wire.[6] Appointed to administer this newly formed segregation camp was Raymond Best, at the time the Leupp isolation camp director. Best's appointment to his new post by WRA officials in D.C. came after those officials had concluded that the Tule Lake project director Harvey Coverley had mishandled the registration-questionnaire affair. Thus on August 1, 1943, Best replaced Coverley.[7]

Best's arrival at Tule Lake did nothing to relieve the tension there. In fact, his testy, unsympathetic attitude toward the Nikkei fed into the already low morale and stoked the camp's volatility. In an interview forty years after the war, Robertson—who came to Tule Lake from Leupp to serve as Acting Assistant Project Director in charge of health, education, recreation, internal security, housing, and other related matters—recalled that Best tended to be "aloof" and "opinionated" and seemed not to understand the Nikkei's responses to their situation at Tule Lake. In this light, Kurihara's fondness for Best was an anomaly.[8]

In October, amidst an atmosphere of continued animosity against the administration, an overturned truck caused serious injury to Nikkei farmworkers and death to one of them. Inmates accused administrators of negligence because of a rumor that an inexperienced minor had driven the truck filled with Nikkei in the truck's bed. The events that followed brought Tule Lake to a state of crisis. In the tension-filled days following the death of the worker, Best refused to permit a public funeral. The inmates held one anyway, which thousands attended, as the death became a symbol of the unjust treatment of the Nikkei. Upon learning that the worker's widow would receive little financial compensation, the farmworkers went on strike. The strikers were led by the

Daihyo Sha Kai (Representative Body), composed of Nikkei recently chosen in camp-wide elections. Because agricultural production at the Tule Lake camp helped feed the army and navy as well as other concentration camps, the strike created an emergency. Best responded by bringing in Nikkei from other WRA camps to harvest the crops. They were housed away from Tule Lake and paid about ten times what Tuleans had received for the same work. On November 1, when the WRA Director Dillon Myer visited Tule Lake, a crowd of more than five thousand inmates demonstrated in the administration area to protest the use of strikebreakers as well as poor food, unsanitary conditions, and administrative incompetence. The crowd, remaining peaceful even if Myer refused to address their grievances, eventually dispersed.[9]

Three nights later, as protesters attempted to prevent the surreptitious transfer of food and supplies to the strikebreakers, floodlights poured onto the protest area as military police with bayonets arrived in jeeps mounted with machine guns. Those suspected of leading the protest were beaten, arrested, and locked in the Tule Lake stockade.

Tokio Yamane, a Kibei-Nisei, later recounted his experiences that night. "We heard the news that some white guys were stealing food from the warehouse. A Japanese American internal security man, Tom Kobayashi, caught them on the spot. . . . Then he got into a fight with them. . . . The news of this incident was brought to our attention during the *Daihyo Sha Kai* meeting." The Reverend Shizue Kai and George Kuratomi, who were leading the meeting, asked Yamane, a young man who had been a high school track star, to run to the warehouse to learn what was happening. Since the *Daihyo Sha Kai* was then negotiating with camp administrators for "better treatment," Yamane was instructed to tell the Nikkei to "calm down and return to their own resident compounds as soon as possible." Yamane and another young man, Koji Todoroko, left immediately in the pitch-dark night. When they arrived at the warehouse, "several Caucasians suddenly came out of the dark and hit [them] with their big fists." "I became unconscious," recalled Yamane. "When I regained my consciousness, I found myself lying bloody in the room with a number of WRA [police] officers standing around me. I was made to stand straight with hands up and back on the wall. Todoroki and I were accused of being the troublemakers. But being the troublemakers for what? We had no clue. . . . Despite our innocence, we were beat up to make us confess 'the crime' from eight in that evening until probably around three in the morning." During their beating, Kobayashi—the Nisei internal security man who had earlier confronted Caucasian men stealing food meant for the Nikkei—was brought into the room. When he refused to stand with hands up and denied committing any crime, a "big, muscular" white man employed by Internal Security swung a baseball bat at him, and the Caucasians in the room "laughed." "I saw the baseball bat break into two and blood came spurting out of his head. . . . Big guys were standing all around us with firearms. . . . [W]e were tortured until morning." Finally a military policeman took them to the military section of the camp, to a "bullpen," which was a tent surrounded by a barbed wire fence and guarded by soldiers. The three men were given a blanket each and a makeshift bed, on which they endured the cold winds blowing from Oregon. "The only topic we discussed was how to die with dignity."[10]

The army took control of the camp that night and in the ensuing days built five watchtowers and a high, impassable fence between the Nikkei barracks and the administration area. A stockade was set up, in which Yamane, Todoroki, Kobayashi, and others were imprisoned. On November 13—less than a month before Kurihara and his fellow Nisei arrived in Tule Lake—martial law was declared; Tule Lake remained in this state of emergency, "crawling with troops, security patrols, and FBI agents," until January 15.[11]

On December 6, Kurihara and the other fifty-two inmates from Leupp arrived. "A very repulsive sight greeted us as we approached [the concentration camp]," Kurihara later recalled. "It was the sight of numerous watch towers lining the perimeter of the camp," the "high fences . . . with meshed wires," and the "search lights beaming throughout the camp, watching us . . . as if we were incorrigible murderers." Kurihara and the other transplants from Leupp knew nothing of the beatings and other events that had occurred earlier.[12]

Despite efforts by Robertson and Best to prevent it, Colonel Meek, commander of the military force guarding the camp, dispatched the newcomers to the stockade. There they sat for two days. "[A]fter long discussions and arguments," Robertson noted, "the Colonel—who had previously encountered Kurihara—asked what Robertson thought of [him]." Although Robertson assured Meek that "Joe was completely rehabilitated and would cause no trouble at Tule," Meek remained unconvinced, and he had Kurihara brought to him for an interview. "They connected me with the start of the trouble [at Tule Lake] while I was in Leupp," recalled Kurihara. "I said if I were the instigator of the trouble here while I was in Leupp, I should be a general." Kurihara convinced Meek that he was no longer interested in involving himself in the politics of camp life, and as a result, Meek released him and all but ten men who Meek believed would cause trouble for the army.[13]

After Kurihara was released from the stockade, Best told him that he would support him in any position of leadership he desired. Kurihara declined the offer, stating, "[I]f I knew you were going to continue to be here I would attempt some kind of leadership, but I'm afraid that just about the time I established a constructive group here you would be reassigned and I would be in the same fix in which I found myself at Manzanar. I would prefer to just retire to my apartment here and read my Bible . . . and study the Japanese language." Moreover, he continued, he would never "be able to act and feel freely as an American, because America was not willing to allow him to act and feel that way."[14]

Martial law at Tule Lake continued for two months. As soon as it began, administrators issued orders to arrest suspected dissident leaders, who—upon hearing of these orders—went into hiding. On November 26, military police combed the entire camp looking for the men. In doing so, they entered living quarters and seized such personal items as "wooden canes, binoculars, hatchets, short wave radios, rice, homemade sake," all of which they pronounced contraband.[15]

During martial law, crowds that refused to disperse were met with tear gas. Suspected dissidents, including leaders of the *Daihyo Sha Kai*, were picked up in the middle of the night. So numerous were those arrested that a larger stockade had to be built, consisting of four barracks that included a mess hall, washroom, and latrine cordoned off by a barbed-wire fence and secured by its own guard towers. Eventually three hundred and fifty Nikkei were held there, while another twelve hundred Issei were sent to Justice Department internment camps. From mid-November through mid-January high tension filled the air, and life in Tule Lake was one of "turmoil, idleness, impoverishment and uncertainty." Schools were closed and recreational activities suspended. Except for mess hall operations and hospital services, work came to a standstill. Living conditions became dire with lack of food and milk as well as shortages of coal, warm clothes, and shoes for the children, who had to brave the freezing winter weather.[16]

Suspicion, fear, and anger grew among the Nikkei, dividing one from another, as inmates accused each other of collaborating, informing, or fence sitting. Demoralized by the situation, Tuleans voted into office a newly formed group called the Coordinating Committee, composed of Nikkei vetted by the WRA. By a small margin—473 out of 8,713 votes cast—Tuleans elected the committee, and in so doing, they seemed to agree to cooperate with the administration and seek to return the camp as best as possible to "normalcy." Four days after the election, on January 15, 1944, the army announced the end of martial law and withdrew most of its troops. Except for the stockade, the army returned administrative control of the camp to the WRA.[17]

Recognized by the administration as spokespersons for the Nikkei, the Coordinating Committee confronted the task of unifying a split community. As shown by the narrow margin of the committee's victory, Tuleans did not necessarily favor its accommodationist view to that of the more confrontational *Daihyo Sha Kai*, but the vast majority of them were disheartened by the suffering that resulted from the lack of food, work, and earning capacity. At the same time, they remained hostile to the administration and the military. The status quo broke, according to Kurihara, "not because [Tuleans] didn't want to stick with the Negotiating Committee [of the *Daihyo Sha Kai*] but—one of the main reasons was lack of finance [in other words, income]. Another reason [was that] they didn't want to loaf along doing nothing. Time lags so monotonous." Kurihara believed, in fact, that the Coordinating Committee's position did not reflect the sentiments of the Nikkei. "Many who favored the status quo did not vote. They thought [voting] was the way to go to the stockade. . . . A lot of people feared they might be pulled in. They had a soldier by the vote box." Kurihara had a dim view of the Coordinating Committee members: "Among those seven are several people whose record is so black that I even flatly refuse to talk to them. My profession is a public accountant. I nearly sent [one of them] to jail for defrauding the company of 40,000 dollars. . . . The Administration doesn't know their past."[18]

Although the committee was widely viewed with mixed feelings, it did attempt to improve conditions at Tule Lake. It had two goals: full employment and release of the stockade prisoners. However, it faced obstacles. Work divisions such as the Mail and Files Section and the Statistics Section in the administration, for example, had replaced Nikkei with Caucasian workers during the period of martial law, and they now resisted the return of the Nikkei, suspicious that important information might get to the "wrong" people. Other divisions, likewise, refused to re-employ Nikkei or refused to hire as many as had been hired before martial law, explaining that they wanted to avoid instances of insubordination. Despite these problems, the committee was able to find some employment for the Nikkei. And while the military at first refused to release the prisoners from the stockade, by April they released some, although not entirely due to the committee's efforts. Somewhat reluctantly, the committee accepted its role as mediator between the WRA and the Nikkei, well aware that the people it sought to help saw its members as collaborators with administrators. Kurihara spoke for many when he said, "The Coordinating Committee . . . is the unconscious tool of either the army or WRA." "From our point of judgment, [its members] are loyals." "The people consider [them] *inu*. Yet [the administrators] continue to employ these people. They should know better." Aware that it did not have the support of the people it ostensibly represented, the committee in February proposed another election for a new committee. But WRA officials and the military balked, fearing that anti-administration dissidents would be elected. Finally, on April 30, after it became obvious that it lacked the confidence of the Nikkei, and after accomplishing as much as it thought possible, the Committee dissolved itself.[19]

Rosalie Hankey and JERS

In stark contrast to his behavior at Manzanar, and similar to his behavior at Moab and Leupp, at Tule Lake Kurihara refrained from speech making and distanced himself from intra-Nikkei rivalries. Ueno, who had by then reconciled with Kurihara, recalled that the latter "didn't talk about what was going on. [He] just asked me about Japanese characters, how to talk and how to write." Ueno, too, had decided to remove himself from the politics at Tule Lake. Realizing now that his previous activities had brought great hardship to his wife and children, he was determined to cause them no further suffering.[20]

While avoiding an active role in the goings-on at Tule Lake, Kurihara nonetheless listened, observed, discussed issues with friends, and offered his views to Rosalie Hankey, a field researcher with the Japanese Evacuation and Resettlement Study (JERS), a U.S. government-approved research effort independent of the WRA and funded by private foundations.[21]

One of the main results of that effort was *The Spoilage*, by the project's director Dorothy Swaine Thomas and her assistant Richard S. Nishimoto. Critics of both Thomas and the book have pointed to what they believe was an overreliance on Rosalie Hankey's research at Tule Lake. In my examination of eyewitness accounts of events at Tule Lake, however, I found that they generally agreed with the field notes Hankey made at the time. Moreover, discussions of Tule Lake in secondary sources do not contradict a basic strength of *The Spoilage*, namely, its outline of events at the camp. To be sure, specific assertions in the book are debatable. Nevertheless, to single out Hankey's field notes as the source of distortions in *The Spoilage* misses the role of the book's authors, Thomas and Nishimoto. They had their own conceptual framework, which led to their own conclusions.[22]

Thomas first became aware of the wealth of information Kurihara could provide when she read what he had written. Francis Frederick, who had handled security at Moab and Leupp, and believed that Kurihara had a "strong character" and "plenty of guts," and was "highly respected," told Kurihara about the JERS project and gave him JERS researcher Robert Spencer's name. Knowing that Kurihara was "given to letting off steam by writing," Frederick "suggested that he send his writings and thoughts" to Spencer. Kurihara eventually took that suggestion and in December 1943, before being transferred to Tule Lake, wrote a letter to Spencer. He then gave his essays in which he denounced the forced exile and incarceration of Nikkei, to the Leupp Project Director Paul Robertson, whom he trusted, and Robertson forwarded them to Thomas.[23]

Spencer wrote Frederick that Kurihara's letter caused "a special meeting of the minds," at which time it was deemed "of extreme value, and an overt statement made by one of those individuals to whom evacuation has meant the frustration of every hope." It was in this way that Thomas and her researchers became aware that Kurihara might be a powerful informant for their project.[24]

The researcher who contacted Kurihara at Tule Lake was thirty-two-year old Rosalie Hankey. In late January 1944, while working at the Gila camp as one of Thomas's researchers, Hankey was asked by Thomas to visit Tule Lake, which she subsequently did several times before moving there more permanently. A large and tall woman, six feet two inches, she was described in masculine and unattractive terms by males at Tule Lake—for example, as a "hard drinker" who was "built like a Sherman tank."[25]

These descriptions point to Hankey's efforts to situate herself within the Caucasian, male-dominated milieu of WRA administrators at Tule Lake. Heather Fryer has argued that Hankey developed a persona that displayed either feminine or masculine characteristics, "whichever . . . furthered her purposes." Indeed, her field notes include vignettes that support such a characterization. As a case in point, at the end of her first day at Tule Lake, she called on the WRA anthropologist Marvin Opler. "I felt extraordinarily tired but elated at the amount of material I had been able to get," she wrote. "I cudgeled my brain as to how I might avoid giving [Opler] confidential information and still remain on friendly terms. . . . I decided that I would feign disappointment at my progress and play the part of a discouraged, puzzled, female anthropologist, whose hopes to get information had been frustrated. Since I felt ready to blow my top to the first intelligent listener this was difficult. Yet it worked better than I had anticipated. When I said I had received almost no information he looked very satisfied and said, 'Now I know by that statement that you're a good field worker.' Thereupon he proceeded to show me how vast his knowledge of the situation was."[26]

When masculine characteristics suited her purposes, she exhibited "tough-girl qualities": The ability to drink "like a man," for example, served to demonstrate that she could hold her own among men. Months after her initial visit to Tule Lake, she met with John Burling, the assistant director of the Alien Enemy Control Unit. In her notes to Thomas she wrote, "By God—if I don't become a chronic alcoholic getting dope out of Burling I shall be very much surprised. In any case, here is the latest development, obtained at God only knows what detriment to my kidneys. . . . [A]nd Burling told me this while [he was] still sober."[27]

That she could laugh at herself is seen in her recounting of a meeting with a Mr. Tada: "Kuratomi [a dissident leader at Tule Lake] arranged for me to have a long talk with Mr. Tada, who hospitably opened our discussion by pouring out for me a large water tumbler of distilled *sake,* which, I soon discovered, had about the same potency as a strong brandy. But I had a very good head for liquor then and I came away with a fine interview, though I noticed later that my handwriting had become larger and larger as the interview progressed."[28]

Hankey performed her job as field researcher with enthusiasm and energy. From February 1944 to May 1945 she visited each of thirty Nisei every seven to fourteen days, recording their views of events at Tule Lake. She also visited many other Nisei less regularly. Her respondents ranged from those who distanced themselves from the politics of camp life to those who were avid members and leaders of one political group or another. Knowing that she was not working for the WRA, they spoke with her freely, regarding her as a friend or at least a sympathetic researcher. She also visited WRA staff and administrators, who were more than willing to voice their opinions. Robertson, who sympathized with the Nikkei, proved to be an especially valuable confidant. She took copious notes, writing many statements of her interviewees verbatim. In addition she recorded her own observations as she walked within the camp and attended meetings and other events there. The result was field notes of about a thousand typed pages.[29]

When Hankey approached Tule Lake for the first time on February 2, 1944, she was confronted by a "high, barbed-wire-topped fence" surrounding the camp, with "large watchtowers" and "high-powered search lights." "A short distance from the entrance gate, guarded by armed sentries, I was given a visitor pass by a soldier who telephoned his superior officer to check my statement that I had been invited by Best. I then walked to a WRA office about one-fourth mile away to get another pass which admitted me into the premises of the . . . Military Area." Arriving at Best's office, Hankey was directed to Harry Black, who was in charge of community management. Black informed her that she could enter the "colony"—the section of Tule Lake where the Nikkei were confined—only with an armed soldier. Black also told her that she must take the soldier with her if she went into the barracks, or she could have an inmate "brought to [her] at the office under armed guard." Although these directions "provoked" her, she said nothing about them. While she waited for a meeting with Best, Robertson entered the waiting area. She had met him previously at the Gila camp, and as they chatted briefly, he advised her "to employ the ruse he [used to see inmates without the armed escort]: get the soldier to stay in the car." He then gave her Kurihara's address.[30]

On the day she was to meet Kurihara, her armed escort was a Mr. Johnson, "who did not object to remaining outside in the car reading mystery stories" she provided him. She spent the day first visiting Nikkei she had known at Gila. She then made the day's final call on Kurihara, who lived in a barracks room with two other men. "With its tables holding neatly stacked papers, well-made cots and suspended lights," she noted, "the room might have been a well-kept army-officer's quarters. A young man was reading a newspaper spread out on a table. Kurihara, a short, slightly bald stocky man, was extremely polite." Hankey told him of the aims of the JERS project and said she and other staff members had been impressed with the article he had sent them. "Fixing me with a steady gaze," she recalled, "he asked me point blank why I personally had liked his article. I said that honesty shone out of it and that I admired honesty. I also realized that anyone who would make the statements he did must be very courageous or else crazy. He was pleased."[31]

This meeting began Kurihara's role as Hankey's "best informant." From time to time he wrote reports for her that discussed "many significant and interesting" attitudes of Tuleans. Occasionally and when necessary, he wrote letters to her that were formal and abrupt, "evidently written with possible censorship in mind"—a contrast to his "cordial and obliging" manner whenever they discussed matters in person. Calling him "stern-principled," she grew to respect him considerably. His willingness to "gather information for me," Hankey wrote in her field notes, "delights me."[32]

That Kurihara was Hankey's "best informant" meant that she found him to be a most trustworthy source of information. Yet she avoided an over-dependence on him, instead meeting and conversing with a variety of Tuleans. As a result, her field notes discussed him and quoted him less substantially than I had hoped. For me, someone particularly interested in Kurihara's thoughts and words, this was understandably a disappointment. Yet Hankey did what a good researcher should do—avoid an over-reliance on one or a few sources.

The Push for Resegregation

Although Tule Lake was a "segregation" camp intended for "disloyals" only, many of the inmates there fit no such label. In fact, the Nikkei there held a wide variety of attitudes toward both the United States and Japan. First, there were those embittered toward the United States for the indignities and hardships they had suffered, including financial losses, resulting from the forced removal from their homes and livelihoods, and for their treatment as prisoners who had committed no crimes. The most vocal of this group spoke vociferously of their loyalty to Japan and their disparagement of the United States. Second, there were those who remained ambivalent about their future in the United States as well as in Japan. Among these were many who considered themselves American but who chose not to answer the loyalty questions or to answer them negatively. This ambivalent group was by far the largest. One young Nisei woman in this second group called those in the first group "trouble makers." She stated, "They really make life miserable for the nisei." Third, there were those who despised the discrimination they had experienced in the United States but felt no desire to leave it for a life in Japan. Finally, there were Nisei who were minors without political preferences. That there was a wide range of attitudes resulted from the fact that more than several thousand nondissident Tuleans had refused to leave the camp when Tule Lake was made a segregation center. Also, in order to keep their families together, the original Tuleans who had been labeled loyal were permitted to remain at Tule Lake with their dissident family members, while nondissidents in other camps were permitted to accompany their dissident family members when the latter were transferred to Tule Lake.[33]

Those in the first of the four groups just enumerated developed a strong underground movement. Composed largely of Nikkei who had been transferred from other camps, they viewed the Coordinating Committee with contempt. Calling themselves "resegregationists" *(Saikakuri Seigan),* they pushed doggedly for their own segregation from other Tuleans in a separate section within the camp and demanded that they be given priority in repatriation (if they were Issei) or expatriation (if they were U.S. citizens).[34]

The resegregationists believed that they were the only true Japanese among the Nikkei at Tule Lake. They had no use for fence-sitters or for those living there under false pretenses—that is, claiming to want expatriation or repatriation but choosing Tule Lake because they wanted to avoid the draft or were afraid of leaving the camps and knew that Tule Lake would remain in operation after the other camps were closed. "We don't care which [side] wins or loses," declared the resegregationist Mrs. Tsuchikawa of the outcome of the war. "We're going to stick to Japan."[35]

Her statement notwithstanding, the Nikkei did care about the war's outcome. They kept abreast of its progress as best they could, using shortwave radios they assembled themselves. A Kibei-Nisei recalled, "We used to get shortwave news from Japan. . . . We used to listen to the Imperial Japanese Army headquarters news. . . . How many ships they [sank], how many planes they shot down. . . . We used to write it down and pass it out." Good news from Japan heartened the "demoralized, imprisoned population," "offering hope and salvation" to them. However, "[t]owards the end of the war," he noted, "I started getting some doubts about the validity of our news reports because they were sinking too many battleships."[36]

The sentiments of resegregationists captured the friction between old and new Tuleans. The dissidents who arrived from other camps had expected to find themselves among like-minded Nikkei and were dismayed to learn otherwise. Noboru Shirai, an old Tulean who served as a block manager, recalled the September 1943 arrival of the newcomers: "A shadowy character with a thin moustache, dark glasses, and a chip on his shoulder stalked into our office. Without so much as a friendly word, he ripped an administrative bulletin off the board and tore it up. 'What's this?' he barked. 'Who wants to read this kind of crap?'" For many old Tuleans, the newcomers from Jerome and Manzanar seemed especially troublesome. Using intimidation, threats, and even beatings, they worked their way into positions of power in the midst of "internal strife" and "chaos" created by their arrival.[37]

To be sure, the Nikkei from Jerome and Manzanar did not speak with one voice, and dissident leadership also came from other camps. Indeed, factions existed among activists, and disagreements arose among them.[38] Moreover, alignments with one group or another were fluid.

To complicate matters further, not all who agitated were clear in their intentions. A Kibei-Nisei explained his ambivalence this way: "In Japan, I [had been] shunned as a foreigner. I came back to the U.S. and I wasn't treated like a U.S. citizen. . . . I felt I didn't have a country. . . . I would say about 90 percent of Kibei-Nisei had problems with their families. We were away from our parents so long and felt they deserted us. When I went to Japan, I was 10 years old and I couldn't understand why. It wasn't easy when I was there. . . . I swore to myself that if I ever saw my parents again, I would tell them they were not my parents any longer. So, with this kind of background going into camp, I had all this built up and every chance I got, I raised some hell." Indeed, recalled Hiroshi Kashiwagi, many of the Kibei-Nisei were single and were "very aggressive and very arrogant to our eyes." A Kibei-Nisei who at the time was unmarried, recalled, "If you have your own children, you would refrain for the sake of your wife and children. . . . But we were single, and we could go as far as we liked."[39]

By late March the resegregationists had agreed that they no longer needed to operate totally in secret. From April 7 to 9, with the approval of the administration, they circulated a petition for signatures of those who wished to be segregated from the rest of the Tuleans with the goal of early departure to Japan. Although sixty-five hundred Tuleans signed the petition, the petition itself was the subject of great confusion and turmoil in the camp. Many of those approached feared that signing it would lead to their arrest, while others feared that not signing it would close the door to their future repatriation or expatriation. Still others sought to avoid separation of family members. Although Kurihara himself intended to depart for Japan after the war, he refused to sign the petition. "I objected because . . . no clear cut explanation was made.

It was given to the people in a haphazard manner." "I would not sign my name to anything," he continued, "unless I know thoroughly what it means. Many now regret signing the petition." Of the resegregationists, he said their "attitude was take it or leave it. It was too much of a high pressure group." Pressure to sign the petition led to arguments and physical clashes. The resulting mayhem alarmed WRA officials, who withdrew their earlier approval of the petition's circulation, causing further confusion and distrust of administrators.[40]

As food and living conditions improved, interest in the petition decreased and tension subsided. At the same time, Best eased restrictions and endeavored to improve relations with residents.[41] Nevertheless, from April through mid-June 1944, the continued existence of the stockade (although prisoners were being released almost daily) and a lack of employment, as well as unsanitary living conditions, left a persistent feeling of dissatisfaction and with it an attitude of indifference to administration proposals.[42]

When the Coordinating Committee resigned, the WRA began to encourage Tuleans to elect a representative committee that would serve as a liaison between the residents and the administration. But few Nikkei attended block meetings called to nominate candidates, and few agreed to be nominated, so that the effort floundered. Kurihara's reaction to having his name put forward as a candidate was common. "I was home and they came for me," he recalled. "But I refused to attend [the meeting]. . . . I flatly refused to accept the nomination." It was difficult to find nominees for several reasons, but the major one was the continual existence of the stockade. A Nisei woman explained that "as long as the men whom they had once elected were in the stockade, there was no reason to elect another committee." Other reasons were fear of being called a collaborator, skepticism about the benefits of having a representative committee, continued resentment that the administration had refused to recognize and work with the earlier elected *Daihyo Sha Kai*, and general unwillingness to cooperate with the administration. Eventually administrators dropped their effort to have a new committee elected.[43]

On May 24 an incident occurred that could have erupted into yet another major crisis. A sentry shot and killed a Nisei worker named Shoichi James Okamoto. By all accounts the shooting was unprovoked. The incident shook Kurihara profoundly. In her field notes, Hankey wrote, "I . . . inquired how the man was. Kurihara told me he was dead. I expressed my regret. His eyes filled with tears and he began to cry, repeating over and over again: 'I wonder if there is a God.' I was much moved and did not know what to say." Later, Kurihara refused to discuss the incident with Hankey; it may have been too strong a reminder of the Manzanar revolt, which ended in the fatal shooting of two young men.[44]

In the aftermath of this shooting, a crisis was avoided, largely due to WRA officials' sympathetic efforts to understand and support the Nikkei perspective. In contrast to his directives in the aftermath of the earlier fatality of the farm worker, Best immediately issued a public statement of regret and, together with other officials, visited the Okamoto family. Radio and newspaper coverage of the incident quoted Secretary of the Interior Harold Ickes condemning the shooting as "completely unwarranted and without provocation." Officials promptly processed employment compensation papers for Okamoto's survivors, and the WRA approved a public funeral; four thousand to nine thousand Nikkei attended and heard Best give a memorial address. These actions served to distance WRA administrators from the military and calmed the situation. Nevertheless, many Nikkei expressed outrage when they learned that the court-martialed sentry was acquitted. Kurihara articulated their sentiments when he wrote, "[American] laws are mockery to civilization. They can shoot and kill an innocent man for no reason whatever and be acquitted. . . . The resentment over this very unfavorable verdict is great. . . . A cowardly shooting and a shameless verdict. This is America, hypocritical America."[45]

While outward calm prevailed during these months, suspicions toward so-called collaborators grew steadily. Anyone who worked cooperatively with the administration was called *inu*, and many so called were mistakenly labeled. Kurihara told Hankey that some of the inmates had questioned him about her and Robertson's visits to his barracks. He told the questioners that "his conscience was clear." Hearing this, Hankey told herself that she would visit him less often for fear that he would be called *inu*.[46] Such an attribution, were it directed at him, would have repelled Kurihara. The *inu* "sell their soul for a few pennies," he once told Hankey. "They make my blood boil."[47]

Violence among Inmates

In mid-June, the frequency of violence intensified. One beating caused a concussion, another a fractured skull. Kurihara interpreted this situation insightfully. "The Japanese have grievances against the Administration," he said, "but they know as a fact that they're helpless. Naturally, the only thing they can think of is how to get back at those who spy on them." This assessment cut through the tangled mess of lawlessness. Feelings of uncertainty coupled with resentment and bitterness over their situation bred hostility. Trapped in a cage with no hope for a promising future, many Nikkei became so frustrated that they turned on each other rather than against the perpetrators of their plight. Contributing to the violence, moreover, was the pervasiveness of gambling, with huge "losses and gains" that encouraged vicious attacks.[48]

To help quell the violence, the administration endeavored to have the inmates elect their own police commissioners. But as with the previous attempt to hold elections for representatives, this one failed, and for the same reasons. Few blocks nominated candidates. Kurihara had predicted that the election would be "a resounding failure. Nobody with any self respect would take the position," he explained, "because they would invariably be labeled as *inu*."[49]

The continual violence became the central topic of nervous conversations and gossip among the Nikkei. With little control over the violence, it was not long before murder occurred. On the night of July 2, Yaozu Hitomi, general manager of Cooperative Enterprises, which managed the general merchandise stores for inmates called canteens, was stabbed and killed near the entrance of his unit. New Tuleans accused the cooperative, operated by old Tuleans, of profiting from the sale of fruits, vegetables, and other goods. Reflecting this view, Kurihara stated, "The Co-op is charging an exceedingly high price." For an aluminum teapot, for example, "probably worth 50 cents now, they are charging $1.25." In addition to complaints about high prices, rumor had it that Hitomi and other cooperative officials and employees had embezzled canteen funds. Additionally, many inmates had long detested Hitomi as an *inu*. The murderers fled the scene and were never identified.[50]

According to one Issei, Hitomi "was one of the most hated men in the camp." Similarly, Kurihara told Hankey, "I can say that 99 percent of the people are happy over the killing." Speculation ran wild about the identity of the murderers. Administrators suspected that stockade prisoners had instigated the killing, and as a result, further isolated them from the rest of the camp. They had plaster boards attached to the fence around the stockade so that the prisoners could not see other Nikkei, and had mail between the prisoners and other Tuleans stopped. These measures angered the Nikkei and kept alive the issue of the stockade.[51]

Anxiety reigned. With threats to other suspected *inu*, about fifteen of them moved into the administrative area for protection; some of them were then transferred to other camps. Kurihara opined that their transfers helped relieve the tension at Tule Lake. "But I feel sorry for them," he added. "They're branded for good. People from Tule are writing to [other camps], telling their friends all about them.[52]

In the wake of Hitomi's murder and with tensions high, officials of the cooperative resigned, as did the entire Nikkei police force, which was responsible for safety within the barracks blocks. It took much effort by both concerned administrators and well-meaning Nikkei to find Tuleans willing to serve on the cooperative's board of directors, which after all oversaw an agency intended to benefit the inmates. Eventually a new board was constituted, and its first item of business was to adopt procedures aimed at avoiding Hitomi's alleged misuse of cooperative funds.[53]

Kurihara played a vital but behind-the-scenes role, helping to reorganize the cooperative and serving as the board's unofficial advisor and unpaid accountant.[54] This shows how adroit he was in keeping a low profile while involving himself in selected aspects of Tule Lake's community life in which he could be helpful. This also shows how he was able to keep informed of daily happenings and concerns.

Like reorganizing the cooperative, reconstituting the police force proved difficult. Those who had resigned en masse did so because they feared that they would be called on to help find and arrest Hitomi's murderers and thus become targets of anger from those who had hated Hitomi and wanted his murderers to go free. In the stalemate, administrators warned block managers that without a police force, there would be no protection whatsoever for the Nikkei. Rumors of rape began circulating, frightening girls and women, who refused to attend night school or go to see a movie after dark. Recognizing the need for public safety, most of the blocks eventually elected policemen. But members of the new police force refused to intrude into any incident in which their intrusion might be seen by fellow Nikkei as collaboration with the administration, or which involved politics.[55]

Most of the leaders of the various factions or interest groups—*Daihyo Sha Kai*, the Coordinating Committee, the Cooperative Enterprise, and the resegregationists—were Kibei-Nisei. This was due largely to their ability to speak in both Japanese and English, which enabled them to communicate with Issei as well as Nisei and Caucasian administrators. Then, too, they constituted a sizeable proportion of the second-generation population at Tule Lake. While the ratio of Kibei-Nisei to other Nisei had been 1 to 4 before the war, at Tule Lake it was at times almost 1 to 1.[56]

With the new police force in place, the reorganization of the cooperative completed, and the removal of many of the suspected *inu*, tensions began to subside. But then the resegregationists began to engage openly in activities that earlier would have led to their arrest and incarceration in the stockade.[57]

The Stockade

The stockade issue was never far from the minds of most Tuleans, and it remained a bone of contention, especially among families and friends of those imprisoned.

Life in the stockade was dire: Each of the four barracks housed over forty men without partitions and therefore without privacy. Meals consisted of bread or rice, carrots, and rotting fruit that they refused to eat. Mail was censored. Family visits were denied. Lack of sanitation was pervasive. The men were without bucket, broom, or mop; they had blankets but no sheets or pillows; and only on occasion was soap issued to the men. Morgan Yamanaka recalled that some of those in the stockade were "known leaders" of various groups that administrators found objectionable, which explained their presence there. But most did not know why they were there. "What the hell was I?" Yamanaka asked. "[T]he majority of the hundred plus people in the stockade were in there for the same reason I was—we didn't know.[58]

Everyone knew of the situation, but it was the resegregationists who undertook the task of doing something about it. They made release of stockade prisoners their top priority. In 1944 they succeeded in contacting Ernest Besig, the director of the Northern California American Civil Liberties Union (NCACLU). By this time most of the stockade prisoners had been released back into the camp population, but sixteen remained incarcerated, all U.S. citizens.[59]

Besig's attempts to visit Tule Lake met roadblocks, yet he persisted and eventually was permitted in July to enter the camp and interview relatives of stockade prisoners. But he could meet with the prisoners themselves only in the presence of the WRA Internal Security staff. Besig evidently rejected this option; Kurihara noted that the Tuleans were "disappointed" that Besig did not "see the men individually." "I wish he would put up a fight," Kurihara remarked to Hankey, "so that the American public will be informed of the facts," adding, however, that publicizing the issue would probably not amount to much. When Kurihara made these comments, he was unaware that after visiting Tule Lake, Besig had written a letter of protest to Secretary of the Interior Harold Ickes, emphasizing that the men were being held with no charges filed against them. He had then contacted the press, stating, "These people are entitled to a hearing and a trial. If they are guilty, put them in prison or anywhere. But they have the basic right of every citizen for a fair trial."[60]

On July 19, after eight months in the stockade and discouraged by prospects of being kept there indefinitely, fourteen prisoners (two others had just been released) began a long and difficult hunger strike. Most of them were eventually hospitalized but then returned to the stockade when they refused to eat. "I think the hunger strike has made a very strong impression on the people," stated one Nisei. "Those boys have been kept in there unjustly when they should have been released. The only solution which would bring the camp back to normal is release from the stockade."[61]

In an effort to pressure Best to release the hunger strikers, the resegregationists circulated a petition that was signed by more than eight thousand Tuleans. Soon after the signatures were collected, however, a rift developed among the resegregation leaders. Some wanted to present the petition to Best immediately, while others preferred waiting. Assured by Besig that a habeas corpus hearing would result in the release of the men, the latter preferred using legal means to win the men's release. George Kuratomi, one of the stockade prisoners, later commented of this group, "[They] were afraid that the petition might successfully bring our releases. They didn't want that. They wanted the lawsuit so that they could say, 'We got releases for those detainees.' They were after laurels for themselves. They didn't care if we were kept in the stockade and suffered." Others believed that advocates of the delay wanted to collect funds to help pay attorney fees as well as finance their organization. Kurihara advised waiting, but for a different reason. He told Hankey what Best had told him, that "the boys [would] be released within a month." Hearing this, Kurihara decided to try "to kill the agitation" to avoid "trouble and hardship to the Japanese." So he counseled those circulating the petition to wait for Best to release the men and have the signatures ready in case Best did not "live up to his word." If they presented the petition prematurely, Kurihara believed, "Mr. Best [would] feel he's being forced" and would possibly decide against releasing the men. As these comments indicate, Kurihara's perspective had changed since his time at Manzanar. No longer did he believe in agitating his fellow inmates. Now, a year-and-a-half later, Kurihara instead told them, "I don't believe in high pressuring a man if you can avoid it." In the end the petition was never presented to Best. Apparently in an argument between the two factions within the resegregationist group, those who wanted to use legal means grabbed a portion of the signatures and threw it into a fire.[62]

The hunger strike ended finally, when the prisoners realized that one of the men was near death and several others were seriously ill. In August they were allowed to leave the stockade in quick succession, and by month's end all had been released.[63]

How did this come about? Upon his return to San Francisco from Tule Lake, Besig contacted the NCACLU attorney Wayne Mortimer Collins for help. The forty-four-year-old Collins, who was working on the Fred Korematsu case, which challenged the constitutionality of the exclusion order that forced the Nikkei out of their homes, immediately called Robert Cozzens of the WRA office in San Francisco. If the men were not released immediately and unconditionally from the stockade, Collins threatened, he would expose the beatings inflicted on the inmates and the brazen violation by the WRA of the constitutional rights of U.S. citizens. He also threatened to file a habeas corpus lawsuit. These threats led to a meeting that included WRA Director Dillon Myer, Chief Solicitor Philip Glick, Best, and Cozzens. Confronted with Collins's threats, they decided to release all the inmates. When Collins visited

Tule Lake a few days later, he found the stockade and the fence surrounding it demolished. Kurihara followed these events closely. Although he was deeply grateful to Best for treating him humanely at Moab and Leupp, he did not hesitate to criticize the director in this instance. "Mr. Best should have released the men [months earlier]," he said, "when the Army turned over the stockade to the WRA."[64] This opinion reflected the sentiments of his fellow Tuleans. Releasing the stockade inmates would have reduced the turmoil and violence that had long marked life in this segregated camp for dissidents. The eventual demolition of the stockade helped lessen that turmoil. But anxiety and confusion soon returned in response to a new law that allowed Nisei and Kibei-Nisei to renounce their U.S. citizenship.

CHAPTER 8

Renunciation

On July 1, 1944, President Franklin Roosevelt signed Public Law (PL) 405, which amended the Nationality Act of 1940 to allow U.S. citizens living in the United States to renounce their citizenship during wartime. Although not stated explicitly, the law was aimed at dissident Nisei.[1]

As Manzanar Project Director Ralph Merritt remarked of the statute, "This is the first time in the history of a civilized nation that a government has permitted a citizen, during a state of war, to renounce his citizenship." That such an action had never been taken, he said, was due to a general recognition of the influence of "war hysteria." With this law, Merritt believed, "the Government [was] violating its own most sacred principles of citizenship rights."[2]

Officials had several motives for favoring such a law. Some sought to have renunciants exchanged for U.S. citizens detained in Japan. The chairman of the House Immigration and Naturalization Committee, Samuel Dickstein, suggested that the law's provisions be publicized in the camps, to be followed by notices "calling for volunteers to go to Japan in trade for Americans."[3]

In 1939 the State Department had created an office called Special Division to handle the return of U.S. citizens from Europe, and in some cases from German or Italian internment. Once war was declared between the United States and Japan, Special Division coordinated the exchange of citizens stranded in each other's country. After protracted negotiations involving much haggling, two exchanges of American and Japanese nationals occurred, one in June 1942 and another in September 1943. But the U.S. government was generally unsuccessful in enlisting a large number of Nikkei to apply for repatriation or expatriation under this program. Only after the Tule Lake resegregationists began to agitate for a return to Japan did the U.S. government's effort get a fresh impetus. By allowing Americans of Japanese ancestry to renounce their citizenship, advocates of the law believed that the United States would have a ready pool of people to exchange for its citizens stranded in Japan.[4]

In favoring the renunciation law, Attorney General Francis Biddle had a different motive. He knew that challenges to the mass incarceration of Japanese Americans, who were U.S. citizens, were moving through the courts, and he was aware that the Mitsuye Endo case in particular might be successful. In response to the Endo litigation, Biddle—with the support of Best and other WRA officials at Tule Lake—sought a means to release most Nikkei while keeping those he considered troublemakers. Once the latter renounced their citizenship, as he expected they would, they would be sent to the Justice Department internment camp for "enemy aliens" at Santa Fe and later deported to Japan. Some forty years later, Edward Ennis, former director of the Alien Enemy Control Unit, confirmed this planned use of PL 405.[5]

Passage of the renunciation law encouraged the resegregationists. In August they formed the *Sokoku Kenkyu Seinen-dan* (Young Men's Association for the Study of the Mother Country), referred to as *Sokoku.* Most of its leaders were Kibei-Nisei, but about 60 percent of its members were Nisei who had never been to Japan. Its purpose was to prepare its members, who were expected to renounce their U.S. citizenship, for their new life in Japan. To this end its members studied Japanese history, language, culture, and political ideology. *Sokoku* sponsored lectures that emphasized emperor worship and the glorification of Japan. Each morning before dawn, its members participated in morning exercises, with bugles blaring and youths marching, wearing headbands adorned with the symbol of the rising sun. "Even when it rained, even when it snowed," recalled Issei Tom Nagasawa, "they would do Japanese Army exercises." Noboru Shirai remembered, "Most of us were still sound asleep at 5 o'clock in the morning. We were annoyed to be awakened by the yelling, "*wa shoi, wa shoi*" and the blaring of the bugle." A Nisei confided at the time, "A lot of people are against [the activities of the *Sokoku*], but they are afraid to say anything."[6]

Tokio Yamane, one of the leaders of the youth group, recalled, "I proposed a head shave to show others we were truly united in spirit. First it was only a crew-cut head, but it became shorter and shorter until being totally shaved. It was a self-imposed symbol of 'pro-Japan/disloyal' re-segregation since the camp administration did not make our living quarters separate from the 'pro-American/loyal.'"[7]

Kenge Kobayashi, who participated in the morning drill, recalled the social pressure to join. "We had to shave . . . our head," he remembered. "I hated it. I didn't want to be part of it, but everybody else was in it so I just kind of endured it." Others like Sumiko Yamamoto, however, recalled that marching "was fun." Arthur Ogami explained, "[W]hen [we] get in a group like that, we get very enthusiastic and perform." Tom Akashi remembered that he "really enjoyed" the "drilling and marching and [doing] physical exercises. . . . [T]hey ordered the bugles from Sears Roebuck. . . . [T]here was a lot of camaraderie; it felt like I was Japanese. . . . I thought it was great."[8]

While youths took these activities at face value, Kurihara suspected bad intent on the part of the adults who supported the *Sokoku*. "I don't know the true motive behind it," he said. "I don't care to take any interest in it." He continued, "This sounds funny, but they wanted my leadership. But my intention is, if I'm going to do any fighting, I'm going to fight all alone. If anybody is going to get beaten up or killed, then I'll be the only one."[9] While this individualistic approach ran counter to the Japanese idea of group solidarity, Kurihara's memories of Manzanar served as a painful reminder of crowd behavior that could cost the lives of innocent people.

By August 24 Best had received word that his superiors had rejected the idea of resegregation. Robertson favored an immediate public announcement of this rejection, but Best waited a number of days before making it. Not surprisingly, the resegregationists reacted angrily when he did so.[10] In response they began circulating still another petition that professed loyalty to Japan and the desire to move there. With as many as ten thousand signatures, the petition was submitted to the U.S. State Department and the Spanish embassy, which served as the diplomatic intermediary between Japan and the United States during the war. While the number of names on the petition was large, more than half of them were those of minors, a number of whom were infants. In addition, one Nisei noted, "The majority of people signed under intimidation or ignorance."[11]

The truth or falsity of this last assertion cannot be verified, but the advertisement of "10,000 signatures" certainly inflated the strength of the resegregationists, who, despite their effort to attract fellow Nikkei, remained a minority group. Although they had garnered ten thousand names on their petition, their membership in late October was only about two thousand, of which seven hundred fifty were members of the *Sokoku*, the youth group.[12]

By September 1944, the resegregationists had emerged from the underground to become a formal organization. They were also making a concerted effort to convince Nisei to renounce their U.S. citizenship to signify their solidarity with Japan. "My brother and sister renounced their citizenship," Kenge Kobayashi recalled. "I think they were afraid. The [resegregationists] weren't that big of a group, but they were most powerful. . . . [E]verybody was scared of them."[13] Yet the pressure to renounce was inconsistent. While some Nisei spoke of it, others spoke instead of personal, family, and other reasons for renouncing, which I discuss later in this chapter.

The sense of being pressured, however, caused some Nisei to complain. "I want to get out of [Tule Lake]," a young man told Robertson. "[But] I don't want to go to Japan." He added that "many of the boys from Leupp who are supposed to be pro-Japanese" felt the same way. Another woman noted that although "the future was very dark for the Japanese in this country . . . she, personally, had no desire to go . . . to Japan."[14]

Hoshi Dan

In November the resegregationists renamed themselves the *Sokuji Kikoku Hoshi Dan* (Organization to Return Immediately to Serve the Homeland), popularly referred to as *Hoshi Dan*. "They felt that Japan was going to win the war," Hiroshi Kashiwagi remembered of the group, "and that they were Japanese, and they were going to act like Japanese and prepare themselves." At the same time, the young Nisei group, the *Sokoku*, renamed itself the *Hokoku Seinen Dan* (Young Men's Patriotic Organization). Guided by the parent group, this youth group, often referred to as the *Seinen Dan*, emphasized service to the mother country instead of language and cultural study. The young women's group was the *Hokoku Joshi Seinen Dan*. I refer to these three groups collectively as *Hoshi Dan*.[15]

Not everyone who hoped to relocate to Japan was interested in *Seinen Dan* activities. One Nisei remarked, "A lot of people are disgusted at the way they (pressure group) act. . . . My family of five [has] applied already through the Spanish ambassador to go back to Japan. So what more do we need?"[16]

In January 1945, after many *Seinen Dan* leaders had been removed from Tule Lake and membership had declined considerably, the remaining members pressured others to join the group. "Seinen Dan is now going about making people sign up for membership again," one Nisei said. "Those who refuse to sign, they call 'dog.'" Kashiwagi recalled similarly, "[T]hey tried to recruit people, force them to join." Another said, "A week ago my husband met a friend who had a bozo [*bozu*: shaven head] hair cut. 'What! Are you bozo [*bozu*] too?' he asked. 'Sh-h-h,' said the friend. 'This is camouflage—otherwise nobody in my block will talk to me.' When he came home, my husband laughed his head off." In reaction to this pressure, a Nisei said, "The more [*Seinen Dan* leaders] they take out [of Tule Lake] the better."[17]

Others, however, felt no such pressure. In "'Skeleton in the Closet,'" Teruko Kumei writes that former *Seinen Dan* youth group members she interviewed from 1986 to 1995 told her that they were not pressured to join the *Seinen Dan*, nor did they pressure others to join. Other *Seinen Dan* members said the same.[18]

While *Hoshi Dan* members seemed united in their aims, under the surface there was a deep split. According to Tom Akashi, whose father was among the *Hoshi Dan* leaders, one faction led by Reverend Shizue Kai and George Kuratomi favored resegregation but not renunciation, while the other faction led by Kinzo Ernest Wakayama and Zenshiro Tachibana favored both resegregation and renunciation. In the midst of the "struggle" between these groups and the resulting "dissension" within the *Hoshi Dan*, Akashi's father was forced to resign as chair of the leadership group. "Wakayama . . . had about a hundred of these ruffians [fishermen from San Pedro]," recalled Akashi, "and they're tough people." "[T]hey . . . threatened my father." In *Betrayed Trust*, Akashi noted that once Wakayama and Tachibana had taken control of *Hoshi Dan*, they committed the organization to renunciation. He wrote, "I frequently saw Kibei-Nisei leaders intimidate the young Nisei into joining and forcing them into renouncing their citizenship."[19]

Kurihara himself had renounced his citizenship, but he refused to align himself with *Hoshi Dan*. "Just because I don't join their organization," he protested, "they say I'm not loyal [to Japan]. How could they measure my loyalty that way?" Of the group, he said, "They are not leading the residents on the right path or the right way." "They are always saying, 'When we get there.' Whom do they mean? They think they are going to be rewarded [in Japan]. If they think they're going to fool the Japanese officials in Japan, they're [making] a mistake." Of their violence, he declared, "They have carried things too far, knocking in the heads of people who are not for them." He also thought that the Nisei, most of whom were much younger than he, should not be "Japanized." He let it be known that anyone feeling pressured into joining these groups should see him, and his advice would be to stay away from these "trouble-making organizations." He wrote to Best, "It is deplorable to me to see how so many young boys are being misled by these vociferous, glory-seeking, selfish leaders. . . . [A]s I see it, the future of these boys is being ruined." "These groups," he added, "have kept the residents under constant fear and unrest."[20]

Kurihara believed that his open opposition to *Hoshi Dan* made him a target of violence, especially from followers of Wakayama, whom he had known before the war as well as at Manzanar. Kurihara was convinced of this because a friend of his, who had spoken against the activities of the resegregationists, had been beaten along with two other men as they walked home from a meeting one night. To defend himself, Kurihara let it be known that he had written an incriminating denunciation of Wakayama for encouraging force and violence to pressure Nisei to renounce their citizenship and sign the petition for relocation to Japan. Kurihara also revealed that he had entrusted copies of his denunciation to several friends, who promised to give the information to the FBI and Project Director Ray Best if anything untoward happened to him. "[I]f he kills me," Kurihara told Hankey in satisfaction, "I'll speak from the grave." Many knew that Kurihara went out "two nights a week to a class on

Japanese military singing." In case he was attacked on his way to or from class, Kurihara declared, he would attack back. "He opened a drawer of his desk," Hankey recalled of their conversation, "and showed me a curious weapon, a stout club, about six inches long, to which a pipe joint was attached by a leather thong." Fortunately, Kurihara never had to use this weapon.[21]

Kurihara's belief that he had to protect himself was reinforced when one of Wakayama's followers was arrested and tried for knifing the son of a man who had criticized Wakayama. The assailant received a sentence of only ninety days in prison, a leniency that Wakayama and another *Hoshi Dan* leader claimed was due to the weight of their testimonies in court and, implicitly, to their influence in Tule Lake.[22]

Wakayama's enthusiasm for renunciation and relocation to Japan gave Nikkei the impression that he had renounced his own citizenship. In a conversation with Hankey in September, however, he revealed his reluctance to renounce, contending that the renunciation law was unconstitutional and that he did not think that he would be deported. In December 1944, on learning that Wakayama had not renounced his citizenship, a Nisei angrily responded, "Why that dirty son-of-a-gun. I thought he renounced it a long, long time ago."[23]

In her field notes and in *Doing Fieldwork* (with the revealing subtitle, *Warnings and Advice*), Hankey disclosed that she had told the Justice Department's John Burling that Wakayama was dangerous and suggested that Burling "question him about his loyalties in the presence of some of the young *Seinen Dan* officers." More than twenty-five years later, Hankey admitted that passing on this information to Burling had been "very unprofessional." However, caught between professional ethics and issues of life and death, she chose the latter. The anthropologist Dell Hymes wrote, "[A]nthropologists tend to understand and sympathize with the particular peoples they study. When the peoples are in conflict, so may be the sympathies of anthropologists. . . . I know no calculus that does not lead persons of honesty and good will, after serious reflection, to considered judgments that conflict as to where primary duty lies in a given case." "Everyone, including Hankey," Heather Fryer wrote of this episode, "agrees that disclosures from confidential interviews to the Department of Justice violate professional ethics. However, Hankey maintained that she believed that she was protecting Tuleans whose lives were imperiled, which fulfills a higher standard of ethics than that of her academic profession. Whether she saved lives or was complicit in destroying them remains, for the most part, a matter of speculation and the substance of the competing images of Hankey as brave humanitarian, self-serving manipulator, hysterical woman, and incompetent student."[24]

Notwithstanding such ruminations about professional ethics, which express the sometimes-difficult decisions facing researchers, there are two versions of Wakayama's eventual renunciation of his citizenship. According to Wakayama, he was awakened at 3 AM in his barracks apartment when FBI agents arrived with a pistol and told him to sign the renunciation document. He responded that he would do so only "under protest." In the second version, Tule Lake Project Attorney Louis M. Noyes told Hankey that Wakayama signed after John Burling of the Justice Department asked him if he was loyal to Japan, and when Wakayama answered yes, Burling placed the application form in front of him. This occurred in December, more than five months after the renunciation law had taken effect. Perhaps Noyes or Burling wanted Hankey to record this version in her field notes, which they knew she was writing assiduously. Whichever version is accepted, both indicate that Wakayama signed his renunciation application only after it was thrust upon him, a scenario that contrasts notably with his public stance in favor of renunciation and relocation to Japan.[25]

In the dramas played out in Manzanar and Tule Lake, Kurihara and Wakayama found themselves adversaries despite remarkable similarities in their backgrounds and experiences, and personal impressions they made on people who knew them. Both were born in 1895 in Hawai'i. Both served in the medical corps of the U.S. Army during World War I, and both joined the American Legion. Both were incarcerated at Manzanar and then at Tule Lake. Both were bitter over being incarcerated for no other reason than their ethnicity, and both renounced their U.S. citizenship. Finally, both threatened other Nikkei with violence, and both have been portrayed by some as ruthless, by others as heroes.[26]

Unlike Kurihara, however, who had never been to Japan, Wakayama had studied in Tokyo in the late 1930s. Also unlike Kurihara, Wakayama and his wife Toki Wakayama went to court in 1942 to challenge the constitutionality of their incarceration. Due to complications, however, their case was subsequently dropped.[27]

In December 1944 Wakayama was taken to a Department of Justice camp and later deported to Japan. Kurihara, on the other hand, despite having applied for renunciation and having volunteered to leave the United States on the first postwar ship to Japan, remained at Tule Lake under the jurisdiction of the WRA. Kurihara was treated differently because he distanced himself from protestors at Moab and Tule Lake. Wakayama, on the other hand, continued to be in the thick of resistance activities throughout the incarceration period. The reason for Kurihara's change of behavior is reflected in a comment he made to

Hankey, in which he spoke of himself as well as others: "Many have expressed the desire to remain as peacefully as they can in camp until the day of deportation," he told her. "They never forgot the painful incident of Manzanar."[28] Both Kurihara and Wakayama were tragic victims of war and incarceration. Confined behind barbed wire without justification, both became angry and bitter, each in his own way. Unfortunately, at times each of them deflected his anger onto fellow Nikkei instead of the actual perpetrators of the injustices, leaders of the powerful U.S. government.[29]

A Trickle, Then a Rush

Those who decided to renounce their U.S. citizenship had to submit an application to the U.S. Attorney General, attend a hearing on the application, then file a written renunciation for the Attorney General's approval. Among the early renunciants were *Seinen Dan* members who had lost their sense of identity as Americans, largely because of feelings of betrayal by the U.S. government. They saw no hope and no future in America. Despite the uncertainties that awaited the Kibei-Nisei and especially the Nisei, who had never even visited Japan, they were willing to start a new life there.[30]

One Nisei expressed sentiments common among the group: "Why should loyal American citizens be treated as disloyal before any proof of disloyalty was shown? . . . We had worked for and loved our country and then were pushed out, discarded and thrown away. What would a normal person's reaction be? . . . I [renounced] because with everything gone . . . I thought that the only thing that I could do was to go to Japan, though never have I been there." Another Nisei recalled, "I wasn't eager to renounce. . . . Then, people started to talk. . . . You get kind of drawn into it. . . . During camp you get very confused . . . because you're angry about one thing—about being put into camp.[31]

Minoru Kiyota, a Kibei-Nisei who was "equally repelled" by both *Seinen Dan* activities and the government's "oppressive measures," stated, "It was the government of the United States that threw me into this place. Why should I want to be a citizen of a country like that? . . . Renunciation was . . . the last act of defiance available to human beings who found themselves in an intolerable situation."[32]

This sense of betrayal was reflected in the "autobiography" Kurihara penned just before departing for Japan. In it he wrote that his decision to renounce dated "back to the day when General DeWitt ordered evacuation." "It was confirmed," he continued, "when he flatly refused to listen even to the voices of the former World War Veterans and it was doubly confirmed when I entered Manzanar. We who already had proven our loyalty by serving in the last world war should have been spared. The veterans asked for special consideration but their requests were denied. . . . I expected that at least the Nisei would be allowed to remain. But to General DeWitt, we were all alike. 'A Jap's a Jap, always a Jap.' . . . My decision to renounce my citizenship there and then was definite and absolute."[33] Since at that time renunciation was not possible while a person was on U.S. soil, Kurihara meant that his anger at the government in early 1942 caused him to reject the idea of a future life for himself in the United States.

What caused Kurihara—someone who had lived all of his fifty years in the country of his birth—to decide to move to another country, one that he had not been to before, that had little experience in democracy, that had been ruled by militarists, and that was in a state of devastation after the war? Evidence suggests that he had been ridden with guilt over the death in Manzanar of two innocent young men, bystanders who were shot by sentries standing on guard before the large crowd that had been protesting loudly and angrily. Kurihara had riled the Nikkei with his incendiary speeches that threatened death to those suspected of reporting others to the FBI. In rousing the crowd, he had not expected innocent people to be killed. After this episode, he stopped resisting camp authorities, stopped making speeches, kept to himself, and began serious, systematic study of the Japanese language to prepare for life in Japan. The tragic death of the two men profoundly affected him, leaving him with a bitterness that reinforced his earlier belief that a future life for him in America was not an option.

On November 1, 1943, before the renunciation law was passed and while he was confined at the Leupp Isolation Center, he applied for expatriation. Because this was after the *Gripsholm*—the Swedish ship carrying repatriates—had made its second and final exchange of Japanese and American nationals during the war, the Department of Justice (DOJ) took no action on Kurihara's application. A year later, however, five months after the renunciation law was passed and eight days after Kurihara had completed his "Application for Permission to Renounce United States Nationality," the DOJ set in motion the procedure for his departure. After requesting an FBI report on him, and after the required formal hearing, on March 22, 1945 the Attorney General's office gave written approval on his request for renunciation. With this approval, Kurihara was no longer a U.S. citizen.[34]

Kurihara's actions notwithstanding, and despite efforts by *Seinen Dan* members to convince Nisei to renounce their citizenship, only about one hundred submitted applications in the months following the legalization of renunciation. Most of those who renounced were Kibei-Nisei; Kurihara was one of the few Nisei. Then, in mid-December, the government issued two directives that affected the subsequent course of events. First, the WRA announced its decision to close all of its camps within a year. Second, the Western Defense

Command canceled its order excluding Nikkei from the West Coast. In the wake of these changes, Tuleans learned that most of them would be able to resettle anywhere in the country. The exceptions were "those who . . . definitely indicated that they [were] not loyal to the U.S. or [those] considered potentially dangerous to military security." It was not *Hoshi Dan* pressure, as some scholars have believed, but the announcement of these exceptions to unrestricted resettlement that led to a virtual stampede toward renunciation.[35]

Hankey has been mistakenly pointed to as the cause for the exaggerated emphasis on *Hoshi Dan* as the source of the mass renunciation. To the contrary, according to Hankey's own notes, its influence had waned by December 1944, before the on-rush of renunciations. Instead, Hankey describes the heightened anxiety and increase in applications for renunciation that followed the WRA announcement that Tule Lake would be closed.[36]

When people learned of the directives, they panicked. "They [said], 'Wait a minute. We don't want to go out. . . . We want to stay in the security of the camp,'" recalled Tom Akashi. "So all of a sudden, there was a whole avalanche of people renouncing their citizenship. . . . [They said], 'Hey, if we go outside, where are we going? No home, no job, no skills, what are we going to do?'" Moreover, rumor was that Nikkei were getting "shot at" and "houses [were] burned. . . . [T]hey were scared."[37]

"We wouldn't mind going back to San Francisco if we had everything as when we left," a young Nisei woman said in a somewhat different vein. "But we've lost everything." Another stated, "After kicking me around, they can't kick me out with 25 dollars and train fare and say, 'Find yourself a job.'" An old-Tulean Nisei explained his renunciation: "I've got six children and my wife and my father and mother. . . . If they want me to go out the least they can do is give me some kind of set up. . . . I've lost everything. It's somewhere in the U.S. That's where I lost it."[38]

Besides having no means of support outside the camp, Tuleans believed that danger awaited them were they to leave. "We are from Hood River and that was a dangerous place," explained N. K. "My wife was afraid to go there if we were made to leave. She felt that some way she must fix things so the family could stay here together and her 'fixing' was to renounce." A young woman told a U.S. Army interviewer, "What do you want us to do, go back to California and get filled [with] lead?" Her fears were based on good reason. On the day before she posed that question, the *San Francisco Examiner* reported a California Congressman as saying that the return of Nikkei to the West Coast would bring "wholesale bloodshed and violence." A day later the JACL newspaper *Pacific Citizen* reported that three buildings "owned or formerly occupied by persons of Japanese ancestry" had burned in Placer County, California. Rumors at Tule

Lake abounded: Kurihara reported that "[one was] being circulated that five Japanese were killed in Fresno or Stockton, [California]." He explained, "The true motive behind the renunciation of citizenship is that they don't want to get out. They want to remain in camp for the remainder of the war."[39] Another cause for worry was that young men would be drafted into the military. As a young Nisei woman hinted, "You know why the boys are renouncing." Another said it more bluntly: "Some Nisei boys are renouncing because they definitely refuse to go into the Army."[40]

Of major concern to Nikkei was family unity. "Parents want their sons and daughters to renounce so that they can go to Japan with them," explained Kurihara. Renunciant Arthur Ogami stated, "I did what my parents wanted me to do." Hiroshi Kashiwagi recalled, "We had decided as a family. . . . My mother wanted us all to be together. . . . I was going to let the whole thing ride, but then . . . everyone else around us [was] doing it and so we went through that and had a hearing." Aster Kikuye Mayetani's husband, an Issei, applied for repatriation because he was worried about his aging parents in Hiroshima. Believing that she had to renounce her citizenship in order to remain with her husband, and "having no concept of the seriousness of the act, she . . . signed the [renunciation] papers." Sarah Sato, a Sansei, third-generation Japanese American, renounced in order to keep her parents together. Her Nisei father wanted to go to Japan to take care of his father, who was in Japan without any means of support. Sato's mother resisted going to Japan, but when Sarah agreed to accompany them, her mother agreed to go. "So when people say only 'no-nos' . . . renounced," Sarah recalled, "that's not true."[41]

Family concerns could force an "agonizing decision" to renounce. Taeko Okamura's mother was a Nisei whose four children had been visiting their grandparents in Japan when war broke out. When Hiroshima was bombed, she and her husband "were frantic" about their children stranded in Japan, with whom they had had no contact since the outbreak of war. Since it would have been otherwise impossible to travel immediately to Japan as an independent civilian, Okamura's mother felt that her only option was to renounce her U.S. citizenship in order to see if her children and parents-in-law were alive.[42]

As Tuleans anxiously awaited responses to their requests for renunciation, a rumor spread in February that membership in *Seinen Dan* was the only way to guarantee that applications for renunciation would be accepted. "[The rumor] is going over like a wildfire," noted Kurihara. "Those who were strongly opposed to the *[Seinen] Dan* are [now] trying everything to get in it." "[P]arents are advising their sons to join the *[Seinen] Dan* to avoid being drafted." "The membership is growing by leaps and bounds." Kurihara had no patience for those who believed the rumor. "Several people have come around to see me and ask for advice," he told Hankey. "I gave them hell for not being able to judge the situation for themselves. Because it is nothing but outright lies which ordinary common sense could tell. I told them, 'You're like a bunch of sheep.'"[43]

To dispel the rumor, Project Attorney Louis Noyes placed an announcement in the camp newspaper, the *Newell Star.* "The Japanese section," a relieved Nisei said, "stated that '99 percent of the renunciations in Tule Lake will be accepted, and that there is no worry about the draft.'" Another Nisei reported, "The statement . . . certainly clarified many . . . points that have been bothering the [Nikkei] for weeks. . . . Since publication of the statement, many malicious rumors have mysteriously disappeared, especially the drafting for military service."[44]

In the midst of this turmoil, the Justice Department began removing dissident leaders from Tule Lake. On December 27, 1944, seventy *Hoshi Dan* leaders were removed abruptly to a Department of Justice camp for enemy aliens at Santa Fe, New Mexico. Then on January 26, and again in February and March, more leaders were taken to Santa Fe or to another Justice Department camp at Fort Lincoln, North Dakota. During these months, 1,086 active dissidents were removed. With most of the leadership gone, the effectiveness of these organizations largely dissipated.[45]

Change of Mind

Barbara Takei argues that the Western Defense Command (WDC) deliberately initiated the renunciation rush. The WDC, she states, had a secret list of 4,963 Japanese Americans, including 3,066 Tuleans, whom it wanted to keep confined, but it knew that it had no legal basis for doing so. The flood of applications for renunciation solved the WDC's problem.[46]

Beginning in late December 1944 and continuing for two-and-a-half months thereafter, army representatives took applications and held perfunctory hearings for four hundred to five hundred Tuleans a day. By mid-March 1945, Kurihara and well over fifty-four hundred others—seven of every ten citizen Tuleans who were eighteen years or older—received hearings. In all, 5,725 Nisei and Kibei-Nisei renounced their citizenship, of which 128 were in camps other than Tule Lake. This meant that about 10 percent of Nisei and Kibei-Nisei in all the concentration camps renounced their citizenship.[47]

Shortly after renouncing, however, misgivings began. "Soon after we had signed the papers we knew it was a mistake," one Nisei recalled. "But I think we were under a lot of group pressure and we weren't thinking straight."[48] As these second thoughts mounted, on July 14, 1945, President Harry Truman issued Proclamation 2655. Based on the Alien Enemy Act of 1798, the proclamation allowed the Attorney General during wartime to deport alien enemies considered dangerous to public safety. This alarmed many renunciants, who had not thought seriously about deportation. Many wrote letters to the Justice Department, pleading to have their renunciations voided. Kurihara was not among them. His decision to renounce had been made earlier, and apparently he never wavered.[49]

After Hiroshima and Nagasaki were bombed and Japan lost the war, renunciants intensified their effort to have their renunciations rescinded. "[S]pending these long years in camp with all kinds of rumors," wrote Yoshiko Matsuura to Director of the Alien Enemy Control Unit Edward Ennis, "I lost all sense of reality . . . and foolishly renounced my citizenship. . . . I honestly believe that it is very un-American to accept one's application for renunciation after placing a good law-abiding citizen into a wired fence by force." In responses to her, to her husband, and to the thousands of others who wrote such letters, Ennis stated in form letters, "Under the law, the Attorney General has no authority whatsoever to permit you to reconsider your action. . . . Immediately upon the approval . . . of your renunciation, you ceased to be a United States national."[50]

Ennis's form letters prompted renunciants and their supporters to form the Tule Lake Defense Committee, through which they turned to the Northern California ACLU Director Ernest Besig, who in turn asked the indefatigable Wayne Mortimer Collins for help. Collins's entrance into the effort came none too soon. Two days before the first deportation date of November 15, 1945, Collins filed two habeas corpus suits, *Abo v. Williams* and *Furuya v. Williams*, in federal court, requesting the court to free renunicants from detention and prevent their deportation. Because of their similarity, the two cases were later combined. Collins also filed two equity suits, *Abo v. Clark* and *Furuya v. Clark*, which sought to cancel the renunciations; these cases were likewise combined.[51]

In June 1947, nineteen months after the suits were filed, Judge Louis Goodman of the U.S. District Court of San Francisco decided the habeas corpus cases by freeing all renunciants and declaring that none of them could be deported involuntarily. The Department of Justice filed an appeal; it took three-and-a-half years before the Ninth Circuit Court of Appeals handed down its verdict, essentially reversing Goodman's decision and returning the cases to the district court for separate proceedings for each renunciant. Despite this setback, Hiroshi Kashiwagi exulted, "Wayne Collins . . . saved us [when] we were so close to being deported." When the peace treaty of 1952 between the United States and Japan ended the threat of deportation, Collins placed his energies on the issue of renunciation.[52]

In the equity case *Abo v. Clark*, Collins's basic argument was that the renunciations were invalid because when the Nikkei made them, they were confined in the camps and thus suffered from government duress—forced removal from their homes and jobs and incarceration for no reason other than their ethnicity. In addition, Collins argued, government officials had done nothing to stop

Hoshi Dan members from pressuring and even coercing Nisei to renounce their citizenship. Yet, Collins argued, even members of the *Hoshi Dan* were victims of duress. In April 1948 Judge Goodman ruled on the equity suits, agreeing with Collins that government duress had led to the renunciations, but adding other forms of duress: pressure and threats from resegregationists, pressure from parents to keep families together, fear of leaving Tule Lake with no resources to support themselves, and the desire of young men to avoid the draft.[53]

Wary of possible legal consequences of Collins's emphasis on government duress as the cause for renunciation, the ACLU national board and its director Roger Baldwin, friends and sympathizers of the Roosevelt administration, sought to shield the government from charges that it had been responsible for the renunciations. Toward that end, Baldwin convinced Abraham Wirin of the Southern California ACLU to represent three renunciants who claimed duress from other Nikkei rather than from the government. The victory of the renunciants in this case, *Acheson v. Murakami*, in the Ninth Circuit Court of Appeals, threw monkey wrenches into two aspects of Collins's renunciation efforts. First, the Appeals Court accepted the charge that duress from pro-Japan pressure groups at Tule Lake was responsible for the litigants' renunciation. This placed in jeopardy Collins's charge that government duress was the primary cause of renunciation and endangered the efforts of *Seinen Dan* renunciants to regain their citizenship. Second, the *Murakami* ruling treated each of the three renunciants separately, weakening Collins's efforts to group all renunciants in a single case. Sure enough, when the Ninth Circuit Court of Appeals decided Collins's mass equity case in 1950, it returned the case to the District Court for individual hearings. As a result, Collins was required to file thousands of individual cases.[54]

To avoid the drawn out and cumbersome process of hearing so many cases, the Attorney General's office and Collins negotiated an administrative procedure in which renunciants would file individual affidavits requesting restoration of citizenship on a case-by-case basis. While less cumbersome than the judicial alternative, this in itself proved to be a protracted process. Moreover, one of the stipulations required by the Department of Justice was that applicants state that they renounced because of fear and coercion from fellow Nikkei.[55]

Under this process, a total of 5,409 Nisei, including 1,143 who had already expatriated to Japan, eventually sought to restore their citizenship. Most of them succeeded, but only after years of effort, many cases extending for more than a decade.[56] Collins persevered with unflagging commitment to the cause. He sent to the renunciants detailed memoranda on what was required of them in the affidavits, prodded them when they failed to send him the necessary information, and encouraged them when they were despondent.[57] Tex Nakamura and other assistants who were active with the Tule Lake Defense Committee visited renunciants in the United States and in Japan to help them navigate the cumbersome procedures. All who requested assistance received it, even if they could not or would not pay the necessary legal fees.[58]

When Collins concluded his efforts in 1968, twenty-three years after he had begun, only forty to fifty renunciants were unable to have their citizenship restored. Masaru Hashimoto was one of them. Records of his activities as a *Hoshi Dan* leader at Tule Lake, he believed, had led the Department of Justice to reject his application.[59]

In discussing Nikkei actions concerning renunciation, Mae M. Ngai has argued that dual loyalties—"a set of allegiances that sustained commitment to life in America alongside affective and cultural ties, even patriotic sympathies, with Japan"—should be understandable. Also understandable are their responses to the hostility and threat of danger beyond the barbed wire enclosure. Even at the nadir of their despair over incarceration, most Nikkei were pragmatic and non-ideological. By July 1945 they realized that Japan was losing the war, and the bombing of Hiroshima and Nagasaki hit them with the dire consequences of renunciation and relocation to Japan. In behaving out of "self-interest," Ngai has noted, "they were no different from most ordinary people, who are concerned more with their individual and family's well-being than with the interests of the nation-state."[60]

Kurihara would have had none of that kind of reasoning. In the months before it was clear to incarcerated Nikkei that Japan was going to lose the war, he refused to sympathize with their ambivalence as they wrestled with the consequences of renouncing. He was especially critical of those who could not make up their minds. "The [I]ssei are really on the fence," he said. "If it looks as if Japan is going to win—they jump to Japan. If it looks as though things will go the other way, they will jump the other way. . . . Many [I]ssei and families are forcing their sons to join the *[Seinen] Dan* merely to escape the draft. I told them, when they get back to Japan they will use some means to keep their sons out of the Japanese Army. They were very surprised to hear me say that." "These persons who will change their minds," he concluded, "are no good to either country. . . . It's disgraceful. It makes me ashamed of the Japanese race."[61]

Kurihara was among the no more than three hundred or so renunciants who rejected the idea of regaining their U.S. citizenship. Hidekazu Tamura, a former leader of *Seinen Dan*, recalled that an attorney assisting Collins urged him to join those who wanted to regain their citizenship, but he refused. So did Tokio Yamane, who had been brutally beaten by Tule Lake security officers and then imprisoned in the stockade for a year for a crime he did not commit. Like Kurihara, Yamane turned from identifying as an American to identifying as a Japanese. "I had . . . made up my mind . . . in Tule Lake [after being beaten for no cause] to live as a Japanese citizen," he explained. Consequently he said "no" when the U.S. embassy contacted him in Japan in 1951 when the occupation ended, about applying to restore his citizenship, and he said "no" again in 1954, when "two Japanese American Nisei working for Mr. Wayne Collins" contacted him. Kurihara, having also moved to Japan, likewise refused to apply to restore his citizenship. Perhaps his sense of pride prevented him making the request. As Francis Frederick, Moab's security officer, had noted over a decade earlier, Kurihara was "very proud and for this reason [did not] ask favors." Kurihara would have agreed with Frank Ego, who said it this way in 1955, when a member from Collins's team asked Ego if he wanted to request restoration of his citizenship: "No way. I'm waiting [for] the government to give it to me automatically."[62]

Had Kurihara applied to have his citizenship restored, would he have been successful? Even some of the *Seinen Dan* leaders at Tule Lake, after initial difficulties, were able to regain their U.S. citizenship.[63] Although FBI and WRA officials at Manzanar had considered Kurihara a troublemaker, his behavior changed after the Manzanar revolt such that at Moab, Leupp, and Tule Lake, WRA officials regarded him as a model of cooperation and restraint. Nevertheless the odds were stacked against Kurihara. Department of Justice officials were well acquainted with his case. In a September 1956 memo from Enoch Ellison, Chief of the Japanese Claims Section, to George Cochran Doub, Assistant Attorney General, Ellison wrote, Kurihara "would be among the last to whom I would extend administrative relief [to allow restoration of U.S. citizenship]." As if Kurihara's personality should be grounds for poor citizenship, Ellison wrote, "[H]e was the kind of man who had to take sides fervently and vigorously." Ellison acknowledged indirectly the U.S. government's role in prohibiting the Nikkei from full participation in the larger society. At the same time, he ignored its responsibility in provoking Kurihara's behavior at Manzanar. "Upon being denied the opportunity to be an actively patriotic American," Ellison wrote, Kurihara "became all Japanese and openly promoted physical violence toward our citizens of Japanese ancestry who actively counseled other evacuees to hold fast in their loyalty to the United States." Following the official government stance of refusing to fault itself as the cause for Nisei renunciation, Ellison continued, "I know of no legal principle that would permit us to treat simple embitterment, involving no mistake or fear, as a coercive influence sufficient to relieve [a person] of the consequences of his act." Ellison concluded with satisfaction, "So far as we know he remains content with his choice and would not accept United States citizenship now if it were offered to him." Attached to Ellison's memo were documents on five Nisei renunciants who named Kurihara as one of those who "coerced or otherwise influenced" their decision to renounce their citizenship. Also attached was a copy of a memo that quoted incendiary statements that Kurihara had made to FBI agents several months after the Manzanar revolt. According to the FBI, Kurihara had stated, "I have done everything that I could to help Japan. . . . I want Japan to win the war and I will do anything or commit any act which would help Japan attain this end. . . . I would willingly fight in the Japanese Army although I would never again fight for the United States." Doub responded that he agreed with Ellison's assessment of Kurihara.[64]

Whatever their ultimate decision would have been, Kurihara never put Justice Department officials in a position to have to decide whether or not to restore his citizenship. For Kurihara, making the request would have meant disavowing what he stood for and what he had said, done, and written about the incarceration. But had Kurihara applied, the U.S. government would probably have said no, as Ellison's assessment indicated. For Kurihara this would have been another humiliation added to the humiliation of having to apply in the first place. Conversely, a yes response would have been equally unacceptable to Kurihara because of the implications of the response, that despite all the trouble he had caused, a kind-hearted U.S. government would agree to restore his citizenship. This response would have enabled the government to pose as his generous benefactor, negating Kurihara's position that it was anything but generous, was in fact a blatant violator of its professed principles. Thus, through the remaining years of his life, Kurihara never requested restoration of his citizenship and therefore remained a renunciant, a noncitizen, an alien.

If Kurihara had had any doubts about his decision to renounce his citizenship, he never mentioned them. While Nisei and Kibei-Nisei Tuleans had been swept up in the rush to renounce their citizenship and then to rescind their renunciations, Kurihara had remained on the sidelines, steadfast in his decision and impatient with the quandary in which others found themselves. Perhaps being unmarried and without dependents made it easier for him than for many others to make his decision to renounce, to stick to it, and to volunteer to depart on the first available transport to Japan.

While some scholars have claimed that the renunciation law was repealed, as of this writing, the law still stands. A provision was added to it in September 1961, after Collins and his team had helped Nisei renunciants regain their citizenship; the provision allows for the regaining of one's citizenship if it can be shown "by a preponderance of the evidence" that renunciation was not voluntary. In this way Collins's efforts helped not only the Nisei renunciants of World War II but also future generations of citizens who might unwittingly renounce their citizenship and later attempt to rescind their action.[65]

CHAPTER 9

Japan

Kurihara's refusal to seek restoration of his citizenship did not mean that he was enthusiastic about the idea of living in Japan. He believed that he understood the daunting implications of doing so. Pointing out to Hankey his frankness and outspoken ways, he sensed that such forthrightness might spell trouble for him in Japan. "[I]f I weren't in love with Japan I wouldn't criticize her," he said. "Yet if I did [it publicly in Japan], I should be thrown in jail."[1] Such were the prospects of his new life, after years of senseless incarceration in America!

This anticipated loss of personal freedom, his lack of fluency in Japanese, and the anxiety of adjusting to radical cultural reorientation at the age of fifty gave Kurihara pause about his decision to leave the country of his birth. At a pre-departure orientation meeting called by WRA officials, a staff member noticed a "doleful" Kurihara. In order "to distract" him, the staff person asked why Kurihara, who had been designated leader of this departing group, "was not speaking to the crowd, or interpreting for them." Kurihara responded "disconsolately that every time he spoke Japanese he 'put his foot in [his mouth].' He said that he believed it would take several more years, perhaps as many as ten, before he could make himself well enough understood in Japan to gain respect there."[2]

Despite these misgivings, Kurihara remained determined to leave the United States. He had asked to be on the first postwar transport to Japan, and his request had been granted. "It is my sincere desire to get over there as soon as possible to help rebuild Japan politically and economically," he wrote Dorothy Thomas on the eve of his departure. "The American Democracy with which I was infused in my childhood is still unshaken. My life is dedicated to Japan with Democracy my goal."[3]

It was an idealized and lofty aspiration. He needed only to look at the United States to know that achieving the ideals of democracy was no easy task. As he had said at his renunciation hearing ten months before his departure, "Until [the removal order and the ensuing incarceration,] I tried to be a good American. . . . [B]ut when the Government will discriminate [against] you, and even being a veteran, throw you in camp, then I would ask you, how would you feel? . . . I have come to realize there is no such thing as democracy in the United States with the exception for the white people."[4]

He may have truly believed that he would participate actively in the building of a democratic Japan, but his fifty years in the United States failed utterly to prepare him for the reality and complexity of life in postwar Japan. He found, stunningly, that he lacked the resources necessary to contribute to the kind of movement toward democracy in which he had naively believed he would participate. American-style democracy, he learned, could not be transplanted in Japan. But all that was in the future as he prepared to embark for Japan. On a picture postcard "yellowed with age," he sent Best a poem he had composed, and which reached the Tule Lake Project Director on the day of Kurihara's departure:

> Let's not say goodby bon Ami
> 'Twas but yesterday we just but met
> Let us say au revoir bon Ami
> For tomorrow we again will meet.
> 'Tis true the land I've sworn to build
> Is far across the great divide
> However wide it's just a leap
> So far but so near, We'll always be.[5]

On November 25, 1945, the day of his group's departure, Kurihara approached some of his traveling companions. Knowing that he had more money than most in his group, he "peeled off bills from a roll he was carrying and gave cash" to those "who did not have any." The overcast, rainy day in Seattle did nothing to brighten their spirits, as Kurihara and the other fifteen hundred Nikkei—423 of them from Tule Lake, the others from Department of Justice camps—boarded the USS *Randall.* Most of those departing were single men, mainly Kibei-Nisei, plus some Issei. Kurihara was the only adult Nisei. In the next few months, two more transports would follow, making a total of about seven thousand Nikkei, a fifth of them renunciants, who left for Japan soon after the end of the war.[6]

Placed in steerage that held "rows upon rows of bunks," the Nikkei were "packed like sardines," recalled Takeo Okamura of the ship's facilities. "Just about everyone got seasick." Of the journey, Arthur Ogami remembered, "At high seas it was pretty rough. . . . [T]he bow would come up at least fifty-six feet and go down sixty feet."[7] After two weeks at sea, on December 8, 1945, Kurihara and the others arrived at the port of Uraga, in Tokyo Bay. A multitude of U.S. and Japanese ships greeted the passengers. A U.S. bomber hovered overhead. The Japanese battleships were "anchored without flags or cannons," noted Tokio Yamane, "and [we saw] submarines made of bamboo trees. The Japanese defeat was more than clear to everybody on board."[8]

Landing transports took the Nikkei to shore, where they were trucked to a nearby repatriation center. Reaching the "stench-ridden" and "filthy" room confronting him, Robert Tsuida lamented, "This place is terrible! Why can't the American army disinfect these buildings? . . . We never thought we were coming back to anything as bad as this." Tom Akashi was similarly appalled. "Everywhere we looked we saw . . . filth [and] death," he recalled. "People were . . . begging, stealing, salvaging and fighting for food and a place to stay." "[T]alk about misery and dirtiness[!]. . . . For a while, we were elated because they fed us what we thought was red rice," which was "supposed to be good luck, special. . . . But it was korian . . . hard beans. Everybody got diarrhea. . . . It was just terrible. . . . And . . . you see around you . . . these families, the repatriate families huddled together. It's cold, no fire, no warmth, no food. . . . It was a dismal situation." Tad Yamakido called it "chaos." "There was no sanitation," he said. "The bathrooms were holes in the ground and overflowing. The food was horrible."[9]

To make matters worse in a country literally devastated by war, in addition to the relative trickle of Nikkei from the United States, a veritable flood of hundreds of thousands of civilians and soldiers were returning to Japan—from China, Manchuria, Korea, Formosa (Taiwan), and throughout Southeast Asia, as well as islands scattered over half of the Pacific Ocean. These were among the 6.5 million Japanese in Asia and the Pacific at the end of the war, of which almost half were civilians, including women and children. The Nikkei were shocked to see bodies of repatriated dead children. The bodies were lying "on the ground," recalled Tokio Yamane, "naked, and their bellies were swelled as a result of malnutrition." "If I had [had] a chance," noted Mitsuo Aoyama, who was nineteen years old when he arrived with his family, "I would have been on the first ship back to the States." Tom Yoshiyama voiced similar sentiments to a reporter roaming the docks writing stories for the Los Angeles ethnic newspaper, *Rocky Shimpō*.[10]

In these wretched conditions, Kurihara lost most of his possessions. Before leaving the United States, he had "bought lots of bed sheets" because "he knew they didn't have that in Japan," Ueno recalled. Kurihara had also brought with him a number of other goods. But in the "temporary detention camp, he lost everything. The people were so hungry and stole them."[11]

A few months after Kurihara and the Nikkei traveling with him had arrived in Tokyo Bay, Raymond Best (still at Tule Lake) received a report on the dismal conditions in Japan. "Best told me," Ueno remembered, "'Look at this report. Children had one rice bowl and sour pickle. They're miserable out there. You don't want to expose your children to that.'" Like Kurihara, Ueno had renounced his citizenship with the intention of living in Japan. Best's advice, however, made Ueno recall a friend of his who had renounced his citizenship and was sent to the INS internment camp in North Dakota. Of the man's departure from Tule Lake, Ueno said, "It was miserable. His wife had just miscarried and was in the hospital. He had three children, one only a year old." Ueno and his wife took care of the youngest child until the child's mother regained her strength. These thoughts, together with more information on renunciants who had arrived in Japan, led Ueno to change his mind about leaving the United States.[12]

Unlike Ueno, those who were already in Japan could not change their minds. Furthermore, once in Japan, their first concern was to find their families in their home towns and villages. As soon as transportation was available, they boarded trains bound for their home prefectures. "We were packed like sardines," recalled James Nakamura, whose trip with his family to their home prefecture took two days. "It was really, really bad. [The train] was shaking back and forth, and you were standing all the way. You couldn't sleep or anything." Taeko Okamura recalled, "The train was so crowded that one could not get up to even use the bathroom." Sarah Sato noted, "When the train stopped at the stations, people . . . jump[ed] out the windows and [did] their duty and jump[ed] back." "And every time the train made a stop at a station," Okamura said, "there were Japanese soldiers pounding on the windows with their shoes to let them in. These soldiers had no way of getting home since the Japanese railway system was not in operation at that time. Our train was run by the Occupation Forces."[13]

As the trains took them to their destinations, the Nikkei passed devastation upon devastation. Most of the major cities had been fire bombed into "urban rubble." Allied bombs had destroyed from a fourth to a third of Japan's wealth. Compared to prewar levels, living standards had fallen 65 percent in rural areas, and 35 percent in cities. As many as nine million people were homeless.[14]

Kurihara's train took him southwestward to his family's home in the village of Ōshima in Yamaguchi prefecture. There he stayed temporarily with his older sister Kawayo Kawamoto and her husband and children. His sister's family had moved to Japan in 1920, shortly after Kurihara's parents had returned there. As mentioned earlier, Kurihara's father had died upon reaching Japan in 1919, and Kurihara's mother had died in the 1930s. Kurihara saw at once how dire life was for the Kawamotos. There was little food available. Kurihara's sister did her best to find vegetables for her younger brother, for which he was very thankful.[15]

Kurihara was more fortunate than most expatriates and repatriates. As Taeko Okamura, recalled, "We were not welcomed. We were scornfully asked, 'Why did you come here?'" Okamura, who was a young girl when she went with her family to Japan, remembered, "I broke out with boils all over the palms of both my hands. The doctor said it was malnutrition." Grace Asakura, who was twenty-five when she went to Japan with her family, said that life there was "miserable." "We [had] had no idea that living conditions in Japan were so backwards. And relatives, they really were not happy to see us. . . . You see, they were living on our property." Ben Ogami recalled, "They didn't want us. . . . [M]ore mouths to feed. . . . There was a lot of animosity."[16]

"My uncle initially welcomed us," Tom Akashi remembered, "but then that lasted about, maybe two days. . . . [H]e fed us one time, rice, but then he said, 'Fend for yourself.' You know, he had his own family to take care of," and "[we had] a family of eight to feed. . . . But he was good enough to give us [a] place [to stay]. . . . We had to sell our clothes, whatever, on the black market . . . to feed ourselves. . . . [W]e were considered Americans, so we . . . couldn't get what they call *haikyuu,* which is rations . . . that the army had."[17]

Kurihara had been correct at Moab and Tule Lake to concern himself about his lack of fluency in Japanese. Tom Akashi recalled dialect differences he encountered on his way to his family village. "[T]hey [didn't] understand us, when we asked for directions. . . . [W]e'd catch bits of words, but we really [didn't] know what they were saying." Even in their home prefecture, the spoken Japanese of Nikkei sounded strange, even to their relatives. Sumiko Yamamoto "thought [she] was speaking good Japanese," and felt "insulted" when her cousin laughed at her and said, "'Your Japanese is funny.'"[18]

Language was not the only problem. "[People] gave us a strange look because we were dressed differently," Akashi recalled. "You know, our American clothes had color, and they . . . had tattered clothing. . . . [S]ome of 'em said, '*Keto.*' You know, *keto*, 'white man.' . . . They . . . thought we were Americans. Not Japanese Americans."[19]

While Nikkei adjustment to their new cultural environment proved difficult at best, that difficulty paled when compared with the physical destruction, abject poverty, and emotional trauma they confronted. "[E]xhausted, dispirited," "bewildered," and starving, the people of Japan did what they could to cope with the devastation that bore down on them. With poverty pervasive, the homeless begged in the streets and found shelter in the subways. And with occupation forces everywhere, prostitution flourished.[20]

"Food was scarce," recalled James Nakamura. "You didn't have any rice at all unless you were a farmer. All the people in the city were selling their kimonos, stuff like that, or bartering to get rice. It was real rough." In their desperation, city dwellers roamed the countryside to trade their cherished kimonos, jewelry, and other valuables for rice and other basic foods. Black markets flourished, with staples such as rice selling for thirty times more than the official price set by occupation authorities.[21]

Working for the Occupation

Realizing that he could not stay with his sister and her family, Kurihara sought a job in the city of Sasebo in Nagasaki prefecture, on the southern island of Kyushu. There he found work with the U.S. military, which was under the command of General Douglas MacArthur, head of the occupation forces as Supreme Commander of the Allied Powers (SCAP). The absurdity of this situation would not have been lost on Kurihara. After having rejected the United States, the country that had rejected him, he found himself not only among Americans again, but working for the very government that had only recently imprisoned him and other Nikkei for ostensibly threatening the nation's security.[22]

As one of the more than fourteen hundred renunciants in Japan after the war, Kurihara was far from unique in his newfound employment. The occupation forces were desperately in need of bilingual and bicultural personnel, not only translators and interpreters, but also those who could explain each culture to those of the other. During the entire occupation period, from August 1945 to April 1952, the U.S. Army recruited as many as six thousand Nisei and Kibei-Nisei from the U.S. west coast and Hawai'i. Additionally, they employed Nisei and Kibei-Nisei civilians, some from the United States, but most from those who had been living in Japan before and during the war, and many like Kurihara who had only recently renounced their U.S. citizenship. In all, a total of almost ten thousand Nisei and Kibei-Nisei—soldiers and civilians—worked at some point for the U.S. military during the occupation.[23]

In their need for translators and interpreters, U.S. Army officers were waiting at the pier when each transport carrying repatriates and expatriates arrived. Tokio Yamane and other renunciants were approached as soon as they disembarked. Yamane recalled that a high-ranking officer told them, "We need your help here. Your bilingual ability is indispensable for rebuilding Japan." At first, Yamane, still smarting from his bitter memories of torture at Tule Lake, refused. But when a Japanese government official urged him to respond positively to the American request, explaining that doing so would help the Japanese, Yamane consented.[24]

Others were recruited at the repatriation center, where military personnel roamed the area. While soldiers sought to buy dollars at inflated rates, officers searched for bilingual speakers. The U.S. Army "needed interpreters," Mitsuo Aoyama noted, and he needed a job. Within a few weeks, he found himself working for the Military Railway Service alongside other Nisei renunciants.[25]

Both William and Grace Asakura found jobs as translators in Fukuoka. "We got jobs with the military," Grace remembered. "They were all over Japan." The couple worked for the Allied forces until they regained their citizenship and returned to the United States. Osamu Hasegawa and his brother, who had joined the *Seinen Dan* and subsequently renounced their U.S. citizenship, found jobs as translators at the Imperial Hotel, where officers of the occupation forces lived. They commuted daily for over an hour from Kamakura to Tokyo and then another hour back to Kamakura on the Yokosuka Line. "Everything was disorganized," Hasegawa recalled. "People crowded into the train, sometimes through windows or hung on outside."[26]

Although the Nisei had some capability in Japanese, many like Kurihara were not sufficiently fluent to meet many of the needs of occupation authorities. SCAP needed bilinguals who could translate complex legal, scientific, and administrative documents, as well as serve as censors, court interpreters, and translators in sensitive political transactions. Only a small percentage of Nisei could perform these jobs well. As a result, SCAP was forced to hire thousands of native Japanese who possessed a higher level of bilingual skills. Because their nationality made them suspect to white American officers, however, the Japanese nationals, who did the bulk of the translations, had to work under the supervision of Nisei, who compiled "reports and summaries based on the materials gathered by their subordinates." "Their brokering position between clueless white administrators and right-less Japanese civilians," argued Eiichiro Azuma, "made it possible for [Nisei] to [engage in] the exploitative practice of taking sole credit for the work completed."[27]

However limited their mastery of Japanese language and culture, the Nisei continued to be seen as vital to the functioning of occupied Japan. This led MacArthur's General Headquarters (GHQ) to make decisions that sometimes contradicted U.S. policy. In September 1947, for example, because of a directive declaring that no renunciants could work for the military, they were let go. However, that proved impractical and the rule was subsequently rescinded. "The Occupation Forces couldn't function without [us]," noted Ben Ogami. "We got rehired immediately," affirmed Grace Asakura, "because the U.S. military needed us."[28]

Even more vital were Kibei-Nisei such as Roy Takamine, a renunciant fluent in both Japanese and English, who had been an active resegregationist at Tule

Lake. He was at first denied the high level of security clearance required for a sensitive job. Because the GHQ needed him, however, U.S. military officers gave him the clearance and hired him. At the same time, the U.S. government refused to allow him to regain his citizenship.[29]

In a study on Nisei in war-torn Japan, Azuma analyzed the complexities and ambiguities of their experiences. At the same time that they struggled for acceptance in white America, the land of their birth, they found themselves as cultural brokers with "uncontested power and privileges" in the "semi-colonial context of the military occupation." "While Japanese nationals lived their everyday lives in hunger and deprivation, Nisei who worked for the occupation had abundant nutritious foods, got their hands on all they wanted in the form of commissary supplies, and visited places of recreation and entertainment."[30]

Indeed, it was because of the scarcity of food and jobs in the civilian economy that so many Nisei and Kibei-Nisei felt lucky to be working for the occupation. They ate their meals at the Army mess halls, and if they commuted, carried home extra food as well as food they purchased at post exchanges. Tokio Yamane and other Kibei-Nisei renunciants who had been *Seinen Dan* members worked for GHQ for four or five years because of the scarcity of other jobs available to them. As Japanese nationals, they earned less than Americans, but what they earned was enough to sustain them.[31]

Kurihara, too, benefited from his employment with the military. "[I] am doing exceedingly well," he wrote in September 1946 to Dorothy Thomas, who kept in contact with him after his arrival in Japan. A few months later he told her, "Food [for me] is not a problem at present. . . . Having been considered an essential, the Army is generously taking care of me."[32]

In contrast to Kurihara and others hired by the occupation forces, most Japanese nationals in the early postwar years struggled to make ends meet. A year after the war's end, the cost of living was twice the average person's income. "He eats less, wears poorer clothes than in the last months of the war," reported *Rocky Shimpō* of the average Japanese. "And his money reserves are almost gone. . . . Black market rice to feed [a] family one week costs a month's salary." "Everything is rationed," wrote a renunciant in May 1946 to Mary Kitano, a columnist with *Rafu Shimpō*. "There is no salt, sugar, rice, shoyu or vinegar. . . . Black markets flourish all over the place. . . . There are a lot of hold-ups. . . . [Y]ou can't walk around at night-time. Some of the gangs even bring trucks and take the rice from the warehouses. Since they come in big groups, the police can't do a thing to them."[33]

Gasoline, lumber, steel, copper, aluminum, farm equipment, and many other items also found their way into the black market via "militarists, industrialists, bureaucrats, and politicians who had looted military stockpiles." "[T]he black market flourished," noted the historian John Dower, "because this was exceedingly profitable for a large number of well-placed people." In this milieu, Nisei who wanted to take unfair advantage of their insider position could do so with impunity. Kurihara told his grandnephew Joe Wilfred Fujita, a U.S. navy reservist who visited him in the years after the occupation, that Nisei civilians with whom Kurihara worked during the occupation made money "hand over fist" by selling truckloads of army surplus on the black market. Kurihara refused to participate. "Sometimes I think about it and wonder," he told Fujita. "But then I say, no. I'm glad that I didn't do that. I sleep well."[34]

Later Years

Perhaps Kurihara decided that he lacked sufficient fluency in Japanese to be of further help to the GHQ. Whatever the reason, after about a year with the occupation forces, he left his job in Sasebo and moved to Tokyo.[35] There he found a job as an accountant for a large drafting firm that had connections with officials in the occupation forces. With the increasing threat of Communism in East Asia, the U.S. government had set as its priority the goal of supporting the restoration of the Japanese economy. Because of their unique position as cultural brokers, Nisei were among those able to venture into new businesses, such as drafting and foreign trade, which supported the reconstruction effort.[36]

In his new job Kurihara got along well with company officials and co-workers until he discovered what he called "the swindling of a large sum of money," which should have been paid to his fellow employees, but which was instead funneled to the company's top brass. According to a friend, Kurihara "exposed the boss in front of his colleagues in an employee-management conference." "Just like the crusader that he is," opined his friend, Kurihara sought to report the case to the American authorities in Japan. He quit his job "in the belief that he had to be a free, unobligated man to carry the fight to the 'bitter end.'" His friend did not provide information on the outcome of Kurihara's efforts, and that outcome is unknown.[37]

That incident added to Kurihara's difficulty in adjusting to life in Japan. Despite having renounced his U.S. citizenship and declaring himself Japanese, he was never fully comfortable in his adopted land. A year after arriving in Japan, he wrote Thomas, "I am making a study of the Japanese people. Very, very interesting. These Japanese in Japan and those abroad can be considered as two different species."[38]

One of the differences was the "strong pressure on homogenization" in Japan. In order to feel comfortable socially, the Nisei had to assimilate fully into Japanese culture. Those who succeeded in doing so were able to "merge into the

Japanese mainstream community and keep their invisibility."[39] This requirement went against the grain of Kurihara's nature, his self-identity as an individual with freedom to express himself and to live according to his beliefs. Like Kurihara, Ben Ogami had never been to Japan before renouncing his citizenship and moving to Japan. Unlike Kurihara, however, Ogami admitted his mistake and returned to the United States in 1955. He stated flatly, "I lost ten years in Japan."[40]

Nisei renunciants like Ogami and Kurihara had more difficulty than Kibei-Nisei in adjusting to Japanese society. Gladys Ishida, who interviewed both Nisei and Kibei-Nisei in the 1950s, found that the Kibei-Nisei she interviewed, who had spent only a few years in the United States before war broke out, had a much easier time than the Nisei in adjusting to life in Japan.[41]

Kurihara eventually moved to Meguro, a wealthy section of Tokyo. There he boarded with the Kobayashi family, who lived in a quiet, upscale neighborhood, which Kurihara found to be a "most comfortable place to live." Several other single men also boarded with the family. Mr. Kobayashi, who had been an executive in a large corporation, was retired. Kurihara rented two rooms in the large house, one to live in and another for his belongings. Sakae Kobayashi, who was then a young mother and daughter-in-law of the elder Kobayashis, recalled that Kurihara was polite, uncomplaining, and cheerful. Whenever she summoned him to join the family for dinner, she noticed that his room was always neat. He told her that he liked everything to be in its place and at hand when he needed it.[42]

Lack of facility in Japanese remained a problem for Kurihara. Especially during the early years of his arrival, reading and writing were difficult. Like other Nisei in Japan, he continued to read English-language newspapers published in Japan and continued to think in English rather than in Japanese.[43] Still, his facility with the Japanese language improved during his two decades in Japan so that, according to his barber Inose Makoto, who met him in 1957, Kurihara's conversational Japanese was good enough to lead one to think that he was a native speaker. Inose's barbershop, which Kurihara frequented, was located within a five-minute walk from the Kobayashi home. There the sixty-two-year old and the twenty-seven-year-old began an eight-year friendship that lasted until Kurihara's death.[44]

This sustained friendship was one of the few that Kurihara maintained with a Japanese national. In the Kobayashi household, Kurihara kept to himself and was generally quiet during mealtimes. While other boarders and the family chatted about baseball, television drama, and events of the day, Kurihara seemed to have little interest in joining the conversation or getting to know the others.[45]

On the other hand, Kurihara formed friendships with individuals he would not have befriended in Manzanar. One of these was the Kibei-Nisei David

Itami. Three years after Kurihara's expatriation, Itami, who worked for the occupation, wrote to Dorothy Thomas, saying that he had read *The Spoilage*, which Kurihara had lent him with the suggestion that he read about Kurihara's role in the camps. Itami had known Kurihara since March 1942 when they were among the volunteers who helped prepare Manzanar for the influx of exiled Nikkei. He was not, however, at Manzanar during the December revolt because he had left for Camp Savage to become a civilian Japanese-language instructor. He later volunteered for the U.S. Army, and served in its Pacific Military Intelligence Research Section. He told Thomas that his Nisei friends at Manzanar would certainly "condemn" him for writing to her, because he, like they, had been accused by Nikkei dissidents like Kurihara of being spies for the U.S. government. But hearing of the effort by renunciants to regain their U.S. citizenship, he felt "compelled to at least look into the situation to see if anything [could] be done on behalf of Joe, who," Itami wrote, "does not belong here and does not deserve to be left forgotten." "I have come to know him rather intimately only in the recent months," he continued. "Apparently Joe is not too happy being a Japanese citizen, and perhaps due to his honesty and sincerity, he is finding it a hard going to live and get along in this confused and bewildered community." "He still maintains that he wants to remain a loyal Japanese contributing to the democratization of Japan," noted Itami. "Yet in the cold reality of life . . . he is still unknown in this huge metropolis of 4 million people. . . . To my wife . . . he has been confiding his secret hope that someday he may be able to go back to his native land, Hawaii. But in facing me, his pride would not have it. He still claims that he would not accept a trip to the states unless he is given a clean slate bill and 'invited' to become a citizen again."[46] As the U.S. government extended no such invitation, he remained in Japan, alienated from his native country.

Kurihara did, however, maintain close contact with his family in Hawai'i, especially with his older sister, Kikuno, who in 1954 visited him in Japan. He also maintained close ties with his nephew, Jack Kawamoto, a Kibei-Nisei who had not been incarcerated during the war because he lived in Hawai'i. After Kawamoto moved to Tokyo in the 1950s, Kurihara visited him frequently. During one of Kurihara's visits, Jack's wife Haruko happened to be writing to her Aunt Kikuno. Remarking on Kurihara's fastidiousness, Haruko wrote affectionately, "Uncle Joe is here today, typing some letters. Same ole guy, everything must be so, so." This close relationship led Kurihara and his nephew to partner in a business venture selling pots for orchid plants. The business, however, was unsuccessful.[47]

Also in the 1950s, in keeping with his interest in plants, Kurihara befriended Kawamoto Toshio (no relation to Jack Kawamoto) of the Nippon Bonsai-Saikei

Art Institute. Kawamoto, the son of Kawamoto Tokichi, a renowned bonsai expert, had mastered the special art of *saikei*, miniature landscaping. In an effort to spread the knowledge and practice of *saikei* to the English-speaking world, Kawamoto and Kurihara collaborated to produce a book, *Bonsai-Saikei: The Art of Japanese Miniature Trees, Gardens, and Landscapes*, which Kurihara translated into English. In the book's introduction, Kurihara expressed his enthusiasm for this art form. "As [saikei] spreads in this world," he wrote, "jealously, hatred, suspicion, intimidation, and provocation will be superseded by peace and good will everywhere. Talk to the trees, nourish the soil, and play with the rocks for an hour a day. You will find it soothing, peaceful, and joyous. Let us hope that all the people of the world will indulge in saikei and once again bring Paradise back onto this earth."[48]

Despite these activities, Kurihara's renunciation was never far from his mind. Fourteen years after having arrived in Japan, he showed his friend and barber, Inose Makoto, a copy of a newspaper article that his brother had sent him. The article noted that President Dwight Eisenhower's administration admitted that the U.S. government had made a "mistake" in incarcerating innocent people on the basis of their ethnicity. Kurihara proudly noted to his friend that he was one of the leaders who had fought against this injustice, and that the government's admittance of wrongdoing vindicated him.[49]

Three years later during John Kennedy's presidency, Kurihara wrote U.S. Attorney General Robert Kennedy and quoted from the article: "At a moving ceremony attended by high Government officials," the article stated, "the Justice Department formally completed a program to return U.S. citizenship to most of those Nisei who renounced it in a wave of bitterness against their confinement. Attorney General William P. Rogers [of the Eisenhower administration] said the program was an attempt to 'make up for a mistake our nation made' toward a group of its citizens. Assistant Attorney General George C. Doub hoped the Nisei would 'have the charity to forgive their Government.'" Kurihara then addressed Kennedy: "Regarding it may I ask what the government had done to right the wrong after she asked the Nisei to forgive their Government? . . . Personally I would like to ask why were those who have not as yet made application for the return of their citizenship are [*sic*] not contacted and consulted? . . . Amongst the 357 remaining [who have not applied for restoration of citizenship], there are men who served in the United States Army and gallantly fought to save democracy during the First World War. As a democratic government, did she [take] any step to compensate them? . . . I fought for justice in the relocation centers and was branded a disloyal nisei, but I immediately forgave with joy when the announcement [by Attorney General Rogers] was made. Since then three years have passed without anything [being done] by the U.S.

government." It seemed that Kurihara had expected the U.S. government, in the evident spirit of Rogers's announcement, to go one step further and offer him and other renunciants like him the restoration of their citizenship.[50]

Paul Grumbly, Special Litigation Counsel in Kennedy's office, responded by sending Kurihara a copy of the press release that Kurihara had quoted in his letter. Hinting at the difficulty Kurihara would have in regaining his citizenship, Grumbly wrote, "I believe you will find the statements contained therein to be self-explanatory and particularly so with reference to the type of cases in which citizenship was restored administratively and those in which this Department [denied restoration administratively and] would vigorously defend its adverse determination in the courts."[51]

Kurihara responded by stating that the point he raised in his letter to Kennedy was "completely ignored or overlooked" by Grumbly. Confessing the wrong done to the Nikkei in World War II, he wrote, "is a great deed [on the part of the U.S. government], but that alone is not enough." "I am not interested in the restoration of my citizenship status," he continued, "because I am now too old to return to the United States." What, then, did he want from the government? "Frankly," he told Grumbly, "it is the soldiers' compensation I believe ought to be settled." What Kurihara sought, in other words, was to be awarded compensation from the government for the wrongful incarceration of a veteran. Obviously, the injustice accorded him by the U.S. government still rankled him as much as it had during the period of his dissident behavior at Manzanar twenty years before.[52]

Grumbly responded by telling Kurihara that Congress on July 2, 1948, had enacted Public Law 886, "which authorizes the Attorney General to adjudicate certain claims for property damages resulting from evacuation of certain persons of Japanese ancestry during World War II. If by any chance you did occasion any property loss as the result of your evacuation," he continued in his best bureaucratic mode, "the time for filing such claims expired January 3, 1950." Obviously, Grumbly either did not or chose not to understand Kurihara's point, and with that realization, Kurihara ceased the correspondence.[53]

A year later and soon after the publication of *Bonsai-Saikei*, Kurihara attempted to promote the book in the United States. Toward that end, he wrote to Tamotsu Murayama, a columnist with the *Pacific Citizen*, the semi-monthly publication of the Japanese American Citizens League, Kurihara's nemesis at Manzanar. In announcing the book's publication, Murayama wrote, "[It] will be very useful to bonsai enthusiastics and gardeners. Already, orders from Europe as well as America are being received." Kurihara also sent letters announcing the book's publication to university libraries on the West Coast. According to his friend Inose Makoto, Kurihara wanted to promote the book worldwide.

"That was the kind of person that he was," recalled Inose. "Expansive. He never thought on a small scale."[54]

Kurihara subsequently wrote to Ueno, then living in San Jose, California, telling him of the book and of its sales in California, and asking Ueno if he wanted to purchase one. Kurihara then wrote of his plan to travel with Kawamoto to the United States in a couple of years on an "exhibition tour" to promote the book. At that point he may not have been in the best of health, for he noted, "Of course two years from now is a long time to wait and anything can happen in the meantime."[55]

Sure enough, he died of a stroke on November 26, 1965, seven months after writing to Ueno. He was seventy years old. At his deathbed were his seventy-four-year-old brother Taiji, who had traveled from Honolulu, and his seventy-one-year-old sister Kawayo, who had traveled from his family's home in Ōshima. His plans to visit his elder siblings Kikuno and Taiji and their families in Honolulu on his way to California on his proposed book tour never materialized. Among the personal possessions he left behind was the newspaper clipping of May 21, 1959, announcing the restoration of citizenship to Nisei renunciants.[56]

Kurihara's two decades in Japan was a mirror image of his much longer life in the United States. In both countries, bounded by circumstances he never successfully transcended, his life was centered primarily on his cultural subgroup. In the United States, his unwillingness, indeed inability, to confine himself to the "place" that his ethnicity supposedly relegated him, drove him from the country. Yet even in his adopted country Japan, he never melded successfully into the larger society. Indeed, in both places his friends and relatives were mostly Americans of Japanese ancestry. Nonetheless in both countries he befriended and interacted with many individuals in the larger societies.

In the United States, he strove to be accepted as an American, that is, to enjoy the promise of American life, to enjoy fully the rights and opportunities that he learned about in school. He was equally eager to shoulder the responsibilities of American citizenship that made those rights and opportunities possible. In both of these endeavors he symbolized better perhaps than anyone else in his generation, the possibilities and certainly the pitfalls of Nikkei life in America until after World War II. Yet he built a foundation much better than even he perhaps realized. As the story of his role in the resistance to incarceration has become widely known, his example for later generations has been burnished brightly. My hope is that this study continues that burnishing.

AFTERWORD

Three themes coursed through Kurihara's life: high expectations, his distinctiveness, and a strong sense of justice. These themes, especially the third, help to explain who he was, how he saw himself, and why he did what he did.

Throughout his life, Kurihara maintained high expectations of himself and his country. This was borne out in his perfect behavior grades at St. Ignatius, for example, and his anger at the U.S. government in its decision to incarcerate innocent people. At times, however, his expectations of himself led him to unrealistic endeavors. As a case in point, upon his arrival to the West Coast in 1920, he went to San Jose with the idea of enrolling at Santa Clara University to study medicine even if he had only completed the ninth grade. He learned that the university required applicants to hold a high school diploma. Instead of enrolling in the high school division adjacent to the university, he returned to San Francisco, where he enrolled at St. Ignatius High School. After completing only two years there, he departed for Michigan with the idea of entering the University of Michigan at Ann Arbor. However, that university, too, required applicants to have a high school diploma, which he did not have.[1]

His high self-expectations also meant that he would do what he thought was right and just. An example is his response to California's anti-alien land law prohibiting Japanese immigrants from owning and leasing agricultural land. To help the Issei continue with farming, Kurihara and a friend used their status as U.S. citizens to lease thousands of acres of farmland. Three decades later in Japan, in a conversation with his grandnephew, Joe Wilfred Fujita, he recalled this experience, pointing out that he and his friend could have kept the leases in their names. Instead, when the Issei farmers' sons reached adulthood, Kurihara and his friend transferred the leases to them. Another experience he recounted to Fujita was his refusal during the occupation of Japan to participate in confiscating supplies and selling them on the black market (discussed in the previous chapter). Both of these instances show Kurihara's sense of ethics and his pride in being able to meet standards that he placed on himself.[2]

The second theme in Kurihara's life was his distinctiveness. Several instances that set Kurihara apart from others of his generation come to mind. One was his conversion to Catholicism at a time when his family members and most Nikkei were Buddhists, while the relatively small numbers of Christians were primarily Protestants. In 1912 to 1914 he was one of the few Japanese Americans to enroll in the Catholic St. Francis School in Hawai'i, and in 1915 to 1917 the only Japanese American to enroll at St. Ignatius School in San Francisco. Then, too, in World War I he was the only soldier of Japanese descent in his eleven-hundred-member field artillery unit. And after World War II, he was one of the few if not the only Nisei (not Kibei-Nisei) who rejected the opportunity to request cancellation of his renunciation.

These experiences undoubtedly supported his sense of being singular, and they likely contributed to what he told his grandnephew Joe Fujita in 1957, that he had graduated from Columbia University in 1924 as one of the first two Japanese Americans to do so. When I told Fujita that I had records from Southwestern University showing that Kurihara attended the institution in the early 1920s and graduated there in 1924, the same year that he supposedly graduated from Columbia, Fujita was surprised. He said that he was sure that Kurihara had said "Columbia."

Columbia University has no record of Kurihara as a student or graduate. Moreover, during World War II, in response to a government questionnaire, Kurihara provided the names of schools he attended. Southwestern University was the only university he listed, entering in January 1921 and graduating in 1924. Why, then, did he tell his grandnephew a different story? It is possible that Fujita recalled incorrectly. On the other hand, he was correct in giving 1924 as Kurihara's year of graduation. Fujita volunteered the statement about Columbia without my prompting him; that is, I did not ask Fujita if Kurihara mentioned anything about his schooling. Moreover, Fujita had little emotional investment in his statement. To be sure, he was proud of his granduncle, but they did not know each other well. At first I ignored this bit of misinformation, but it stayed with me as a puzzle, and I was left with questions: Did Kurihara intentionally lie to Fujita? Or was the answer more subtle and complex? Was this an instance in which Kurihara's memory created a new version "of past events to suit the immediate interests of the present"? Was Kurihara's story an illustration of the way in which memory can serve to buttress a person's "sense of self"?[3]

Because "memory is a constantly integrative, reconstructive process," what people remember can be influenced by later experiences. Moreover, it is possible for people to believe that they experienced something that did not actually happen to them. This occurs when people imagine the experience.[4] It is in the instances when memory "diverges most clearly from fact" that one can see elements of desire and "clues to unrealized hopes." Near the twilight of life, in particular, when people take stock of themselves and their pasts, the stories they recount about themselves can undergo more extensive reconstruction than in other times of their lives. Kurihara was sixty-two years old when he spoke with his grandnephew; while age sixty-two seems relatively young today, in 1957 people of that age would be considered at the twilight of their lives.[5]

Robert McGlone's term, "aphoristic memory," provides additional insight into Kurihara's claim. Aphoristic memory is a story that illustrates "what the rememberer deems a general truth about himself." This story is "integrated with the broad themes of the rememberer's life story."[6] Having graduated from a university at a time when very few Nisei and Asian Americans did so, his narrative on Columbia can be seen as an embellishment of this achievement. He would have repeated that embellishment to himself enough times to have integrated it into his memory. In saying what he did, Kurihara wanted his grandnephew to understand that he, Kurihara, had an important place in history.

One of the ways in which Kurihara could claim a place in history was in his call for redress. As early as July 1942, in a speech he gave at a meeting of the Manzanar Citizens Federation, he stated, "Let America redeem herself by fully compensating us for the sufferings we were made to endure—mentally, physically, and economically." In the essay that he sent to the *Saturday Evening Post* in November 1943, he wrote, "May I ask what reparations the Government is considering to right the wrong? Let the government pay to each and every one of us a legitimate damage of $5000.00 for every year in camp, and to those who were engaged in business at the time of evacuation, a justifiable damage commensurate to the income they were enjoying." He echoed the same sentiments in a letter to his friend Yoshiko Hosoi, and again in his autobiography.[7]

Kurihara was not the first to seek redress from the U.S. government. In May 1942 James Omura, who had left the West Coast exclusionary zone during the brief period of "voluntary" relocation, sought legal action against the U.S. government for restoration of constitutional rights and compensation for economic losses. He contacted a Colorado law firm, but could not afford their startup charge of $3,500. By 1945 other Nikkei also believed that the federal government should be held accountable for their incarceration.[8]

In 1948 Congress made a gesture in that direction by passing the Japanese Evacuation Claims Act, but it proved to be woefully inadequate. Finally, on August 10, 1988, after two decades of effort on the part of Nikkei activists, President Ronald Reagan signed a redress bill into law, providing for $20,000 to survivors who were alive when the act was passed. Two years later payments began and continued for another nine years, accompanied by a letter of apology signed by President George H. W. Bush.[9] Kurihara would have been pleased with the apology and compensation. He would have been further pleased to learn that for about two years staff members from the Justice Department's Office of Redress Administration were stationed at the U.S. Embassy in Tokyo. As a result, a number of renunciants in Japan received the letter and redress payment. This happened more than two decades after Kurihara had passed away.

The push in the 1970s and 1980s leading to redress also occurred after his death. During those decades, Kurihara was a subject of heated public controversy. In a 1970 column in the *Pacific Citizen*, Reverend Roy Sano of Oakland, California offered Kurihara as a "hero for the 1970s." He praised Kurihara as a dissident who challenged Americans to meet high standards of "justice." He wrote of Kurihara's resistance to "oppression" and "inequities," and his "assertiveness" and "strength." Writing during the Vietnam War, Sano likened Kurihara's departure from the United States to the few Sansei who moved to Canada and Sweden in their opposition to the draft, both of which marked a "loyalty to democratic principles." In an angry response, Karl Yoneda called Sano's article "misinformed," and "a great disservice to those who lived through the turmoil and chaotic Manzanar camp." John Hamada, who was sixteen at the time of the Manzanar revolt, reacted to the two pieces. "Now what about those [Kurihara] tried to have murdered? Others "ate the same bad food, slept in the same tar paper barracks, suffered the same barbed wire enclosure. But who instead of turning sour and preaching defeat said: 'Let's get out of here.'" The people "whose names appeared on Kurihara's death list preached a gospel of hope. It took far more courage to do what they did . . . than it did to assemble hoodlum would-be assassins who manipulated the anxiety of people in confinement."[10]

Others supported Sano's views. William Hohri called Kurihara a "pioneer for redress" and "one of the real heroes" among the Nikkei in the camps. A letter Kurihara sent to a friend, Hohri stated, "reveals not a pro-military Japan fanatic, but a man who is angry . . . who is dedicated to democratic principles, and who suffers from the conflict of feelings of loyalty to America and the inescapable fact of America's betrayal to him, an American citizen and veteran of WWI." Harry Ueno agreed, saying that as soon as war broke out, Kurihara sought to help the United States by applying for a support position, but he was repeatedly rejected. The forced removal and incarceration led him to feelings of betrayal. "Deep in his heart he cried a hundred times for the country he once loved and trusted and fought for." The public controversy about Kurihara continued through the 1980s, more than two decades after his death and until the redress bill became law.[11] As the foregoing indicates, Kurihara has been a symbol for those who admire him as well as those who scorn him. Given the evidence, people have interpreted his statements and actions in different and contrasting ways, influenced in large part on their own personal experiences and worldviews.[12]

The third theme of Kurihara's life, important because it explains his actions in the concentration camps and his refusal to attempt to regain his citizenship, was his strong sense of justice. He did what he believed was right and expected others, including the government, to do the same. Family lore supported this characterization of Kurihara. His older sister Kikuno reflected the pride she had of her brother by recounting a story to her niece, Hanako Marubayashi, decades after it had happened. When Kurihara was eighteen years old and attending St. Francis School in Honolulu, Kikuno recounted, he saw prisoners cleaning the stream near his home on Houghtailing Road. He was surprised to see a Japanese man among them, because in 1913, when this incident occurred, it was almost unheard of to see Nikkei as prisoners. Kurihara asked the man why he was a prisoner, and hearing his response, replied that it was not a good reason to be placed in prison. Marubayashi did not know how Kurihara did it, whether or not he was able to find a lawyer despite being a student on a small budget, but according Kikuno, her brother was successful in having the man freed. "Auntie [Kikuno] said that Uncle Joseph was a kind person," Marubayashi remembered. "He thinks, 'Right is right and wrong is wrong.'" This same image of Kurihara was expressed by his nephew, Raymond Kurihara, son of Kurihara's younger brother Roy, with whom Kurihara had lived in Los Angeles in the 1930s. When asked to recall characteristics of his uncle, Raymond responded, "He always stood up for the underdog." Kurihara's sense of justice also meant that he expected people to treat others with respect, and when this expectation was not met, he took action. His Japanese friend and barber Inose Makoto reminisced,

> K-san [Kurihara] was like a samurai of old Japan . . . a person who is kind to those who are weak, demanding of oneself, who endures in the face of suffering . . . who does his best till the end, who always keeps his promise. . . . He had this kind of spirit. . . . K-san was the kind of person who would challenge any injustice, however slight. For example, when young ruffians crowded their way forcefully to the front of a line where people were waiting for the train, he challenged them, not caring that what they saw was a short, old man. "What's this old shrimp?" they said. And Kurihara took a boxer's pose, and challenged them to a fight. These youths were completely taken aback. . . . This short, old man, challenging them, "Come on over here and fight!" Those hooligans then slunk away.[13]

Kurihara's sense of justice caused him to protest vigorously and vociferously at Manzanar. His bitter response to the U.S. government was to renounce his citizenship and refuse to request that it be reinstated, despite the fact that in his very bones, Kurihara was as American as one could be. He had absorbed his American-ness from an early age growing up in Hawaiʻi, attending public and Catholic schools, and volunteering as a U.S. soldier in World War I. He continued adhering to his American identity as a university student, businessman, and navigator. In his mind he was not an ethnic American nor a Japanese American, but an American.[14]

Then came World War II and incarceration, and his reaction was what one might expect from an American. After the Manzanar debacle, however, he realized that protesting while imprisoned, with power heavily weighted with the government, could have tragic consequences for innocents. So he turned to writing as an alternative way of expressing himself. In this effort, however, he was at first rejected. His attempt to get the *Saturday Evening Post* to print an essay he wrote berating the government for acts of injustice against the Nikkei and African Americans was met with suspicion; instead of printing the essay, the editors of the *Post* sent it to the FBI. He was unable to enter the discourse on incarceration because those who controlled the discourse believed that he was a troublemaker.

A month later, however, he learned about Dorothy Thomas's research project. Here was his opportunity to participate in the writing of the first draft of the history of the incarceration. He sent Thomas a collection of his writing, and later, at her request, penned his "autobiography." Kurihara's writing, like his speeches, demonstrated his understanding of the power of language, something he had learned well during his years at St. Ignatius School. His classes in rhetoric and elocution there taught him the effectiveness of using vivid imagery and well-chosen hyperbole to convey his thoughts. His use of language, coupled with his direct style of communicating and his passion, gave power to what he wrote.[15]

Once Thomas's book *The Spoilage* was published in 1946, he saw that he had succeeded in getting his views included for others to read. However, what followed was two decades of silence, as Nikkei turned inward and refused to discuss the incarceration. But then came the next generation who wanted to know what happened in the U.S. concentration camps. When they searched the documents, they found Kurihara's account. They resurrected him and made him a hero.

Imagine what would have happened had Kurihara, having renunciated, and with all that he had written and declared, then recanted, in effect saying to the U.S. government, "I'm sorry. I was wrong. I apologize." That would have negated all that he had stood for and would have destroyed his decades of effort to have his views taken seriously, that the U.S. government had committed a grave injustice. So he refused to recant. He would instead be an American and stand up in defense of justice.

Were he alive today, he would be pleased to know that scholars writing about resistance in the WRA camps have unearthed what had previously been hidden, shifting the paradigm of shame to one of pride, and bringing a fuller story of the incarceration into the history books. He would be further pleased to know that he had played a part in setting the historical record straight, and that his defense of justice had paid off.

NOTES

Preface

1. Hansen, "A Riot of Voices," 107–39; Miyamoto, "Problems of Interpersonal Style among the Nisei," 29–45; Lyman, "Generation and Character," 279–314; Maykovich, *Japanese American Identity Dilemma*, 30; Caudill, "Japanese-American Personality and Acculturation," 3–102; Kitano, *Japanese Americans*, 124–26; Kikumura, *Through Harsh Winters*, 209–10. On public vs. private display of emotions, see Doi, "Omote and Ura," 258–61. For an in-depth discussion of Nisei and white communication styles, see Miyamoto, "Problems of Interpersonal Style among the Nisei," 29–45. For a heated exchange on the Nisei interpersonal style, see Lyman, "On Nisei Interpersonal Style: A Reply to S. Frank Miyamoto"; Lyman, "'American' Interpersonal Style and Nikkei Realities: a Rejoinder to S. Frank Miyamoto"; and Miyamoto, "Miyamoto Reply to Stanford Lyman."

2. Tamura, *Americanization, Acculturation, and Ethnic Identity.*

Introduction

1. Kurihara, "Niseis and the Government," 19–20. Translation by Ruriko Kumano, August 30, 2005: "Emperor 10,000 Years of Life! 10,000 Years of Life! 10,000 Years of Life! Great Imperial Japan 10,000 Years of Life! 10,000 Years of Life! 10,000 Years of Life! Remain Together Comrades 10,000 Years of Life! 10,000 Years of Life! 10,000 Years of Life!"

2. Hunter, *Buddhism in Hawaii.*

3. Frederick, "Case History, Joseph Yoshisuke Kurihara," 15.

4. Frederick, "Case History, Joseph Yoshisuke Kurihara," 15.

5. Important volumes on the incarceration include Daniels, *Concentration Camps*; Robinson, *A Tragedy of Democracy*; U.S. Commission on Wartime Relocation and Internment of Civilians, *Personal Justice Denied*; Irons, *Justice at War*; Hayashi, *Democratizing the Enemy*; Muller, *American Inquisition*; Drinnon, *Keeper of Concentration*

Camps; and Weglyn, *Years of Infamy*. An authoritative synthesis is Daniels, *Prisoners without Trial*. Earlier works include Grodzins, *Americans Betrayed*; tenBroek, Barnhart, and Matson, *Prejudice, War, and the Constitution*; Thomas and Nishimoto, *The Spoilage*; Girdner and Loftis, *The Great Betrayal;* and Bosworth, *America's Concentration Camps*. Arthur Hansen and his colleagues have produced significant oral histories, including Hansen, *Japanese American World War II Evacuation Oral History Project*; Hansen and Mitson, *Voices Long Silent*; and Embrey, Hansen, and Mitson, *Manzanar Martyr*. Hansen, "Oral History and the Japanese American Evacuation," discusses the many oral history projects, publications, and film documentaries, on the World War II Nikkei experience. Web-based oral history sources include the Densho archive at www.densho.org. Printed oral histories such as *Regenerations Oral History Project*, edited by Japanese American National Museum and other institutions, have been digitized and are available at the California Digital Library website via Calisphere at http://content.cdlib.org. A film worthy of note is Omori, *Rabbit in the Moon*.

Most discussions of Kurihara are brief, with the exceptions of Thomas and Nishimoto, *The Spoilage*, 49+; Hohri, *Repairing America*, 34+; and Bosworth, *America's Concentration Camps*, 153–55+. Works that mention Kurihara include Daniels, *Concentration Camps: North America*, 107; Hayashi, *Democratizing the Enemy*, 128, 134–35; Hosokawa, *Nisei: The Quiet Americans*, 361–62, 378; Bailey, *City in the Sun*, 136; Chin, *Born in the USA*, 343–48; Kurashige, "Resistance, Collaboration, and Manzanar Protest," 398. Errors have appeared in published works. For example Murray, *Historical Memories*, 117, mistakenly says that Kurihara was a Kibei; Spickard, *Japanese Americans*, 126–27, says that Kurihara could not enlist in the army in World War II because he was too old (in fact, he did not want to enlist); Spickard also mistakenly states that Kurihara sailed to Japan in February 1946 (in fact, Kurihara departed in November 1945); and Kiyota, *Beyond Loyalty*, 112–13, contains numerous errors about Kurihara.

6. Toya Miyatake's photography in Manzanar is an example of resistance that was undetected by administrators: see Alinder, *Moving Images*, 75–102. Works on resistance include Hansen and Hacker, "The Manzanar Riot"; Muller, *Free to Die for Their Country*; Lon Kurashige, "Resistance, Collaboration, and Manzanar Protest"; Hansen, "Peculiar Odyssey"; Lyon, *Prisons and Patriots*; Okihiro, "Religion and Resistance in America's Concentration Camps"; Okihiro, "Japanese Resistance in America's Concentration Camps"; Okihiro, "Tule Lake under Martial Law"; Kumei, "'Skeleton in the Closet'"; Hansen, "Cultural Politics in the Gila River Relocation Center"; Jackman, "Collective Protest in Relocation Centers"; Takita-Ishii, "Tokio Yamane"; Hohri, *Resistance*; Thomas and Nishimoto, *The Spoilage*; McKay, "Young Women's Everyday Resistance"; Collins, *Native American Aliens*; Christgau, "Collins versus the World"; Nishimoto, *Inside an American Concentration Camp*; Yatsushiro, "Political and Socio-Cultural Issues at Poston and Manzanar Relocation Centers"; Hansen, "Protest-Resistance and the Heart Mountain Experience"; Nelson, *Heart Mountain*; Emi, "Draft Resistance at the Heart Mountain Concentration Camp and the Fair Play Committee"; Mackey, *Remembering Heart Mountain*; Castelnuovo, *Soldiers of Conscience*; and films by Abe, *Conscience and the Constitution*, and by Shiozaki, *The Manzanar Fishing Club*. Takei,

"Legalizing Detention"; Bailey, *City in the Sun*; and Leighton, *The Governing of Men* discuss issues of resistance.

7. Beechert and Beechert, *From Kona to Yenan*, 71; Yoneda, *Ganbatte*, 148–49.

8. Togo Tanaka, "Post Script," *Rafu Shimpo*, April 25, 1946.

9. Murray, *Historical Memories*, 195–200; Maki, Kitano, and Berthold, *Achieving the Impossible Dream*, 57; Takita, "The Tule Lake Pilgrimage," 62; Alinder, *Moving Images*, 128–30.

10. Morrison, *Beloved*, 35–36; Marker, *Sans Soleil*. Thanks to Roland Sintos Coloma for bringing to my attention the notion of rememory in *Beloved*.

11. Wei, *The Asian American Movement*, 1–43; Maki, Kitano, and Berthold, *Achieving the Impossible Dream*, 57–59; Murray, *Historical Memories*, 200–206.

12. Takita, "The Tule Lake Pilgrimage," 78–97, 104, 124; Murray, *Historical Memories*, 186–87.

13. Collins, *Native American Aliens*, 101; Takei, "Legalizing Detention," 94. Most of the renunciants sought and regained their citizenship after twenty-three years of dogged effort by the attorney Wayne M. Collins.

14. Takita, "The Tule Lake Pilgrimage and Japanese American Internment," 264.

15. Asakura interview by author; Matsushita interview by author. Renunciants contacted in the 1970s and quoted in Tule Lake Committee, Ross, and Ross, *Second Kinenhi*, were anonymous. When I tried to interview former renunciants in the mid-1990s, in most instances I was either refused or told that they would speak to me only on condition of anonymity. Their attitude changed after the turn of the twenty-first century. In the early years after 2000, representatives of the Densho project (http://densho.org) were able to interview former renunciants who allowed their names to be used. Also, in 2004, for the first time at a Tule Lake pilgrimage, three former renunciants spoke publically and emotionally about their acts of renunciation. See Takita, "The Tule Lake Pilgrimage," 271.

16. Takita, "The Tule Lake Pilgrimage," 342.

17. Works that speak to the importance of words are Daniels, "Words Do Matter"; Herzig-Yoshinaga, "Words Can Lie or Clarify"; Okamura, "The American Concentration Camps"; Hirabayashi, "'Concentration Camp' or 'Relocation Center'"; and Nakagawa, "Power of Words Resolution." For discussions on objections to "concentration camps," see Daniels, "Words Do Matter," 200; and Takita, "The Tule Lake Pilgrimage," 98. For publications in the 1970s using "concentration camps," see Daniels, *Concentration Camps: North America*; and Weglyn, *Years of Infamy*.

18. Drinnon, *Keeper of Concentration Camps*, 6; Hayashi, *Democratizing the Enemy*, xv.

19. Daniels, *American Concentration Camps*.

20. Daniels, "Words Do Matter," 190–94. In 1940 there were 695,363 Italians, 314,715 Germans, and 91,858 Japanese—for a total of about one million—living as resident aliens in the United States. The figures given in my narrative, of the number interned of each nationality, are estimates. No precise figures are available. Moreover, the numbers given do not include the 2,264 Japanese, 4,058 Germans, and 288 Italians removed

from fifteen Latin American countries and interned in the United States. It also does not include the 3,300 Japanese sent from the War Relocation Authority camps to the Department of Justice camps.

21. Weglyn, *Years of Infamy*, 202–3.

22. Daniels, "Words Do Matter," 190.

Chapter 1. Growing Up American

1. "Yoshisuke Kurihara Certificate of Hawaiian Birth," Office of the Secretary, Territory of Hawaii, May 2, 1910, Case File 146–54–117. Occupation is a more accurate term than annexation. The overthrow of the Kingdom of Hawaii in 1893 and the subsequent attempts at annexation in 1898 were illegal acts in that they violated treaties between the United States and the Hawaiian Kingdom and therefore violated international law on treaties. The U.S. Constitution states in Article VI that all treaties are the "Supreme Law of the Land." In 1993 Congress passed and President Bill Clinton signed PL 103–150, which admitted that the U.S. government illegally invaded and occupied the Kingdom of Hawaii. See Boyle, "Restoration of the Independent Nation State of Hawaii under International Law"; Sai, "A Slippery Path toward Hawaiian Indigeneity."

2. Moriyama, "The Causes of Emigration," 248–61; Moriyama, *Imingaisha*, 2–6; Irwin and Conroy, "Robert Walker Irwin and Systematic Immigration to Hawaii," 46–47; Kichizo Kurihara family records, Consulate-General of Japan. Although Joseph Kurihara's birth certificate states that his parents arrived in Hawai'i in 1889, his father was on the sugar plantation payroll in 1888: Payroll book 1887–1891, HSPA. For a discussion of contract labor in Hawai'i, see Beechert, *Working in Hawaii*, 40–55.

3. On the first group that arrived in 1868 (called the *Gannenmono*, or "first year people," because that was the first year of the Meiji era), see Van Sant, *Pacific Pioneers*, 97–116. On numbers arriving after 1885, see Adams, *Japanese in Hawaii*, 11.

4. Saito and Campbell, "Lihue Plantation Company History."

5. Payroll book 1887–1891, HSPA; Beechert, *Working in Hawaii*, 102–3. For a discussion of plantation living and working conditions during the 1880s and 1890s, see Tamura, *Americanization, Acculturation, and Ethnic Identity*, 11–17.

6. Saito and Campbell, "Lihue Plantation Company History"; Lo, "Hanama'ulu's Chronology."

7. Payroll book 1887–1891, HSPA.

8. "Yoshisuke Kurihara Certificate of Hawaiian Birth," Office of the Secretary, Territory of Hawaii, May 2, 1910, Case File 146–54–117. For a discussion of laborers' rejection of plantation work, see Tamura, *Americanization, Acculturation, and Ethnic Identity*, 211.

9. Kurihara, "Autobiography," 1.

10. *Polk-Husted's Directory, 1898*, 43; *Polk-Husted's Directory, 1898*, "Map of Honolulu and Vicinity," n.p. By 1910, the population of Honolulu County had increased to 82,028, which was 43 percent of the territory's population; at the same time the territory's population increased to 191,909. See U.S. Bureau of the Census, *Thirteenth Census*,

1910, 5–7. The dominant industry was sugar cane production, with rice and coffee also being produced. In the next few years pineapple would also grow to become a major industry. See U.S. Bureau of the Census, *Thirteenth Census, 1910*, 37, 46; *Polk-Husted's Directory, 1911*, 50; *Polk-Husted's Directory, 1915*, 46. Territorial status had enabled raw sugar to enter the U.S. mainland duty-free, resulting in a boom in the sugar industry.

11. By the mid-1910s a fortunate few were able to benefit from the electricity that had arrived in the area: Houghtailing interview by Kodama, 1103. Paula Rath, "Pioneers of Palama," *Honolulu Advertiser*, 25 September 2005.

12. Mohr, *Plague and Fire*, 3–4, 7–16, 29–34, 125–46.

13. On overcrowding, see Rath interview by Nishimoto, 90–95; and Paula Rath, "Pioneers of Palama," *Honolulu Advertiser*, September 25, 2005. On youth gangs, see Kimura interview by Kodama, 262.

14. Sanborn Fire Insurance Maps, Territory of Hawaii, Honolulu, 1914, sheets 7, 9–10, University of Hawaii Libraries, hereafter cited as Sanborn Maps 1914; Like interview by Nishimoto, 687–93; Joseph interview by Nishimoto, 501; Houghtailing interview by Kodama, 1099–106.

15. Houghtailing interview, 1098–99; Sanborn Maps 1914, sheet 7; Marubayashi interview by author; *Polk-Husted's Directory, 1908*, 345. For a discussion of hack drivers, see Like interview by Nishimoto, 686.

16. *Polk-Husted's Directory, 1914*, 421; *Polk-Husted's Directory, 1917*, 471.

17. Conversation with Grace Fukumoto, May 31, 2007, Honolulu.

18. Hawaii Republic, DPI, *Report of the Minister of Public Instruction, 1897*, 17, hereafter cited as *Report of the Minister of Public Instruction*. For enrollment numbers at Kaiulani, see *Report of the Minister of Public Instruction, 1899*, 128. The name of Kurihara's grammar school is in Kurihara, Individual Record, FBI Report, July 8, 1942, Case File 146–54–117. For information on the Reform School, see *Report of the Minister of Public Instruction, Biennial, 1899*, 9.

19. U.S. Department of the Interior, Bureau of Education, *American Schoolhouses*, plates 31, 43, 85, 178; Brubaker, *Planning and Designing Schools*, 1–5; Graves, *School Ways*, 23–24. For information on materials used to construct Kaiulani School, see *Report of the Minister of Public Instruction, 1897*, 5. For a photo of the newly built Kaiulani school, see *Report of the Minister of Public Instruction, 1899*, 6. Other photos of Kaiulani School, taken in 1900, are in the photo collection at the Hawaii State Archives.

20. Kent, *Hawaii: Islands under the Influence*, 56–68; Coffman, *Nation Within*, 245–61; Mohr, *Plague and Fire*, 17–27.

21. Hawaii Republic, Act 57, 187, 189.

22. During first two decades of the twentieth century, children in the territory often began first grade at age eight or older. Going to school barefoot was also common. Kurihara's walk was less than a mile, in contrast to rural children, who often had to walk four or more miles each way. See Tamura, *Americanization*, 95–96. For Honolulu's population, see *Polk-Husted's Directory, 1903*, 39. For the numbers and types of schools, see Hawaii Territory, DPI, *Report to the Governor and Legislature, 1902–1904*, 100–104, hereafter cited as *Report to the Governor*. According to Article 17, §1, of the

Hawai'i Constitution of 1894, all persons born or naturalized in the Hawaiian islands were citizens of the Republic of Hawaii. For citizenship under the Republic of Hawaii and after the Organic Act was passed, see *U.S. Organic Act*, §4, Citizenship.

23. See *Report to the Governor, 1910–1912*, 223–33. Before World War II, the Territory of Hawai'i hired Asian Americans as public school teachers because there was a need for teachers and Asian Americans constituted a majority of young adults who filled this need. This practice contrasted with the U.S. West Coast, where local school districts refused to hire Asian Americans as teachers.

24. *Report to the Governor, 1902–1904*, 2, 103; *Report to the Governor, 1908–1910*, 28. For enrollment at Kaiulani School, see *Report to the Governor, 1902–1904*, 103; and *Report to the Governor, 1910–1912*, 209.

25. For the names and ethnic breakdown of Kaiulani teachers and teachers of all public schools, see, for example, *Report to the Governor, 1902–1904*, 103, 120–38. For the ethnic breakdown of Kaiulani students, see Kaiulani School Term Report, September 1909, DPI, HSA. *Report to the Governor, 1908–1910*, 74, 78, shows that when Kurihara was in the eighth grade, of the 20,245 public school students in the territory, 32 percent were Japanese, 30 percent were Hawaiians or Part-Hawaiians, 18 percent were Portuguese, and 11 percent were Chinese.

26. *Report to the Governor, 1908–1910*, 74, 78.

27. Tyack, *The One Best System*, 230; *Report to the Governor, 1902–1904*, 64–77; *Report to the Governor, 1904–1906*, 31–45.

28. S.F.S. #1, Schaefer, 1913–14, Tuition Records 1912–1916, File 307, SLC. St. Francis School was established in 1893 and ceased operations in 1916. See Yzendoorn, *History of the Catholic Mission in the Hawaiian Islands*, 230; and Alvarez, "Weaving a Cloak of Discipline," 382.

29. Alvarez, "Weaving a Cloak of Discipline," 202, 265, 269–70; S.F.S. #1, Schaefer, 1913–14, Tuition Records 1912–1916, File 307, SLC.

30. S.F.S. #1 1–4, 1913–14, Tuition Records 1912–1916, File 307, SLC; St. Louis Term Report, December 1913, DPI, HSA. In 1924 the first Japanese American in Hawai'i was baptized a Catholic, followed by more in the next several years; by 1927 there were 600 Nikkei Catholics. See Yzendoorn, *History of the Catholic Mission in the Hawaiian Islands*, 239. When compared with the 139,600 ethnic Japanese in the territory, most of whom were Buddhists, Japanese Catholics as well as Protestants remained a relatively small group. See Tamura, *Americanization*, 118; Alvarez, "Weaving a Cloak of Discipline," 268, 292. For numbers and percentages of ethnic groups in Hawai'i, see Lind, *Hawaii's People*, 28.

31. Kurihara, "Autobiography," 1. In an examination of the religious affiliation of the Nisei in the greater Seattle area, Stephen Fugita and Marilyn Fernandez found that only eight of their 183 survey participants were Catholic, while sixty-six were Protestant and fifty-four were Buddhist. Fujita and Fernandez, *Altered Lives, Enduring Community*, 233n2. These data, while collected in the 1990s, help to explain the lack of discussion of Catholics and the tendency to combine them with Protestants in publications discussing religious affiliations among Japanese Americans before and during World War

II. See, for example, Yoo, "A Religious History of Japanese Americans in California," 121–42; Strong, *Japanese in California*, 352–59, 382; and Thomas and Nishimoto, *The Salvage*, 66–69, 607.

32. Alvarez, "Weaving a Cloak of Discipline," 241–42, 291–92, quote from 207; conversation with Patricia Alvarez, June 7, 2007; Kurihara, Certificate of Baptism, San Francisco, November 16, 1915, Case File 146–54–117.

33. Class Register September 1913 to March 1914, Leo, Class Registers 1904–1916, First Class St. Francis School, File 140, SLC; S.F.S. #1, Schaefer, 1913–14, Tuition Records 1912–1916, File 307, SLC; Kurihara, "Autobiography," 1.

34. Manifest of Alien Passengers from U.S. Insular Possessions, 14498, microfilm M1410, roll 83, National Archives Pacific Region; *Polk-Husted's Directory, 1908*, 63. In 1915 there were seventeen ship companies, each with a number of ships, servicing Honolulu Harbor. See *Polk-Husted's Directory, 1915*, 1120.

35. Kurihara, "Autobiography," 2; Azuma, *Between Two Empires*, 63–69; Iwata, *Planted in Good Soil*, 221–34; Daniels, *Asian America*, 144. A California land law of 1913 forbade Japanese immigrants from owning land; an amendment in 1920 forbade them from leasing agricultural land, and a 1923 amendment prohibited them from sharecropping. For a Japanese immigrant's perspective of Japanese "schoolboys" working temporarily on farms, see Kiyama, *The Four Immigrants Manga*, 52–57.

36. Kurihara, "Autobiography," 2–3.

37. Lee, "Hemispheric Orientalism and the 1907 Pacific Coast Race Riot"; Daniels, *The Politics of Prejudice*, 33–34; Wollenberg, *All Deliberate Speed*, 53; Daniels, *Asian America*, 29–66, 100–154; Chan, *Asian Americans*, 45–61. Other Nisei recounted similar experiences in California in the 1920s and 1930s. See Smith, *Americans in Process*, 16–17, 24. For a discussion of the types of jobs available to Japanese, see Iwata, *Planted in Good Soil*, 111–52.

38. Kurihara, "Autobiography," 2.

39. Quote is from Muscatine, *Old San Francisco*, 420. For occupations in San Francisco, see Issel and Cherny, *San Francisco, 1865–1932*, 57. On the earthquake and exposition, see Cole, *A Short History of San Francisco*, 116–18; and Lewis, *San Francisco*, 222.

40. For anti-Asian hostility among Catholics, see Burns, "Building the Best," 72.

41. "Xavier, Francis, St.," 877; Yamazaki, "St. Francis Xavier School," 56–57; Matsuki, "Golden Era of Our Church," 1–6. Breton also helped lay the groundwork in 1916 for Our Lady Queen of Martyrs parish in Seattle. See Duntley, "Japanese and Filipino Together," 73–98. For discussions of the San Francisco Japanese community in the early decades of the twentieth century, see Okazaki, *Nihonmachi*, 38–82; Kenji G. Taguma, "San Francisco Japantown Properties up for Sale," *Hawaii Herald*, 27: 6, March 17, 2006, 1, 26. The mission was located on 2011 Buchanan Street; in the few months before he left San Francisco, Kurihara lived within a block of the mission, at 2041 Pine Street.

42. Information on Father Egloffstein is in *Catalogus Provinciae Californiae, Societatis Jesu*, 1915, p. 21, RG 1 box 19, USF. The Society of Jesus led the San Francisco mission from 1914 to 1925; then it was transferred to the Society of the Divine Word. See McGloin, *Jesuits by the Golden Gate*, 182–83. The records at St. Francis School in

Hawai'i has Yoshisuke as Kurihara's given name. His certificate of baptism and the records at St. Ignatius School identify him as Joseph Yoshisuke Kurihara. See Kurihara, Certificate of Baptism, San Francisco, November 15, 1915, Case File 146–54–117; and *Registrar's Book, 1906–1927*, 307–8, SIHS, RG1 box 17, USF.

43. In a letter to Harry Ueno, Kurihara said that he visited Santa Clara University before attending St. Ignatius University: Kurihara to Ueno, April 7, 1965, HU. However, he attended St. Ignatius High School, not the university. McKevitt, *The University of Santa Clara*, 170–71; McKevitt, *Brokers of Culture*, 276; McGucken, *The Jesuits and Education*, 276. Established in 1855, the San Francisco school was first called St. Ignatius College. The school used the term "college" in the European sense of the word, a school for students six to eighteen years old. In the late nineteenth century the school began high school and post–high school classes. At the turn of the twentieth century it ended its elementary-level classes; in 1918 it ended grades 7 and 8. In 1909 the high school division was called St. Ignatius High School, and in 1912 the post–high school division was named University of St. Ignatius (later University of San Francisco). See McGloin, *Jesuits by the Golden Gate*, 134–37; Totah, "Spiritus Magis," 3, 7, 30, 42.

44. McGloin, *Jesuits by the Golden Gate*, 96; Totah, "Spiritus Magis," 1–48. Photo Albums, 1907–1925, SIHS, USF. Lists of student names accompany the class photos.

45. In 1885, the San Francisco school board had created a separate school for Chinese, which continued to operate through the 1930s. The creation of the school was in response to *Tape v. Hurley*, 66 California Reports 473–475 (1884–1885), in which the California State Supreme Court upheld a lower court decision that allowed a Chinese American girl, Mamie Tape, to enroll in a regular public school. The court had reasoned that no state law prohibited the Chinese from attending school with whites. In response the California legislature passed a law that allowed school districts to establish segregated schools for "Mongolians." In 1906, when the San Francisco school board directed Japanese and Korean children to attend the Chinese school, uproar in Tokyo led to federal intervention by President Theodore Roosevelt, who feared a diplomatic crisis with the emerging Asian power. The result was the Gentleman's Agreement of 1907–08, in which Japan agreed not to issue passports to laborers intending to travel to the continental United States. In turn, the San Francisco school board agreed to allow the few Nikkei (ethnic Japanese) youths in the city—ninety-three of the twenty-eight thousand students—to attend regular public schools. Congress then passed a bill that allowed Roosevelt to issue an executive order that barred Japanese from entering the continental United States via Hawai'i, Canada, and Mexico. The Gentleman's Agreement stopped the flow of laborers but not family members, and as a result, wives and other family members arrived until a 1924 immigration law stopped their entry into the United States. See Wollenberg, *All Deliberate Speed*, 61, 67; and Daniels, *The Politics of Prejudice*, 43–44, 72–73. Note that in 1915 it was relatively rare for Asian Americans to attend high school: Chinese Americans were relatively few as a result of the Chinese exclusion laws, and most children of Japanese immigrants were not yet of high school age.

46. Wollenberg, *All Deliberate Speed*, 29–47; Low, *The Unimpressible Race*, 59–73; San Francisco Population from the 1920 Census and 1910 Census; Okazaki, *Nihonmachi*, 38–42.

47. Kurihara, "Autobiography," 3.

48. California's 1920 land law forbade Japanese immigrants from leasing and corporations from owning agricultural land. A 1923 law further forbade Japanese from sharecropping. Between 1912 and 1923 Washington, Oregon, Idaho, Arizona, Texas, and Nebraska passed similar laws. See Daniels, *The Politics of Prejudice*, 46–54, 79–91; Ichioka, *The Issei*, 153–56, 226–43; and Tamura, *Americanization*, 78. By 1913 the Chinese were no longer seen as a threat. Chinese laborers had been excluded in 1882 with the Chinese Exclusion Act, which was extended in 1892 and 1902 and made permanent in 1904. During World War II, with China an ally of the United States, the law was rescinded and Chinese were allowed to become naturalized citizens. See Chan, *Asian Americans*, 54–55, 122. Phelan, who attended St. Ignatius High School, was mayor from 1897 to 1903 and U.S. Senator from 1913 to 1919.

49. Kurihara, "Autobiography," 3–4. Kurihara lived at 2095 Fulton Street in a building that was still standing in 2006; the next year he moved to 931 Anza Street. Kurihara's addresses are listed in *Registrar's Book, 1906–1927*, SIHS, 307–308, 331–32, 353–54, RG1, box 17, USF.

50. Yamazaki, "St. Francis Xavier School," 54–73; Pereyra, "The Catholic Church and Portland's Japanese," 399–434. The Maryknoll St. Francis Xavier School included kindergarten, elementary, and junior high grades. The St. Paul Miki School, which opened in 1937, included kindergarten through second grade. Kurihara could not have gone to these schools even if he had known about them, since they opened when Kurihara was a high school student. Nevertheless, my point is that the Catholic schools he attended, both in Hawai'i and San Francisco, were Western-centered, not bilingual-bicultural schools for Japanese Americans students. Ethnic parochial schools are discussed in Walch, *Parish School*, 3–4, 76–81.

51. Quote is from *Catalog of St. Ignatius University*, 1916–17, 113, RG4 Catalogs, USF. During the late nineteenth and early twentieth centuries, the notion of Americanization generally meant Anglo-conformity; it also meant that immigrants and their children would communicate in English, shed their so-called foreign ways, and be infused with ideas of patriotism, Christianity (Protestantism), diligence, and hard work. Catholic leaders vigorously protested the notion that Christianity meant Protestantism but agreed with the other aspects of the Americanization thrust. For a discussion of the Americanization idea during this period, see Tamura, *Americanization, Acculturation, and Ethnic Identity*, 52–55; and Walch, *Parish School*, 28–29. For a discussion of the challenge to Catholic schools, see Walch, *Parish School*, 72–73.

52. Courses and basic textbooks for all four years are in *Catalog*, SIU, 1916–1917, 114–15, RG 4, USF. The high school was attached to St. Ignatius University.

53. *Scholastic Records*, 6th Grade 1912–1913 to Senior High School 1925–1926, SIHS, RG1, box 9, USF; and *Scholastic Records*, 7th Grade 1916–1917 to Senior College 1920–1921,

SIHS, RG1, box 9, USF. For expectations of student behaviors, see *Bulletin*, SIU, 1916–17, 10–11, RG 4, USF. McGucken, *The Jesuits and Education*, 150, 165. While Catholic social doctrine included ideas of justice and the dignity of the human person (see O'Connor, *Catholic Social Doctrine*, 28, 50), Catholic social thought has been essentially traditionalist and conservative. There is a radical strand in Catholicism, but it became prominent well after the time of Kurihara's Catholic schooling. The radical strand, consisting of social reform ideas, evolved among a minority of Catholics in the 1920s and 1930s and became highly visible in the 1960s—for example, movements in Europe and North America and liberation theology in Latin America; there is no evidence that Kurihara was radicalized by Catholic social thinking during the 1920s and 1930s, before the incarceration of Japanese Americans. For discussions on Catholic social thought, see "Social Thought, Catholic," 255–66; and Bryk, Lee, and Holland, *Catholic Schools and the Common Good*, 41–46.

54. Farrell, *The Jesuit Code of Liberal Education*, 342–57; Gleason, *Contending with Modernity*, 5–6, 51–53. Kurihara took six periods of Latin in each of his two years at St. Ignatius School. For a discussion on the conflict between Americanists and traditionalists, see McKevitt, *Brokers of Culture*, 264–67, 276–78. Quote is from McKevitt, *Brokers of Culture*, 211. Even in the 1920s, Catholic high school educators opted to continue the study of the Western Classics, which they believed developed "the student's ability to reason" and promoted "the central moral aims of schooling." See Bryk, Lee, and Holland, *Catholic Schools and the Common Good*, 31.

55. Shuckburgh, *A History of Rome for Beginners*, 35, 38. Kurihara received an average score of 81 percent in his first-year history course and a 91 percent in his second year, which were very good scores in this Jesuit preparatory school. Kurihara's second-year textbook, Robinson's *A Short History of Greece*, focuses on battles and wars.

56. Rhetoric and elocution were important subjects in many schools across the country. R. C. H. Morison, *Chambers's New Reciter*, v, xiii, discusses the growing emphasis of elocution in the schools in the early 1900s and the many books published for recitation, including his *Chambers's New Reciter*. Another example is S. S. Curry's *Little Classics, with Initiative Steps in Vocal Training for Oral English*. For information on the elocution contest, see *Catalog of St. Ignatius University*, 1916–1917, 119, RG4 Catalogs, University of San Francisco Archives. For the elocution program, see *Catalog of St. Ignatius University*, 1917–1918, 102–103, RG 4 Catalogs, University of San Francisco Archives.

57. Mary Russell Mitford (1787–1855) of Hampshire, England, was a poet, playwright, and novelist who saw a number of her plays performed during her lifetime. "Rienzi's Address" is in *McGuffey's Sixth Eclectic Reader* (New York: Wiley, 1907), 221–23; and *Standard Classics, A Fifth Reader* (Boston: Educational Publishing, 1910), 173–75. After introducing many reforms, Rienzi unfortunately abused his power and was eventually assassinated.

58. According to his older sister, before he left for San Francisco, Kurihara had already demonstrated a tendency to take action in the name of justice: Marubayashi interviewed by author. Selections of the other contestants were Elijah Kellogg's "Spartacus to the

Gladiators," in which Spartacus calls on his fellow gladiators to battle their oppressors; Patrick Henry's "Liberty or Death," which speaks of noble struggles and principled action; Eleanor Donnelly's "Gualberto's Victory," which brings together ideas of Christian forgiveness and heroism; and Robert Walker's "The Level Crossing" and James Buckham's "The Race at Devil's Elbow," which present ideas of redemption and heroism. See *Catalog*, SIU, 1917–1918, 102, RG 4 Catalogs, USF.

Chapter 2. A Yank in France, a Jap in America

1. Kurihara, "Autobiography," 4.

2. Kurihara, "Autobiography," 4.

3. Chambers, *To Raise an Army*, 148; Society of the First Division, *History of the First Division during the World War, 1917–1919*, 1–6.

4. Joseph Y. Kurihara, "World War I Draft Registration Card"; Roy S. Kurihara, "World War I Draft Registration Card." A year later, with the dire situation in France demanding a much larger American presence, a second national registration day was held on September 12, 1918. With the age eligibility extended to include men ages eighteen to twenty and thirty-one to forty-five, 13 million more men were registered. Chambers, *To Raise an Army*, 179–89; quotes are from page 184.

5. Chambers, *To Raise an Army*, 200; Kurihara, "Autobiography," 5; Kurihara, "Renunciation of U.S. Nationality," Case File 146-54-117; Kurihara, "The Niseis and the Government of the United States," 6; Savage and Armstrong, "Were Things Really So Cheap in the 'Good Old Days'?"; http://www.inflationdata.com, "Historical Consumer Price Index." *Koku* means country, *on* is gratitude; *koku on* means "a deep sense of gratitude toward one's country." *The Detroit Free Press*, January 13, 1918, printed a photo of Kurihara's five nieces and nephews with this caption: "Joseph Y. Kurihara . . . is the sort of patriot who believes that actions speak louder than words. . . . Kurihara is now at Camp Custer training with others of the selective army. Almost the last thing he did before donning a uniform was to purchase a Liberty bond for each of five little nieces and nephews who reside in Honolulu, Hawaiian Islands, and whose smiling faces appear herewith."

6. Information on his height and weight is in Kurihara, Individual Record, 2864, WWII Internment Case File. The height and weight requirements are in Jay Hayden, "Draft Physical Tests Are Rigid," *Detroit News*, July 24, 1917. Information on Kurihara's brother Roy is from his son Raymond Kurihara, e-mail correspondence, June 26, 2007.

7. *Camp Custer*, 1–4. In 1917 the business section of Battle Creek, a town of twenty-five thousand residents, consisted of one street four blocks long. Three "motion picture houses," two small theaters, and a few modest restaurants would prove inadequate for the thirty-six thousand soldiers at Camp Custer. Edward Speyer, "Battle Creek Wins Disdain," *Detroit News*, September 9, 1917; Speyer, "Camp Custer Remains but the Bayonet Passes," *Detroit Saturday Night*, July 30, 1927; Douglas D. Martin, "Men Get Better Chance to Survive War Rigors," *Detroit Free Press*, November 2, 1941; "100

Buildings Up at Camp Custer," *Detroit Free Press*, July 25, 1917; Speyer, "Selected Men Need Clothing," *Detroit News*, November 14, 1917; "Real Guns Arrive at Camp Custer," *Detroit News*, November 11, 1917.

8. The War Department created the 85th Division soon after the United States entered the war. *Camp Custer*, 1–4; Barry, *Doings of Battery B*, 12; "Splendid Gymnasium for Custer Which Gifts of Michigan and Wisconsin Citizens Made Possible," *Detroit News*, November 11, 1917.

9. U.S. Army Field Artillery 328th, *The Red Guidon*, 123; Kurihara, "Autobiography," 5; Frank Parker, "Custer Begins Trench Work," *Detroit Free Press*, November 7, 1917; Edward Speyer, "Custer Bayonet Classes Taught How to Growl," *Detroit News*, November 4, 1917; "Custer Gives Sham Battle," *Detroit News*, December 18, 1917; "Camp Custer Boosts Sports for Soldiers," *Detroit News*, September 16, 1917; W. J. Cameron, "Yanks Study French; Aliens Study English," *Detroit News*, November 9, 1917; *Camp Custer*, 4.

10. Ford, *Americans All!* 3, 14, 112–36; "Stimulating Loyalty," *Detroit News*, September 11, 1917; "Draft Aliens for U.S. Army," *Detroit News*, September 14, 1917.

11. Shenk, "*Work or Fight!*" 119, 122.

12. Salyer, "Baptism by Fire," 854. Karl Iwanaga, commander of the Commodore Perry Post, composed of ethnic Japanese, reported that more than one thousand Nikkei served in World War I: "California's Japanese Post," *American Legion Monthly*, July 19, 1935, 36. U.S. Army Field Artillery, 328th, *The Red Guidon*, 75–123.

13. While Japan and the United States fought on the same side during World War I, their national interests conflicted in the Pacific, and during the war their relations deteriorated: Kawamura, *Turbulence in the Pacific*. In recalling his experiences during World War I, Kurihara mentions no ill treatment by fellow soldiers or officers, and only warm feelings toward families in Michigan who befriended him.

14. Salyer, "Baptism by Fire," 848; Britten, *American Indians in World War I*, 124, 130.

15. Salyer, "Baptism by Fire," 847–62. In Hawaii, Horace W. Vaughan, a territorial federal district court judge, challenged the refusal of Bureau of Naturalization to grant citizenship to Asian immigrant veterans. After some rancor, the bureau eventually backed down and deferred to the courts. While Judge Vaughn's court naturalized most of the Asian veterans, other courts did their share—in Washington, D.C., Boston, San Francisco, Los Angeles, and Philadelphia.

16. Coffman, *The War to End All Wars*, 355–56; Coffman provides a detailed account of Americans in the war effort, including the critical Meuse-Argonne offensive (pp. 299–356), which lasted from September through November 1918.

17. U.S. Army Field Artillery, 328th, *The Red Guidon*; U.S. Army Center of Military History, *Order of Battle of the United States Land Forces in the World War, American Expeditionary Forces*, 372–79; "The Custer Division in the World War"; Kurihara, "Autobiography," 5–6; and Kurihara, "I Was in the War."

18. Coffman, *The War to End All Wars*, 227–28. Four out of every five soldiers, or 1.6 million of them, departed from New York. Most of the others left from Newport News, Virginia.

19. Kurihara, "I Was in the War"; according to Ferrell, *A Soldier in World War I*, 11, 171n2, each boxcar held either forty men or eight horses.

20. Kurihara, "Autobiography," 6; Kurihara, "I Was in the War"; Ferrell, *A Soldier in World War I*, 63; U.S. Surgeon General's Office, *The Medical Department of the United States Army in the World War*, 389.

21. Kurihara, "I Was in the War"; similar descriptions are in Ferrell, *A Soldier in World War I*, 68, 173n3. Hanson, *World War I*, 88.

22. U.S. Surgeon General's Office, *The Medical Department of the United States Army in the World War*, 844; Coffman, *The War to End All Wars*, 125–26, 283; Scott, *The American Negro in the World War*, 147.

23. Kurihara, "Autobiography," 6; Pencak, *For God and Country*, 41–42, 331n41.

24. Kurihara, "I Was in the War."

25. Ngai, *Impossible Subjects*, 8.

26. Kurihara, "Autobiography," 7; Kurihara, NA Form 13164, Military Personnel Records.

27. Kurihara, "Autobiography," 8.

28. Kurihara, "Autobiography," 8. Kurihara's mother later returned to Hawaii, and after a few years she departed once again for Japan; she died in the 1930s. Marubayashi interview by author.

29. Quotes from Pencak, *For God and Country*, 6; Best, "Joe Kurihara, 'Repatriate,'" 2. On arriving from Hawaii to Los Angeles, see Kurihara, "Renunciation of U.S. Nationality," Case File 146–54–117, 1. His nephew recalled seeing Kurihara wearing the American Legion lapel pin: Raymond Kurihara, e-mail correspondence, July 18, 2007. The American Legion, formed on February 15, 1919 by twenty army officers, drew to its membership over one million World War I veterans by 1940, 25 percent of all who served. See Pencak, *For God and Country*, xii, 26; and Baker, *The American Legion and American Foreign Policy*, 16. In 1935 Japanese American veterans in Los Angeles formed the Commodore Perry Post. See "New Legion Post Active: Japanese Form Own Unit," *Los Angeles Times*, May 31, 1935; and *Sixth Annual Nisei Veterans Reunion*, 72. Ironically, Nikkei veterans of World War I organized posts in Topaz, Gila, Jerome, and Poston, where they were incarcerated during World War II. There was no post in Manzanar. See *Sixth Annual Nisei Veterans Reunion*, 73. The American Legion concentrated its efforts in spreading the "principles of Americanism" to immigrant and citizen youths and adults in schools, in the Boy Scouts, and in the community. See Gellerman, *The American Legion as Educator*, 68–74. Although Americanism was defined in various ways by members of the American Legion, it essentially boiled down to nationalism and patriotism, for which the American flag was a primary symbol.

Established in 1899 by veterans returning from campaigns in Cuba and the Philippines, the VFW was a relatively small organization until returning World War I soldiers increased its membership significantly and transformed it into an influential body. See Mason, *VFW*, 7, 37–39, 45; and Bottoms, *The VFW*, 54–55. Kurihara identified himself as a member of the VFW in Kurihara, "Niseis and the Government," 1.

30. Salyer, "Baptism by Fire," 866.

31. U.S. Commission on Wartime Relocation and Internment of Civilians, *Personal Justice Denied*, 34, 69; Pencak, *For God and Country*, 258–59; U.S. Congress, *Recommendations of the Commission on Wartime Internment*, 477–80.

32. Kurihara, "Niseis and the Government," 4; Kurihara, "Autobiography," 38.

33. Kurihara, "Autobiography," 9.

34. The term ethnoracial is especially appropriate when referring to Asian Americans and African Americans. As Varzally (*Making a Non-White America*, 9) notes, the term indicates the "perceived biological, historical, and behavioral qualities by which groups bounded themselves and were bound by others at different times and different places." In 1920 Los Angeles city included 11,618 Nikkei, 2,062 Chinese, 21,652 Mexicans, and 15,579 blacks. See Modell, *The Economics and Politics of Racial Accommodation*, 23. In 1930 Los Angeles County, the Mexican and nonwhite population was 11.7 percent, with 35,000 Japanese, 3,572 Chinese, 997 Indians, 46,425 blacks, 5,292 all other nonwhites, and 167,024 Mexicans. Population figures for 1930 city and county ethnoracial/linguistic groups are from U.S. Bureau of the Census, *Fifteenth Census, 1930: Population*, vol. 3, pt. 1. In 1930, the 1.2 million residents in Los Angeles made it the fifth largest city in the United States. See Fogelson, *The Fragmented Metropolis*, 77–81.

35. "Restrictive Covenants" is from Widener, "'Perhaps the Japanese Are to Be Thanked?'" 148; Scott Kurashige, *Shifting Grounds of Race*, 37, 40–41. Information on the location of temples in Los Angeles is from Glen Creason, Map Librarian, Los Angeles Public Library, e-mail correspondence, December 19, 2005; and Works Project Administration Writers' Program, *Los Angeles*, 146, 156–57.

36. Kurashige, *Shifting Grounds of Race*, 39–42; Modell, *The Economics and Politics of Racial Accommodation*, 71–75; "Payne's Heart of Downtown," 1931 map, Los Angeles Public Library; "Sims Map of Metropolitan Los Angeles," 1926, Los Angeles Public Library. Kurihara lived at 308 South Flower Street, eight blocks away from city hall. Address in Kurihara, Transcripts, 1924, Southwestern University. Varzally, *Making a Non-White America*, 30–40, provides maps showing the residential distribution of African Americans, Mexican Americans, Nikkei, Chinese Americans, and Filipino Americans, and discusses people's intergroup interactions. See also Wild, *Street Meeting*, 9–14. Wild, *Street Meeting*, 5–6, notes that the interethnic mixing of pre–World War II Eastside Los Angeles gave way to segregation as the norm after World War II.

37. Kurihara, "The Niseis and the Government," 11.

38. Modell, *The Economics and Politics of Racial Accommodation*, 8–9, 70, 94–99; Iwata, *Planted in Good Soil*, 393–448; Kurashige, *Shifting Grounds of Race*, 69–70.

39. Kurihara, "Autobiography," 12; Modell, *The Economics and Politics of Racial Accommodation*, 100–102; Daniels, *The Politics of Prejudice*, 46–54, 79–91; Ichioka, *The Issei*, 153–56, 226–43; Tamura, *Americanization, Acculturation, and Ethnic Identity*, 78. The land laws were ineffective in preventing Japanese immigrants from farming. Kurihara's experience was an example of how Japanese immigrants responded to the land laws: leasing or purchasing the land in the names of their children or friends who were American citizens. Moreover, little effort was made to enforce the laws. See

Daniels, *The Politics of Prejudice*, 88; and Modell, *The Economics and Politics of Racial Accommodation*, 102.

40. Kurihara, "Autobiography," 9; Best, "Joe Kurihara, 'Repatriate,'" 19; Frederick, "Case History, Joseph Yoshisuke Kurihara." Raymond Best was director at the Tule Lake Relocation Center and Francis Frederick was chief of internal security at Leupp Isolation Center.

41. Widener, "'Perhaps the Japanese Are to Be Thanked?'" 146.

42. Kurihara, "Autobiography," 10.

43. Southwestern University School of Law, "History of Southwestern"; Southwestern University School of Commerce, Official Announcement, 1922–1923, 35–39.

44. Kurihara, Transcripts, 1924, Southwestern University.

45. Kurihara, "Autobiography," 10; Southwestern University School of Commerce, Official Announcement, 1925–1926, 34–35; Kurihara, Transcripts, 1924, Southwestern University.

46. Kurihara, "Autobiography," 11–25; Modell, *The Economics and Politics of Racial Accommodation*, 130–33; Kurashige, *Shifting Grounds of Race*, 69.

47. Kurihara, "Autobiography," 11, 15–24; Fujita interview by author.

48. Kurihara, "Autobiography," 12–13, 18–24; Kurihara, Individual Record, 2864, WWII Internment Case File. The Japanese section of Los Angeles was called Little Tokio. See Works Project Administration Writers' Program, *Los Angeles*, 156. Kurihara lived on 788 East Pico Blvd. See U.S. Bureau of the Census, *Fifteenth Census, 1930, Population Schedule*, Los Angeles, Sheet 33A.

49. Kurihara, "Renunciation of U.S. Nationality," Kurihara Case File 146–54–117, 2–3; Kurihara, "Autobiography," 24–25.

50. Raymond Kurihara, e-mail correspondence with author, June 26, 2007.

51. His byline was J. Y. Kurihara: "Go East, Young Man, Go East," *Rafu Shimpō*, 7 March 1937; "Jobs and Leisure," *Kashū Mainichi*, June 23, 1940; "How to Make Best of a College Education," *Kashū Mainichi*, June 30, 1940; "Let's Not Pass the Buck," *Kashū Mainichi*, September 8, 1940.

52. "Sun Suits and Temptation," *Kashu Mainichi*, June 18, 1940.

53. "Strange Facts," *Kashu Mainichi*, June 18, 1940; "Strange but True," *Kashu Mainichi*, August 18, 1940; Kurihara, "Renunciation of U.S. Nationality," Case File 146–54–117, 2–3; Kurihara, "Autobiography," 24–25.

Chapter 3. To Manzanar

1. Godsil, *The High Seas Tuna Fishery of California*, 17, 38; Kurihara, "Autobiography," 25.

2. Godsil, *The High Seas Tuna Fishery of California*,9.

3. Godsil, *The High Seas Tuna Fishery of California*, 24, 26.

4. Godsil, *The High Seas Tuna Fishery of California*, 33.

5. Godsil, *The High Seas Tuna Fishery of California*, 29.

6. Godsil, *The High Seas Tuna Fishery of California*, 26–27, 31. For excellent photos of the excitement and hazards of tuna fishing in the 1920s through the 1950s, see Felando, "California's Tuna Clipper Fleet Part 1," 6–17; and Felando, "California's Tuna Clipper Fleet Part 2," 17–27.

7. Godsil, *The High Seas Tuna Fishery of California*, 11, 26.

8. Dorwart, *Conflict of Duty*, 52–53, 55.

9. Zacharias, *Secret Missions*, 200.

10. Dorwart, *Conflict of Duty*, 68. On MAGIC, see Loureiro, "U.S. Counterintelligence against Japan," 39–40, 119. On MAGIC not implicating Japanese Americans, see Robinson, *By Order of the President*, 277n43. Herzig, "Japanese Americans and MAGIC," refutes accusations that MAGIC intercepts played a role in the decision to incarcerate the Nikkei.

11. Malkin, *In Defense of Internment*, xiii, 37–51.

12. Quote on size of boats from Godsil, *The High Seas Tuna Fishery*, 9. On the men's nationalities, see Estes, "Kondo Masaharu," 15. Quote on shacks from Kumamoto, "Search for Spies," 59. Loureiro, "U.S. Counterintelligence against Japan in Southern California," 57–59.

13. Estes, "'Offensive Stupidity,'" 10. Some of the tuna vessels owned by Abe Tokunosuke, a Japanese national and longtime U.S. resident, for example, were registered in Japan and flew the Japanese flag while at sea. See Loureiro, "U.S. Counterintelligence against Japan in Southern California," 49. In 1939 Abe's twenty-five tuna vessels constituted the largest fleet under a single management in Southern California. Abe also used Baja California as a base of operation for his fleet, and among his crew were more than a hundred contract workers from Japan residing in Mexico. See Estes, "'Offensive Stupidity,'" 3. On the Japanese role in the development of the fishing industry in southern California and western Mexico, and the recruitment of fishermen from Japan, see Estes, "Kondo Masaharu."

14. Zacharias, *Secret Missions*, 200.

15. Kurihara, "Autobiography," 25–27.

16. Kurihara, "Autobiography," 27.

17. Kurihara, "Autobiography," 27–30.

18. Tanaka, "How to Survive Racism in America's Free Society," 93–94; Kurihara, "Autobiography," 30.

19. Kurihara, "Autobiography," 31.

20. Kurihara, "Autobiography," 30–33.

21. Kurihara, "Autobiography," 36–37.

22. Estes, "'Offensive Stupidity,'" 2–4.

23. Estes, "'Offensive Stupidity,'" 9.

24. Loureiro, "The Imperial Japanese Navy and Espionage"; Ichioka, *Before Internment*, 204–26. A slightly different account is in Kumamoto, "The Search for Spies," 55. I use the family name first for Japanese nationals who were not residents of the United States.

25. Malkin, *In Defense of Internment*, 32–34, 132.

26. Loureiro, "U.S. Counterintelligence against Japan in Southern California," 102; Munson, "Japanese on the West Coast"; Robinson, *By Order of the President*, 66–67.

27. Loureiro, "U.S. Counterintelligence against Japan in Southern California," 134–39.

28. Loureiro, "U.S. Counterintelligence against Japan in Southern California," 89–93.

29. Loureiro, "U.S. Counterintelligence against Japan in Southern California," 108.

30. Ichioka, *Before Internment*, 216.

31. Ichioka, *Before Internment*, 197; Unrau, *The Evacuation and Relocation of Persons of Japanese Ancestry during World War II*, 12; Hayashi, *Democratizing the Enemy*, 74–75.

32. Muller, *American Inquisition*, 15–16; Daniels, *Concentration Camps*, 39, 71–72. For analyses of the discussions and activities that led up to forced removal of West Coast Nikkei, see Daniels, *Concentration Camps*, 42–73; Daniels, *The Decision to Relocate the Japanese Americans*; Irons, *Justice at War*, 25–47; U.S. Commission on Wartime Relocation and Internment of Civilians, *Personal Justice Denied*, 72–92; Grodzins, *Americans Betrayed*; and tenBroek, Barnhart, and Matson, *Prejudice, War, and the Constitution*. de Nevers, *The Colonel and the Pacifist*, provides a portrait of Bendetsen and reveals how he conceived, developed, advocated, and executed E.O. 9066. While acknowledging domestic issues—racial antipathy, pressure of lobbyists, and wartime hysteria—Hayashi, in *Democratizing the Enemy*, 8, 39, 80–84, posits national and global security issues, both real and imagined, as further causes for the mass removal of the Nikkei.

33. Azuma, *Between Two Empires*, 209.

34. Executive Order No. 9066, February 19, 1942, Authorizing the Secretary of War to Prescribe Military Areas, Franklin D. Roosevelt Presidential Library and Museum. Available at http://www.fdrlibrary.marist.edu (accessed November 11, 2012) The expansion of exclusion zones to include all of California is discussed in Commission on Wartime Relocation and Internment of Civilians, *Personal Justice Denied*, 111–12.

35. Muller, *American Inquisition*, 21. The forced removal is also discussed in Commission on Wartime Relocation and Internment of Civilians, *Personal Justice Denied*, 100–12; and Unrau, *The Evacuation and Relocation of Persons of Japanese Ancestry*, 63–64.

36. Muller, *American Inquisition*, 17, 19, 154 n12; Robinson, *By Order of the President*, 33–44, 90–91; Daniels, *Concentration Camps*, 72–73.

37. Robinson, *Tragedy of Democracy*, 113–21; Lind, *Hawaii's People*, 28.

38. Hayashi, *Democratizing the Enemy*, 152.

39. Irons, *Justice at War*, 27; Unrau, *The Evacuation and Relocation of Persons of Japanese Ancestry during World War II*, 16; Japanese American Citizens League, *The Case for the Nisei*, 31–34. On submarine attacks on the East and West Coasts, see Baldwin, "Americans at War," 199–200; Gannon, *Operation Drumbeat*, xviii. On military conclusions of no threat, see Muller, "Hirabayashi," 41–42.

40. Japanese American Citizens League, *The Case for the Nisei*, 18. Unease about Japanese American dual nationality was reflected in question 25 of the loyalty questionnaire that those incarcerated were required to answer: "To the best of your knowledge, was your birth ever registered with any Japanese governmental agency for the purpose of

establishing a claim to Japanese citizenship?" Dual citizenship continued to be a heated topic in 1944, as evidenced by the American Legion Hood River Post's removal from an honor roll the names of Nikkei veterans suspected of being dual citizens: "Legion Post Explains Its Anti-Jap Stand" December 22, 1944, *Hood River News*, Roll 7, M1342, Community Analysis Reports, 1942–46, WRA.

41. Huber, "Dual Citizenship," 23–24; Japanese American Citizens League, *The Case for the Nisei*, 15–18; Muller, *American Inquisition*, 11–12. For the 1924 Japanese Nationality law, see Flournoy and Hudson, *A Collection of Nationality Laws of Various Countries as Contained in Constitutions, Statutes, and Treaties*, 382–88. For a discussion of the difficulties of expatriating, see Sakamaki, "Dual Citizenship and Expatriation," 35. Kurihara's dual citizenship is indicated in Kurihara, Removed Koseki; Kurihara, Individual Request for Repatriation, 2864, WWII Internment Case File; and Kurihara, "Murder in Camp Manzanar," 17.

42. American-born children of male citizens of France, Switzerland, Russia, and Turkey were also dual citizens. Japanese American Citizens League, *The Case for the Nisei*, 18–21, 20n79. For nationality laws during this period, see Flournoy and Hudson, *A Collection of Nationality Laws of Various Countries as Contained in Constitutions, Statutes, and Treaties* (304–6 and 361–63 for laws for Germany and Italy). Currently the United States tolerates dual passports, but it continues to refuse to accept explicitly dual citizenship. Those wishing to become naturalized citizens must still swear that they renounce any allegiance to another country. This is in contrast to many other countries, which recognize explicitly dual and multiple citizenships. See Bloemraad, "Much Ado about Nothing?" 159–60, 179–80n2, n4.

43. Kurihara, "Autobiography," 37. Unrau, *The Evacuation and Relocation of Persons of Japanese Ancestry during World War II*, 52–53 discusses the Terminal Island removal.

44. Kurihara to Tanaka, February 21, 1942, Tanaka Journal, frame 342, folder A17.07, reel 011, JAERR.

45. Kurihara, "Autobiography," 38.

Chapter 4. Resistance in Manzanar

1. Unrau, *Evacuation and Relocation of Persons of Japanese Ancestry during World War II*, xxv.

2. Unrau, *Evacuation and Relocation of Persons of Japanese Ancestry during World War II*, xxix, 181; Hayashi, *Democratizing the Enemy*, 17–18. For a detailed discussion of Manzanar site, 1800–1940, see Unrau, *Evacuation and Relocation of Persons of Japanese Ancestry during World War II*, 136–85.

3. Scott Kurashige, *The Shifting Grounds of Race*, 129–30. The *Doho*, a publication of the Communist Party of the United States of America (CPUSA), also publicized the need for volunteers. The support of the CPUSA in America's war effort is discussed in the profile of Yoneda in the next chapter.

4. Brown, "Story of Joe Kurihara," 14.

5. Kurihara, [Speeches], 3; From Merritt to Tozier, Chief Reports Division, January

7, 1946, pp. 1–2, 4, folder 8, box 16, MWRR; Kurihara, Individual Request for Repatriation or Expatriation, 2864, WWII Internment Case File, WRA; Brown, "Story of Joe Kurihara," 18–19.

6. Kurihara, "Autobiography," 39.

7. Unrau, *Evacuation and Relocation of Persons of Japanese Ancestry during World War II*, 187–94.

8. Takemoto, *Nisei Memories*, 126.

9. Unrau, *Evacuation and Relocation of Persons of Japanese Ancestry during World War II*, xxvi, 377. For maps of Manzanar, see Burton, et al., *Confinement and Ethnicity*, 164–65.

10. Wax, "The Destruction of a Democratic Impulse," 12.

11. When the WCCA administered the Manzanar site from March 21 through May 31, 1942, it was called the Owens Valley Reception Center. On June 1, 1942, when it was transferred to the WRA, it was renamed the Manzanar War Relocation Center.

12. Except when otherwise cited, my discussion of the events of the revolt is based on Unrau, *Evacuation and Relocation of Persons of Japanese Ancestry during World War II*, 477–523, which provides much detail; Hansen and Hacker, "The Manzanar Riot: An Ethnic Perspective," an excellent analysis and a persuasive argument that "revolt" is a more appropriate word than "riot"; Mananar-Incident Material, box 69, entry 4b, WRA; and Morris Edward Opler, "A History of Internal Government at Manzanar, March 1942 to December 6, 1942," July 15, 1944, typescript, folder 2, box 12, MWRR.

13. Koichi Tsuji, "A Private Report on the Incident of Dec. 6, 1942, Part I," [December 6, 1942], S1.20c, 67/14c, JAERR. Recognizing the unpopularity of Campbell among the Nikkei, the WRA office in Washington, D.C., had him transferred out of Manzanar about a month after the revolt. Koichi Tsuji, "Manzanar Incident, Exhibit C," [January 1943], S1.20c, 67/14c, JAERR.

14. Kurihara, "Murder in Camp Manzanar," 1, 5; Unrau, *Evacuation and Relocation of Persons of Japanese Ancestry during World War II*, 507.

15. Kurihara, "Murder in Camp Manzanar," 2–3. Tanaka, "Report on the Manzanar Riot," 25, January 10, 1943, O10.12, JAERR, describes Kurihara as "pudgy and rotund," 150 pounds, and semi-bald.

16. The members of the Committee of Five were as follows: Gengi Yamaguchi, a forty-year-old Issei who was a block manager; Shigetoshi Tateishi, a Kibei-Nisei (age unknown) who was a block leader; Sakichi Hashimoto, a forty-two-year-old Issei who was on the Kitchen Workers executive committee; Kazuo Suzukawa, a thirty-eight-year-old Issei who was a chef in the mess hall for Block 8; and Kurihara. Unrau, *Evacuation and Relocation of Persons of Japanese Ancestry during World War II*, 480.

17. Before his appointment as Manzanar project director, Merritt had been a California agriculturalist. Myer, who had been a bureaucrat in the Department of Agriculture before his appointment as WRA Director, appointed Merritt and others from the department to many of the administrative posts in the WRA. Raymond Best, who became project director of Moab and Tule Lake, also worked in the Department of Agriculture. Other administrators in the WRA worked previously in the Bureau of Indian Affairs

(BIA). E. R. Fryer, who had been superintendent of the Navajo Reservation in Arizona and who administered the ten camps from his San Francisco office, hired many people from the BIA. On Myer's stint at the Department of Agriculture, see Drinnon, *Keeper of Concentration Camps*, 18–19. On appointments from the Department of Agriculture and the BIA, see Brown interview by Hansen, 19–21.

18. Kurihara, "Murder in Camp Manzanar," 4; Merritt to Tozier, Chief Reports Division, January 7, 1946, p. 4, folder 8, box 16, MWRR. Both Merritt and Kurihara later recalled the same three points of agreement. With item 2, however, Kurihara said that there would not be another "mob demonstration," while Merritt said that there would not be another "mass meeting." This later led Merritt to conclude that Kurihara had violated one of the terms of their agreement. Merritt recalled three additional areas of agreement that Kurihara did not recall: that Ueno would be taken to the Manzanar jail and stand trial in a manner that Merritt decided; that recognized committees would discuss future grievances with Merritt; and that the Committee of Five would help to find Tayama's assailants. Frederick, "Kurihara Case History," 10; Fryer and Sigler to the Director, December 22, 1943, 6, Manzanar-Incident Material, box 69, entry 4b, WRA.

19. Kurihara, "Murder in Camp Manzanar," 5.

20. Kurihara, "Murder in Camp Manzanar," 5. In recounting the details of the revolt, Kurihara makes no mention of a group going to the hospital, which indicates that he was unaware of it. He and the other committee members were on the oil tank speaking to the crowd, and could not hear everything that was being said in the crowd.

21. Tanaka, "A Report on Manzanar Riot of Sunday December 6, 1942," [January 7, 1943], 71–74, O10.12, 67/14c, JAERR.

22. Matsushita interview with author.

23. Embrey, Hansen, and Mitson, *Manzanar Martyr*, 56.

24. Kurihara, "Murder in Camp Manzanar," 6.

25. The two soldiers who shot into the crowd later testified that they believed that their lives were in danger, and the military Board of Officers who heard their case concluded that there was no wrongdoing. However, at later hearings of a subcommittee of the Senate Committee of Military Affairs, Captain Hall admitted that two rounds of tear gas thrown into the crowd broke it up before the shots were fired, questioning the claim that the soldiers were in physical danger: Unrau, *Evacuation and Relocation of Persons of Japanese Ancestry during World War II*, 519–21.

26. Kurihara, "Murder in Camp Manzanar," 8.

27. Tanaka, "An Analysis of Manzanar Riot and Its Aftermath," January 25, 1943, p. 5, Mananar-Incident Material, box 69, entry 4b, WRA. For a discussion on the Nikkei at Death Valley, see Kashima, Judgment without Trial, 143–44.

28. Ueno, Kurihara, and the others jailed at Bishop, Independence, and Lone Pine were called "troublemakers" by WRA officials and the FBI. The same term was used for all those who were taken to the citizen isolation camps of Moab and Leupp. Most of those jailed were Issei and Kibei-Nisei. Kurihara was one of two Nisei. Unrau, *Evacuation and Relocation of Persons of Japanese Ancestry during World War II*, 490.

29. Tanaka, Project Report No. 79, October 26, 1942, Manzanar-Incident Material, box 69, entry 4b, WRA.

30. Unrau, *Evacuation and Relocation of Persons of Japanese Ancestry during World War II*, 376–81.

31. Hansen and Hacker, "The Manzanar Riot," 121, credits Yatsushiro, "Political and Socio-Cultural Issues at Poston and Manzanar Relocation Centers," for insights into six Nikkei cultural themes, of which two are relevant to Manzanar revolt. In *Japanese American Celebration and Conflict*, 90–91, and in "Resistance, Collaboration, and Manzanar Protest," Lon Kurashige challenges the emphasis on cultural differences and instead highlights differences in class backgrounds: protesters were those who had worked primarily in the produce and fishing industries, in contrast to the JACLers, who were primarily the college-educated, social elite of the Nikkei. My view is that social class interacted with and fed into the different cultural perspectives of the Nikkei.

32. Takemoto, *Nisei Memories*, 101.

33. Lon Kurashige, "The Problem of Biculturalism," 1, 633–34; Hayashi, "*For the Sake of Our Japanese Brethren*," 121–26, 134–36; Stephan, *Hawaii under the Rising Sun*, 35–37, 41–43; Takahashi, *Nisei/Sansei*, 6–9, 48–84. For a discussion of Nikkei sentiments toward a victory by Japan, see Hayashi, *Democratizing the Enemy*, 121–24.

34. Hansen and Hacker, "The Manzanar Riot," 124.

35. Hansen and Hacker, "The Manzanar Riot," 124–25; Kumamoto, "The Search for Spies," 57.

36. For assessments of the JACL, see Takahashi, "Japanese American Responses to Race Relations"; Ichioka, *Before Internment*, 46–47; Daniels, "The Japanese," 36–63; Spickard, "The Nisei Assume Power," 147–74; and Robinson, A *Tragedy of Democracy*, 110–11. For a history of the JACL, see Tanaka, "History of J. A. C. L," n.d., typescript, 67/14c, JAERR.

37. Tanaka, "An Analysis of Manzanar Riot and Its Aftermath," January 25, 1943, p. 5, Mananar-Incident Material, box 69, entry 4b, WRA; Tanaka interview by Hansen, 158; Hansen, "A Riot of Voices," 129–30.

38. Yoneda to Roy Nash, August 24, 1942, folder 4, WRA, Community Government, Block Manager Reports, August 16–31, 1942, box 9, MWRR. On the deathlist and blacklist, see Hansen, "A Riot of Voices," 129.

39. Quote from Miyamoto, "Resentment, Distrust, and Insecurity at Tule Lake," 129. Although Miyamoto was referring to the situation at Tule Lake, his analysis can be applied to Manzanar.

40. Kurihara, [Speeches], 1–2; Yoneda, *Ganbatte*, 135–37.

41. Tanaka and Masaoka, "Project Report No. 36," July 29, 1942, O1.78, 67/14c, JAERR. Togo Tanaka and Joe Masaoka worked for the WRA by taking field notes and writing reports on happenings in the camp. They did this openly.

42. Kurihara, Speeches, 3.

43. Tanaka and Masaoka, "Project Report No. 47," August 12, 1942, 257–58, O10.08, 67/14c, JAERR; Kurihara, "Autobiography," 40.

44. Kurihara, "Autobiography," 41.

45. Hansen and Hacker, "The Manzanar Riot," 131; Tanaka, "An Analysis of Manzanar Riot and Its Aftermath," January 25, 1943, 3, Mananar-Incident Material, box 69, entry 4b, WRA; Tanaka interview with author. Morris Edward Opler, "A History of Internal Government at Manzanar, March 1942 to December 6, 1942," July 15, 1944, 36–37, 40–41, 49, typescript, folder 2, box 12, MWRR, provides a similar interpretation. For discussion on the clash of opposing views, see Tanaka and Masaoka, Project Report No. 45, August 6, 1942, MWRR. In his memoir, Ariyoshi downplayed the resistence to Manzanar Citizens Federation perspective. See Beechert and Beechert, *From Kona to Yenan*, 70–71.

46. The idea behind this countergroup was similar to Kurihara's proposal to change the name Manzanar Citizens Federation to Manzanar Welfare Federation. Odo, *Heroic Struggles of Japanese Americans*, 49, notes that Kurihara's motion for a name change lost by a vote of 112 to 128. See also Unrau, *Evacuation and Relocation of Persons of Japanese Ancestry during World War II*, 513, 517–18.

47. Kurihara, Speeches, 3.

48. Roy Nash was Manzanar's project director from June 1 to November 24, 1942, and was succeeded by Ralph Merritt. Tayama to Rudisill, August 9, 1942, file 323.3 Manzanar, box 12, General Correspondence, 1942–46, WDC. Attached to the letter was the report, "Brief Report of the Kibei-Nisei Meeting Held at Mess Hall 15, Manzanar Relocation Center, August 8, 1942." Odo, *Heroic Struggles of Japanese Americans*, 50–53, provides his version of the meeting.

49. Kurihara recalled his own words in a written statement that he made in 1943. See Frederick, "Case History, Joseph Yoshisuke Kurihara," 4. On "roaring applause," see Tayama to Rudisill, August 9, 1942, file 323.3 Manzanar, box 12, General Correspondence, 1942–46, WDC. Attached to the letter was a report that Tayama sent to the army and to the FBI: "Brief Report of the Kibei Meeting Held at Mess Hall 15, Manzanar Relocation Center, August 8, 1942."

50. Van Wagoner, FBI report, Kurihara et al., Internal Security-Sedition-Public Law 503, September 13, 1942, 10, Assistant Secretary of War 020, Civil Affairs Division, box 9, entry 47, SOW. Yoneda reported on this and other meetings. See Yoneda, "Notes and Observations of 'Kibei Meeting' Held August 8th, 1942 at Kitchen 15—Only Japanese Spoken," folder 2, August 1 to September 30, 1942, box 8, KY; and "Manzanar Citizens' Federation—July 28, 1942" and "Block Meeting, Block 4, July 30, 1942," folder 1, June 1 to July 30, 1942, box 8, KY.

51. Nash, "Official Bulletin," August 10, 1942, folder 1, box 16, MWRR. The ban on speaking in Japanese at meetings had come earlier, on July 4, from the WRA office in Washington, D.C. At the time, Manzanar administrators chose to interpret the directive as allowing spoken Japanese, as long as the meeting included an English translation. Van Wagoner, FBI report, Kurihara et al., Internal Security-Sedition-Public Law 503, September 13, 1942, 2–3, 25, Assistant Secretary of War 020, Civil Affairs Division, box 9, entry 47, SOW.

52. Hoover to Berge, October 14, 1942; Berge to Hoover, November 10, 1942; Berge

to the Director FBI, January 30, 1943: in Classified Subject file 146–28–492, pertaining to Joseph Y. Kurihara et al., box 85, 5/38/20/5, DOJ.

53. Unrau, *Evacuation and Relocation of Persons of Japanese Ancestry during World War II*, 513; Morris Edward Opler, "A History of Internal Government at Manzanar, March 1942 to December 6, 1942," July 15, 1944, 50–51, typescript, folder 2, box 12, MWRR.

54. Tanaka, "Special Report," October 10, 1942, 2–3, microfilm reel 149, 67/14c, JAERR.

55. Tanaka, "Special Report," October 10, 1942, 3–4, microfilm reel 149, 67/14c, JAERR.

56. Robert L. Brown and Ralph P. Merritt, Final Report: Manzanar Relocation Center, vol. 1, 1946, p. 16, 67/14c, JAERR. Similar sentiments were expressed at another meeting held on November 30, 1942. See Tanaka and Masaoka, Project Report No. 76, December 1, 1942, MWRR. On the charter not being ratified, see Morris Edward Opler, "A History of Internal Government at Manzanar, March 1942 to December 6, 1942," July 15, 1944, 119–20, typescript, folder 2, box 12, MWRR.

57. While Ueno and others believed that Campbell and Winchester were taking sugar (and meat) meant for the Nikkei, others said that the Nikkei warehouse workers were taking the sugar. Unrau, *Evacuation and Relocation of Persons of Japanese Ancestry during World War II*, 507.

58. A detailed portrait of Tayama is in Tanaka, "A Report on the Manzanar Riot of Sunday December 6, 1942," [7 January 1943], 1–13, O10.12, 67/14c, JAERR.

59. Quote from Hansen and Hacker, "The Manzanar Riot," 139; Kurihara, "Autobiography," 47.

60. Hansen and Hacker, "The Manzanar Riot," 139, 156n115; Janet Goldberg, "Manzanar 'Incident,' December 5 to December 19," O7.00, 67/14c, JAERR. Goldberg was a teacher who wrote the report under the supervision of Reports Officer Robert Brown. Tayama, who was born in Hawai'i, died on May 9, 1966, at age sixty: See "Final Rites Held for Fred Tayama," *Pacific Citizen*, May 13, 1966.

61. Lotchin, "Japanese Relocation in World War II and the Illusion of Universal Racism"; Kurihara, Speeches, 8. For Kurihara's use of the word "whitewash," see his essay to the *Saturday Evening Post* in chapter 6.

Chapter 5. Stepping Back

1. My profile of Slocum is based on Tanaka, "A Report on the Manzanar Riot," 29–36, O10.12, 67/14c, JAERR; Tanaka interview by Hansen; Hosokawa, *JACL, in Quest of Justice*, 51–55; and Salyer, "Baptism by Fire." Slocum had earlier been married for ten years to a woman of Irish ancestry. On Slocum's membership in the American Legion and the VFW, see Claude B. Washburne, Chief, Inspection and Fiscal Division, WCCA, August 12, 1942, p. 4, file 323.3, box 12, 1942–46, WDC.

2. *Toyota v. United States*, 268 US 302 (1925).

3. Tanaka interview by Mitson and Hacker, 133.

4. Quotes are from Tanaka interview by author. Information for Tanaka's profile is from Tanaka interview by Mitson and Hacker; Lon Kurashige, "Resistance, Collaboration, and

the Manzanar Protest," 403–4; and Hayashi, *Democratizing the Enemy*, 57. After the war, Tanaka worked in Chicago as a journalist and later returned to Los Angeles, where he worked as a businessman: Tanaka interview by Gatewood, 420.

5. Tanaka, "How to Survive Racism in America's Free Society," 92–94.

6. Scott Kurashige, *Shifting Grounds of Race*, 128, 130; Tanaka, "How to Survive Racism in America's Free Society," 94; Tanaka interview by author. For an example of Tanaka's disagreement with WRA officials, see Tanaka to Shoemaker, July 11, 1942, folder 1—Un-American Activities, box 27, MWRR. On Kurihara's view of Tanaka's documentary reports, see Hansen, "A Riot of Voices," 128.

7. These reports are part of JAERR, 010.10, 010.12, 010.14, 010.16.

8. Kurihara, "Autobiography," 46; Hosokawa, *Nisei*, 362.

9. Tanaka interview by author.

10. Yoneda, *Ganbatte*, xi–xiv, 15–16, 40–41, 95. Because of California's anti-miscegenation law, in November 1935 the couple traveled to Seattle to be married. For a biography of Elaine Black Yoneda, see Raineri, *The Red Angel*.

11. Yoneda, *Ganbatte*, 122–23; Claude B. Washburne, Chief, Inspection and Fiscal Division, WCCA, August 12, 1942, p. 3, file 323.3, box 12, WDC.

12. Yoneda to Nash, August 24, 1942, folder 4, box 9, MWRR; Yoneda, "Notes and Observations of 'Kibei Meeting' Held August 8th, 1942 at Kitchen 15—Only Japanese Spoken," folder 2, box 8, KY; Yoneda, "Manzanar Citizens' Federation—July 28, 1942," and "Block Meeting, Block 4, July 30, 1942," folder 1, box 8, KY; Yoneda to Nash and Campbell, July 10, 1942, folder 2, box 9, MWRR.

13. Yoneda, *Ganbatte*, 139, 169.

14. Yoneda, *Ganbatte*, 145–47.

15. Yoneda, *Ganbatte*, 148–49. One of the two men who translated Kurihara's words to Elaine on December 6 later recounted the incident to Karl: Kamikawa interview by Yoneda, folder 1, box 9, KY.

16. Karl Yoneda, Letter to the Editor, *Pacific Citizen*, February 13, 1970, folder 1, box 8, KY; Elaine Black Yoneda, Letter to the Editor, *Hokubei Mainichi*, [May 3] 1983.

17. Takemoto, *Nisei Memories*, 101; Kurihara, "The Niseis and the Government," 8.

18. Frederick, "Kurihara Case History, Statement," 1.

19. Ichioka, *Before Internment*, 170–71; Shibusawa, "'The Artist Belongs to the People'" 259. In *Doing Fieldwork*, 73, Wax said this about the Gila camp Nikkei who were labeled disloyal: "Some talked for hours, telling me again and again that they were not disloyal but they had lost faith in America and felt that they had no future in this country. Some became so distressed they could barely hold back their tears."

20. Muller, *American Inquisition*, 2–4, 143, italics in original.

21. Morris Edward Opler, "A History of Internal Government at Manzanar, March 1942 to December 6, 1942," July 15, 1944, 131–155, folder 2, box 12, MWRR.

22. Brown and Merritt, "Supplement #3 to Report on the Manzanar Incident," January 6, 1943, Mananar-Incident Material, box 69, entry 4b, WRA, emphasis in original; Throckmorton to Merritt, January 2, 1943, Mananar-Incident Material, box 69, entry 4b, WRA; Tanaka, "An Analysis of the Manzanar Riot and Its Aftermath," January 25,

1943, 9–10, Mananar-Incident Material, box 69, entry 4b, WRA; Kurihara, "Niseis and the Government," 18.

23. Thomas, *The Spoilage*, 63; Unrau, *Evacuation and Relocation*, 693. For discussions on the poorly written questions and the confusion and controversy they created, see Commission on Wartime Relocation, *Personal Justice Denied*, 191–97; Thomas and Nishimoto, *The Spoilage*, 53–83; Weglyn, *Years of Infamy*, 134–51; Unrau, *Evacuation and Relocation of Persons of Japanese Ancestry during World War II*, 690–702; and Hansen and Hacker, "The Manzanar Riot," 143n10. For a copy of the questionnaire, see Chin, *Born in the USA*, 349–53.

Manzanar was not the only camp to display open opposition. While the dynamics at each camp differed, anger at their forced removal and incarceration led inmates at other camps to resist. Poston, Heart Mountain, and Tule Lake are the most well known, but there was turbulence also at Gila River and tension in the other camps, too, where inmates rendered their own forms of protest, such as non-cooperation, petitions, strikes, and mass meetings. Moreover, registration teams that visited the camps to administer the questionnaires encountered a general feeling of resentment and hostility. For a helpful discussion on resistance, see Gottlieb, "The Concept of Resistance." Hansen, "Protest-Resistance and the Heart Mountain Experience," uses Gottlieb's theoretical framework to argue that Nikkei resistance was widespread not only during World War II but also before and after the war. For works on Nikkei resistance, see Introduction.

24. For a discussion of the removal of Issei "troublemakers" from WRA camps to INS Internment Camps established for enemy aliens, see Drinnon, *Keeper of Concentration Camps*, 75–76. Earlier, by February 1942, Issei who had been on a list of suspects, as well as suspected German and Italian aliens, had been taken to Internment Camps. See Commission on Wartime Relocation, *Personal Justice Denied*, 284. On the removal to Moab and Tule Lake, see Weglyn, *Years of Infamy*, 126, 157. Okihiro, "Japanese Resistance," argues against the notion of a decline in resistance in the camps and proposes the idea that there was instead a continuation and "rechanneling" of resistance.

25. Kurihara, "Murder in Manzanar," 19; Van Wagoner, FBI report, Kurihara et al., Internal Security-Sedition-Public Law 503, September 13, 1942, 2–3, 25, Assistant Secretary of War 020, Civil Affairs Division, box 9, entry 47, SOW; Tanaka, "A Report on the Manzanar Riot," 26–27, O10.12, JAERR.

26. Tanaka interview by author; Kurihara, "Murder in Camp Manzanar," 21; Hansen and Hacker, "The Manzanar Riot," 141.

27. Tanaka interview by author.

28. Zacharias, *Secret Missions*, 34–35.

29. Yoneda, *Ganbatte*, 133; Raineri, *The Red Angel*, 214; Morris Edward Opler, "A History of Internal Government at Manzanar, March 1942 to December 6, 1942," July 15, 1944, 78, 83–85, 89, 109, typescript, folder 2, box 12, MWRR; "Wake Up the Manzanar Residents!" November 26, 1942, folder 3, box 16, MWRR; "Report on Letters and Posters Circulated at Manzanar," November 17, 1942, folder 3, box 16, MWRR. I have not found evidence that supports Yoneda's accusations. In the following document Yoneda lists Kurihara and Kishi as leaders of the Black Dragons: George Thow Photo, "Long Live

Great Empire of Japan! Manzanar Black Dragon Ass'n Hdqts," 1979, folder 5, box 8, KY. Yoneda made the same accusation in Yoneda to Editor, *Pacific Citizen*, February 13, 1970. Kurihara's denials are reported in Tanaka and Masaoka, Project Report 82, November 11, 1942, MWRR; Tanaka and Masaoka, Project Report 84, November 18, 1942, MWRR. Ueno disavowed any relationship with the Black Dragons in Embrey, Hansen, and Mitson, *Manzanar Martyr*, 44.

30. Yoneda, *Ganbatte*, 134.

31. "In re: Joseph Kurihara, Suggested Findings of Fact, Conclusion and Order, Segregation Docket No. 7, Manzanar Relocation Center," January 7, 1943, box 2864, 5/68/56/4, Kurihara, WWII Internment Case File; "Excerpt from Memo from Board of Review Dated 1/14/43, Joseph Kurihara," box 2864, 5/68/56/4, Kurihara, WWII Internment Case File.

32. Best, "Joe Kurihara, 'Repatriate,'" 19; Frederick, "Kurihara Case History," n.p.

33. Tanaka, "A Report on the Manzanar Riot," 24–25; Van Wagoner, FBI report, Kurihara et al., Internal Security-Sedition-Public Law 503, September 13, 1942, 2–3, 25, Assistant Secretary of War 020, Civil Affairs Division, box 9, entry 47, SOW.

34. HFN, pp. 1–2, September 4, 1944, W 1.61, JAERR.

35. Kamikawa interview by Yoneda.

36. Merritt to Tozier, Chief Reports Division, 7 January 1946, 3–4, folder 8, box 16, MWRR. For one of Tayama's reports, see Tayama to Rudisill, August 9, 1942, file 323.3, box 12, WDC.

37. Frederick, "Kurihara Case History, Statement," 12–13.

38. Frederick, "Kurihara Case History, Statement," 4–5, 13.

39. Frederick, "Kurihara Case History, Statement," 4–5.

40. From Hoover to Wechsler, January 13, 1945, Kurihara, Case File 146-54-117.

Chapter 6. Isolating Citizen Dissidents

1. Ueno, Diary, December 5, 1942–May 9, 1943, HU. Ueno's diary entries are consistent with other sources I found on events in Manzanar, Moab, and Leupp.

2. Federal officials called this citizen isolation camp the "Moab Isolation Center." Fryer and Sigler to Director, December 22, 1943, 35–36, Manzanar-Incident Material, box 69, entry 4b, WRA.

3. Merritt to Kaku, et al., January 8, 1943, Manzanar-Incident Material, box 69, entry 4b, WRA. Members of the Committee of Four were Tom Ozamoto, George Murakami, Ikanda, and Masunaka (I was unable to find the given names for the latter two): A Private Letter from Moab Addressed to the Block Leader of Block 17, February 14, 1943, folder 1, box 12, MWRR.

4. Kurihara, "Murder in Camp Manzanar," 13; Ueno, "Manzanar," 202; Merritt to Myer, January 9, 1943, Mananar-Incident Material, box 69, entry 4b, WRA.

5. *Utah Economic and Business Review*, December 1947, n.p.; Redd and Redd interview by author.

6. Quote from Sam Taylor, who was ten years old when the Nisei arrived at the

isolation camp: Taylor, "Community Comments," *Times-Independent*, September 1, 1994; Louthan, "Dalton Wells CCC Camp," 5; Louthan and Pierson, "Moab Japanese-American Isolation Center," 28–29; Burton, et al., *Confinement and Ethnicity*, 327. In 1994 the Moab Isolation Center was put on the National Register of Historic Places, and the following year Lloyd M. Pierson, former federal government archaeologist and former curator-director of the Dan O'Laurie Museum in Moab, Utah, succeeded in placing an anodized aluminum interpretive sign at the entrance of the camp. Pierson, "Dalton Wells CCC/internment Site North of Moab," *Times-Independent*, September 1, 1994; conversation with Lloyd Pierson, Moab, Utah, July 16, 1999.

7. Disposition of Cases Involved in Manzanar Incident of December 6, 1942, February 26, 1943, Manzanar-Incident Material, box 69, entry 4b, WRA; Ruth E. McKee, "History of W.R.A., Pearl Harbor to June 30, 1944," 154, box 3, WRA. For the quote from Ennis to Hoover and a discussion of the informal agreement between the WRA and the Alien Enemy Control Unit, see Drinnon, *Keeper of Concentration Camps*, 75.

8. Drinnon, *Keeper of Concentration Camps*, 103–4; Louthan and Pierson, "Moab Japanese-American Isolation Center," 29; Burton, et al., *Confinement and Ethnicity*, 325; Weglyn, *Years of Infamy*, 126. Yoshiro Kaku, who was among the Manzanar sixteen, is an example of one wrongly sent to Moab. Unaware of the events of December 5 and 6 until after he was jailed, he was removed from Manzanar because, as a warehouse worker, he had tried to enforce the rationing of sugar, for which he came into direct conflict with Chief Steward Joe Winchester and Assistant Project Director Ned Campbell, who confiscated sugar that was well beyond the quota for the Caucasian mess hall. Both Best and Frederick noted in separate reports that the twenty-seven-year-old Kaku was "honest, sincere and trustworthy," "one of the most cooperative" individuals. Despite threats by other Nikkei who did not want him to cooperate, Kaku proved to be "practically indispensible" to the smooth running of the isolation camps at Moab and Leupp. There he worked in the warehouse, which meant that, as in Manzanar, he had to enforce the rationing of food and supplies. See Frederick, Yoshio Kaku Case History, n.d., S1.20c, JAERR; Best to Myer, February 28, 1943, 5/68/56/4, box 2864, Kurihara WWII Internment Case File, WRA. Kaku was returned to Manzanar on July 9, 1943: D'Ille to Merritt, August 13, 1943, entry 16, file 39.055, box 289, Isolation Cases General, WRA.

9. Kurihara, "Murder in Camp Manzanar," 13.

10. Kurihara to the People of Manzanar, January 18, 1943, 5/68/56/4, Kurihara WWII Internment Case File, WRA, emphasis in original; Best to Myer, February 28, 1943, 5/68/56/4, Kurihara WWII Internment Case File, WRA; Kurihara to Best, November 20, 1945, in Best, "Joe Kurihara, 'Repatriate,'" 18.

11. Kurihara, "Murder in Camp Manzanar," 9. Kurihara filed an application for expatriation in November 1943, while he was at the Leupp Isolation Center, but he had thought about it seriously while in Manzanar, and his decision became solidified while at Moab, as demonstrated by his focused study of the Japanese language. Kurihara, Individual Request for Repatriation or Expatriation, November 1, 1943, Kurihara WWII Internment Case File.

12. Embrey, Hansen, and Mitson, *Manzanar Martyr*, 81; Sasaki interview by author; Kurihara, "Murder in Camp Manzanar," 20.

13. Kurihara, "Murder in Camp Manzanar," 14; Kurihara to Kanemoto, February 26, 1943, Law and Order Incident Moab, folder 6, box 16, MWRR.

14. Kurihara, "Murder in Camp Manzanar," 18–19, emphasis in original.

15. Supplement 4, Manzanar "Incident" December 5 to December 19, folder 3—Law and Order—Incident—Events Leading Up to and Including Incident—December 21, 1942, box 16, MWRR;

16. Residents of Moab Camp to Negotiation Committee, February 14, 1943, folder 6—Law and Order—Incident—Moab, box 16, MWRR; Best to Meyer, April 3, 1943, file 39.053, box 289, Headquarters, Subject Classified General Files, 1942–46, WRA; Ueno, Ego, and Tsuji to Best, April 5, 1943, file 39.053, box 289, Headquarters, Subject Classified General Files, 1942–46, WRA.

17. Private Letter from Moab Addressed to the Block Leader of Block 17, February 14, 1943, folder 1, box 12, MWRR.

18. Private Letter from Moab Addressed to the Block Leader of Block 17, February 14, 1943, folder 1, box 12, MWRR.

19. Frederick, "Kurihara Case History," 23; Ego interview with author. Yoshio Kaku, in a letter to the author, September 11, 1996, described Kurihara at Moab similarly: "He was a very quiet person. All he talk[ed] about [was] the way the Japanese people were treated after . . . Pearl Harbor."

20. Special Meeting of the Negotiating Committee of 105 Rep. at 13–15, February 19, 1943, folder 1, box 12, MWRR; Document Report No. 88, July 23, 1943, folder 1, box 12, MWRR.

21. Sigler to Provinse, April 12, 1943, 39.053, box 289, Headquarters, Subject-Classified General Files, 1942–46, WRA; Embrey, Hansen, and Mitson, *Manzanar Martyr*, 48.

22. Unless otherwise indicated, information on this incident is from Frederick to Best, Facts Leading to the Arrest and Disposition of Twenty-One Residents of Moab Isolation Center for Unlawful Assembly, April 19, 1943, S1.10, JAERR. Frederick enjoyed being in a position to wield his power. See Drinnon, *Keeper of Concentration Camps*, 100.

23. Spencer to Frederick, July 20, 1943, S1.10, JAERR.; Frederick to Spencer, July 22, 1943, S1.10, JAERR.

24. Unrau, *The Evacuation and Relocation of Persons of Japanese Ancestry during World War II*, 490; Memorandum to the Chief or Administrative Service, "Current Requirements for Prisoner of War and Alien Enemy Internment Camps in Continental United States," March 22, 1942, in Daniels, *American Concentration Camps*, vol. 3, n.p.

25. Embrey, Hansen, and Mitson, *Manzanar Martyr*, 74–75; Ueno, Diary, April 14, 1943; Drinnon, *Keeper of Concentration Camps*, 100n; Ueno interview by Ng, 497.

26. William J. McCormick, FBI Report re: Joseph Y. Kurihara and Harry Yoshio Uyeno [*sic*], May 6, 1943, box 85, DOJ. Ueno's letter was dated March 29, 1943. Ego interview by author. By the end of 1943 the men realized that Japan was going to lose the war: Ueno interview by author.

27. Myer to Best, March 10, 1943, file 39.053, box 289, Headquarters, Subject Classified

General Files, 1942–46, WRA; Fortas to Myer, March 24, 1943, entry 16, file 39.055, box 289, Isolation Cases General, WRA. On Kishi, see Myer to Merritt, March 26, 1943, file 39.055, box 289, Headquarters, Subject Classified General Files, 1942–46, WRA.

28. Ego interview by author.

29. Robertson interview by Hansen and Bell, 232, 237; Unrau, *The Evacuation and Relocation of Persons of Japanese Ancestry during World War II*, 490. A total of eighty-three men were sent to Leupp, but all of them were not there at the same time. Twenty-seven were originally from Manzanar, twenty from Tule Lake, sixteen from Gila River, and thirteen from Topaz. Other camps sent from one to three men. See Centers of Origin and Destination of All Residents from Inception (1–11–43) to Closing (12–4–43), December 12, 1943, entry 16, file 39.055, box 289, Isolation Cases General, WRA. Men arrived at different times, while others departed at other times. In October 1943, for example, there were fifty-seven men at Leupp. See Robertson to Myer, October 23, 1943, entry 16, file 39.055, box 289, Isolation Cases General, WRA.

30. Ego interview by author; Ueno interview by author.

31. Kurihara, "Autobiography," 50; Frederick to Spencer, August 20, 1943, S1.10, JAERR; Robertson to Myer, August 11, 1943, entry 16, file 39.055, box 289, Isolation Cases General, WRA.

32. Frederick, Personal Narrative Report, March 13, 1946, S1.00, JAERR; Drinnon, *Keeper of Concentration Camps*, 99; Hansen, "Cultural Politics in the Gila River Relocation Center," 358.

33. Drinnon, *Keeper of Concentration Camps*, 99. While Frederick's letters to Spencer seemed to indicate a close friendship between the two, Spencer's view was that it was a working relationship. See Spencer interview by Hansen, 274–75, 15–17. "Tough guy" from Frederick to Spencer, July 22, 1943, S1.10, JAERR. "Release nearly" from Frederick to Spencer, September 9, 1943, S1.10, JAERR. Frederick wrote many letters to Spencer, from July 20, 1943, to January 9, 1945, S1.10, JAERR. Robertson recalled that Frederick tended to promote himself. See Robertson interview by Hansen and Bell, 225. Documents that follow are from S1.10, JAERR. As Associate Chief of Internal Security, Frederick received a temporary draft deferment. Had he been named Chief of Internal Security, he would have received a permanent deferment. Despite Robertson's request to have him promoted to chief, however, the WRA office in D.C. refused, and thus Frederick remained vulnerable to the draft. Frederick believed that Bennett, who was project director at Gila, and with whom Frederick had had conflicts when he worked there, was behind the refusal by the WRA to promote Frederick: Frederick to Spencer, October 1, 1943. In October Frederick was to be drafted into the army as a sergeant whose job was to investigate crimes such as murder, rape, desertion, and black marketing, and involving army personnel: Jane Frederick to Spencer, October 25, 1943. However, he was able to postpone his induction to December. Meanwhile he continued to work at Leupp: Frederick to Spencer, November 5, 1943. He was inducted December 3, 1943 at Salt Lake: Frederick to Spencer, December 7, 1943.

34. Myer to Field Assistant Directors and Project Directors, re: Leupp Center, June 5, 1943, entry 16, file 39.055, box 289, Isolation Cases General, WRA.

35. Robertson to Myer, August 11, 1943, entry 16, file 39.055, box 289, Isolation Cases General, WRA.

36. Robertson to Myer, August 11, 1943, entry 16, file 39.055, box 289, Isolation Cases General, WRA; Myer to Robertson, September 2, 1943, file 39.055, box 289, WRA.

37. Frederick, Personal Narrative Report, March 13, 1946, S1.00, JAERR.

38. Frederick to Spencer, August 30, 1943, S1.10, JAERR.

39. Ueno interview by author; Kurihara, "Autobiography," 48–49; Frederick's assessment is in Frederick, "Kurihara Case History," 23. Ueno made a similar comment about Kurihara: "He was honest, straightforward; whatever he said he stuck to." See Embrey, Hansen, and Mitson, *Manzanar Martyr*, 41.

40. Brown, "Story of Joe Kurihara," 46.

41. Brown, "Story of Joe Kurihara," 45–46.

42. Kurihara to Higashi, November 1, 1943, folder 6—Law and Order-Incident-Moab, box 16, MWRR. Slacker refers to a person who evades military service. Kurihara liked to express himself in poetry, and sometimes included a poem in letters and essays. Hankey said of his poems, which often expressed defiance to America, "It is strong stuff for a *hakujin* (white person)." She wrote in her field notes, "I praised the sentiment, helped him with the grammar, and suggested that he try blank verse for power. . . . He was very pleased with the result. I left him happily working on a new one, denouncing the lies of the American press." Before departing for Japan, Kurihara asked Hankey if the study would keep his album of photos and poems: HFN, June 26, 1944, 2; and October 30, 1944, 6, W 1.61, JAERR.

43. Kurihara, "Niseis and the Government," 1, 10–11, 15; Kurihara to Editor, *Saturday Evening Post,* November 2, 1943, HU.

44. Memorandum for the Files, Kurihara, December 17, 1942, 5/68/56/4, Kurihara WWII Internment Case File.

45. Myer interview by Grodzins; Drinnon, *Keeper of Concentration Camps*, 118. For an analysis of Myer, see Drinnon, *Keeper of Concentration Camps*, 29–159, especially 76–77.

46. Provinse and Glick to Myer, October 12, 1943, entry 16, file 41.142, Opening and Closing of Projects, Leupp, box 296, WRA.

47. Robertson to Frederick, December 27, 1943, S1.10, JAERR; Centers of Origin and Destination of All Residents from Inception (1–11–43) to Closing (12–4–43), December 12, 1943, entry 16, file 39.055, box 289, Isolation Cases General, WRA. Robertson returned to Leupp from Tule Lake on December 18 to close it officially, but the closing was delayed because the INS was considering using Leupp as a war prisoner camp: Robertson to Frederick, December 27, 1943, S1.10, JAERR. When this idea was abandoned, Myer considered reopening Leupp in order to house about a hundred Nisei who had been placed in the Tule Lake stockade because of their role as "agitators or troublemakers" in the Tule "disturbance" of November 4, 1943. Issei involved in the conflict had been sent to INS internment camps. Tule Lake Project Director Raymond Best was to head the Leupp camp. This idea was abandoned, apparently because of the legal problems that the reopening would entail. See "WRA to Reopen Leupp Center," press release, April 26, 1944, S1.10, JAERR; Drinnon, *Keeper of Concentration Camps*,

116. For memos on the use of Leupp, see entry 16, file 41.142, Opening and Closing of Projects, Leupp, box 296, WRA. The WRA returned Leupp to the Interior Department on September 20, 1944. See Kashima, *Justice without Trial*, 158.

Chapter 7. Turmoil at Tule

1. Burton, et al., *Confinement and Ethnicity*, 279. For a concise history and visiting guide to the Tule Lake site, see Takei and Tachibana, *Tule Lake Revisited*.

2. Burton, et al., *Confinement and Ethnicity*, 282.

3. Weglyn, *Years of Infamy*, 134–51, quotes from 134 and 157; Commission on Wartime Relocation, Personal Justice Denied, 191–97.

4. Burton, et al., *Confinement and Ethnicity*, 282; Entry 25—Lists of Evacuees Transferred from, Remaining at, and Transferred to Tule Lake Segregation Center, 1943–44, folders "Manzanar Trip 35–39," WRA.

5. HFN, p. 20, April 1944, W1.61, JAERR; Shirai, *Tule Lake*, 112. See also Kumei, "'Skeleton in the Closet,'" 72.

6. Burton, et al., *Confinement and Ethnicity*, 282.

7. Robert Belligmeier, "Segregation Report," 1–6, August 27, 1943, R20.14, JAERR.

8. Weglyn, *Years of Infamy*, 158–60. For Robertson's role at Tule Lake, see Robertson to Frederick, December 27, 1943, S1.10, JAERR. For Robertson's recollection of Best, see Robertson interview by Hansen and Bell, 229, 245. According to Frederick, with the exception of Kurihara and a few others, the Nikkei at Leupp and Tule Lake "hate[d] Best": Frederick to Spencer, November 5, 1943, S1.10, JAERR; Frederick to Spencer, November 29, 1943, S1.10, JAERR.

9. Hankey, "Report, Tule Lake," December 24, 1943, W1.60, JAERR. The events of October 1943 through the end of martial law on January 15 is discussed in Takei, "Legalizing Detention," 76–83; Thomas and Nishimoto, *The Spoilage*, 113–83; Weglyn, *Years of Infamy*, 160–73; and Burton, et al., *Confinement and Ethnicity*, 283.

10. Takei, "Legalizing Detention," 79; Takita-Ishii, "Tokio Yamane," 167–69; see also Takita, "The Tule Lake Pilgrimage and Japanese American Internment," 321–30, 375–99. The horrendous torture is described in detail in a 1945 FBI report quoted in Takei, "Legalizing Detention," 98n13; and HFN, p. 1, August 19, 1944, and p. 3, August 24, 1944, W1.61, JAERR. After two weeks, the three young men were transferred to a barracks in the stockade. In December 1945, after the war ended, Yamane and Todoroki were transported to Japan with other renunciants. The terrible emotional cost of the incarceration and beatings were evident when, eight months after their arrival, Todoroki committed suicide. Kobayashi was eventually confined "in a mental hospital somewhere in the U.S." See Takita-Ishii, "Tokio Yamane," 180.

11. Quote from Weglyn, *Years of Infamy*, 165; Shirai, *Tule Lake*, 118.

12. "Statement by Joe Kurihara, Tule Lake, Written for Miss Hankey," March 1944, CAR.

13. Robertson to Frederick, December 27, 1943, S1.10, JAERR; HFN, p. 16, March 15, 1944, W1.60, JAERR.

14. Best, "Joe Kurihara 'Repatriate,'" 12.

15. Weglyn, *Years of Infamy*, 166.

16. Thomas and Nishimoto, *The Spoilage*, 147. The stockade was a military prison used by the army after martial law was declared on November 4, 1943. It continued to be used by the military until August 24, 1944. Adjacent to the stockade was a steel-reinforced concrete jail, built in late 1944 after the stockade had been closed. The jail was used in 1945 to imprison renunciants awaiting removal to DOJ camps. The foregoing information on the stockade and jail is from an anonymous reviewer, and Takei and Tachibana, *Tule Lake Revisited*, 30–33.

17. Weglyn, *Years of Infamy*, 205–6; Takei, "Legalizing Detention," 82–83. The vote by secret ballot was 4,593 against and 4,120 in favor of the status quo—in other words, a continuation of resistance to the military: Thomas and Nishimoto, *The Spoilage*, 181.

18. HFN, p. 15, March 15, 1944, and p. 50, March 21, 1944, W1.61, JAERR; Thomas and Nishimoto, *The Spoilage*, 186–87.

19. HFN, p. 49, March 21, 1944, W1.61, JAERR; HFN, p. 3, April 12, 1944; Thomas and Nishimoto, *The Spoilage*, 184–220. For details on the discussion rejecting the proposed resignation of the committee, held at a meeting of committee members and WRA and military officials, see HFN, pp. 38–40, February 2–3, 1944, W1.61, JAERR.

20. Ueno interview by author.

21. Goss to Shirrell, June 26, 1942, roll 7, M1342, CAR, 1942–46; Ichioka, "JERS Revisited," 6.

22. For discussions of other research groups and background on Thomas and the JERS project, see Ichioka, "JERS Revisited"; Murray, *Historical Memories of the Japanese American Internment and the Struggle for Redress*, 140–84; and Miyamoto, "Dorothy Swaine Thomas as Director of JERS." For criticism of the JERS project, *The Spoilage*, and accusations that it relied too heavily on Hankey, see, for example, Suzuki, "The University of California Japanese Evacuation and Resettlement Study"; and Opler, book review of *The Spoilage*. In discussing Thomas's use of reports from her field researchers, Hirabayashi, *The Politics of Fieldwork*, 169, argues that Thomas "forced the raw data that JERS fieldworkers had gathered back into a conceptual framework with which she was familiar." For the prominent role of Richard Nishimoto in JERS and in the authorship of *The Spoilage*, see Hirabayashi and Hirabayashi, "The 'Credible' Witness." For a defense of the JERS project, see Miyamoto, "Dorothy Swaine Thomas as Director of JERS." Gudridge, in "The Constitution Glimpsed from Tule Lake," 111, noted, "[P]erhaps *The Spoilage* is a somewhat different book from the book that its critics suppose it to be or the book that they think it should be."

23. From Frederick to Spencer, December 9, 1943, S1.10, JAERR; Wax, *Doing Fieldwork*, 103.

24. From Spencer to Frederick, December 2, 1943, S1.10, JAERR; from Thomas to X, January 13, 1944, W1.25A, JAERR.

25. Wax, *Doing Fieldwork*, 94–95; "Wax, Rosalie H.," in *American Men and Women of Science*, 2,584; Shallit, *Song of Anger*, 57.

26. Fryer, "'The Song of the Stitches,'" 691. My use of the term "WRA administrators" includes those who were not technically WRA administrators, such as the WRA re-

searcher Marvin Opler and the JERS researcher at Gila, Robert Spencer. HFN, pp. 16–17, February 2, 1944, W1.61, JAERR. Social scientists like Opler were hired by the WRA to live in the camps and "furnish WRA administrators with information to enable them to administer the concentration camps efficiently": Ichioka, "JERS Revisited," 3.

27. Fryer, "'The Song of the Stitches,'" 695; HFN, p. 3, January 1945, W1.63, JAERR.

28. Wax, *Doing Fieldwork*, 169.

29. Wax, Project Description, 5–6, National Endowment for the Humanities Application, RHW. On Robertson's supportive relationship with Hankey, see, for example, HFN, pp. 5–6, May 28, 1944, W1.61, JAERR. In Wax, *Doing Fieldwork*, 124, Hankey states that her respondents "fell into three categories": those who avoided camp politics, those intensely interested but not active in camp politics (Kurihara was in this group), and those active in camp politics.

30. HFN, pp. 1–4, February 2–3, 1944, W1.61, JAERR.

31. HFN, pp. 5, 15–16, February 2–3, 1944, W1.61, JAERR.

32. HFN, p. 4, July 20, 1944, W1.61, JAERR. The phrase "best informant" is in Wax, *Doing Fieldwork*, 102; the phrase "stern-principled" is in HFN, pp. 30–31, December 16, 1944, W1.63, JAERR.

33. HFN, p. 1, August 17, 1944, W1.61, JAERR. For similar sentiments critical of the first group, see HFN, pp. 2–4, August 21, 1944, and p. 1, August 22, 1944, W1.61, JAERR; Thomas and Nishimoto, *The Spoilage*, 226–27; Akashi, *Betrayed Trust*, 120; Shirai, *Tule Lake*, 107.

34. Akashi, *Betrayed Trust*, 129–31; Thomas and Nishimoto, *The Spoilage*, 229–30; Weglyn, *Years of Infamy*, 230.

35. HFN, pp. 8–11, April 1944, W1.61, JAERR, quote on p. 10. Mrs. Tsuchikawa, a pseudonym given by Hankey, spoke freely and openly. See, for example, HFN, pp. 1–2, May 23, 1944, and August 1944, W1.61, JAERR. In "J'Accuse," Violet Kazue de Cristoforo stated that she was Mrs. Tsuchikawa/Kazue Matsuda at Tule Lake. She argued that Hankey betrayed her trust and reported falsehoods about her. de Cristoforo was born in Hawai'i in 1917. A Kibei-Nisei, she was married to an Issei (Shigeru Matsuda) and had transferred to Tule Lake from Jerome. She had three children. One of her brothers served in the U.S. Army; the other was Tokio Yamane, who was brutally beaten and kept in the stockade for months. She renounced her citizenship and was deported to Japan. Later she married Wilfred H. de Cristoforo. See HFN, ed., p. 2, 21 March 1944, RHW. de Cristoforo recounts her tragic story in Tateishi, *And Justice for All*, 124–40. For a discussion of de Cristoforo's angry charges, see Murray, *Historical Memories of the Japanese American Internment and the Struggle for Redress*, 337–38.

36. Tule Lake Committee, *Second Kinenhi*, 67; Takei, "Legalizing Detention," 84. Harry Ueno and Mamoru Sasaki were among those who had "hand-assembled" radios with which they could monitor news from Tokyo: Ueno interview by author; Kumei, "'Skeleton in the Closet,'" 83.

37. Shirai, *Tule Lake*, 112–14, 128. For expressions of disappointment in seeing "loyals" at Tule Lake, see Kumei, "'Skeleton in the Closet,'" 71.

38. Shirai, *Tule Lake*, 128; Wax, *Doing Fieldwork*, 170; Kumei, "'Skeleton in the Closet,'" 76. Dissident leaders also came from Poston, Topaz, and other camps: HFN,

pp. 2, 6, March 6, 1945, and p. 3, April, 13, 1945, W1.63, JAERR; Akashi, interview by Ikeda and Omori, denshovh-atom-01-0030. For an example of internal strife resulting in serious beating, see HFN, ed., pp. 29–30, 39, December 15 and 19, 1944, RHW. Nikkei from Jerome arrived in September 1943, with more arriving in February and May 1944. Those from Manzanar arrived in February and May 1944. See Thomas and Nishimoto, *The Spoilage*, 107.

39. Tule Lake Committee, et al., *Second Kinenhi*, 66–67; Kashiwagi, interview by Ito, denshovh-khiroshi-02-0018; Kibei-Nisei, quoted in Kumei, "'Skeleton in the Closet,'" 90. For the Kibei-Nisei sense of alienation from parents, see Kumei, "'Skeleton in the Closet,'" 88; and Ueno, *Manzanar Martyr*, 2–5, 13–14.

40. HFN, p. 19, April 14, 1944, W1.61, JAERR; Akashi, *Betrayed Trust*, 131–34; Thomas and Nishimoto, *The Spoilage*, 230–34.

41. HFN, pp. 1, 5, May 22, 1944, W1.61, JAERR.

42. Thomas and Nishimoto, *The Spoilage*, 236–38.

43. Kurihara's quote from HFN, p. 5, May 21, 1944, and p. 1, May 22, 1944, W1.61, JAERR; Nisei woman's quote from HFN, p. 3, May 22, 1944, W1.61, JAERR; Thomas and Nishimoto, *The Spoilage*, 241–48. Hankey's field notes included many others who said that the stockade remained a major issue.

44. HFN, ed., p. 36, May 1944, RHW; HFN, p. 2, May 28, 1944, W1.61, JAERR.

45. Thomas and Nishimoto, *The Spoilage*, 249–60; quotes from 252 and 260.

46. HFN, p. 2, June 8, 1944, W1.61, JAERR.

47. HFN, p. 15, March 15, 1944, W1.61, JAERR.

48. HFN, p. 1, 17 June 1944, W1.61, JAERR; Akashi, *Betrayed Trust*, 120; Thomas and Nishimoto, *The Spoilage*, 264–65. On WRA's hiring of spies, see Thomas and Nishimoto, *The Spoilage*, 205. On the pervasiveness of gambling, see Takei, "Legalizing Detention," 81.

49. HFN, p. 1, June 26, 1944, W1.61, JAERR; Thomas and Nishimoto, *The Spoilage*, 266–68.

50. HFN, p. 15, March 15, 1944, W1.61, JAERR; Takei, "Legalizing Detention," 83; Thomas and Nishimoto, *The Spoilage*, 270–71. For Hitomi's identity, see Akashi, interview by Ikeda and Omori, denshovh-atom-01-0032. On the structure of the cooperative and its canteens, see Miyamoto, "Resentment, Distrust, and Security at Tule Lake," 134–35.

51. HFN, p. 1, August 8, 1944, W1.61, JAERR; HFN, p. 2, July 20, 1944, W1.61, JAERR; Thomas and Nishimoto, *The Spoilage*, 273.

52. HFN, p. 1, August 21, 1944, W1.61, JAERR.

53. Thomas and Nishimoto, *The Spoilage*, 275.

54. HFN, p. 2, July 20, 1944, W1.61, JAERR.

55. HFN, p. 1, July 24, 1944, W1.61, JAERR; Thomas and Nishimoto, *The Spoilage*, 277–82.

56. Akashi, *Betrayed Trust*, 121; Thomas and Nishimoto, *The Spoilage*, 370.

57. Thomas and Nishimoto, *The Spoilage*, 277–82.

58. Yamanaka, quoted in Tule Lake Committee, et al., *Second Kinenhi*, 63; Thomas and Nishimoto, The *Spoilage*, 284–85; Weglyn, *Years of Infamy*, 208–12.

59. Thomas and Nishimoto, *The Spoilage*, 291, 302.

60. HFN, p. 1, July 20, 1944, W1.61, JAERR; *San Francisco Chronicle*, July 15, 1944, quoted in Thomas and Nishimoto, *The Spoilage*, 292; Weglyn, *Years of Infamy*, 209; Drinnon, *Keeper of Concentration Camps*, 130–31.

61. HFN, p. 7, July 30, 1944, W1.61, JAERR; Thomas and Nishimoto, *The Spoilage*, 293–97; Takita-Ishii, "Tokio Yamane," 170. The hunger strike that began on July 19 was resumed in early August after strikers were hospitalized and then returned to the stockade. There are some differences in dates and numbers of hunger strikers between the account given in *The Spoilage*, largely based on the diary of Kato (pseudonym), and Tokio Yamane's later recall of events.

62. HFN, pp. 1–2, July 31, 1944, W1.61, JAERR; Thomas and Nishimoto, *The Spoilage*, 297, 298n41, Kuratomi's statement on 298; Akashi, *Betrayed Trust*, 146.

63. HFN, pp. 2–3, August 12, 1944, and p. 2, August 13, 1944, W1.61, JAERR; Thomas and Nishimoto, *The Spoilage*, 299.

64. HFN, p. 1, August 21, 1944, W1.61, JAERR; Weglyn, *Years of Infamy*, 215–16. The Korematsu case, and the Hirabayashi, Yasui, and Endo cases that Collins also participated in, challenged the constitutionality of the curfew, forced removal, and incarceration of the Nikkei. The scholarly literature on these cases, which reached the U.S. Supreme Court, is large; important publications include Irons, *Justice at War*; and Daniels, "The Japanese American Cases." For a colorful portrait of Collins, who devoted a large part of his career to seeking justice for the Nikkei and who called the JACL "a cowardly group," see Drinnon, *Keeper of Concentration Camps*, 133–34.See also Takei, "Legalizing Detention," 94.

Chapter 8. Renunciation

1. Public Law 405, folder 3—Department of Justice, box 12, MWRR. The 1940 law (76th Cong., 3rd Sess., Ch. 876. 14 Oct. 1940) permitted a person to apply for renunciation to a foreign consul while outside the United States.

2. Merritt to Fisher, November 27, 1945, pp. 3–5, folder 3—Department of Justice, box 12, MWRR.

3. Dickstein quoted in Weglyn, *Years of Infamy*, 313n11.

4. "Ship Sails to Return Captives," June 19, 1942, file 014.33, box 8, WDC; "Letters of Protest Regarding Repatriation," October 25, 1942, file 014.33, box 8, WDC; "Repatriation [Gripsholm, September 2, 1943]," September 11, 1943, file 36.310, box 249, WRA; Corbett, *Quiet Passages*, 1, 41, 60–95. Because of its errors, Corbett's *Quiet Passages* should be read with caution; see Daniels, "A Tragedy with a Happy Ending?" 134–36.

5. On Endo, see Irons, *Justice at War*, 144; on Biddle, see Ngai, *Impossible Subjects*, 187; on Best, see Weglyn, *Years of Infamy*, 212; on Ennis's confirmation, see Kashima, *Judgment without Trial*, 169.

6. Nagasawa, quoted in Tule Lake Committee, et al., *Second Kinenhi*, 66; Shirai, *Tule Lake*, 149–50; HFN, p. 8, September 11, 1944, W1.61, JAERR; Kumei, "'Skeleton in the Closet,'" 77–78; Thomas and Nishimoto, *The Spoilage*, 311–13; Weglyn, *Years of Infamy*,

232–33. According to Kumei, "'Skeleton in the Closet,'" 78, in order to avoid annoying people, the start time for the exercises was later moved to 6 AM.

7. Takita-Ishii, "Tokio Yamane," 171.

8. Kobayashi interview by Ito, denshovh-kkenge-01–0013; Yamamoto interview by Ikeda and Takei, denshovh-ysumiko-01–0018; Ogami interview by Ito; Akashi interview by Ikeda and Omori, denshovh-atom-01–0031.

9. HFN, pp. 4–5, August 14, 1944, W1.61, JAERR.

10. HFN, p. 6, August 24, 1944, p. 4, August 30, 1944, and p. 1, September 1, 1944, W1.61, JAERR.

11. HFN, p. 1, October 10, 1944, W1.61, JAERR; Shirai, *Tule Lake*, 150; Thomas and Nishimoto, *The Spoilage*, 315–17.

12. Thomas and Nishimoto, *The Spoilage*, 321.

13. Kobayashi interview by Ito, denshovh-kkenge-01–0014.

14. HFN, p. 1, September 13, 1944, and p. 1, September 14, 1944, W1.61, JAERR.

15. Kashiwagi, interview by Ito, denshovh-khiroshi-02–0020; Akashi, *Betrayed Trust*, 169. The Tuleans referred to these groups collectively as the *Hoshi Dan, Hokoku Dan,* or *Hoshi Dan*: Akashi, interview by Ikeda and Omori, denshovh-atom-01–0033.

16. HFN, pp. 2–3, October 10, 1944, W1.61, JAERR.

17. HFN, p. 1, February 1, 1945, and pp. 2, 4, February 8, 1945, W1.63, JAERR; Kashiwagi, interview by Ito, denshovh-khiroshi-02–0020.

18. Kumei, "'Skeleton in the Closet,'" 81; Nakagawa, "Renunciants," 151.

19. Akashi interview by Ikeda and Omori, denshovh-atom-01–0033; Akashi, *Betrayed Trust*, 170–76, 340n50. This split is also discussed in Wax, "In and Out of Tule Lake Segregation Center," 23. Tachibana later left Wakayama's faction for that of Akashi's father. In Thomas and Nishimoto, *The Spoilage*, Wakayama is given the pseudonym Kira. Suzuki, "The University of California Japanese Evacuation and Resettlement Study," 195, identifies Kira as Kinzo Ernest Wakayama and portrays him as a heroic figure who challenged the constitutionality of his incarceration.

20. HFN, p. 1, November 6, 1944, W1.61, JAERR; Best, "Joe Kurihara 'Repatriate,'" 13–17. In an interview forty-one years after Tule Lake was closed, the Assistant Project Director Paul Robertson stated that Tule Lake was not in constant turmoil, as scholarly accounts would have one believe. Instead, he said, it was a "small element that kept things stirred up . . . trying to get people to show loyalty to Japan": Robertson, interview by Hansen and Bell, 248. While Robertson believed that the "element" was small, those affected by violence believed that it was no small matter.

21. HFN, p. 5, October 16, 1944, W1.61, JAERR; HFN, ed., p. 1, November 13, 1944, RHW. On the beating of the three men, see HFN, pp. 5–6, October 23, 1944, and p. 1, November 9, 1944, W1.61, JAERR. On Kurihara and Wakayama knowing each other before the war and at Manzanar, see HFN, ed., p. 2, December 14, 1944, RHW. Multiple entries in Hankey's field notes include Kurihara's depiction of Wakayama as leader of a violent gang. See, for example, HFN, pp. 5–6, September 29, 1944, and p. 2, November 6, 1944, W1.61, JAERR. On another Nisei's statement of Wakayama's encouragement of violence, see HFN, p. 1, November 9, 1944, W1.61, JAERR.

22. Wax, *Doing Fieldwork*, 158.

23. HFN, p. 1, September 21, 1944, W1.61, JAERR: Wakayama stated, "I think that it (renunciation of citizenship) is unconstitutional. . . . You can't discriminate against a certain portion of the people just because of their color and race. They evacuate them and then they try to pin them down to citizenship. They say it is voluntary, but once a person is thrown into camp and pushed around he looks at the thing emotionally. They are not responsible. . . . But when they force me to sign my name for the benefit of the Administration, I won't stand for it. But after the war the entire picture will be changed. Although I might be deported to Japan, I don't think that the U.S. will do that." On the Nisei's angry response, see HFN, p. 1, December 14, 1944, W1.63, JAERR.

24. HFN, ed., p. 19, December 12, 1944, RHW; Wax, *Doing Fieldwork*, 168; Hymes, "The Use of Anthropology," 52–53; Fryer, "'The Song of the Stitches,'" 693. Suzuki, "The University of California Japanese Evacuation and Resettlement Study," offers a scathing and instructive criticism of Wax's unprofessional conduct. Miyamoto, "Dorothy Swaine Thomas as Director of JERS," 52–58, provides a thoughtful and likewise instructive rebuttal. While I do not exonerate Hankey for her misdeeds, I do note that she recognized her own shortcomings. In fact, in criticizing her, Suzuki quotes from Wax's own book, *Doing Fieldwork*, in which she attempted to be as transparent as possible about her biases and unprofessional thoughts and actions while engaged in fieldwork, with the expressed purpose of providing "warnings and advice" (the subtitle of her book) for others to learn from her misdeeds and from the ethical dilemmas that confronted her. (For an earlier publication on her experiences as a field researcher, this one focused on the Gila camp, see Wax, "Twelve Years Later.") Suzuki's positivistic stance led him to assume mistakenly that researchers can know "what precisely took place at Tule Lake" (205), and that there can be a "complete and objective history" (207) of the camp.

25. Wakayama gave his version in 1957 in Hakata, Japan, to the Nisei attorney Tex Nakamura: see Weglyn, *Years of Infamy*, 143. Noyes's version is in HFN, ed., p. 19, December 12, 1944, RHW.

26. Wakayama's profile is in Suzuki, "The University of California Japanese Evacuation and Resettlement Study," 195–96; and Thomas and Nishimoto, *The Spoilage*, 375–76. See also Hohri, *Repairing America*, 113–14. I was unable to find evidence of direct encounters between Kurihara and Wakayama while they were in Manzanar. However, Kurihara told Hankey (HFN, p. 2, November 6, 1944, W1.61, JAERR) that Wakayama was a key figure in the Manzanar revolt, despite protestations that "he had nothing to do with [it]. . . . Such deliberate lies . . . just to get out of it!" Kurihara's distrust of Wakayama stemmed from the 1930s, when the latter was secretary-treasurer of the Fishermen's Union of Los Angeles.

27. Suzuki, "The University of California Japanese Evacuation and Resettlement Study," 195–96, argues for the importance of the Wakayamas' legal challenge, but as Miyamoto points out in "Dorothy Swaine Thomas of JERS," 57, Suzuki does not explain "why the case was not pressed on to the U.S. Supreme Court as the other test cases [Korematsu, Hirabayashi, Yasui, and Endo] were." Kumei, "'Skeleton in the Closet,'" 75, discusses her 1987 and 1988 interviews with Wakayama in which he stated that he and his wife dropped the suit. No explanation is given for this action. However, Irons, in *Justice at War*, 114–15, provides the following information. The Southern California ACLU attorney A. L. Wirin

represented the Wakayamas in their court challenge, which at first was supported by the New York head office. But complications ensued, which led the ACLU to question this challenge as an ideal test case, among them Wakayama's arrest for participating in a secret meeting at the WCCA temporary camp at Santa Anita, and his subsequent application for expatriation in 1943, both of which led the ACLU director Roger Baldwin to end his support. As a result, Wirin felt that he could no longer pursue the case.

28. Quote on "painful incident" is in HFN, p. 2, November 6, 1944, W1.61, JAERR. Thirty-five years after the war ended, Hankey wrote, "Mr. Kurihara never spoke to me of his role in the Manzanar riot. . . . In Tule Lake Mr. Kurihara was to become an uncompromising opponent of violence and terrorism." In Hankey's view, his apparent confession in 1945 to Merritt, in which he stated that he had organized the group that beat up Tayama, reveals "the burden he was carrying during the many months in which [he and Hankey] conversed and became friends." See HFN, ed., p. 25, February 2–3, 1944, RHW. In late December, Wakayama was removed with sixty-nine other men to the Department of Justice camp for aliens in Santa Fe: see Thomas and Nishimoto, *The Spoilage*, 339n27; and Akashi, *Betrayed Trust*, 194.

29. In 1982, when Congress held hearings on the question of redress for Nikkei who had been wrongly incarcerated, Wakayama, who had maintained that the United States was obligated to apologize for its wrongs, returned to the United States for the first time since his departure in 1946 to testify before a congressional committee. In 1993, the ninety-three-year-old Wakayama, still living in Japan, was awarded the 75th Anniversary World War I Commemorative Medal for his service in France. "I have no bad feeling against the Army or the U.S. at the present," he said. "There is no country like the United States." He passed away in Fukuoka, Japan, at age 102. Seven years later his ashes were interred at the National Memorial Cemetery of the Pacific in Honolulu, where he was given full military honors in recognition of his service during World War I. See Gregg Kakesako, "America Exiled Him but He Still Loves His Country," *Star-Bulletin*, February 15, 1994; Karen Feldscher, "The Patriot," *Northeastern University Magazine*, March 2004, available at www.historyplace.com/pointsofview/patriot.htm (accessed November 12, 2012); Eileen McCluskey, "The Heart of Patriotism," *Northeastern University Arts + Sciences Chronicle,* Summer 2004, 10; Martha Nakagawa, "An American Comes Home," *Hawai'i Herald*, May 5, 2006.

30. "Nationality Regulations," October 6, 1944, Immigration and Naturalization Service, Circular No. 3886, folder 3—Department of Justice, box 12, MWRR; Kumei, "'Skeleton in the Closet,'" 84–97.

31. Ishida, "Background and Effect of Renunciation of Citizenship by Japanese Americans during World War II," 100; Tule Lake Committee, *Second Kinenhi*, 96–97.

32. Kiyota, *Beyond Loyalty*, 107, 111–12. In "Review of *Beyond Loyalty*," Daniels appropriately calls it "an autobiographical novel" (635). For me, the book's value lay in Kiyota's personal experiences and reflections, not for information about others. On pp. 112–13, for example, his statements on Kurihara are erroneous.

33. Kurihara, "Autobiography," 51.

34. Kurihara, "Individual Request for Repatriation or Expatriation," November 1,

1943, Kurihara WWII Internment Case File; Kurihara, "Application for Permission to Renounce United States Nationality," November 20, 1944, Kurihara Case File 146–54–117; Rhetts to Hoover, December 1, 1944, HU; Kurihara, "Renunciation of United States Nationality," March 22, 1945, Case File 146–54–117.

35. Takei, "Legalizing Detention," 86. Quote on exceptions from *Newell Star*, December 19, 1944, in Thomas and Nishimoto, *The Spoilage*, 334. The U.S. Supreme Court had decided in Mitsuye Endo's case, one of four cases challenging deprivation of liberty, that she should be allowed to return to California. Before the decision was announced, however, the army, having been informed of the Court's decision by Chief Justice Stone and Justice Frankfurter, declared the end of the exclusion of "loyal" Nikkei from the West Coast. See Daniels, "The Japanese American Cases," 161.

Pressure from the *Hoshi Dan* was not the primary reason for the mass renunciations that began in December 1944 and continued through mid-March 1945. Kumei, "'Skeleton in the Closet,'" 80, argues that Collins (no relation to Wayne Collins), *Native American Aliens*, and Weglyn, *Years of Infamy*, placed too much emphasis on pressure from *Seinen Dan* in influencing renunciation. I would add that Thomas and Nishimoto, *The Spoilage*, 324, 341–42, on which Collins relies for his evidence, does the same.

36. In *Impossible Subjects*, Ngai (198) states that "conventional thinking on renunciation exaggerates the influence of the nationalists" in causing the large number of renunciations, because scholars have relied on *The Spoilage*, which depended on the work of "field research" that "gave disproportionate attention to the views of certain pro-Japan loyalists." Ngai seems to have been unaware of Kumei's "'Skeleton in the Closet.'" Kumei, like Ngai after her, argued that the attorney Wayne Collins used the argument of *Seinen Dan/Hoshi Dan* pressure to help his clients regain their citizenship. Moreover, Hankey's field notes make it clear that her notes were not the cause of emphasis in *The Spoilage* of *Seinen Dan/Hoshi Dan* pressure leading to mass renunciation. The statements in *The Spoilage* that *Seinen Dan/Hoshi Dan* pressure was a major reason for the mass renunciations was likely the result of conclusions made by the book's coauthor, Richard Nishimoto, who had a leading role in JERS as well as on the book manuscript. For a discussion on Nishimoto's role in JERS and *The Spoilage*, see Hirabayashi and Hirabayashi, "The 'Credible' Witness."

37. Akashi, interview by Ikeda and Omori, denshovh-atom-01–0034, 0037.

38. HFN, p. 4, January 2, 1945; p. 2, January 3, 1945; and p. 5, January 8, 1945, W1.63, JAERR.

39. Ishida, "Background and Effect of Renunciation of Citizenship by Japanese Americans during World War II," 99; HFN, p. 2, January 14, 1945, W1.63, JAERR; *San Francisco Examiner*, December 13, 1944, quoted in Thomas and Nishimoto, *The Spoilage*, 345; *Pacific Citizen*, January 13, 1945, quoted in Thomas and Nishimoto, *The Spoilage*, 346; HFN, p. 1, January 15, 1945, W1.63, JAERR; HFN, p. 2, January 22, 1945, W1.63, JAERR.

40. HFN, p. 1, January 24, 1945, and p. 1, January 27, 1945, W1.63, JAERR. Also HFN, p. 5, February 10, 1945, W1.63, JAERR; Ishida, "Background and Effect of Renunciation of Citizenship by Japanese Americans during World War II," 41.

41. HFN, p. 2, February 13, 1945, W1.63, JAERR; Ogami interview by Ito, denshovh-oarthur-01–0019; Kashiwagi interview by Omori and Omori, denshovh-khiroshi-01–005; on Mayetani, see George Ishihara to Ivan Williams, [October 1945], Japanese Repatriation and Relocation Correspondence, Tule, box 2, INS; Sato interview by Goto, denshovh-ssarah-01–0024; see also Ishida, "Background and Effect of Renunciation of Citizenship by Japanese Americans during World War II," 37–38.

42. Okamura, "Testimony for the Commission on Wartime Relocation and Internment of Civilians."

43. HFN, pp. 1–2, February 13, 1945, and p. 5, February 28, 1945, W1.63, JAERR.

44. HFN, p. 7, February 16, 1945, W1.63, JAERR.

45. Kumei, "'Skeleton in the Closet,'" 79; Kashimi, *Judgment without Trial*, 278n37; Akashi, interview by Ikeda and Omori, denshovh-atom-0034–37; HFN, p. 1, April 10, 1945, W1.63, JAERR.

46. Takei, "Legalizing Detention," 86–89.

47. Collins, *Native American Aliens*, 101; Takei, "Legalizing Detention," 94; Kurihara, "Renunciation of United States Nationality," January 15, 1945, Kurihara Case File 146-54–117. Since no exact numbers are available on the number in 1945 of Nisei and Kibei-Nisei who were age eighteen or older, I derived the 10 percent in the following way: It is estimated that there were 117,000 Nikkei who were in the ten concentration camps, and two-thirds (78,000) of them were Nisei and Kibei-Nisei. Of the 78,000, I estimate that in 1945 there were about 50,000 who were age eighteen and older. With 5,725 renouncing, my estimation is that 10 percent of all Nisei and Kibei-Nisei renounced.

48. Tule Lake Committee, *Second Kinenhi*, 98.

49. Collins, *Native American Aliens*, 110; Nakamura interview by Ikeda and Takei, denshovh-ntetsujiro-01–0006; Takei, "Legalizing Detention," 94. For a copy of Proclamation 2655, see Weglyn, *Years of Infamy*, 181. While the following account suggests that Kurihara may have wavered, I was not able to find confirmation of Tanaka's letter to the Red Cross. The account comes from Tanaka: Letter from Tanaka to author, August 30, 1996; and Tanaka interview by Mitson and Hacker, May 19, 1973, 136. According to Tanaka, the American Friends Service Committee (AFSC) took it as its mission to encourage Nisei who had renounced their U.S. citizenship to reconsider their decision. The AFSC staff believed that the renunciants would later regret their loss of American citizenship. With the cooperation of the WRA, Bill McKee of the AFSC's Midwest Office in Chicago learned who had renounced their citizenship. His job was to contact these Nisei and let them know that the AFSC wanted to help. According to Tanaka, with the encouragement of McKee, Kurihara agreed to request that a letter be written on his behalf. In spring 1945 and again in fall 1945, when Kurihara was at Tule Lake, McKee discussed the idea with Tanaka and other Nikkei of writing supporting letters for Kurihara and other renunciants. The letter would state whether or not the renunciant had been a law-abiding citizen before the war. With the encouragement of the AFSC staff, Tanaka wrote a letter to the Red Cross on Kurihara's behalf.

50. Yoshiko Matsuura is a pseudonym: Correspondence with Ennis and Collins, August 13, 1945–May 5, 1958, box 14, reel 17, WC. This is just one set of many such letters. See also letters to Ennis from renunciants, August-September 1945, R9.05, JAERR.

51. "Resumé of Meeting with Mr. Collins," October 8, 1945, folder 4, box 1, reel 1, WC; Collins, *Native American Aliens*, 125.

52. Kashiwagi interview by Omori and Omori, denshovh-khiroshi-01-005; Collins, *Native American Aliens*, 126–28. According to Ben Ogami (interview by author), when he and others were embarking on the second transport to Japan on December 30, 1945, they were told that they did not have to go to Japan, so a number of people left the transport.

53. Collins, *Native American Aliens*, 124, 128–29; Collins to Clark, November 1, 1945, file 014.33, WDC. Collins told his son that the *Hoshi Dan* did not have the kind of influence that *The Spoilage* attributed to it. Phone conversation with Wayne Merrill Collins, the son of Wayne Mortimer Collins, December 2, 1996.

54. Kutulas, "In Quest of Autonomy," 206–19; Kutulas, *The American Civil Liberties Union and the Making of Modern Liberalism*, 99–100, 118–23; Collins, *Native American Aliens*, 132–39. For a scathing critique of Baldwin, see Drinnon, *Keeper of Concentration Camps*, 117–26, 146–47.

55. Collins, *Native American Aliens*, 139–43.

56. The number 5,409 is in Girdner and Loftis, *The Great Betrayal*, 453; and in Kurihara to Attorney General Robert Kennedy, October 20, 1962, Kurihara Case File 146-54-117, which quotes Attorney General William Rogers. Wayne Collins provides a list of 1,143 persons in Japan joining the suit to rescind their renunciations in "Alphabetical List of Person in Japan Who are Parties Plaintiff," n.d., folder 8, reel 28, WC. Correspondence with Collins, August 3, 1955–September 1, 1969, box 12, reel 14, WC; Correspondence with Ennis and Collins, August 13, 1945–May 5, 1958, box 14, reel 17, WC.

57. Memoranda, 19 pp., n.d., box 10, reel 12, WC; Personal Questionnaire, pp. 1–21, July 8, 1955, box 7, reel 7, WC; Correspondence with Collins, May 14, 1947–April 27, 1959, box 7, reel 7, WC.

58. Correspondence with Collins, et al.: July 2, 1948–October 1, 1959, box 7, reel 7; September 24, 1945–September 13, 1960, box 7, reel 7; October 19, 1945–August 19, 1960, box 9, reel 10; February 19, 1948–January 23, 1953, box 10, reel 12, WC.

59. "Tex" Nakamura gives the estimate of forty to fifty unsuccessful applicants in Takei, "Legalizing Detention," 97; Hashimoto cited in Kumei, "'Skeleton in the Closet,'" 88. The Department of Justice denied restoration of citizenship to renunciants who had been leaders of the *Hoshi Dan* and who were said to have pressured Nisei to renounce their citizenship. In such cases, Collins worked with the renunciant to prepare a supplemental affidavit that provided clarification and explanation, often leading to a successful outcome. Correspondence with Collins, et. al.: August 17, 1948–February 6, 1958, box 10, reel 12; March 20, 1958–July 6, 1959, box 7, reel 8, WC.

Collins's deeply felt animosity toward the JACL was evident twenty years after the end of the war. In rejecting a 1967 JACL banquet invitation honoring "friends . . . actively concerned and sympathetic with Japanese Americans before, during and immediately following . . . evacuation," he responded that he held "an intensive hostility toward" the JACL, which he called a "wretched organization." He continued, "The arrival of the Issei . . . was a signal honor to our country," which "owes them a debt it cannot repay. . . . [The] evacuation was unjustified, vicious and criminal action taken by our government against a loyal segment of our population." He continued, "I do not intend to overlook the fact that the JACL," "the pretended spokesman for the affected people," "was indifferent to what happened to them and that it did nothing to help them. . . . I believe that the JACL would be doing the members of our population who are of immediate or remote Japanese ancestry a service were it to disband and disperse." From Doi to Collins, September 16, 1967, and Collins to Doi, October 20, 1967, folder 9, box 1, reel 1, WC.

60. Ngai, *Impossible Subjects*, 200. Stephan, *Hawaii under the Rising Sun*, 35–43, and Shibusawa, "'The Artist Belongs to the People,'" 259, offer similar analyses in their separate discussions of Nikkei loyalties.

61. HFN, p. 4, February 28, 1945, W1.63, JAERR; HFN, p. 1, June 26, 1944, W1.61, JAERR.

62. Kumei, "'Skeleton in the Closet,'" 84; Takita-Ishii, "Tokio Yamane," 174; Frederick, "Kurihara Case History," 23; Ego interview by author. The number three hundred—more specifically, 316—comes from subtracting 5,409 applications for restoration of citizenship (Girdner and Loftis, *The Great Betrayal*, 453) from 5,725 total renunciations (Takei, "Legalizing Detention," 94).

63. Collins worked with former *Seinen Dan* leaders in preparing supplemental affidavits that were successful in restoring their U.S. citizenship. See Collins's correspondence: August 17 1948–February 6, 1958, box 10, reel 12; March 20, 1958–July 6, 1959, box 7, reel 8, WC.

64. Ellison to Doub, September 7, 1956, and Doub to Ellison, September 11, 1956, Kurihara Case File 146–54–117; Hoover to Wechsler, January 13, 1945, Case File 146–54–117.

65. A number of authors have ignored the continued viability of the renunciation law. For example, Ngai, *Impossible Subjects*, 329n46, states that the renunciation law was repealed in 1947; no citation is provided. Christgau, "Collins versus the World," 23, also states that Congress repealed the renunciation law and provides no date or citation. Others, such as Takei, "Legalizing Detention," 97, and the Tule Lake Committee website, www.tulelake.org/history.html, state that the renunciation law was repealed in 1971, with no citation. Perhaps the latter two confused the renunciation law with the Emergency Detention Act of 1950, which allowed the U.S. president to detain suspected persons in times of war and or insurrection, and which was repealed in 1971: see Daniels, "The Japanese American Cases," 165–66. Kashima, *Judgment without Trial*, 172, correctly recognizes the continued viability of the renunciation law, and the influence of Collins's actions in bringing about the provision that was added in 1961. For the law's provisions, see Title 8 U.S. Code § 1481(a)(6) and (b). For a case filed in 2010 using the 1944 renunciation law as justification for renunciation, see *Kaufman v. Holder*, Case 1:05-cv-01631-RWR, document 91, filed 02/25/10, https://ecf.dcd.uscourts.gov/cgi-bin/show_public_doc?2005cv1631-91.

Chapter 9. Japan

1. HFN, p. 2, June 26, 1944, W 1.61, JAERR.
2. Brown, "Story of Joe Kurihara," 53.
3. Kurihara to Thomas, November 7, 1945, Reel 090, JAERR.

4. Kurihara, Renunciation of United States Nationality, January 15, 1945, Kurihara Case File 146–54–117.

5. Best, "Joe Kurihara, 'Repatriate,'" 17. He sent the same poem to Thomas: Kurihara to Thomas, November 16, 1945, Reel 090, JAERR.

6. Brown, "Story of Joe Kurihara," 54; "Japanese Boarding Ship for Nippon," *Los Angeles Times*, November 25, 1945; "1500 Voluntary Repatriates," *Pacific Citizen*, December 15, 1945; Conrat and Conrat, *Executive Order 9066*, 102, 120; "Deportees from Tule, Santa Fe," *Rocky Shimpō*, November 26, 1945; Ego, [Autobiography], 5; Ego interview by author. From 1942 to 1946, a total of 4,724 Nikkei from WRA camps, primarily from Tule Lake, were transported to Japan; this figure does not include Nikkei from INS camps. The second transport, the USS *Gordon*, which carried most of the deported Nikkei, departed on December 30, 1945; the third transport left on February 23, 1946. Kurihara was not the oldest renunciant, but among the three who were older than age fifty: U.S. Department of the Interior, *The Evacuated People*, 196. The number seven thousand is an estimate, based on figures given by the WRA: Stauber to Director, Repatriation to Japan, January, 2, 1946, file 36.310, box 251, WRA. Since 1,143 renunciants in Japan sought to regain their citizenship ("Alphabetical List of Person in Japan Who are Parties Plaintiff," n.d., folder 8, reel 28, WC), and about three hundred did not, I estimate that about fifteen hundred of the seven thousand departees were renunciants. Girder and Loftis, *The Great Betrayal*, 450, say that about eight thousand Nikkei left at war's end, but provide no citation.

7. Okamura, "Testimony for the Commission on Wartime Relocation and Internment of Civilians," August 11, 1981, typescript, 6–7, Okamura family papers; A. Ogami interview by Ito, denshovh-oarthur-01.

8. Takita-Ishii, "Tokio Yamane," 173; Ego, [Autobiography], 5; Akashi interview by Ikeda and Omori, denshovh-atom-0042; Ego interview by author.

9. "A Disappointed Expatriate," *Rocky Shimpō*, December 11, 1945; Akashi interview by Ikeda and Omori, denshovh-atom-0042; Akashi, *Betrayed Trust*, 328; Yamakido, quoted in Nakagawa, "Renunciants," 155.

10. Takita-Ishii, "Tokio Yamane," 174; Aoyama, correspondence with author; "Yes, He Would Like Nothing Better Than to Return to U.S.—But Can't," *Rocky Shimpō*, December 15, 1945; Dower, *Embracing Defeat*, 48–50.

11. Ueno interview by author. According to Ueno, Kurihara received money occasionally during the war; for example, when he was at Leupp, he received a check for $800 from "a Portuguese tuna clipper." Ueno learned about Kurihara's loss of his possessions when Best shared with him the contents of a report describing the arrival in Japan of Kurihara's group.

12. Ueno interview by author; Ueno phone conversation with author; Embrey, Hansen, and Mitson, *Manzanar Martyr*, 83, 92. After the war Ueno and his family moved to San Jose, where he worked in strawberry and cherry orchards. Through the efforts of Wayne Collins, Ueno was eventually able to regain his citizenship. He died in 2004 at age 97. See Katherine Corcoran, "Manzanar Martyr Dies," *Mercury News*, December 16, 2004.

13. Nakamura interview by author; Okamura, "Testimony for the Commission on

Wartime Relocation and Internment of Civilians," August 11, 1981, typescript, 6–7, Okamura family papers; Sato interview by Goto, denshovh-ssarah-0025.

14. Dower, *Embracing Defeat*, 43–47.

15. Marubayashi interview by author.

16. Okamura, "Testimony for the Commission on Wartime Relocation and Internment of Civilians," August 11, 1981, typescript, 6–7; Asakura interview by author; B. Ogami interview by author.

17. Akashi interview by Ikeda and Omori, denshovh-atom-0043.

18. Akashi interview by Ikeda and Omori, denshovh-atom-0043; Yamamoto interview by Ikeda and Takei, denshovh-ysumiko-0027.

19. Akashi interview by Ikeda and Omori, denshovh-atom-0042.

20. Reischauer, *Japan: Story of a Nation*, 204–205; Tomita, *Dear Miye*, 179, 187; Dower, *Embracing Defeat*, 123–39.

21. Nakamura interview by author; Dower, *Embracing Defeat*, 94–95.

22. Fujita interview by author.

23. Azuma, "Brokering Race, Culture, and Citizenship," 191–92. See also McNaughton, *Nisei Linguists*, 427, 454.

24. Takita-Ishii, "Tokio Yamane," 173–74.

25. Aoyama correspondence with author.

26. Asakura interview by author; Hasegawa interview by author; "Citizenship Renunciants Regret Their Act, Amazed at High Costs," *Rocky Shimpō*, 29 Jan. 1946.

27. Azuma, "Brokering Race, Culture, and Citizenship," 193–94. See also McNaughton, *Nisei Linguists*, 453–54. Kurihara discussed his lack of fluency in written Japanese with his Tokyo barber: Inose interview by Monkoski-Takamure.

28. B. Ogami interview by author; Asakura interview by author; McNaughton, *Nisei Linguists*, 430, 447.

29. Takamine interview by author.

30. Azuma, "Brokering Race, Culture, and Citizenship," 194.

31. Ishida, "Japanese American Renunciants," 166; Takita-Ishii, "Tokio Yamane," 174.

32. Kurihara to Thomas, September 29, 1946, reel 090, JAERR; Kurihara to Thomas, December 24, 1946, reel 090, JAERR.

33. "Taro Tanaka Barely Keeping Body and Soul Together, Living Cost Twice Income," *Rocky Shimpō*, November 4, 1946; Mary Kitano, "Japan Front," *Rafu Shimpō*, May 18, 1946.

34. Dower, *Embracing Defeat*, 116; Fujita interview by author.

35. Kurihara to Thomas, February 4, 1947, reel 090, JAERR.

36. Azuma, "Brokering Race, Culture, and Citizenship," 194–95.

37. Itami to Thomas and Nishimoto, April 4, 1949, Correspondence—Dr. Thomas, carton 2, 78/53c, JAERR.

38. Kurihara to Thomas, December 24, 1946, reel 090, JAERR.

39. Takita-Ishii, "Tokio Yamane," 177.

40. B. Ogami interview by author.

41. Ishida, "Japanese American Renunciants," 101–3.

42. Inose correspondence with author; Maezawa phone interview by author; S. Ko-

bayashi phone interview by Monkoski-Takemure. Meguro is one of twenty-three special municipal wards of Tokyo.

43. S. Kobayashi phone interview by Monkoski-Takemure, September 10, 1997; Ishida, "Japanese American Renunciants," 155.

44. Inose phone interview by Monkoski-Takamure.

45. Maezawa phone interview by author.

46. Itami to Thomas and Nishimoto, April 4, 1949, Correspondence—Dr. Thomas, carton 2, 78/53c, JAERR. At Manzanar, Itami worked for Robert Brown, the reports officer in charge of public relations and communications with the outside press. To this end, Brown began the *Manzanar Free Press*, which also provided information to the Nikkei in the camp. "[W]e found very soon after we started the newspaper that we had to have a Japanese section," recalled Brown, "and so . . . Dave did all the calligraphy by hand. He would do all that scratching on a stencil and we'd mimeograph it. That went out to all the Issei who couldn't read English." See Brown interview by Hansen, December 13, 1973, February 20, 1974, 96.

47. Haruko to Aunty, August 16, 1954, Grace Fukumoto family collection; Marubayashi interview by author.

48. Kawamoto and Kurihara, *Bonsai-Saikei*, 1963, 24.

49. Inose interview by Monkoski-Takemura.

50. Kurihara to Kennedy, October 20, 1962, Kurihara Case File 146–54–117; "U.S. Seeks Forgiveness for Relocation of Nisei," *Honolulu Star-Bulletin*, May 21, 1959.

51. Grumbly to Kurihara, November 9, 1962, Kurihara Case File 146–54–117.

52. Kurihara to Grumbly, December 11, 1962, Kurihara Case File 146–54–117.

53. Grumbly to Kurihara, January 9, 1962, Kurihara Case File 146–54–117.

54. Tamotsu Murayama, "Nisei Translates Book on Bonsai," *Pacific Citizen*, January 11, 1963; Inose interview by Monkoski-Takamure; Kurihara to Directors of Library, 1964.

55. Kurihara to Ueno, February 3, 1965, April 7, 1965, HU.

56. Kurihara, Removed Koseki; Murayama, *Hawaii Nisei*, 129–32; Fujita interview by author. Murayama, a Nisei living in Japan, knew Kurihara personally. The date of death on his family records in Japan (removed koseki) and on his cemetery plaque in Nuuanu Cemetery, Honolulu, is November 26, 1965.

Afterword

1. Kurihara to Ueno, April 7, 1965, HU; McKevitt, *The University of Santa Clara*, 170; Kurihara, "Autobiography," 4; *Catalogue 1917–1918*, University of Michigan, 85, Bentley Historical Library, University of Michigan.

2. Kurihara, "Autobiography, 12; Fujita interview by author.

3. Kurihara, Individual Record, Kurihara Internment Case File. There is no mention of Kurihara in Columbia University's 1924 commencement program, nor is he listed in the student directories of 1922–1925: e-mail correspondence with Katie Henningsen, Butler Library, Columbia University, September 3, 2008. Quotes from Lupton, "Memory's Apostle," 11. Ironically, Kurihara's contemporary and arch-foe Tokie Slocum,

with whom he had had many altercations, did attend Columbia. Did the university's name thus sit in the recesses of Kurihara's memory?

4. Nurius, "Human Memory," 266; Mazzoni and Memon, "Imagination Can Create False Autobiographical Memories," 186–89.

5. Samuel and Thompson, "Introduction," 7; Conway and Rubin, "The Structure of Autobiographical Memory," 113–14.

6. McGlone, "Deciphering Memory," 424.

7. Kurihara, Speeches, 8; Kurihara, "Niseis and the Government," 15; Hohri, *Repairing America*, 32; Kurihara, "Autobiography," 38.

8. Hohri, *Repairing America*, 29–30. In a forthcoming work, Arthur Hansen edits, annotates, and writes a critical introduction to a memoir that Omura was completing before his death. I have seen no evidence of contact between Omura and Kurihara on this or on any other issue. Lane Ryo Hirabayashi, in Nishimoto, *Inside an American Concentration Camp*, 165, states that in 1945 Nikkei delegates to the All Center Conference articulated the idea of "monetary reparations for losses and damage."

9. Smith, "Wartime Internment," 106–108; Maki, Kitano, and Berthold, *Achieving the Impossible Dream*, 52–55. For a copy of Public Law 886 (the 1948 Act), see Girder and Loftis, *The Great Betrayal*, 535–37. For details of the redress effort, see Maki, Kitano, and Berthold, *Achieving the Impossible Dream*; Murray, *Historical Memories of the Japanese American Internment and the Struggle for Redress*; Shimabukuro, *Born in Seattle*; Hohri, *Repairing America*.

10. Roy Sano, "A New Hero for Future Historians," *Pacific Citizen*, January 30, 1970; Yoneda to Editor, *Pacific Citizen*, February 13, 1970; Hamada to Editor, *Pacific Citizen*, March 13, 1970.

11. Hohri, "Joe Kurihara: Pioneer for Redress," *New York Nichibei*, August 14, 1980; Hohri to Editor, *New York Nichibei*, October 23, 1980; Ueno to Editor, *Rafu Shimpō*, October 7, 1981; Name Withheld, "Heel or Hero?" Letter to Editor, *Hokubei Mainichi*, April 26, 1983; Elaine Black Yoneda to Editor, *Hokubei Mainichi*, [May 3] 1983; "Murder at Camp Manzanar," *Rafu Shimpō*, December 21, 1982; "Murder at Camp Manzanar: The Other View," *Rafu Shimpō*, December 21, 1983; Peter Suzuki to Editor, *Pacific Citizen*, September 19, 1986.

12. This notion of constructivism corresponds with reader-response theory, which has existed since the 1930s and continues to have relevance. See, for example, Shuman, "The Past as Present," 30; Steinfirst, "Reader-Response Criticism," 114.

13. Marubayashi interview by author. Maps of the period confirm Marubayashi's account of a stream near the family home, which was located on Houghtailing Road. Raymond Kurihara, e-mail correspondence, June 26, 2007; Inose interview by Monkoski-Takamure.

14. My thoughts on Kurihara in this and the following paragraphs are the result of helpful critique and suggestions from Idus Newby.

15. Kurihara to Thomas, October 19, 1945, and November 10, 1945; Thomas to Kurihara, October 17, 1945, and October 23, 1945, Reel 090, JAERR. Kurihara's typescript autobiography is fifty-two pages long, double spaced.

GLOSSARY

Besig, Ernest: Executive Director, American Civil Liberties Union of Northern California.

Best, Raymond R.: Project Director, Moab and Leupp Citizen Isolation Camps, and Tule Lake Segregation Center.

Biddle, Francis: Attorney General under President Franklin D. Roosevelt.

Burling, John: Assistant Director, Alien Enemy Control Unit, Justice Department.

Campbell, Ned: Assistant Project Director, Manzanar.

Clark, Tom: Attorney General under President Harry Truman.

Collins, Wayne Mortimer: Attorney who represented renunciants who sought to regain their U.S. citizenship. He also represented Fred Korematsu, Iva Toguri D'Aquino, and Japanese Peruvians.

Daihyo Sha Kai: Representative Body. This was a group elected to represent the Nikkei at Tule Lake.

DeWitt, John: Lieutenant General and Commanding General, Western Defense Command.

Ennis, Edward J.: Director, Alien Enemy Control Unit, Justice Department.

Glick, Philip M.: Chief Solicitor, War Relocation Authority.

Hankey, Rosalie: Field researcher, Tule Lake, Japanese Evacuation and Resettlement Study; later Rosalie Hankey Wax.

Hoshi Dan: The collective name for the dissident groups at Tule Lake. *Hoshi* means "volunteer"; *Dan* means "group." The Issei group was called the *Sokuji Kikoku Hoshi Dan* (Organization to Return Immediately to Serve the Homeland). The Nisei and Nisei-Kibei group was called the *Hokoku Seinen Dan* (Young Men's Patriotic Organization; literally, Serve the Country Youth Group), and the young women's group was called the *Hokoku Joshi Seinen Dan.*

Ickes, Harold: Secretary of the Interior.

Issei: "I" means first; "sei" means generation. Issei refers to the immigrant generation.

Kai, Reverend Shizue: Leader among Nikkei dissidents at Tule Lake.

Kibei-Nisei: "Ki" means return; "bei" means America (Beikoku). Kibei refers to those

Nisei (immigrants' children who were born in the United States) who spent part of their young lives in Japan and who later returned to the United States. To make it clear that they were Nisei and therefore U.S. citizens, I use the term Kibei-Nisei instead of Kibei.

Kuratomi, George: Leader among Nikkei dissidents at Tule Lake.

McCloy, John J.: Assistant Secretary of War.

Merritt, Ralph: Project Director, Manzanar, from November 25, 1942, until its closure on November 21, 1945.

Myer, Dillon: Succeeded Milton Eisenhower as director of the War Relocation Authority.

Nakamura, Tetsujiro "Tex": Assistant legal officer, Tule Lake; assistant to Wayne Collins in renunciation cases.

Nash, Roy: Project Director, Manzanar, from June 1 to November 24, 1942.

Nikkei: "Ni" refers to Nippon (Japan) and "kei" refers to genetic lineage. Nikkei refers to anyone of Japanese ancestry who lives outside Japan.

Nisei: "Ni" means second; "sei" means generation. Nisei refers to the immigrants' children, who were born in the United States and were therefore U.S. citizens.

Noyes, Louis: Project Attorney, Tule Lake.

Opler, Marvin: Community Analyst, Tule Lake, WRA. His brother, Morris Opler, was Community Analyst at Manzanar.

Robertson, Paul: Project Director, Moab and Leupp Citizen Isolation Camps, succeeding Raymond Best. When the Leupp camp closed, he became Assistant Project Director, Tule Lake.

Sansei: "San" means third; "sei" means generation. Sansei refers to the Nisei's children.

Stimson, Henry L.: Secretary of War.

Tayama, Fred: Chair, JACL Southern California chapter. His beating led to the Manzanar revolt.

Thomas, Dorothy Swaine: Professor and Director of the Japanese Evacuation and Resettlement Study.

Ueno, Harry: Dissident Kibei-Nisei, leader of the Kitchen Workers Union, Manzanar.

Wakayama, Kinzo Ernest: Dissident Kibei-Nisei, a leader in the *Hoshi Dan*, Tule Lake.

Yamane, Tokio: Dissident Kibei-Nisei, beaten by WRA security officers, Tule Lake.

BIBLIOGRAPHY

Abbreviations

CAR — Community Analysis Reports and Community Analysis Trend Reports of the War Relocation Authority, 1942–1946. Reel 7. Microfilm Publication M1342. National Archives. Washington, D.C.

DOJ — Department of Justice. General Records. RG 60. National Archives. Washington, D.C.

DPI — Department of Public Instruction. Hawaii Territory

HFN — Hankey Field Notes, Tule Lake. There are two versions of the Field Notes of Rosalie Hankey (Wax). The first is composed of notes recorded in 1944–45, during her research time in Tule Lake. They are part of the Japanese American Evacuation and Resettlement Records. The full citation is Rosalie Hankey, Field Notes, Tule Lake, p. #, date, W 1.61 (or W 1.63), 67/14c, JAERR. The second version is an edited set of her original notes. In 1981–82, under a grant from the National Endowment for the Humanities, she retyped her field notes, providing explanations and clarifications, and deleting what she considered to be extraneous. This set is housed with the Rosalie H. Wax Papers. The full citation is Rosalie Hankey, Field Notes, ed., Tule Lake, p. #, date, 83/115c, RHW.

HAS — Hawai'i State Archives. Honolulu.

HSPA — Hawaiian Sugar Planters' Association Archives. LPC PV.4–14. Special Collections, Hamilton Library. University of Hawai'i Manoa. Honolulu.

HU — Harry Ueno Personal Files. This includes miscellaneous documents and diary entries of December 5, 1942–May 9, 1943. (Diary entries translated by Mary Monkoski-Takemure and Reiko Monkoski, December 23, 1998, in author's possession.)

INS — Immigration and Naturalization Service. RG 85. National Archives. Washington, D.C.

JACL — Japanese American Citizens League

JAERR Japanese American Evacuation and Resettlement Records. 67/14c. The Bancroft Library. University of California Berkeley.
JERS Japanese American Evacuation and Resettlement Study
KY Karl G. Yoneda Papers. Collection 1592. U.S. War Relocation Records. Department of Special Collections, Charles E. Young Research Library. University of California Los Angeles.
MWRR Manzanar War Relocation Records. Collection 122. Department of Special Collections, Charles E. Young Research Library. University of California Los Angeles.
ONI Office of Naval Intelligence.
RHW Rosalie Hankey Wax Papers. 83/115c. The Bancroft Library. University of California Berkeley.
SIHS St. Ignatius High School.
SIU St. Ignatius University.
SLC St. Louis College and St. Francis School. St. Louis College Records. St. Louis School Archives. Honolulu.
SOW Secretary of War. RG 107. National Archives. Washington, D.C.
USF University of San Francisco Archives. San Francisco.
WC Wayne Collins Papers. 78/177c. The Bancroft Library. University of California Berkeley.
WCCA Wartime Civilian Control Administration.
WDC Western Defense Command. Wartime Civil Control Administration. RG 338. National Archives. Washington, DC.
WRA War Relocation Authority Records. RG 210. National Archives. Washington, D.C.

Selected Documents on or by Kurihara

Best, Raymond R. "Joe Kurihara, 'Repatriate.'" [December 1945.] Typescript. JAERR.
Brown, Emily. "Story of Joe Kurihara." [December 1945]. Typescript. File 24.052B, box 223 Final Reports, Headquarters, WRA. Lacks documentation and includes some erroneous information. I use it when its contents agree with other documents.
Frederick, Francis S. "Case History, Joseph Yoshisuke Kurihara." World War II Internment Case File, Joseph Y. Kurihara. August 17, 1943. Box 2864, 5/68/56/4, WRA.
Kawamoto, Toshio and Joseph Y. Kurihara. *Bonsai-Saikei: The Art of Japanese Miniature Trees, Gardens, and Landscapes*. Tokyo: Nippon Saikei, 1963.
Kurihara, J. Y. "I Was in the War." *Kashu Mainichi*, May 19, 1940, and May 26, 1940, n.p.
Kurihara, Joseph Y. "World War I Draft Registration Card." June 5, 1917. Available at http://search.ancestry.com (accessed December 1, 2006).
———. Transcripts, 1924. Southwestern University. Los Angeles, California.
———. Speeches. Unpublished typescript. [1942]. JAERR.
———. "Murder in Camp Manzanar." Unpublished typescript. April 16, 1943. Received from a member of Kurihara's family, in author's possession. A copy with a different

typescript is housed at the Bancroft Library, 67/14c, O8.10. University of California Berkeley.

———. "The Niseis and the Government of the United States." Unpublished handscript. [1943]. Charles and Lois Ferguson Collection, Japanese American National Museum, Los Angeles.

———. "Autobiography." Unpublished typescript. 1945. JAERR.

———. NA Form 13164, Military Personnel Records. National Archives, St. Louis, Mo. Freedom of Information Act.

Kurihara, Joseph Yoshisuke. Case File 146–54–117, Civil Division, U.S. Dept. of Justice. Freedom of Information Act.

———. WWII Internment Case File. Box 2864. WRA.

Kurihara, Kichizo Family Records. Consulate-General of Japan, Honolulu, n.d.

Kurihara, Roy S. "World War I Draft Registration Card." June 5, 1917. Available at http://search.ancestry.com (accessed July 6, 2005).

Kurihara, Yoshisuke. Removed Koseki (trans.). Ōshima-cho, Ōshima-gun, Yamaguchi, Japan. This document is from Kurihara's family records in Japan. It includes dates of birth and death.

Newspapers and Newsletters

American Legion Monthly, 1935
Detroit Free Press, 1917–1918, 1941
Detroit News, 1917
Detroit Saturday Night, 1927
Hawaii Herald, 2006
Hawaii Times, 1959
Hokubei Mainichi, 1983
Honolulu Advertiser, 2005
Honolulu Star-Bulletin, 1959
Inyo Independent, 1942
Kashū Mainichi, 1937, 1940
Los Angeles Times, 1935, 1942, 1945
New York Nichibei, 1980
Pacific Citizen, 1945, 1948, 1966, 1970, 1986
Rafu Shimpō, 1946, 1981, 1983
Rocky Shimpō, 1945–46
Times Independent, 1942–43, 1994
Utah Zephyr, 1989

Interviews and Correspondence

Akashi, Tom. Interview by Tom Ikeda and Chizu Omori, July 3, 2004, denshovh-atom-01. Densho Visual Histories. Densho Digital Archive.

Aoyama, Mitsuo. Correspondence with author, April 20, 1997.

Asakura, William and Grace (pseudonyms). Interview by author, April 15, 1997, undisclosed location.

Brown, Robert. Interview by Arthur A. Hansen, December 13, 1973, transcript. In *Camp and Community: Manzanar and the Owens Valley*, edited by Jesse A. Garrett and Ronald C. Larson, 17–41. Fullerton, Calif.: California State University Japanese American Oral History Project, 1977.

Brown, Robert. Interview by Arthur A. Hansen, February 20, 1974, transcript. In *Japanese American World War II Evacuation Oral History Project, Part II: Administrators* edited by Arthur A. Hansen, 73–130. Westport, Conn.: Meckler, 1991.

Collins, Wayne Merrill (son of Wayne Mortimer Collins). Phone conversation with author, December 2, 1996.

Creason, Glen. E-mail correspondence with author, December 19, 2005. Map Librarian, Los Angeles Public Library.

Ego, Frank. Phone interview by author, October 16 and 17, 1997.

Fujita, Joe Wilfred (Kurihara's grandnephew). Interview by author, September 21, 2005, Honolulu.

Hasegawa, Osamu. Phone interview by author, April 27, 1997.

Houghtailing, George. Interview by Michiko Kodama, January 30, 1984, Honolulu, transcript. In *Kalihi, Place of Transition*, Ethnic Studies Oral History Project, vol. 3, 1097–120. Honolulu: ESOHP, University of Hawai'i Manoa, 1984.

Inose, Makoto. Phone interview by Mary Monkoski-Takamure, July 30, 1997.

Inose, Makoto. Correspondence with author, August 18, 1997. Translated by Mary Monkoski-Takamure.

Joseph, Joe A. Interview by Warren Nishimoto, February 16, 1984, Honolulu, transcript. In *Kalihi, Place of Transition*, Ethnic Studies Oral History Project, vol. 2, 501–25. Honolulu: ESOHP, University of Hawai'i Manoa, 1984.

Kamikawa, Satoru. Interview by Karl G. Yoneda, August 27, 1972. Folder 1—Manzanar Diary—Joe Kurihara and Harry Ueno Controversies, box 9, KY.

Kashiwagi, Hiroshi. Interview by Alice Ito, July 3, 2004, denshovh-khiroshi-02. Densho Visual Histories. Densho Digital Archive.

Kimura, Minoru. Interview by Michiko Kodama, December 20, 1983, Honolulu, transcript. In *Kalihi, Place of Transition*, Ethnic Studies Oral History Project, vol. 1, 255–98. Honolulu: ESOHP, University of Hawai'i Manoa, 1984.

Kobayashi, Kenge. Interview by Alice Ito, July 4, 1998, denshovh-kkenge-01. Densho Visual Histories. Densho Digital Archive.

Kobayashi, Sakae. Phone interview by Mary Monkoski-Takemure, September 10, 1997 and January 6, 1998.

Kurihara, Raymond (Kurihara's nephew). E-mail correspondence. June 26, 2007, June 27, 2007, July 15, 2007, July 18, 2007, January 31, 2008.

Like, Albert Nawahi. Interview by Warren Nishimoto, January 12, 1984, Honolulu, transcript. In *Kalihi, Place of Transition*, Ethnic Studies Oral History Project, vol. 2, 685–726. Honolulu: ESOHP, University of Hawai'i Manoa, 1984.

Maezawa, Yuji. Phone interview by author, March 28, 1998.

Marubayashi, Hanako (Kurihara's niece). Interview by author, September 21, 2005, Honolulu.

Matsushita, Robert (pseudonym). Interview by author, October 15, 1995, undisclosed location.

Myer, Dillon. Interview by Morton Grodzins, September 29, 1943, E2.10, 67/14c, JAERR.

Nakamura, James (pseudonym). Phone interview by author, September 8, 1997.

Nakamura, Tetsujiro "Tex." Interview by Tom Ikeda and Barbara Takei, September 24, 2009, denshovh-ntetsujiro-01. Densho Visual Histories. Densho Digital Archive.

Ogami, Arthur. Interview by Alice Ito, March 10, 2004, denshovh-oarthur-01. Densho Visual Histories. Densho Digital Archive.

Ogami, Ben. Phone interview by author, September 19, 1997.

Rath, Robert H., Sr. Interview by Warren Nishimoto, October 17, 1996, Honolulu, transcript. In *Reflections of Palama Settlement*, Center for Oral History, vol. 1, 90–95. Honolulu: COH, University of Hawai'i Manoa, 1998.

Redd, Annaley, and Hardy Redd. Phone interview by author, June 11, 1999.

Robertson, Paul G. Interview by Arthur A. Hansen and Regan J. Bell, August 12, 1987, transcript. In *Japanese American World War II Evacuation Oral History Project, Part II: Administrators*, edited by Arthur A. Hansen, 205–81. Westport, Conn.: Meckler, 1991.

Sasaki, Mamoru (pseudonym). Phone interview by author, January 24, 1997.

Sato, Sarah. Interview by Dee Goto, April 9, 1998, denshovh-ssarah-01. Densho Visual Histories. Densho Digital Archive.

Spencer, Robert F. Interview by Arthur A. Hansen, July 15–17, 1987, transcript. In *Japanese American World War II Evacuation Oral History Project, Part II: Analysts*, edited by Arthur A. Hansen, 177–292. Westport, Conn.: Meckler, 1994.

Takamine, Roy (pseudonym). Interview by author, April 22, 1997, Honolulu.

Tanaka, Togo. Interview by Betty E. Mitson and David A. Hacker, May 19, 1973, transcript. In *Japanese American World War II Evacuation Oral History Project, Part 3, Analysts*, edited by Arthur A. Hansen, ed., 115–43. New Providence, N.J.: Saur, 1994.

———. Interview by Arthur A. Hansen, August 30, 1973, transcript. In *Japanese American World War II Evacuation Oral History Project, Part 3, Analysts*, edited by Arthur A. Hansen, ed., 151–71. New Providence, N.J.: Saur, 1994.

———. Interview by author, May 13, 1996, Los Angeles.

———. Letter to author, August 30, 1996.

———. Interview by James Gatewood, December 13, 1997, transcript. In *Regenerations Oral History Project: Rebuilding Japanese American Families, Communities, and Civil rights in the Resettlement Era, Los Angeles Region, Volume II*, Japanese American National Museum, 419–64. Los Angeles: JANM, [1999].

Ueno, Harry Y. Interview by author, April 2, 1994, Sunnyvale, California; phone conversation with author, April 26, 1997.

———. Interview by Wendy Ng, January 23, 1998, and May 9, 1998, transcript. In *Regenerations Oral History Project: Rebuilding Japanese American Families, Communities, and Civil rights in the Resettlement Era, San Jose Region: Volume IV*, edited by the Japanese American National Museum, 457–530. Los Angeles: JANM, 2000.

Yamamoto, Sumiko M. Interview by Tom Ikeda and Barbara Takei, December 8, 2009, denshovh-ysumiko-01, Densho Visual Histories, Densho Digital Archive.

Other Sources

Abe, Frank. *Conscience and the Constitution*. Videorecording. Hohokus, N.Y.: Transit Media, 2000.

Adams, Romanzo. *Japanese in Hawaii*. New York: National Committee on American Japanese Relations, 1924.

Akashi, Motomu. *Betrayed Trust: The Story of a Deported Issei and His American-Born Family During WW II*. Bloomington, Ind.: AuthorHouse, 2004.

Alinder, Jasmine. *Moving Images: Photography and the Japanese American Incarceration*. Chicago: University of Illinois Press, 2009.

Alvarez, Patricia. "Weaving a Cloak of Discipline: Hawaii's Catholic Schools, 1840–1941." Ph.D. diss., University of Hawaii Manoa, 1994.

Ambrosius, Lloyd E. *Wilsonian Statecraft: Theory and Practice of Liberal Internationalism during World War I*. Wilmington, Del.: SR Books, 1991.

Azuma, Eiichiro. "Brokering Race, Culture, and Citizenship: Japanese Americans in Occupied Japan and Postwar National Inclusion." *Journal of American-East Asian Relations* 16, no. 3 (Fall 2009): 183–211.

———. *Between Two Empires: Race, History, and Transnationalism in Japanese America*. New York: Oxford University Press, 2005.

Bailey, Paul Dayton. *City in the Sun: The Japanese Concentration Camp at Poston, Arizona*. Los Angeles: Westernlore, 1971.

Baker, Roscoe. *The American Legion and American Foreign Policy*. Westport, Conn.: Greenwood, 1954.

Baldwin, Hanson W. "Americans at War." *Foreign Affairs* 22, no. 1 (January 1943): 200.

Barraclough, Geoffrey, ed. *The Times Concise Atlas of World History*. Maplewood, N.J.: Hammond, 1982.

Barry, Edward M., ed. *Doings of Battery B: Humorous Happenings and Striking Situations and Experiences of Its Members*. Grand Rapids, Mich.: Dean-Hicks, 1920.

Beechert, Alice M., and Edward D. Beechert, eds. *From Kona to Yenan: The Political Memoirs of Koji Ariyoshi*. Honolulu: Biographical Research Center, University of Hawai'i, 2000.

Beechert, Edward D. *Working in Hawaii: A Labor History*. Honolulu: University of Hawaii Press, 1985.

Bloemraad, Irene. "Much Ado about Nothing? The Contours of Dual Citizenship in the United States and Canada." In *Dual Citizenship in Global Perspective: From Unitary to Multiple Citizenship*, edited by Thomas Faist and Peter Kivisto, 159–86. New York: Palgrave Macmillan, 2007.

Bonjour La France. "France Map—Map of SNCF National Railway Network in France." Available at http://bonjourlafrance.net/france-map/sncf-map-large.htm (accessed November 13, 2012).

Borden, Penn. *Civilian Indoctrination of the Military: World War I and Future Implications for the Military-Industrial Complex.* New York: Greenwood, 1989.

Bosworth, Allan. *America's Concentration Camps.* New York: Norton, 1967.

Bottoms, Bill. *The VFW: An Illustrated History of the Veterans of Foreign Wars of the United States.* Rockville, Md.: Woodbine House, 1991.

Boyle, Francis A. "Restoration of the Independent Nation State of Hawaii under International Law." *St. Thomas Law Review* 7 (1994–95): 727–38.

Britten, Thomas A. *American Indians in World War I: At Home and at War.* Albuquerque: University of New Mexico Press, 1997.

Brubaker, C. William. *Planning and Designing Schools.* New York: McGraw-Hill, 1998.

Bryk, Anthony S., Valerie E. Lee, and Peter B. Holland. *Catholic Schools and the Common Good.* Cambridge, Mass.: Harvard University Press, 1993.

Burns, Jeffrey. "Building the Best: A History of Catholic Parish Life in the Pacific States." In *The American Catholic Parish,* vol. 2, edited by Jay Dolan, 15–17. New York: Paulist, 1987.

Burton, Jeffery F., Mary M. Farrell, Florence B. Lord, and Richard W. Lord. *Confinement and Ethnicity: An Overview of World War II Japanese American Relocation Sites.* Washington, D.C.: National Park Service, U.S. Department of the Interior, 1999.

Camp Custer: A University of Democracy. Battle Creek, Mich.: Atkins and Jones, 1918.

Castelnuovo, Shirley. *Soldiers of Conscience: Japanese American Military Resisters in World War II.* Westport, Conn.: Praeger, 2008.

Caudill, William. "Japanese-American Personality and Acculturation." *Genetic-Psychology Monographs* 45 (1952): 3–102.

Chamberlain, Mary. "Narrative Theory." In *Thinking about Oral History: Theories and Applications,* edited by Thomas L. Charlton, Lois E. Myers, and Rebecca Sharpless, 142–65. New York: Altamira, 2008.

Chambers, John Whiteclay. *To Raise an Army: The Draft Comes to Modern America.* New York: Free Press, 1987.

Chan, Sucheng. *Asian Americans: An Interpretive History.* Boston: Twayne, 1991.

Chin, Frank. *Born in the USA: A Story of Japanese America, 1889–1947.* Lanham, Md.: Rowman & Littlefield, 2002.

Christgau, John. "Collins versus the World: The Fight to Restore Citizenship to Japanese American Renunciants of World War II." *Pacific Historical Review* 54 (February 1985): 1–31.

Christian, Carole E. "Joining the Mainstream: Texas's Mexican Americans during World War I." *Southwestern Historical Quarterly* 92 (April 1989): 559–95.

Coffman, Edward M. *The War to End All Wars: The American Military Experience in World War I.* New York: Oxford University Press, 1968.

Coffman, Tom. *A Nation Within: The Story of America's Annexation of the Nation of Hawai'i.* Kaneohe, Hawaii: Epicenter, 1998.

Cole, Tom. *A Short History of San Francisco.* San Francisco: Lexikos, 1981.

Collins, Donald E. *Native American Aliens: Disloyalty and the Renunciation of Citizenship by Japanese Americans during World War II.* Westport, Conn.: Greenwood, 1985.

Americans Remember Their World War II Incarceration. Seattle: University of Washington Press, 2004.

Gannon, Michael. *Operation Drumbeat: The Dramatic True Story of German's First U-Boat Attacks along the American Coast in World War II*. New York: Harper & Row, 1990.

Gellerman, William. *The American Legion as Educator*. New York: Teachers College, 1938.

Girder, Audrie, and Anne Loftis. *The Great Betrayal: the Evacuation of the Japanese-Americans during World War II*. London: Macmillan, 1969

Gleason, Philip. *Contending with Modernity: Catholic Higher Education in the Twentieth Century*. New York: Oxford University Press, 1995.

Godsil, Harry Carr. *The High Seas Tuna Fishery of California*. Fish Bulletin No. 51. Division of Fish and Game of California, Bureau of Marine Fisheries, 1938. Available at http://content.cdlib.org (accessed May 30, 2008).

Gottlieb, Roger S. "The Concept of Resistance: Jewish Resistance during the Holocaust." *Social Theory and Practice* 9 (Spring 1983): 31–49.

Grant, Glen, and Bennett Hymer. *Hawai'i Looking Back: An Illustrated History of the Islands*. Honolulu: Mutual, 2000.

Graves, Ben E. *School Ways: The Planning and Design of America's Schools*. New York: McGraw-Hill, 1993.

Grodzins, Morton. *Americans Betrayed: Politics and the Japanese Evacuation*. Chicago: University of Chicago Press, 1974 [1949].

Gudridge, Patrick O. "The Constitution Glimpsed from Tule Lake." *Law and Contemporary Problems* 68, no. 81 (Spring 2005): 82–118.

Hansen, Arthur A. "Cultural Politics in the Gila River Relocation Center, 1942–1943." *Arizona and the West* 27 (Winter 1985): 327–62.

———. ed. *Japanese American World War II Evacuation Oral History Project*. Parts 1–4. Westport, Conn.: Meckler, 1991–1995.

———. "A Riot of Voices: Racial and Ethnic Variables in Interactive Oral History Interviewing." In *Interactive Oral History Interviewing*, edited by Eva M. McHahan, 107–39. Hillsdale, N.J.: Erlbaum, 1994.

———. "Oral History and the Japanese American Evacuation." *Journal of American History* 82 (September 1995): 625–39.

———. "Protest-Resistance and the Heart Mountain Experience: The Revitalization of a Robust Nikkei Tradition." In *A Matter of Conscience: Essays on the World War II Heart Mountain Draft Resistance Movement*, edited by Mike Mackey, 81–117. Powell, Wyo.: Western History, 2002.

———. "Peculiar Odyssey: Newsman Jimmie Omura's Removal from and Regeneration within Nikkei Society, History, and Memory." In *Nikkei in the Pacific Northwest: Japanese Americans and Japanese Canadians in the Twentieth Century*, edited by Louis Fiset and Gail M. Nomura, 271–307. Seattle: University of Washington Press, 2005.

———. ed. *James Omura Memoir* [working title]. Forthcoming.

Hansen, Arthur A., and David A. Hacker. "The Manzanar Riot: An Ethnic Perspective." *Amerasia Journal* 2 (Fall 1974): 112–57.

Hansen, Arthur, and Betty E. Mitson, ed. *Voices Long Silent: An Oral Inquiry into the Japanese American Evacuation*. Fullerton, Calif.: Oral History Program, California State University, Fullerton, 1974.

Hanson, William, L. *World War I, I Was There*. Gerald, Mo.: Patrice, 1982.

Hawaii Republic. Act 57. In *Laws of the Republic of Hawaii Passed by the Legislature at Its Session, 1896*, 181–95. Honolulu: Republic of Hawaii, 1896.

———. Department of Public Instruction. *Report of the Minister of Public Instruction, Biennial, 1897*. Honolulu: MPI, 1898.

Hawaii Territory. Department of Public Instruction. *Report to the Governor and Legislature, 1902–1904*. Honolulu: DPI, 1905.

———. Department of Public Instruction. *Report to the Governor and Legislature, 1908–1910*. Honolulu: DPI, 1905.

———. Department of Public Instruction. *Report to the Governor and Legislature, 1910–1912*. Honolulu: DPI, 1913.

———. Department of Public Instruction. *Report to the Governor and Legislature, 1920*. Honolulu: DPI, 1921.

———. "Revised School Laws, 1905." In *School Laws*, 1–35. Honolulu: Department of Public Instruction, 1928.

Hayashi, Brian Masaru. *"For the Sake of Our Japanese Brethren": Assimilation, Nationalism, and Protestantism among the Japanese of Los Angeles, 1895–1942*. Stanford, Calif.: Stanford University Press, 1995.

———. *Democratizing the Enemy: The Japanese American Internment*. Princeton: Princeton University Press, 2004.

Herzig, John A. "Japanese Americans and MAGIC." *Amerasia Journal* 11, no. 2 (1984): 47–65.

Herzig-Yoshinaga, Aiko. "Words Can Lie or Clarify: Terminology of the World War II Incarceration of Japanese Americans." 2009 (rev. 2010). Available at http://pnwjacl.org/POW-1.htm (accessed June 4, 2011).

Hirabayashi, James. "'Concentration Camp' or 'Relocation Center': What's in a Name?" *Japanese American National Museum Quarterly* (Autumn 1994): 5–10.

Hirabayashi, Lane Ryo. *The Politics of Fieldwork: Research in an American Concentration Camp*. Tucson: The University of Arizona Press, 1999.

Hirabayashi, Lane Ryo, and James Hirabayashi. "The 'Credible' Witness: The Central Role of Richard S. Nishimoto in JERS." In *Views from Within: The Japanese American Evacuation and Resettlement Study*, edited by Yuji Ichioka, 65–94. Los Angeles: Asian American Studies Center, UCLA Los Angeles, 1989.

Hohri, William Minoru. *Repairing America: An Account of the Movement for Japanese-American Redress*. Pullman, Wash.: Washington State University Press, 1988.

Hohri, William Minoru, with Mits Koshiyama, Yosh Kuromiya, Takashi Hoshizaki, and Frank Seishi Emi. *Resistance: Challenging America's Wartime Internment of Japanese-Americans*. Lomita, Calif.: Epistolarian, 2001.

Hosokawa, Bill. *JACL in Quest of Justice.* New York: Morrow, 1982.

———. *Nisei: The Quiet Americans,* revised ed. Boulder: University Press of Colorado, 2002.

Huber, S. C. "Dual Citizenship." *Paradise of the Pacific* 50 (January 1938): 23–24.

Hunter, Louise. *Buddhism in Hawaii: Its Impact on a Yankee Community.* Honolulu: University of Hawaii Press, 1971.

Hymes, Dell. "The Use of Anthropology: Critical, Political, Personal." In *Reinventing Anthropology,* edited by Dell Hymes, 3–82. New York: Vintage, 1974 [1969].

Ichioka, Yuji. *Before Internment: Essays in Prewar Japanese American History.* Edited by Gordon H. Chang and Eiichiro Azuma. Stanford, Calif.: Stanford University Press, 2006.

———. *The Issei: the World of the First Generation Japanese Immigrants, 1885–1924.* New York: Free Press, 1988.

———. "JERS Revisited: Introduction." In *Views from Within: The Japanese American Evacuation and Resettlement Study,* edited by Yuji Ichioka, 3–27. Los Angeles: Asian American Studies Center, UCLA, 1989.

InflationData.com. "Historical Consumer Price Index." http://inflationdata.com/inflation/Consumer_Price_Index/HistoricalCPI.aspx (accessed November 13, 2012).

Irons, Peter. *Justice at War: The Story of the Japanese American Internment Cases.* Berkeley: University of California Press, 1993 [1983].

Irwin, Yukiko, and Hilary Conroy. "Robert Walker Irwin and Systematic Immigration to Hawaii." In *East across the Pacific: Historical and Sociological Studies of Japanese Immigraton and Assimilation,* edited by Hilary Conroy and T. Scott Miyakawa, 40–55. Santa Barbara, Calif.: ABC Clio, 1972.

Isenberg, Nancy. "The Personal Is Political: Gender, Feminism, and the Politics of Discourse Theory." *American Quarterly* 44, no. 3 (September 1992): 449–58.

Ishida, Gladys. "The Background and Effect of the Renunciation of Citizenship by Japanese Americans during World War II. M.A. thesis. Universitiy of Chicago, 1946.

———. "The Japanese American Renunciants of Okayama Prefecture: Their Accommodation and Assimilation to Japanese Culture." Ph.D. diss. University of Michigan, 1955.

Issel, William, and Robert Cherny. *San Francisco, 1865–1932: Politics, Power, and Urban Development.* Berkeley: University of California Press, 1986.

Iwata, Masakazu. *Planted in Good Soil: A History of the Issei in United States Agriculture.* Vol. 1. New York: Peter Lang, 1992.

Jackman, Norman R. "Collective Protest in Relocation Centers." *American Journal of Sociology* 63, no. 2 (September 1957): 264–72.

Japanese American Citizens League. *The Case for the Nisei.* N.p.: JACL, [1945].

Kashima, Tetsudan. *Judgment without Trial: Japanese American Imprisonment during World War II.* Seattle: University of Washington Press, 2003.

Kawamura, Noriko. *Turbulence in the Pacific: Japanese-U.S. Relations during World War I.* Westport, Conn.: Praeger, 2000.

Kent, Noel J. *Hawaii: Islands under the Influence.* Honolulu: University of Hawaii Press, 1993.

Kikumura, Akemi. *Through Harsh Winters: The Life of a Japanese Immigrant Woman.* Novato, Calif.: Chandler, 1981.

Kinkead, Thomas L. *An Explanation of the Baltimore Catechism of Christian Doctrine.* New York: Benziger, 1891.

Kitano, Harry H. L. *Japanese Americans: Evolution of a Subculture.* 2nd ed. Englewood Cliffs, N.J.: Prentice Hall, 1976.

Kiyama, Henry. *The Four Immigrants Manga: A Japanese Experience in San Francisco, 1904–1924.* Translated, with an introduction and notes by Frederik L. Schodt. Berkeley: Stone Bridge, 1999.

Kiyota, Minoru. *Beyond Loyalty: The Story of a Kibei.* Honolulu: University of Hawaii Press, 1997.

Kumamoto, Bob. "The Search for Spies: American Counterintelligence and the Japanese American Community, 1931–1942." *Amerasia Journal* 6, no. 2 (1979): 45–75.

Kumei, Teruko Imai. "'Skeleton in the Closet': The Japanese American *Hokoku Seinendan* and Their 'Disloyal' Activities at Tule Lake Segregation Center during World War II." *Japanese Journal of American Studies* 7 (1996): 67–102.

Kurhashige, Lon. "The Problem of Biculturalism: Japanese American Identity and Festival before World War II." *Journal of American History* 86 (March 2000): 1,632–54.

———. "Resistance, Collaboration, and Manzanar Protest." *Pacific Historical Review.* 70, no. 3 (2001): 387–417.

———. *Japanese American Celebration and Conflict: A History of Ethnic Identity and Festival, 1934–1990.* Berkeley: University of California Press, 2002.

Kurashige, Scott. *The Shifting Grounds of Race: Black and Japanese Americans in the Making of Multiethnic Los Angeles.* Princeton: Princeton University Press, 2008.

Kutulas, Judy. "In Quest of Autonomy: The Northern California Affiliate of the American Civil Liberties Union and World War II." *Pacific Historical Review* 67 (May 1998): 201–31.

———. *The American Civil Liberties Union and the Making of Modern Liberalism, 1930–1960.* Chapel Hill: University of North Carolina Press, 2006.

Lee, Erika. "Hemispheric Orientalism and the 1907 Pacific Coast Race Riot." *Amerasia Journal* 33, no. 2 (2007): 19–47.

Lee, Ulysses. *The Employment of Negro Troops.* Washington, D.C.: Center of Military History, 1966.

Leighton, Alexander Hamilton. *The Governing of Men.* Princeton, N.J.: Princeton University Press, 1945.

Lewis, Oscar. *San Francisco: Mission to Metropolis.* 2nd ed. San Diego: Howell-North, 1980.

Lind, Andrew W. *Hawaii's People.* 3rd ed. Honolulu: University of Hawaii Press, 1967.

Lo, Catherine Pascual. "Hanama'ulu's Chronology." Hanama'ulu Town Celebration, 2004. Available at http://poipuwebdesigns.tripod.com/id6.html (accessed November 13, 2012).

Los Angeles Public Library. "Sims Map of Metropolitan Los Angeles." 1926. Los Angeles, Calif.

———. "Payne's Heart of Downtown." 1931 map. Los Angeles, California.

Lotchin, Roger W. "Japanese Relocation in World War II and the Illusion of Universal Racism." *Journal of the Historical Society* 11, no. 2 (June 2011): 155–81.

Loureiro, Pedro. "U.S. Counterintelligence against Japan in Southern California, 1933–41." M.A. thesis. San Diego State University, 1987.

———. "The Imperial Japanese Navy and Espionage: The Itaru Tachibana Case." *International Journal of Intelligence and Counterintelligence* 3, no. 1 (1989): 105–21.

Louthan, Bruce D. "Dalton Wells CCC Camp." *Canyon Legacy* 19 (Fall/Winter 1993): 5–14.

Louthan, Bruce D., and Lloyd M. Pierson. "Moab Japanese-American Isolation Center: The Dark Postlude in the History of Dalton Wells CCC Camp." *Canyon Legacy* 19 (Fall/Winter 1993): 28–31.

Low, Victor. *The Unimpressible Race: A Century of Educational Struggle by the Chinese in San Francisco.* San Francisco: East/West, 1982.

Lupton, Catherine. "Memory's Apostle: Chris Marker, La Jetée, and Sans Soleil." In *La Jetée Sans Soleil*, videodisc by Chris Marker with accompanying booklet, 7–13. Irvington, N.Y.: Criterion, 2007.

Lyman, Stanford. "Generation and Character: The Case of the Japanese-Americans." In *East across the Pacific*, edited by Hilary Conroy and T. Scott Miyakawa, 279–314. Santa Barbara: ABC-Clio, 1972.

———. "On Nisei Interpersonal Style: A Reply to S. Frank Miyamoto." *Amerasia Journal* 14 (1988): 105–8.

———. "'American' Interpersonal Style and Nikkei Realities: a Rejoinder to S. Frank Miyamoto." *Amerasia Journal* 14 (1988): 115–23.

Lyon, Cherstin M. *Prisons and Patriots: Japanese American Wartime Citizenship, Civil Disobedience, and Historical Memory*. Philadelphia: Temple University Press, 2012.

Mackey, Mike, ed. *Remembering Heart Mountain: Essays on Japanese American Internment in Wyoming*. Powell, Wyo.: Western History, 1998.

Maeda, Daryl J. *Chains of Babylon: The Rise of Asian America.* Minneapolis: University of Minnesota Press, 2009.

Maki, Mitchell T., Harry H. L. Kitano, and S. Megan Berthold. *Achieving the Impossible Dream: How Japanese Americans Obtained Redress.* Urbana: University of Illinois Press, 1999.

Malkin, Michelle. *In Defense of Internment: The Case for "Racial Profiling" in World War II and the War on Terror*. Washington, D.C.: Regnery Publishing, 2004.

Marker, Chris. *San Soleil.* Videodisc. Irvington, N.Y.: Criterion, 2007.

Mason, Herbert Molloy. *VFW: Our First Century*. Lenexa, Kan.: Addax, 1999.

Matsuki, Kyoko. "Golden Era of Our Church." Unpublished typescript. St. Francis Xavier Japanese Catholic Mission, 1992.

Maykovich, Minako K. *Japanese American Identity Dilemma*. Tokyo: Waseda University Press, 1972.

Mazzoni, Giuliana, and Amina Memon. "Imagination Can Create False Autobiographical Memories." *Psychological Science* 14, no. 2 (March 2003): 186–89.

McGloin, John Bernard. *Jesuits by the Golden Gate: The Society of Jesus in San Francisco, 1849–1969*. San Francisco: University of San Francisco, 1972.

McGlone, Robert E. "Deciphering Memory: John Adams and the Authorship of the Declaration of Independence." *Journal of American History* 85, no. 2 (September 1998): 411–38.

McGucken, William J. *The Jesuits and Education: The Society's Teaching Principles and Practice, Especially in Secondary Education in the United States*. New York: Bruce, 1932.

McKay, Susan. "Young Women's Everyday Resistance: Heart Mountain, Wyoming." In *Guilt by Association: Essays on Japanese Settlement, Internment, and Relocation in the Rocky Mountain West,* edited by Mike Mackey, 203–16. Powell, Wyoming, 2001.

McKevitt, Gerald. *The University of Santa Clara: A History, 1851–1977*. Stanford, Calif.: Stanford University Press, 1979.

———. *Brokers of Culture: Italian Jesuits in the American West, 1848–1919*. Stanford: Stanford University Press, 2007).

McNaughton, James C. *Nisei Linguists: Japanese Americans in the Military Intelligence Service during World War II*. Washington, DC: Department of the Army, 2007.

Miyamoto, S. Frank. "Problems of Interpersonal Style among the Nisei." *Amerasia Journal* 13:2 (1986–87): 29–45.

———. "Miyamoto Reply to Stanford Lyman." *Amerasia Journal* 14 (1988): 109–113.

———. "Dorothy Swaine Thomas as Director of JERS: Some Personal Observations." In *Views from Within: The Japanese American Evacuation and Resettlement Study,* edited by Yuji Ichioka, 31–63. Los Angeles: Asian American Studies Center, UCLA Los Angeles, 1989.

———. "Resentment, Distrust, and Insecurity at Tule Lake." In *Views from Within: The Japanese American Evacuation and Resettlement Study,* edited by Yuji Ichioka, 127–40. Los Angeles: Asian American Studies Center, UCLA Los Angeles, 1989.

Modell, John. *The Economics and Politics of Racial Accommodation: The Japanese of Los Angeles, 1900–1942*. Urbana: University of Illinois Press, 1977.

Mohr, James C. *Plague and Fire: Battling Black Death and the 1900 Burning of Honolulu's Chinatown*. New York: Oxford University Press, 2005.

Morison, R. C. H. *Chambers's New Reciter*. London: Chambers, 1901.

Moriyama, Alan T. "The Causes of Emigration: The Background of Japanese Emigration to Hawaii, 1885–1894." In *Labor Immigration under Capitalism: Asian Workers in the United States before World War II,* edited by Lucie Cheng and Edna Bonacich, 248–76. Berkeley: University of California Press, 1984.

———. *Imingaisha: Japanese Emigration Companies and Hawaii, 1894—1908*. Honolulu: University of Hawaii Press, 1985.

Morrison, Toni. *Beloved*. New York: Alfred Knopf, 1987.

Muller, Eric L. *Free to Die for Their Country: The Story of the American Draft Resisters in World War II*. Chicago: University of Chicago Press, 2001.

———. *American Inquisition: The Hunt for Japanese American Disloyalty in World War II*. Chapel Hill: University of North Carolina Press, 2007.

———. "Hirabayashi: The Biggest Lie of the Greatest Generation." UNC Legal Studies Research Paper No. 1233682. August 18, 2008. Available at www.ssrn.com/abstract=1233682 (accessed November 13, 2012).

Munson, Curtis B. "Japanese on the West Coast." In *American Concentration Camps, Volume 1, July 1940—December 31, 1941*, edited by Roger Daniels, 1–17. New York: Garland, 1989.

Murayama, Tamotsu. *Hawai Nisei: Kutsujoku Kara Eikōhe* [*Hawaii Nisei: From Struggle to Glory*]. N.p.: Jijitsu-shinsa, 1966.

Murray, Alice Yang. *Historical Memories of the Japanese American Internment and the Struggle for Redress*. Stanford: Stanford University Press, 2008.

Murray, Arthur Mordaunt. *The "Fortnightly" History of the War*. New York: Stokes, 1917.

Muscatine, Doris. *Old San Francisco: The Biography of a City*. New York: Putnam's, 1975.

Nakagawa, Mako (primary author). "Power of Words Resolution." Japanese American Citizens League, 2010. http://pnwjacl.org/POW-1.htm. Accessed June 4, 2011.

Nakagawa, Martha. "Renunciants: Bill Nishimura and Tad Yamakido." *A Question of Loyalty: Internment at Tule Lake, Journal of the Shaw Historical Library* 19 (2005): 137–59.

Nelson, Douglas W. *Heart Mountain: The History of an American Concentration Camp*. Madison: State Historical Society of Wisconsin, 1976.

Ngai, Mae M. *Impossible Subjects: Illegal Aliens and the Making of Modern America*. Princeton, N.J.: Princeton University Press, 2004.

Nishimoto, Richard S. *Inside an American Concentration Camp: Japanese American Resistance at Poston, Arizona*. Edited by Lane Ryo Hirabayashi. Tucscon: University of Arizona Press, 1995.

Nurius, Paula S. "Human Memory: A Basis for Better Understanding the Elusive Self-Concept." *Social Service Review* 67, no. 2 (1993): 261–78.

O'Connor, Daniel A. *Catholic Social Doctrine*. Westminster, Md.: Newman, 1956.

Oda, James. *Heroic Struggles of Japanese Americans: Partisan Fighters from America's Concentration Camps*. North Hollywood, Calif.: James Oda, 1980.

Okamura, B. Taeko Sakai. "Testimony for the Commission on Wartime Relocation and Internment of Civilians." August 11, 1981. Typescript, in author's possession.

Okamura, Raymond Y. "The American Concentration Camps: A Cover-Up through Euphemistic Terminology." *Journal of Ethnic Studies* 10, no. 3 (Fall 1982): 95–109.

Okazaki, Suzie Kobuchi. *Nihonmachi: A Story of San Francisco's Japantown*. San Francisco: SKO, 1985.

Okihiro, Gary Y. "Japanese Resistance in America's Concentration Camps: A Re-evaluation." *Amerasia Journal* 2 (Fall 1973): 20–34.

———. "Tule Lake under Martial Law: A Study in Japanese Resistance." *Journal of Ethnic Studies* 5 (Fall 1977): 71–85.

———. "Religion and Resistance in America's Concentration Camps." *Phylon* 45, no. 3 (1984): 220–33.

Omori, Emiko. *Rabbit in the Moon*. Videorecording. N.p.: Wabi-Sabi, 2004.

Opler, Marvin K. Book Review of *The Spoilage*. *American Anthropologist* 50 (1948): 307–10.

Panzer, Joseph J. *Educational Traditions of the Society of Mary*. Dayton, Ohio: The University of Dayton Press, 1965.

Pencak, William. *For God and Country: The American Legion, 1919–1941*. Boston: Northeastern University Press, 1989.

Pereyra, Lillian A. "The Catholic Church and Portland's Japanese: The Untimely St. Paul Miki School Project." *Oregon Historical Quarterly* 94 (Winter 1993–94): 399–434.

Polk-Husted's Directory of Honolulu and Territory of Hawaii. Honolulu: Husted, 1896–97, 1898, 1903, 1908, 1911, 1915.

Pratt, Richard C. *Hawai'i Politics and Government: An American State in a Pacific World*. Lincoln: University of Nebraska Press, 2000.

Pukui, Mary Kawena, Samuel H. Elbert, and Esther T. Mookini. *Place Names of Hawaii*. Honolulu: University Press of Hawaii, 1974.

Raineri, Vivian McGuckin. *The Red Angel: The Life and Times of Elaine Black Yoneda, 1906–1988*. New York: International, 1991.

Rawls, Walton. *Wake Up, America! World War I and the American Poster*. New York: Abbeville, 1988.

Reischauer, Edwin O. *Japan: Story of a Nation*, 4th ed. New York: McGraw Hill, 1990.

Robinson, Greg. *By Order of the President: FDR and the Internment of Japanese Americans*. Cambridge, Mass.: Harvard University Press, 2001.

———. *A Tragedy of Democracy: Japanese Confinement in North America*. New York: Columbia University Press, 2009.

Robinson, William S. *A Short History of Greece*. New York: Macmillan, 1895.

Rubin, David C. "Definitions of Autobiographical Memory." In *Theoretical Perspectives on Autobiographical Memory*, edited by Martin A. Conway, David C. Rubin, Hans Spinnler, and Willem A. Wagenaar, 495–99. Dordrecht, Netherlands: Kluwer, 1992.

———. "Beginnings of a Theory of Autobiographical Remembering." In *Autobiographical Memory: Theoretical and Applied Perspectives*, edited by Douglas Herrmann, Darryl Bruce, J. Don Read, David Payne, and Michael Toglia, 47–68. Mahwah, N.J.: Erlbaum, 1998.

———. "Introduction." In *Remembering Our Past: Studies in Autobiographical Memory*, edited by David C. Rubin, 1–15. Cambridge: Cambridge University Press, 1999.

Sai, David Keanu. "A Slippery Path toward Hawaiian Indigeneity: An Analysis and Comparison between Hawaiian State Sovereignty and Hawaiian Indigeneity and its Use and Practice in Hawai'i Today." *Journal of Law and Social Challenges* 10 (Fall 2008): 68–133.

Saito, Deborah, and Susan Campbell. "Lihue Plantation Company History." Honolulu: University of Hawaii Manoa Library Hawaiian Collection, 2004. Available at http://www2.hawaii.edu/~speccoll/p_lihue.html (accessed November 13, 2012).

Sakamaki, George. "Dual Citizenship and Expatriation." *Paradise of the Pacific* 50 (April 1938): 35.

Salyer, Lucy E. "Baptism by Fire: Race, Military Service, and U.S. Citizenship Policy, 1918–1935." *Journal of American History* 91 (December 2004): 847–76.

Samuel, Raphael, and Paul Thompson. "Introduction." In *The Myths We Live By*, edited by Raphael Samuel and Paul Thompson, 1–22. London: Routledge, 1990.

Sanborn Fire Insurance Maps. Territory of Hawaii, Honolulu. 1914. Sheets 7, 9–10. University of Hawaii Libraries.

Sanborn Maps. San Francisco, California. 1915. Sheet 404, reel 3. San Francisco Public Library, San Francisco.

San Francisco Population from the 1920 Census and 1910 Census, March 18, 2005. San Francisco Public Library.

Savage, Tom V., and David G. Armstrong. "Were Things Really So Cheap in the 'Good Old Days'? Using Index Numbers to Determine the Meaning of Historical Prices." *The Social Studies* 93, no. 4 (July/August 1992): 155–59.

Scott, Emmett J. *The American Negro in the World War*. Chicago: Homewood, 1919.

Shallit, Barney. *Song of Anger: Tales of Tule Lake*. Fullerton: Oral History Program, California State University, 2001.

Shenk, Gerald E. *"Work or Fight!" Race, Gender, and the Draft in World War One*. New York: Palgrave Macmillan, 2005.

Shibusawa, Naoko. "'The Artist Belongs to the People': The Odyssey of Taro Yashima." *Journal of Asian American Studies* 8 (October 2005): 257–75.

Shimabukuro, Robert Sadamu. *Born in Seattle: The Campaign for Japanese American Redress*. Seatttle: University of Washington Press, 2001.

Shiozaki, Cory. *The Manzanar Fishing Club*. Film. Los Angeles: From Barbed Wire to Barbed Hooks, 2012.

Shirai, Noboru. *Tule Lake: An Issei Memoir*. Translated from Japanese by Ray Hosoda, edited by Eucaly Shirai and Valerie Samson. Sacramento: Muteki Press, 2001.

Shuckburgh, Evelyn S. *A History of Rome for Beginners: From the Foundation of the City to the Death of Augustus*. London: Macmillan, 1913 [1897].

Shuman, R. Baird. "The Past as Present: Reader Response and Literary Study." *English Journal* 82, no. 5 (Septemebr 1993): 30–32.

Sixth Annual Nisei Veterans Reunion: July 1–6, 1970. Los Angeles: Commodore Perry Post, [1970]. Casey Kasuyama Collection.

Smith, Cindy K. "Wartime Internment of Japanese-Americans: An Examination of Current Reparations Proposals." *University of Puget Sound Law Review* 6 (1982): 97–121.

Smith, William C. *Americans in Process*. Ann Arbor: Edwards, 1937.

"Social Thought, Catholic." *New Catholic Encyclopedia*. 2nd ed. Vol. 13. Detroit and Washington, D.C.: Thomson/Gale and Catholic University of America, 2003.

Society of the First Division. *History of the First Division during the World War, 1917–1919*. Philadelphia: Winston, 1922.

Southwestern University. School of Commerce. Official Announcement, 1922–1923, 1925–1926. Los Angeles: Southwestern University.

———. School of Law. "History of Southwestern," 2005. Available at http://www.swlaw.edu/about (accessed November 13, 2012).

Spickard, Paul R. “The Nisei Assume Power: The Japanese [American] Citizens League, 1941–42.” *Pacific Historical Review* 52 (1983): 147–74.

———. *Japanese Americans: The Formation and Transformations of an Ethnic Group*. Rev. ed. New Brunswick, N.J.: Rutgers, 2009.

Stamps, T. Dodson, and Vincent J. Esposito, eds. *A Short Military History of World War I*. New York: U.S. Military Academy, West Point, 1954. Available at http://www.firstworldwar.com/maps/graphics/maps_69_wfront_final_off.jpg (accessed November 13, 2012).

Steigerwald, David. *Wilsonian Idealism in America*. Ithaca, N.Y.: Cornell University Press, 1994.

Steinfirst, Susan. “Reader-Response Criticism.” *School Library Journal* n.v. (October 1986): 114–15.

Stephan, John J. *Hawaii under the Rising Sun: Japan's Plans for Conquest after Pearl Harbor*. Honolulu: University of Hawaii Press, 1984.

Strong, Edward K. *Japanese in California, Based on a Ten Percent Survey of Japanese in California and Documentary Evidence from Many Sources*. Stanford: Stanford University Press, 1933.

Suzuki, Peter T. “The University of California Japanese Evacuation and Resettlement Study: A Prolegomenon.” *Dialectical Anthropology* 10 (1986): 189–213.

Takahashi, Jere. “Japanese American Responses to Race Relations: The Formation of Nisei Perspectives.” *Amerasia Journal* 9, no. 1 (1982): 29–57.

———. *Nisei/Sansei: Shifting Japanese American Identities and Politics*. Philadelphia: Temple University Press, 1997.

Takei, Barbara. “Legalizing Detention: Segregated Japanese Americans and the Justice Department's Renunciation Program.” *A Question of Loyalty, Internment at Tule Lake: Journal of the Shaw Historical Library* 19 (2005): 75–105.

Takei, Barbara, and Judy Tachibana. *Tule Lake Revisited: A Brief History and Guide to the Tule Lake Concentration Camp Site*. 2nd ed. San Francisco: Tule Lake Comm., 2012.

Takemoto, Paul Howard. *Nisei Memories: My Parents Talk about the War Years*. Seattle: University of Washington Press, 2006.

Takita, Sachiko. “The Tule Lake Pilgrimage and Japanese American Internment: Collective Memory, Solidarity, and Division in an Ethnic Community.” Ph.D. diss. University of California, Los Angeles, 2007.

Takita-Ishii, Sachiko. “Tokio Yamane: A Renunciant's Story.” *A Question of Loyalty, Internment at Tule Lake: Journal of the Shaw Historical Library* 19 (2005): 161–85.

Tamura, Eileen H. *Americanization, Acculturation, and Ethnic Identity: The Nisei Generation in Hawaii*. Urbana: University of Illinois Press, 1994.

Tanaka, Togo. “How to Survive Racism in America's Free Society.” In *Voices Long Silent: An Oral Inquiry into the Japanese American Evacuation*, edited by Arthur A. Hansen and Betty E. Mitson, 84–109. Fullerton: Oral History Program, California State University, Fullerton, 1974.

Tateishi, John. *And Justice for All: An Oral History of the Japanese American Detention Camps*. New York: Random House, 1984.

tenBroek, Jacobus, Edward N. Barnhart, and Floyd W. Matson. *Prejudice, War and the Constitution.* Berkeley: University of California Press, 1968 [1954].

"The Custer Division in the World War." *Infantry Journal* 29 (July 1926): 22–24.

Thomas, Dorothy Swaine, with the assistance of Charles Kikuchi and James Sakoda. *The Salvage.* Berkeley: University of California Press, 1975 [1952].

Thomas, Dorothy Swaine, and Richard S. Nishimoto, with contributions from Rosalie A. Hankey, James M. Sakoda, Morton Grodzins, Frank Miyamoto. *The Spoilage.* Berkeley: University of California Press, 1969 [1946].

Tomita, Mary Kimoto. *Dear Miye: Letters Home from Japan, 1939—1946.* Stanford, Calif.: Stanford University Press, 1995.

Totah, Paul. "Spiritus Magis: 150 Years of St. Ignatius College Preparatory, Part 1." *Genesis IV, The Alumni Magazine, History Supplement* 42, no. 1 (Spring 2005): 1–48.

Tule Lake Committee, John R. Ross, and Reiko Ross. *Second Kinenhi: Reflections on Tule Lake.* San Francisco: Tule Lake Committee, 2000.

Tuttle, William M., Jr. *Race Riot: Chicago in the Red Summer of 1919.* Urbana: University of Illinois Press, 1996.

Tyack, David. *The One Best System: A History of American Urban Education.* Cambridge, Mass.: Harvard University Press, 1974.

Ueno, Harry. "Manzanar." In *And Justice for All: An Oral History of the Japanese American Detention Camps,* edited by John Tateishi, 186–207. New York: Random House, 1984.

Unrau, Harlan D. *The Evacuation and Relocation of Persons of Japanese Ancestry during World War II: A Historical Study of the Manzanar War Relocation Center, Vols. 1 and 2.* Washington, D.C.: U.S. Department of the Interior, National Park Service, 1996.

U.S. Army Center of Military History. *Order of Battle of the United States Land Forces in the World War, American Expeditionary Forces: Divisions, Vol. 2.* Washington, D.C.: Center of Military History, 1988.

U.S. Army Field Artillery, 328th. *The Red Guidon.* Milwaukee, Wisc.: Hammersmith-Kortmeyer, [1919].

U.S. Bureau of the Census. *Thirteenth Census, 1910: Statistics for Hawaii.* Washington, D.C.: GPO, 1913.

———. *Fifteenth Census, 1930: Population.* Volume 3, Pt. 1. Washington, D.C.: GPO, 1931.

U.S. Commission on Wartime Relocation and Internment of Civilians. *Personal Justice Denied.* Seattle: University of Washington Press, 1997.

U.S. Congress. Senate. Committee on Governmental Affairs. *Recommendations of the Commission on Wartime Internment and Relocation of Citizens.* Washington, D.C.: GPO, 1986

U.S. Department of Defense. *Hispanics in America's Defense.* Washington, DC: GPO, 1990.

U.S. Department of the Interior. Bureau of Education. *American Schoolhouses.* Bulletin 1910, no. 5. Washington, D.C.: GPO, 1910.

———. National Park Service, *Story of Human Conservation.* Washington, D.C.: GPO, 1946.

———. War Agency Liquidation Unit. *People in Motion: The Postwar Adjustment of the Evacuated Japanese Americans.* New York: AMS, 1975 [1947].

———. War Relocation Authority, *The Evacuated People: A Quantitative Description.* Washington, D.C.: GPO, 1946.

U.S. Hawaiian Commission. *The Report of the Hawaiian Commission Appointed in Pursuant of the "Joint Resolution for Annexing the Hawaiian Islands to the United States," Approved July 7, 1898.* Washington D.C.: GPO, 1898.

U.S. Organic Act: An Act to Provide a Government for the Territory of Hawaii, C 339, 31 Stat 141. (Includes amendments up to 1958.) No date. Available at http://www.hawaii-nation.org/organic.html (accessed November 13, 2012).

U.S. Surgeon General's Office. *The Medical Department of the United States Army in the World War, Vol. VIII, Field Operations.* Washington, D.C.: GPO, 1925.

Van Sant, John E. *Pacific Pioneers: Japanese Journeys to America and Hawaii, 1850–80.* Urbana: University of Illinois Press.

Varzally, Allison. *Making a Non-White America: Californians Coloring Outside Ethnic Lines, 1925–1955.* Berkeley: University of California Press, 2008.

Villahermosa, Gilberto. "America's Hispanics in America's Wars." *Army Magazine* 52, no. 9 (September 2002). http://www.valerosos.com/HispanicsMilitary.html (accessed November 13, 2012).

Walch, Tim. *Parish School: American Catholic Parochial Education from Colonial Times to the Present.* New York: Crossroad, 1996.

"Wax, Rosalie H." In *American Men and Women of Science: The Social and Behavioral Sciences,* vol. 2, L-Z, edited by Jaques Cattell Press, 2,584. New York: Cattell & Bowker, 1973.

Wax, Rosalie H. "The Destruction of a Democratic Impulse." *Human Organization* 12, no. 1 (Spring 1953): 11–21.

———. "Twelve Years Later: An Analysis of Field Experience." *American Journal of Sociology* 63, no. 2 (September 1957): 133–42.

———. *Doing Fieldwork: Warnings and Advice.* Chicago: University of Chicago Press, 1971.

———. "In and Out of Tule Lake Segregation Center: Japanese Internment in the West, 1942–1945." *Montana: the Magazine of Western History* 37, no. 2 (Spring 1987): 12–25.

Weglyn, Michi Nishiura, *Years of Infamy: The Untold Story of America's Concentration Camps.* Updated edition. Seattle: University of Washington Press, 1996 [1976].

Wei, William. *The Asian American Movement.* Philadelphia: Temple University Press, 1993.

Widener, Daniel. "'Perhaps the Japanese Are to Be Thanked?' Asia, Asian Americans, and the Construction of Black California." *positions* 11, no. 1 (Spring 2003): 135–81.

Wild, Mark. *Street Meeting: Multiethnic Neighborhoods in Early Twentieth-Century Los Angeles.* Berkeley: University of California Press, 2005.

Wilson, Woodrow. *War Messages.* 65th Cong., 1st Sess. Senate Doc. No. 5, Serial No. 7264. Washington, D.C. (April 2, 1917): 3–8+. Available at http://wwi.lib.byu.edu/index.php/Wilson%27s_War_Message_to_Congress (accessed November 13, 2012).

Wist, Benjamin O. *A Century of Public Education in Hawaii.* Honolulu: Hawaii Educational Review, 1940.

Wollenberg, Charles. *All Deliberate Speed: Segregation and Exclusion in California Schools, 1855–1975.* Berkeley: University of California Press, 1976.

Work Projects Administration Writers' Program. *Los Angeles: A Guide to the City and Its Environs, Compiled by Workers of the Writers' Program of the Work Projects Administration.* New York: Hastings, 1941.

"Xavier, Francis, St." *New Catholic Encyclopedia.* Vol. 14. Detroit and Washington, D.C.: Thomson/Gale and Catholic University of America, 2003.

Yamazaki, Yuki. "St. Francis Xavier School: Acculturation and Enculturation of Japanese Americans in Los Angeles, 1921–1945." *U.S. Catholic Historian* 18, no. 1 (Winter 2000): 54–73.

Yatsushiro, Toshio. "Political and Socio-Cultural Issues at Poston and Manzanar Relocation Centers: A Themal Analysis," Ph.D. diss. Cornell University, 1953.

Yoneda, Karl G. *Ganbatte: Sixty-Year Struggle of a Kibei Worker.* Los Angeles: Asian American Studies Center, University of California, 1983.

Yoo, David. "'Read All about It': Race, Generation and the Japanese American Ethnic Press, 1925–41." *Amerasia Journal* 9, no. 1 (1993): 69–92.

———. "A Religious History of Japanese Americans in California." In *Religions in Asian America: Building Faith Communities*, edited by Pyong Gap Min and Jung Ha Kim, 121–42. Walnut Creek, Calif.: AltaMira, 2002.

Yzendoorn, Reginald. *History of the Catholic Mission in the Hawaiian Islands.* Honolulu: Honolulu Star-Bulletin, 1927.

Zacharias, Ellis M. *Secret Missions: The Story of an Intelligence Officer.* Annapolis, Md.: Naval Institute Press, 2003 [1946].

INDEX

Abo v. Clark. See Wayne Mortimer Collins, and *Abo v. Clark*
Abo v. Williams. See Wayne Mortimer Collins, and *Abo v. Williams*
Acheson v. Murakami. See A. L. Wirin
ACLU. *See* American Civil Liberties Union
Akashi, Tom, 116–19, 124, 134, 136
aliens: resident, numbers of, 155–56n20
American Civil Liberties Union (ACLU): of Northern California, 112; and silence on isolation camps, 94; of Southern California, 128. *See also* Roger Baldwin; Ernest Besig; Abraham Wirin
Americanization: defined, 161n51; of World War I recruits, 26–27
American Legion: and Asian Americans, 32–33, 165n29
Aoyama, Mitsuo, 134, 138
Ariyoshi, Koji: as chair of the Manzanar Citizens' Federation, 61; as a Communist, 60; as a volunteer soldier, 71
Asakura, William and Grace, 136, 138, 155n15
Assembly Centers. *See* detention centers, temporary
Azuma, Eiichiro, 46, 138–39

Baldwin, Roger, 94, 128
Bendetsen, Karl R., 46
Besig, Ernest, 112–13, 127
Best, Raymond: on Kurihara, 76, 83; at Tule Lake, 97–99, 108–9, 113
Biddle, Francis, on renunciation law, 116
Bishop, town of, 58
Black Dragons, 75–76
blacklist, 60
block leaders. *See* Manzanar, block leaders at
Blood Brothers. *See* Black Dragons
Brown, Robert, 74, 196–97n46
Burling, John, 103, 120–21

California Commercial College, 33
Campbell, Ned, 54, 62, 66, 73–74, 77, 179n8
canteens. *See* Tule Lake, Cooperative Enterprises
Catholic school. *See* St. Francis School; St. Ignatius School
Catholic social thought, 162n53
citizenship, U.S., 13; through naturalization, 27
Collins, Wayne Mortimer: and *Abo v. Clark,* 127; and *Abo v. Williams,* 127; on the JACL, 193n59; and Korematsu, 113; and Nisei regaining citizenship, 127–29, 191n36; and release of stockade inmates, 113–14; and stopping deportation, 127
Committee of Five. *See* Joseph Yoshisuke Kurihara, and Committee of Five
Committee of Four. *See* Manzanar, Committee of Four
Communists: on blacklist, 60; and JACL, 60
concentration camps: v. internment camps, 6–7; Nikkei perspectives on, 5; publications on, 153–54n5. *See also* internment camps
Coordinating Committee. *See* Tule Lake Coordinating Committee
Coverley, Harvey, 97

Daihyo Sha Kai, 100, 108; and truck incident, 97–98
deathlist, 60
de Cristoforo, Violet Kazue. *See* Mrs. Tsuchikawa
detention centers, temporary, 47
DeWitt, John L.: and exclusion zones, 46–47; and view of Nikkei, 47–48
Dies Committee, 91
disloyalty. *See* loyalty
dissent. *See* resistance
dissidents: possible prosecution of, 61
Doub, George Cochran, 130–31, 143
Dower, John, 139–40
Drinnon, Richard, 94
dual citizenship, 48–49, 169n40, 170n42
due process: lack of, 82

education. *See* California Commercial College; Kaiulani School; Southwestern University; St. Francis School; St. Ignatius School
Ego, Frank, 85–87, 130
Eisenhower, Milton: as WRA director, 47
Ellison Enoch, 130–31
Emmons, Delos, 48
Endo, Mitsuye, 116
Ennis, Edward J.: and denial of citizenship reinstatement, 127; on renunciation law, 116; and transfer of Issei to internment camps, 82
espionage: and white Americans, 45. *See also* Nikkei, as suspected spies
ethnoracial: defined, 166n34
evacuation. *See* removal, forced; terminology
exchange: of Japanese and U.S. nationals, 115, 123
expatriation. *See* renunciation; Kurihara and renunciation

farming: in the Sacramento valley, 16–17
FBI. *See* Federal Bureau of Investigation
Federal Bureau of Investigation (FBI): investigation at Manzanar, 64; and Nikkei, 46; report on Kurihara, 79–80
fishermen, Nikkei: as suspected spies, 40–42. *See also* Nikkei, in fishing
Frederick, Francis: background on, 89–90, 181n33; and decision to imprison Moab dissidents, 86–87, and Dies Committee, 91–92; on inmate refusal to work, 85; on Kurihara, 76, 85, 92, 102, 130; and Robert Spencer, 89–90; as viewed by inmates, 92
Fryer, Heather, 103, 120
Fujita, Henry, xiv
Fujita, Joe Wilfred, xiv, 140, 146–47
Fukumoto, Grace, xiv

Gentleman's Agreement, 160n45
Gilkey, John, 55
Glick, Philip, 94, 113
Goodman, Judge Louis, 127–28
Gripsholm, 123. *See also* exchange of Japanese and U.S. nationals
Grodzins, Morton: and interview with Dillon Myer, 94
Grumbly, Paul, 144
Gullion, Allen W., 46

Hacker, David, 59, 62
Hall, Captain Martyn, 55, 57
Hamada, John, 149
Hankey, Rosalie: and arrival at Tule Lake, 104; description of, 103; field notes of, 102–4; on John Burling, 103; on Kurihara, 104–5; on Marvin Opler, 103; and professional ethics, 120, 189n24; wrongly blamed, 124, 191n36
Hansen, Arthur, 59, 62
Hasegawa, Osamu, 138
Hashimoto, Kiyoshi, 63
Hashimoto, Masaru, 129
Hawai'i: and occupation by the United States, 156n1. *See also* Nikkei, in WWII Hawai'i
Hayashi, Brian Masaru, 59, 169n32
Higash, Kiyoshi: at JACL national convention, 66; as recipient of Kurihara's ire, 92–93
Hirai, Raymond, 63
Hitomi, Yaozu, 110–11
Hohri, William, 149
Hokoku Joshi Seinen Dan, 118
Hokoku Seinen Dan: and efforts for renunciation, 123, 125; in Japan, 139; newly named, 118; and regaining citizenship, 128, 130; as renunciants, 122
Honolulu: fire of 1900, 11–12

Hoover, J. Edgar: and inquiry on sedition, 64. *See also* Federal Bureau of Investigation
Horton, Kenneth, 79
Hoshi Dan: factions within, 118–19; pressure from, 118–19, 127–28; removal of, 126. *See also* Resegregationists
Hymes, Dell, 120

Ickes, Harold, 112
immigrants, children of: as aliens, 3–4
incarceration. *See* concentration camps
Independence, town of, 51, 58
Inose, Makoto, 141, 143, 150
internment camps: aliens from Latin America in, 155–56n20; defined, 7; Issei from WRA camps to, 82; numbers of aliens in, 7. *See also* concentration camps
inu (dog). *See* stool pigeon
Ishida, Gladys, 141
isolation camps. *See* Moab Isolation Camp; Leupp Isolation Camp
Issei: cultural perspective of, 59; loss of power, 64
Itami, David, 141–42, 196–97n46
Ito, James, 57, 83

JACL. *See* Japanese American Citizens League
Japan: arrival in, 134–37; departure for, 132–33, 194–95n6; and postwar devastation, 135–37; as victor in war, 88
Japanese American Citizens League (JACL), 53; and Communists, 60; cultural perspective of, 59–60; on deathlist, 60; and FBI, 46, 60; opposition to, 5, 60, 65–66, 74. *See also* Kurihara, on the JACL
Japanese Evacuation and Resettlement Study (JERS), 102–5
JERS. *See* Japanese Evacuation and Resettlement Study

Kai, Shizue, 98, 118–19
Kaiulani School, 13
Kaku, Yoshiro, 87, 179n8
Kanagawa, Jim, 57, 83
Kashiwagi, Hiroshi, 107, 118, 125, 127
Kawamoto, Jack, 142
Kawamoto, Toshio, 142–43
Kibei-Nisei: cultural perspective of, 59; as employees of the occupation forces, 137; and feelings of rejection, 107; as Kitchen Workers Union members, 65; meeting of, 63–64; as Tule Lake leaders, 111; and work furloughs, 62
Kishi, Ben, 63, 72, 76, 84, 88
Kitchen Workers' Union. *See* Manzanar Kitchen Workers' Union
Kiyota, Minoru, 122
Knox, Frank: and view of Nikkei, 47
Kobayashi, Kenge, 116–17
Kobayashi, Sakae, 141
Kobayashi, Tom, 98–99; 183n10
Kono, Tamotsu, 84–85
Kumei, Teruko, 118, 191n35, 191n36
Kurashige, Lon, 59
Kuratomi, George, 98, 103, 113, 118–19
Kurihara, Joseph Yoshisuke: on Americanism, 60, 77, 132; and the American Legion, 32–33; and arrival in Japan, 134–37; and beating of Tayama, 77–80; and behavior at Leupp, 92–93, 95; and behavior at Moab, 83, 95; and behavior at Tule Lake, 100, 102, 111, 113, 117, 121–22; on being "Japs," 61–63; as best informant, 105; birth of, 9; and bonsai, 143–45; and Catholicism, 14–16, 18–19, 21, 84; character of, 64, 76–79, 85, 92, 130, 141–42, 145–52, 180n19; and Committee of Five, 55–59, 171n16; confession of, 78–80; as controversial4, 149; on the Coordinating Committee, 101; as cultural bridge, 37; death of, 145; on deaths of Ito and Kanagawa, 83, 123; on democracy, 62, 132; and departure from the United States, 132–33; and distinctiveness, 147–50; as early volunteer to Manzanar, 52; as an employee of the Occupation, 137–40; and ethical behavior, 140, 146–47; and Father Hugh Lavery, 52; on Hawai'i Nisei, 77; and high expectations, 146–47; identity of, 3, 140–41, 145, 151; on *inu*, 109–110; on the JACL, 50; on John DeWitt, 122–23; on justice, 61, 77, 79, 83, 93, 109–10, 143–44, 150–51; as leader, 3, 54–58, 61–62, 75, 83; in Los Angeles, 32–37; on loyalty, 6; as navigator, 37, 39–40, 44; occupations of, 36; and oratory, 22, 61, 65; parents of, 9–11, 32; on protecting himself from violence, 119–20; publications on, 4, 154n5; on racism, 17, 20, 34–35; and Ray-

mond Best, 83, 99, 114, 133; and renunciation, 83, 122–23, 125, 129–30; on reparations, 93, 144, 148; on Resegregationists, 107–8, 117, 119; and restoration of U.S. citizenship, 130–31, 143–44; on rights of blacks, 34; in San Francisco, 16–23; schooling of (*see* California Commercial College; Kaiulani School; Southwestern University; St. Francis School; St. Ignatius School); and sedition, 64, 76; on shooting of Okamoto, 108; siblings of, 11–13, 32, 37, 52, 135, 141, 145, 150; as a soldier in World War I, 25–32; soon after Pearl Harbor, 39, 42–43; on Terminal Islanders, 49; and Togo Tanaka, 49, 55, 65, 70; as U.S. citizen, 13; and the Veterans of Foreign Wars, 32–33; on war, 31; as writer, 37–38, 83, 92–94, 182n42; and WWI liberty bonds, 163n5, as a youth, 9–16. *See also* Dorothy Swaine Thomas; Francis Frederick; Harry Ueno; Kinzo Ernest Wakayama; Leupp; Moab; renunciation; reparations; resistance; Rosalie Hankey; Tule Lake
Kurihara, Raymond, xiv, 150

land laws, alien, 16–17, 34, 159n35, 161n48, 166n39
Lavery, Father Hugh, 52
Leupp Isolation Camp, 88–95, 182n47; and closure, 95
Little Tokyo: in Los Angeles, 33–34
Lone Pine, 58, 61, 84
Los Angeles: ethnic group population in 1920 and 1930, 33, 166n34; Nikkei in, 34
Lotchin, Roger, 67
loyalty, 61, 73–75; of Nisei (*see* Nisei, loyalty of); questionnaire, 74–75, 96

MAGIC, 41
Malkin, Michelle, 41, 45
Manzanar: block leaders at, 65; Committee of Four, 81, 84–86, 178n3; death at, 57; described, 2, 51–53; Kitchen Workers' Union, 54–55, 65; low morale at, 58–59; Negotiating Committee, 81, 85–86; Nikkei arrival at, 52; and proposed charter, 64–65; revolt at, 53–66; WRA employee living conditions at, 53. *See also* Issei; Japanese American Citizens League; Kibei-Nisei
Manzanar Citizens' Federation, 61–62
Marker, Chris, 5
martial law. *See* Tule Lake, martial law at
Marubayashi, Hanako, xiv, 150
Masaoka, Joe Grant, 55, 60
Matsuda, Bob, 85–87
Matsushita, Robert, 56, 155n15
McCloy, John J., 46, 48
McCormick, William, 64, 78
McGlone, Robert, 148
Meek, Colonel, 99
Meiklejohn, Alexander: and silence on isolation camps, 94
memory, 147–48
Merritt, Ralph: and Committee of Four, 84; on Kurihara, 76; and Manzanar revolt, 55–58, 74; and proposed charter changes, 65; on renunciation law, 115
Miyatake, Toya, 154n6
Moab Isolation Camp, 61–87; and Dies Committee, 91–92
Morrison, Toni, 5
Muller, Eric, 73
Munson, Curtis B., 45–46
Murayama, Tamotsu, 144
"Murder in Camp Manzanar," 83
Myer, Dillon: and letter to inmates at Moab, 84; on Leupp, 88, 90, 94; and stockade, 113; at Tule Lake, 98

Nagasawa, Tom, 116
Nakamura, James, 135, 137
Nakamura, Tex, 128, 193n59
Nash, Roy, 63, 76
Nativism. *See* Nikkei, nativist views on
naturalization: of Asian immigrant veterans, 27, 164n15
Naval Intelligence, Office of (ONI): and Nikkei, 40–42, 44–46
Negotiating Committee. *See* Kurihara and Negotiating Committee
Ngai, Mae M., 31, 129, 191n36
Nikkei: different cultural perspectives of, 59–61; as fishermen, 40, 44; job opportunities for, 36; in Los Angeles, 34; nativist views on, 47; perspectives on incarceration, 5; as suspected spies, 40–46, 48; on Terminal Island, 49; in WWII Hawai'i, 47–48. *See also* espionage; Issei; Kibei-Nisei; Nisei; reparations

Nisei: cultural perspective of, 59; as employees of occupation forces, 137; loyalty of, 46. *See also* dual citizenship; renunciants; renunciation
"Niseis and the Government of the United States," 93–94
Nishimoto, Richard S., 102, 191n36
Noyes, Louis M., 121, 126

occupation forces in Japan, 137–40
Ogami, Arthur, 116, 125, 133
Ogami, Ben, 136, 138, 141
Okamoto, Shoichi James: shooting of, 108
Okamura, Taeko, 125, 133, 135–36
Omura, James, 148
ONI. *See* Naval Intelligence, Office of
Opler, Marvin, 103
Opler, Morris, 73–74
Organic Act, 13
Ozamoto, Tom, 85–86

Palama district: in early 20th century, 11–12
Pearl Harbor: attack of, 39, 42
plantations, sugar, 9–10
Provinse, John, 94

racism: in California: 17, 32, 34–35; in the U.S. West, 17, 19–20. *See also* Nikkei, nativist views of
Rafu Shimpō, 49
redress. *See* reparations
relocation. *See* removal, forced; terminology
Relocation Centers. *See* concentration camps; terminology
removal, forced, 46–50
renunciants: and denial of requests to rescind, 129; as employees of occupation forces, 137–40; interviews with, 6, 155n15; in Japan, 137; number of, 126; refusing to regain U.S. citizenship, 129–30
renunciation: efforts to rescind, 126–29
renunciation: law, 115–16, 131; perspectives on, 6; pressure for, 117; procedure for, 122; reasons for, 122–26; stampede toward, 124. *See also* Kurihara, and renunciation
reparations, 5, 148–49
Resegregationists: and effort to segregate themselves, 105–8; as minority group, 117; pressure from, 124; renamed *Hoshi Dan,* 118; on renunciation, 117; and stockade prisoners, 112; and Young Men's Association for the Study of the Mother Country, 116–17. See also *Hoshi Dan*
resistance, 3, 74, 108, 145, 177n23; publications on, 154–55n6. *See also* revolt
revolt: at Manzanar, 53–58
Robertson, Paul: on Kurihara, 92, 99; at Leupp, 89–92, 102; on Raymond Best, 97; at Tule Lake, 104
Roosevelt, Franklin D.: and E.O. 9066, 46; and view of Nikkei, 47

Sacramento. *See* farming
Sano, Roy, 149
Sasaki, Mamoru, 83
Sato, Sarah, 125, 135
schooling. *See* California Commercial College; Kaiulani School; Southwestern University; St. Francis School; St. Ignatius School
sedition. *See* Kurihara, and sedition
Seinen Dan. See Hokoku Seinen Dan
shikata ga nai, 72–73
Shirai, Noboru, 97, 107, 116
shortwave radios, 88, 106
Slocum, Tokutaro Nishimura, 55–56, 68–69, 76, 78–79
Southwestern University, 35–36
Spencer, Robert, 102–3; and Francis Frederick, 89–90
spies. *See* espionage
Spoilage, The: criticism of, 102
Stephan, John, 59
St. Francis School, 14–16
St. Francis Xavier Japanese Catholic Mission, 18
St. Ignatius School, 19–23
Stimson, Henry L., 46–48
stockade. *See* Tule Lake stockade
stool pigeons (aka *inu*), 54, 57, 60, 79, 86, 109–10
submarines: attacks by, 48

Tachibana, Itaru, 44–45
Tachibana, Zenshiro, 119
Takahashi, Jere, 59
Takamine, Roy, 138
Takei, Barbara, 126

Tamura, Hidekazu, 129
Tanaka, Masaji, 63
Tanaka, Togo: on allegiance to Japan, 65; and anti-Axis Committee, 60; arrested by FBI, 43, 69; background on, 69–70; on Kurihara, 4–5, 62, 69–70, 75; and Manzanar mob, 56; as *Rafu Shimpō* editor, 49, 69. *See also* Kurihara, and Togo Tanaka
Tape v. Hurley, 160n45
Tayama, Fred: and Anti-Axis Committee, 60; assault on, 53–54, 56, 66–67, 77–80; before Pearl Harbor attack, 66; and FBI, 63; at JACL national convention, 66; and Manzanar Citizens Federation, 61
Terminal Islanders. *See* Nikkei, on Terminal Island
terminology: importance of, 7, 155n17; use of, 6
Thomas, Dorothy Swaine: criticism of, 102; and Kurihara, 102–3
Throckmorton, Robert, 74
Todoroki, Koji, 98–99, 183n10
Tokunosuke, Abe, 168n13
Truman, Harry: and deportation of alien enemies, 126
Tsuchikawa, Mrs., 106, 185n35
Tsuida, Robert, 134
Tsuji, Koichi, 85–87
Tule Lake: attitudes and friction within, 105–7; before Kurihara's arrival, 96–99; Cooperative Enterprises, 110–11; Coordinating Committee, 100–101; description of, 96; Kurihara's arrival at, 99; martial law at, 99–100; police force, 110–11; resistance at, 108; as segregation camp, 96–97; stockade, 99–100, 108, 110–11, 184n16; and truck incident, 97–98; violence at, 109–10. *See also Daihyo Sha Kai*; Kibei-Nisei; renunciation; Resegregationists
Tule Lake Defense Committee, 127–28
tuna fishing, 39–40

Ueno, Harry Y.: accused of Tayama beating, 86; being transported to Leupp in a box, 88; and Kurihara, 87, 102, 149; at Manzanar, 53–58, 65–66, 79–80; at Moab, 84–87; and renunciation, 88, 135; at Tule Lake, 102
Uyeno, Tad, 55, 60

Van Wagoner, Robert, 64
Veterans of Foreign Wars, 165n29; and redress, 33

Wakayama, Kinzo Ernest, 119–20, 188n23, 189n27, 190n29
War Relocation Authority (WRA): creation of, 47; at Manzanar, 53, 59; policy on block leaders, 64
Wartime Civilian Control Administration (WCCA), 47, 53, 58
Weglyn, Michi, 96
Winchester, Joseph, 54, 179n8
Wirin, A. L. (Abraham), 128
World War I, 24–32; Asian American servicemen in, 27

Yamakido, Tad, 134
Yamamoto, Sumiko, 116, 136
Yamanaka, Morgan, 112
Yamane, Tokio, 98–99, 116, 129–30, 134, 137, 139, 183n10
Yoneda, Elaine, 71–72
Yoneda, Karl: background on, 70–71; and camouflage net factory, 62; as a Communist, 60, 70; and Kibei-Nisei meeting, 63, 71; on Kurihara, 76–78, 149
Yoshiyama, Tom, 134

EILEEN H. TAMURA is an associate professor in the Department of Educational Foundations, College of Education, at the University of Hawaiʻi Manoa. She is the author of *Americanization, Acculturation, and Ethnic Identity: The Nisei Generation in Hawaii* and coeditor of *The Rise of Modern Japan*.

THE ASIAN AMERICAN EXPERIENCE

The Hood River Issei: An Oral History of Japanese Settlers in Oregon's Hood River Valley *Linda Tamura*
Americanization, Acculturation, and Ethnic Identity: The Nisei Generation in Hawaii *Eileen H. Tamura*
Sui Sin Far/Edith Maude Eaton: A Literary Biography *Annette White-Parks*
Mrs. Spring Fragrance and Other Writings *Sui Sin Far; edited by Amy Ling and Annette White-Parks*
The Golden Mountain: The Autobiography of a Korean Immigrant, 1895–1960 *Easurk Emsen Charr; edited and with an introduction by Wayne Patterson*
Race and Politics: Asian Americans, Latinos, and Whites in a Los Angeles Suburb *Leland T. Saito*
Achieving the Impossible Dream: How Japanese Americans Obtained Redress *Mitchell T. Maki, Harry H. L. Kitano, and S. Megan Berthold*
If They Don't Bring Their Women Here: Chinese Female Immigration before Exclusion *George Anthony Peffer*
Growing Up Nisei: Race, Generation, and Culture among Japanese Americans of California, 1924–49 *David K. Yoo*
Chinese American Literature since the 1850s *Xiao-huang Yin*
Pacific Pioneers: Japanese Journeys to America and Hawaii, 1850–80 *John E. Van Sant*
Holding Up More Than Half the Sky: Chinese Women Garment Workers in New York City, 1948–92 *Xiaolan Bao*
Onoto Watanna: The Story of Winnifred Eaton *Diana Birchall*
Edith and Winnifred Eaton: Chinatown Missions and Japanese Romances *Dominika Ferens*
Being Chinese, Becoming Chinese American *Shehong Chen*
"A Half Caste" and Other Writings *Onoto Watanna; edited by Linda Trinh Moser and Elizabeth Rooney*
Chinese Immigrants, African Americans, and Racial Anxiety in the United States, 1848–82 *Najia Aarim-Heriot*
Not Just Victims: Conversations with Cambodian Community Leaders in the United States *Edited and with an introduction by Sucheng Chan; interviews conducted by Audrey U. Kim*
The Japanese in Latin America *Daniel M. Masterson with Sayaka Funada-Classen*
Survivors: Cambodian Refugees in the United States *Sucheng Chan*
From Concentration Camp to Campus: Japanese American Students and World War II *Allan W. Austin*
Japanese American Midwives: Culture, Community, and Health Politics *Susan L. Smith*

In Defense of Asian American Studies: The Politics of Teaching and Program Building *Sucheng Chan*

Lost and Found: Reclaiming the Japanese American Incarceration *Karen L. Ishizuka*

Religion and Spirituality in Korean America *Edited by David Yoo and Ruth H. Chung*

Moving Images: Photography and the Japanese American Incarceration *Jasmine Alinder*

Camp Harmony: Seattle's Japanese Americans and the Puyallup Assembly Center *Louis Fiset*

Chinese American Transnational Politics *Him Mark Lai, edited and with an introduction by Madeline Y. Hsu*

Issei Buddhism in the Americas *Edited by Duncan Ryûken Williams and Tomoe Moriya*

Hmong America: Reconstructing Community in Diaspora *Chia Youyee Vang*

Pacific Citizens: Larry and Guyo Tajiri and Japanese American Journalism in the World War II Era *Edited by Greg Robinson*

Indian Accents: Brown Voice and Racial Performance in American Television and Film *Shilpa S. Davé*

Yellow Power, Yellow Soul: The Radical Art of Fred Ho *Edited by Roger N. Buckley and Tamara Roberts*

Fighting from a Distance: How Filipino Exiles Helped Topple a Dictator *Jose V. Fuentecilla*

In Defense of Justice: Joseph Kurihara and the Japanese American Struggle for Equality *Eileen H. Tamura*

The University of Illinois Press
is a founding member of the
Association of American University Presses.

Composed in 10.5/13 Minion Pro
by Celia Shapland
at the University of Illinois Press
Manufactured by Thomson-Shore, Inc.

University of Illinois Press
1325 South Oak Street
Champaign, IL 61820-6903
www.press.uillinois.edu